A PLUME BOOK

ESSENTIALS OF SCREENWRITING

RICHARD WALTER has been chairman of UCLA's graduate screenwriting program for more than thirty years. A novelist and screenwriter himself, he lectures and offers master classes throughout the nation and the world.

Praise for Richard Walter, *Screenwriting*, and *The Whole Picture*

"The prime broker for Hollywood's hottest commodity: new writing talent." —*Wall Street Journal*

"The Jewish mother of screenwriting." —*Variety*

"*Screenwriting* is full of the expertise of someone who knows what makes movies worth writing, making, and seeing . . . [Richard Walter] instructs with wit, common sense, and love for his art and craft."
—Steven Bach, author of *Final Cut*

"In the gold rush atmosphere of screenwriting, Richard Walter is a wise guide. A lively and provocative book."
—Andrew Bergman, writer/director of
The Freshman and *Honeymoon in Vegas*

"Richard Walter, a writer himself, is the only person teaching screenwriting who knows what the f*^% he's talking about."
—Joe Eszterhas, writer of *Basic Instinct* and *Flashdance*

www.RichardWalter.com

ESSENTIALS
of
SCREENWRITING

- - - - - - - - - - - -

The Art, Craft, and Business of Film and Television Writing

- - - - - - - - - -

RICHARD WALTER

Professor and Screenwriting Chairman, UCLA

A PLUME BOOK

PLUME
Published by the Penguin Group
Penguin Group (USA) Inc., 375 Hudson Street, New York, New York 10014, U.S.A. •
Penguin Group (Canada), 90 Eglinton Avenue East, Suite 700, Toronto, Ontario, Canada
M4P 2Y3 (a division of Pearson Penguin Canada, Inc.) • Penguin Books Ltd., 80 Strand,
London WC2R 0RL, England • Penguin Ireland, 25 St. Stephen's Green, Dublin 2, Ireland
(a division of Penguin Books Ltd.) • Penguin Group (Australia), 250 Camberwell Road,
Camberwell, Victoria 3124, Australia (a division of Pearson Australia Group Pty. Ltd.) •
Penguin Books India Pvt. Ltd., 11 Community Centre, Panchsheel Park, New Delhi – 110
017, India • Penguin Group (NZ), 67 Apollo Drive, Rosedale, North Shore 0632, New
Zealand (a division of Pearson New Zealand Ltd.) • Penguin Books (South Africa) (Pty.)
Ltd., 24 Sturdee Avenue, Rosebank, Johannesburg 2196, South Africa

Penguin Books Ltd., Registered Offices: 80 Strand, London WC2R 0RL, England

First published by Plume, a member of Penguin Group (USA) Inc.

First Printing, July 2010
10 9 8 7 6 5 4 3 2

Portions of this book appeared in *Screenwriting: The Art, Craft and Business of Film and
Television Writing* (Plume, 1988) and *The Whole Picture: Strategies for Screenwriting
Success in the New Hollywood* (Plume, 1997). Copyright © Richard Walter, 1988, 1997.

℗ REGISTERED TRADEMARK—MARCA REGISTRADA

LIBRARY OF CONGRESS CATALOGING-IN-PUBLICATION DATA

Walter, Richard, 1944-
    Essentials of screenwriting : the art, craft, and business of film and television writing /
Richard Walter.
        p. cm.
    Includes material previously published in Screenwriting and the Whole Picture.
    Includes bibliographical references.
    ISBN 978-0-452-29627-5 (pbk. : alk. paper)   1. Motion picture authorship.
2. Motion picture plays—Technique.   3. Television authorship.   4. Television plays—
Technique.   I. Title.
    PN1996.W245   2010
    808.2'3—dc22   2010005304

Printed in the United States of America
Set in Minion Pro • Designed by Eve Kirch

For Danny and Susanna

Contents

Professionalism
A Final Word about Agents

PART IV: THE WHOLE PICTURE

Acknowledgments

My experience editing hundreds upon hundreds of screenplays over the decades positions me uniquely well to appreciate the importance of editing and also the qualities characterizing a worthy editor. There is none worthier than Nadia Kashper, wise beyond her years, without whose support this book would constitute not much more than a catalogue of Richie's Greatest Hits.

I salute also the attention and consideration afforded me by my earlier editors at Plume: Arnold Dolin, Gary Luke, and Peter K. Borland.

For my leonine agent, Peter Miller: roars.

Eternal gratitude to my longtime pal and partner in Westwood Professor Hal Ackerman and also to Lew Hunter and all our UCLA colleagues over many wonderful years.

My writing and teaching continues to be informed and expanded by the spirit of my own teacher, the late and legendary Irwin R. Blacker.

Finally, as always, with love to Pat, for reminding me daily just who I am and what it is that truly matters, and for providing me with more fun and inspiration than any mere movie.

A Note Regarding Credits

When citing movies and television shows, the names of all credited writers are provided the first time the title appears in the book.

Introduction

The God Game

In the early 1970s, while I was still nominally a film student but had been writing professionally for a couple of years, the Writers Guild went on strike.

May I confess here and now that I loved the strike?

By that time I'd written half a dozen feature screenplays for the studios and had earned a steady, even a substantial living. At that precise moment, however, I was "between assignments"—Hollywood's euphemism for out of work—and I did not, therefore, have to abandon any post.

The bright side of unemployment is that you cannot be fired.

It was springtime in Los Angeles and, notwithstanding my still-fresh New York chauvinism, I could not deny the season's sweetness. I resided in a comfy, cozy cottage with a bright yard and plentiful fruit trees. There were birds, possums, raccoons, and skunks. I even liked the skunks. I noodled around in my head with a notion for a novel, but mainly, from my knotty-pine-paneled, north-light study, I stared serenely at the snow-capped San Gabriel Mountains.

Twice a week Guild members were required to present ourselves at a particular studio—my assignment was Paramount—and walk the picket line for three hours. I eagerly anticipated each round. It got me out of doors and into the sunshine, caused me ever so slightly to utilize my muscles. Best of all, for the first time in my life I met regularly with other writers.

Parading with my colleagues up and back before the studio's Bronson

Gate, conversation was endless. We talked sports. We talked weather. We talked cars. We talked Watergate.

Mainly we talked writing; not the profound, penetrating issues regarding beauty and truth but the hard-bitten nuts/bolts considerations, working writers' shoptalk: hand-cranked versus electric pencil sharpeners, standard versus legal-size ruled yellow pads, felt-tipped markers versus ballpoint pens, liquid Wite-Out versus cut-rate bulk generic correction fluid available by the half gallon at an office supply outlet on Lake just north of Colorado in Pasadena.

Spoiled brats that we were, as all writers are and have been since the invention of writing in ancient Sumer five thousand years ago, we inventoried the injustices visited upon us by our oppressors: agents, actors, executives, the pal-of-the-producer hack who had rewritten and wrecked our latest draft, the director who had botched and butchered our otherwise flawless triumph, the literary manager who had refused to take or return our calls, the spouse, offspring, parent, pal, pet, or potted plant who had neglected to pay ample homage to our timeless and eternal genius.

Walking that line, talking with my fellows, amid all of the showbiz gossip I discovered a startling, liberating precept. I present it here as the first among many essential principles we'll underscore from time to time throughout this volume.

Principle 1: All writers hate to write.

It is not I alone who dreads the blank page, who struggles daily to drag himself to his desk, who dawdles and procrastinates and picks lint from the carpet to avoid applying fingers to keys. Those nasty habits belong, I realized, to all writers.

Writers love having written, but we hate to write.

This may appear cynical, but it is simply a statement of observed fact. To sit hour upon hour in an empty room, attempting to fill blank paper—or, these days, glowing LCD screens—with story, character, and dialogue worthy of the time, attention, and consideration of an audience is as lonely as life gets. Writing, like banging your head against the wall, feels terrific mainly when you stop.

On the picket line, putting one foot in front of the other along Melrose, turning the corner at Van Ness, we inventoried the clever and elaborate methods by which the lot of us evade our task. One writer described a technique he had developed whereby he gazed blankly from his window at traffic; as soon as the fourteenth car bearing Nebraska plates drove past, he started writing. Another claimed he would put cool, quiet jazz on the stereo in the background, sharpen all his pencils, lay out neat, fresh stacks of heavy-gauge rag-content bond, test his typewriter ribbon, and then, at long last . . . defrost his refrigerator.

This is not to deny that there are soaring, triumphant moments attendant to writing. Professional screenwriters are paid, after all, for the very same activity that earns civilians reprimand: daydreaming.

To write, however, is far more than merely to dream.

Principle 2: To write is to play God.

As God created the universe, writers create the universe of our screenplays. If we want it to rain, it rains. If we are weary of rain and covet sunshine, out comes the sun. If we get mad at somebody and want to kill him—who has never wanted to kill somebody?—a screenwriter kills him. Afterward, should he experience remorse, with the click of a mouse he can bring him back to life.

After too many decades of auteurism, the alien notion falsely anointing the director as film's first artist, screenwriters are coming into our own, at long last winning the recognition properly due movies' authentic prime movers. The writer is film's first artist if for no other reason than that she is just that: first. The vast, sprawling army of artists and craftspeople who gather to make a movie are lost, every one of them, without the writer. The fanciest state-of-the-art cameras, the latest high-tech editing suite, the finest actors, the most highly respected producers, the whole host of paraphernalia required for the production of a film are useless until a writer writes a plan.

That plan is the screenplay.

Legendary director Frank Capra was asked in an interview to explain precisely how he achieved in his movies that legendary quality called "the Capra touch." In the interview he rambles on about this technique and that one: clues he whispered to the actors, cues offered to the crew, wisdom shared with the editor. Nowhere in the article does he mention the name Robert Riskin, who had merely written all the referenced films.

The afternoon the interview appeared in the press there arrived at Capra's office a script-size envelope. Inside was a document very closely resembling a screenplay: a front cover, a back cover, and one hundred and ten pages. The cover and pages, however, were all blank. Clipped to the "script" was a note from Robert Riskin. It read: "Dear Frank, put 'the Capra touch' on this!"

Writing, like all creative expression, for all its struggle represents ultimately structured, organized, orchestrated dreaming. That's why writers' most basic task—before tale, before character and dialogue—is to learn how to let ourselves dream in a free yet orderly fashion.

Can people really be taught how to dream?

As a screenwriting educator I am frequently asked the twin questions: Can writing be taught at all? Can formal instruction help a writer compete in the film and television industry?

The second answer first. Yes.

There is one strategy—the only strategy—for writers seeking success in film, television, and digital media: good writing. To that end, any support that helps writers structure their narratives, focus their characters, render their dialogue palpable and provocative, any clue that helps writers create screenplays worthy of audiences, ought to help bridge the chasm between amateur and professional.

Can writers be taught to write well?

Again, yes.

Nobody expects an unschooled clarinetist to go into the closet and emerge a professional. No one expects a composer to master musical theory and notation by means of a miraculous religious vision. Even Mozart had a teacher. Likewise, many new painters have mentors, just as experienced painters have protégés.

Like all creative expression, writing depends not upon talent alone but also discipline. Each is rare all by itself. The two in tandem, however, are exponentially rarer still. Copious talent and paltry discipline will not carry a writer nearly so far as the converse combination. Naturally, no teacher or book can provide talent; at UCLA's Master of Fine Arts program writers are required to supply their own. Neither can writers have inspiration unwillingly thrust upon them; they must discover motivation within themselves. Happily, however, if teachers cannot provide talent, neither can they take talent away. While no book can supply a freeze-dried formula for concocting the perfect screenplay, there are challenges both narrow and broad that can be usefully addressed.

An Overview of the Present Volume

As underscored in chapter 7, "Story: Tale Assembly," there is a vast difference between assembling a child's tricycle fresh from the shipping crate and constructing an integrated screen story. Notably, the latter requires a considerable measure of magic.

There is so much more to screenwriting than knowing how far to indent dialogue. Readers seeking to learn proper screenplay format can turn to chapter 11. Format aside, screenwriting's central challenge remains, as always, finding the writer's unique voice.

Chapter 13, "The Writing Habit," deals with writers' attitudes regarding the daily struggle to structure their dreams into coherent dramatic narratives meriting the time, attention, and consideration of audiences.

And since the movie not produced, the film not released and not viewed by audiences has precisely the same effect as the movie not written in the first place, chapter 17, "Script Sales Strategies," addresses issues pertinent to integrating screenplays into the professional community—agents, managers, producers, actors, directors, lawyers, the complete cast of craftspeople and collaborators.

Too often these latter items preoccupy the attention of inexperienced writers. For writers to begin writing from the standpoint of marketing is a self-defeating prophesy. There is no marketing of material that has yet to be written. It's useless for writers to concern themselves about sales before they have something to sell.

Principle 3: Finding an agent is easy; what is hard is writing a screenplay worthy of an agent's representation.

Finally, having fractured screenwriting into shreds and shards and fragments, we need at the same time to remain mindful of "the Whole Picture"; part 4 of the book puts all those fragments back together again. In the end, screenwriting, notwithstanding its inevitable agonies, and for all its loneliness, is seen also to be a most delicious addiction.

Principle 4: Writing is schizophrenic.

Writing requires its practitioners temporarily to shatter themselves into a widely varying cast of characters, each possessing unique traits.

They need also simultaneously to accomplish assorted sets of tasks that endlessly contradict one another.

They must deal with seemingly separate items—story, character, dialogue, and so many others—that are not separate at all but exist only in combination with one another. Writers must wander freely among scattered, chaotic details even as their narratives proclaim a clear, logical, inevitable order. They must write films that are fantastic even as they are plausible. Like all artists, even as they lie through their teeth they must tell nothing but the truth.

Principle 5: Art is the lie that tells the bigger truth.

Chaim Potok, in his timeless novel *The Chosen*, describes a rabbi in conversation with his son. The Hebrew word for God, the rabbi explains, is *mel*, which means also "king" and "head." The reverse, *lem*, means precisely the opposite: "fool." *Lem* also has another meaning: "heart."

If you want to live as a king, the rabbi advises, if you want to emulate God, you must be ruled not by the heart but the head. That is sage advice for a rabbi's son, but not for a writer.

Writing is a heart-oriented enterprise, more a creation of hands, of belly, of groin, than of intellect. Writing for the screen is from top to bottom a wondrously silly endeavor, a sweetly ridiculous way for grown women and men to ply their trade and live their lives.

If you want to be God or a king, therefore, let your head guide you. Should you wish to write for the screen, however, live by your heart: Seize the courage to be something of a fool.

PART I

. . . .

Art

Chapter 1

· · · · · · · ·

Seven Naughty Words

As longtime Screenwriting chairman and cochairman of UCLA's Department of Film, Television and Digital Media I possess the authority to compel legions of students to purchase screenwriting books. Not surprisingly, publishers send me every title touching even remotely upon the subject. These seem to flow nowadays at the rate of perhaps two a week. Among all these books some are fine, some are not. Some are serious and self-important, others are lighthearted and breezy. There is a single component, however, uniting virtually all of them: a glossary.

Inevitably the glossaries are replete with precisely the kind of technical film jargon I urge screenwriters to eschew: angles, lenses, camera moves, editing effects, film graphics.

Screenplays should contain nothing besides clear, everyday language. It doesn't hurt a bit, of course, for a writer to be a genius of invention and imagination. What he needs to know first of all, however, is English. Moreover, he needs to know it quite well, since language is the sole tool available for transporting a screen story from the writer's head into the heads of others. Of particular importance is precision in the choice of words.

To that end, I present a glossary of precisely seven commonly misconstrued terms. In our modern age these words have taken on new meanings, but here I wish to argue for restoration of their original denotations, as current connotations engender snobbism, a danger to any art, and especially destructive to public and popular art such as film and television.

A note of caution is in order. In some circles the words that follow are

considered obscene; reader discretion is advised. Remember also, however, that polite language, as legendary producer Samuel Goldwyn said
years ago, makes for polite pictures. Polite pictures violate movies' one
inviolable rule: Don't be boring.

1. Entertainment

Year after year, upon the release of the latest James Bond installment,
the late producer Albert Broccoli offered interviews reassuring the critics
that he fully appreciated that his 007 films represent "not *Macbeth*, just
entertainment."

Had he never seen *Macbeth*? Did he not know how entertaining
Macbeth is? That it has witches and riddles and special effects ("Is this a
dagger I see before me?") and murder, mayhem, lust, greed, intrigue,
sword fights, blood, vengeance, and horror?

But surely there is more to *Macbeth*, scholars and critics will remon-
strate, than these mere surface tensions. They are not wrong. Indeed,
beneath the play's veneer lie profound insights into the most fundamental
aspects of the human condition.

Entertainment and art are not, however, mutually exclusive. To the contrary, they walk together in lockstep. No artist—notably no film or television
writer—need apologize for entertaining an assembled mass of people.

Over many years "entertainment" has acquired an undeserved connotation that is pejorative; it has come to signify that which is fleeting, superficial, trivial, insubstantial. Truly to comprehend the term, however, a
writer could do a lot worse than to check out a worthy dictionary.

There is none worthier than the *Oxford English Dictionary*, wherein
"entertainment" enjoys an honorable, venerable tradition. To entertain is
to occupy, to hold, to give over to consideration, as in "entertaining a
notion." This does not mean painting one's face and performing a tap
dance for the notion, but cradling it in one's cortex, hefting its mass, regarding it, weighing it, investing it with value and contemplation.

"Entertain" derives from "intertwine." Entertainment is intertwine-
ment in two special ways. First is the weaving of all the elements—plot,
character, dialogue, action, setting, and all the rest—into a unified body
within a single work. Second is a film's union with its viewers. Ideally, the
viewer of any art becomes in a certain sense part of the creation.

To entertain, it is unfairly asserted, is merely to divert. A film most certainly should achieve more than only that, but it cannot accomplish anything at all unless first of all it entertains.

2. Commercial

"Commercial" derives, of course, from "commerce." Decent, sensitive, genuine, inspired artists no sooner engage in commerce than in pedophilia. Commerce is, after all, lowly trade. It is not for nothing that respectable homes and hostelries have separate entrances—down the alley, around back, below stairs—for tradesmen.

Ought not the serious, self-respecting writer be free of the constraints associated with trafficking? How else is he to find—and ultimately to share with viewers—the profound truths lying at his core? How do we reconcile worthy art with sucking for bucks?

Once again, turn to the dictionary.

"Commerce," notwithstanding its most common connotation, means a great deal more than merely dealing. Like "entertainment," the word possesses a respectable history. "Commerce" means first of all "to communicate physically," which all by itself is no shabby description of movies. More significantly, "commerce" suggests "intercourse or converse with God, with spirits, passions, thoughts." "Commerce" denotes "association, communication," especially with regard to "the affairs of life." It represents an "exchange between men of the products of nature or art."

One could travel light-years in search of a loftier, nobler definition of artistic integrity. To be sure, a film's commercial success alone does not establish its merit. By the same token, however, broad commercial success does not on its face constitute worthlessness. Likewise, remoteness and obscurity do not assure a film's value.

"A poet," said Orson Welles, "needs a pen, a painter a brush, and a filmmaker an army." Armies cost money. Commerce in movies and TV represents the vital mechanism necessary to communicate expression whose production happens to be costly.

Commerce's lowly reputation, therefore, is undeserved. If a writer is too fancy to slug it out in the down-and-dirty trenches of commerce, that's his prerogative, but I advise him urgently to avoid trafficking in film and television.

3. Voyeurism

Critics relentlessly assail certain films as voyeuristic, but what are movies if not that? The viewers hide in the theater's darkness peering through the window of the screen into the personal and private lives of strangers. They paw their effects, scrutinize their moves, eavesdrop on their conversations.

We know better than to prowl real alleys peeping into real houses. That's why we hire filmmakers to peep for us. If a film appears brazenly, heavy-handedly voyeuristic, it fails to exercise sufficient craft. To condemn film for voyeurism is like reprimanding water for its wetness.

4. Contrivance

Film is the single most contrived enterprise in the history of the universe.

What is more disjointed, manipulated, choreographed, orchestrated, arranged and rearranged than film? As audiences, we view scenes containing intercut shots and seemingly synchronous dialogue, even as we appreciate that the different pieces were recorded in many places and at diverse times.

Contrivance, like all craft, should never show. A skillful screenplay appears, quite falsely, to be seamless. This notion is discussed in various chapters of this book; it is sufficient here simply to say that if you can't live with grandly crafted appearances, if you disdain fantasy and artifice, you ought not to pursue screenwriting, for it is above all the art of maximum contrivance.

5. Exploitation

As a screenwriter you are in the wrong place, also, if you are too highly bred ever to engage in anything so low class as exploitation.

In fact all art—not film alone—wallows in exploitation. To exploit means simply to make the most of something, to extract the finest, richest resources, to achieve the highest expression. Good scripts are hard enough to construct without pulling punches, for screenwriting is basically a bare-knuckles enterprise. Writers seeking maximum effect need not fear to exploit their resources.

6. Hollywood

Hollywood—which is to say the professional film and television community in Southern California—remains more than ever the center of world filmmaking. Is it the sunshine? Los Angeles has no monopoly on sunshine. Is it tradition? Film is still too young a medium to have much in the way of tradition. Is it the abundance of skilled craftsmen?

Possibly.

Even if most Hollywood films fail, however, if so many among them are shallow and superficial, so also are most books, poems, music, paintings. If you turn up your nose at mention of the word "Hollywood"; if you can't tolerate tinsel—if you don't like bright, brash, brassy, attention-craving spectacle; crisp, crazy dialogue; broad, sprawling action; and fleshy, flashy effects—probably somewhere you took a wrong turn in your development as a practitioner of public, popular art.

7. Audience

"Audience" is the naughtiest word of all. It deserves its own chapter.

Chapter 2

. . . .

Audience: The Status of the Observer

Movies are for audiences.

In elitist circles audience is often disdained.

Should a painting find even a single patron it may survive throughout the ages. Should a poem be published by even the most obscure pushcart press, it may eventually be celebrated by masses of readers.

This is not true for film.

Public and popular art is for the public and populace. To fulfill their natural purpose, movies require a collected group, not an observer but a broad multiplicity of observers, all of them viewing the work together in congregations, the lot of them watching the work unfold at a steady, single pace.

A movie without an audience has the same effect as a movie that does not exist. Of course it may exist in some technical form—clumps of silver halide crystals clouding a chemical emulsion, patterns of light and shadow married to a celluloid base. Without viewers, however, a film has the same effect as if it had never been created. It touches nobody. It moves no one. Without an audience to observe it, all the talent and toil, the art and the craft embedded within it add up to zero.

No screenwriter, therefore, may ignore audience.

Consider a remote radio station of limited broadcast range. Imagine a lone disc jockey with a late-night jazz show. The program enjoys but a handful of listeners.

Just possibly, one night, at one moment or another, there is not a soul listening.

Does the deejay communicate?

To answer this question we have to examine the nature of communication itself. Today there are scores of fancy, convoluted, newfangled models of communication. In my view none comes close to the communications model devised by Aristotle over two millennia ago. Communication, he said, requires three components: a Source, a Message, and a Receiver. Without any one of these core components, communication fails to occur.

Our lonely deejay in his remote radio station with nobody listening does not communicate, because there is no receiver. He hasn't a clue, of course, while broadcasting whether or not anybody is tuned to the program. On blind faith alone he presumes at least a handful of scattered jazz fan insomniacs are out there, radio dials aglow. He chats his chat, spins his discs, never truly knowing whether his music and his patter are exclusive to himself or actually shared with living, breathing listeners. In either case his behavior is the same.

Yet in one instance he communicates and in the other he does not. His ability to communicate depends not on himself alone but also the existence of an audience.

Screenwriters bear the same burden. In keeping with Aristotle's model, the writer is the Source, his screenplay is the Message, and the audience is the Receiver. No writer knows for certain that his script will be produced. This is as true for the humblest beginner as it is for the most experienced practitioner. This is true even for scripts that are sold for substantial sums.

Studio story department shelves are lined with screenplays—optioned, commissioned, purchased—that have yet to be produced. Even among scripts that are produced, many fail to see the light of screen, even after filming. They may, for example, fail to win a distribution deal. In such cases, which represent the vast majority of screenplay sales, the writers' movies have all the impact they would have had if they had not been written at all.

Screenwriters are compelled to ignore this. They are required to leap a chasm of faith and take as given that what they write is surely to be acted by actors, photographed by cinematographers, edited by editors, and exhibited to audiences. For that, and for other reasons, it's useful for writers to be just a little crazy.

For that, too, it's possible to formulate the screenwriter's first, last, and only commandment: Be worthy of an audience. The good movie is that which merits the time, attention, and consideration of a collected group of people. Write a movie that from beginning to end is not boring and people will queue up around the block; they will stand in line outdoors for hours in rotten weather for the opportunity to trade their dollars for the privilege of spending approximately a hundred minutes with a writer's projected fantasy.

Principle 6: Screenwriting's one unbreakable rule: Don't be boring.

If all that is required of a successful screenplay is to avoid boring an audience, why do so few screenwriters eke out even a middle-class living? Why aren't there thousands, even millions more? How difficult can it be, after all, merely to avoid boring an audience for a couple of hours?

Extremely difficult indeed.

To invent a story and characters worth caring about, to assign them action and dialogue that engage and sustain an audience's interest from eight o'clock until nine forty, is a task that is truly Herculean.

To suggest that a film ought to be worthy of the time and attention of an audience should not provoke any kind of controversy. Nevertheless, legions of scholars and critics disdain and even revile this notion. To acknowledge audience at all, they complain, is to pander. The authentic artist cares not a whit for audiences. His task is surely loftier than catering to the lowest common denominator. Respectable writers do not care if their work plays in Peoria. True artists enter a joyful, spiritual trance; they set their creative juices to flowing, their imaginations to soaring.

There's not a whole lot more to it than that, or so we're told.

When I arrived at UCLA's film school in the 1970s, the third worst thing a writer could do was to write a script that actually sold. To do so was to sully artistic expression with filthy lucre. The second worst thing a writer could do was to write a screenplay that not only sold but was actually produced as a film. That's just copping to the system, working for The Man, becoming a cog in the corrupt and corrosive capitalist machine.

The worst thing a writer could do? Write a movie that was a hit. Audiences aren't smart, pundits and academics opine, they're stupid. Why do so many educators who characterize themselves as Marxist appear to hate the masses?

An authentic film artist at UCLA during the 1960s and 1970s didn't consider audience at all. You strapped a Portapak on your back, sprayed the camera lens with whatever caught your fancy (I call it the garden-hose school of cinematography), and anything you did was beautiful because *you're* beautiful.

This is, of course, narcissistic claptrap.

Principle 7: Audiences are not stupid; they are smart.

Throughout the millennia audiences have demonstrated an uncanny knack for finding the worthy stuff. This is not to suggest that all popular movies are good and unpopular ones bad. I'm simply saying that in order to last, movies need to succeed both artistically and commercially.

The burden weighs upon the artist to provide for the audience, and not the other way around. Artists who scorn audience, who regard the public with contempt, should renounce any ambition to write for the screen.

The screenwriter's basic mission is first of all to divert an assembled mass of civilians from life's natural and inevitable tedium. If the most we expect from a work of art is that it forever change our lives, the least we require is that it keep us awake.

If from time to time audiences embrace works that are superficial and silly, throughout the ages they have demonstrated also a marked capability for recognizing greatness. Since the earliest recorded popular expression, the ancient Greek classics, among works performed and celebrated century after century not one was unknown or unpopular contemporaneously, none failed to reach audiences during its author's lifetime.

Oedipus Rex is no obscure, misplaced work that languished in Sophocles' trunk awaiting the attention of some plucky graduate student in search of a subject for a dissertation. *Hamlet* was not ignored during its own day, finally to be resurrected by modern scholars and critics. Shakespeare's best plays were broad, brawling, blockbuster hits in his own day. From their earliest performances audiences flocked eagerly and repeatedly to see them.

Certainly I do not argue that a movie is as good as its audience is large. Even Aristotle recognized there is such a thing as misfortune. Picture for picture, the reason particular audiences spark to particular films is forever a mystery. No screenwriter, however, need apologize for reaching people. If past is prologue, a work of public and popular expression that fails in its own time to find an audience, good or bad as it may well be, it will for all time be lost.

Chapter 3

. . . .

The Personal Screenplay

Self-Revelation

Screenwriting education in recent years has not merely burgeoned but exploded. This phenomenon is by no means limited to accredited film schools. An itinerant army of self-appointed instructors treks back and forth across the nation and the globe. Indeed, so many amateurs now dabble in the discipline that screenwriting might well be considered the new millennium's macramé.

Certainly there are differences among various teachers' approaches. One lecturer preaches that the properly constructed screenplay contains five stations on the story continuum. Another refers to these as "plot points" and "turning points" (I've never quite figured out the distinction) and asserts that there are not five but nine—or is it eleven?—more or less. Still another pundit identifies no fewer than two dozen "building blocks" at the core of story structure.

These differences all pale, however, beside commonly agreed-upon principles. For example, virtually all the popular screenwriting teachers concur that among the myriad screen elements—character, dialogue, setting, and more—preeminent among them is story. All of us agree furthermore that underlying every story is something called "structure."

From my own point of view, these other worthy teachers provide merely their own particular spin on Aristotle's timeless *Poetics*, which argues that story structure is divided into not five or nine or two dozen but just three essential parts. This is often wrongly referred to as the three-act paradigm (a hot word in the academy), but in fact Aristotle never mentions "acts." Aristotle writes instead of beginnings, middles, and ends. Perhaps the time has come finally to deconstruct all that canonical Greek dogma, but personally, if I have to choose among an array of approaches, I'm going with Aristotle.

I predict the old fellow will last.

We'll examine this critical issue in chapter 7, "Story: Tale Assembly."

Even among prickly, crotchety screenwriting instructors there is for the most part agreement on the preeminence of story. One popular pundit, however, suggests a couple of linked notions with which I vigorously disagree. My purpose here is not to engage in a pedagogical turf war but to demonstrate two essential principles that lie at the heart of screenwriting.

This particular independent educator insists that whatever else writers may write, what they must *not* write.is their own personal story. Nobody cares a whit, he cautions, about writers' private, personal plights except, of course, the writers themselves.

Here, then, is our fundamental disagreement. Decades spent writing and teaching have taught me that writers' own personal stories are the only story they *should* write.

> ### Principle 8: Whenever writers sit down before blank paper or glowing pixels, they should write their own personal story.

Even if a writer attempts vigorously to do otherwise, even if he works on an assignment writing a script for hire based on someone else's idea, even an idea totally alien to his experience, he will nonetheless end up telling nothing other than his own personal tale. Whatever the original concept, however specific, however narrow, in all instances it is filtered through the peculiar sensibilities of the specific writer. In the end, despite himself, the writer will create a tale that is personal.

Why fight it?

My advice: Surrender.

It is one battle in which defeat actually amounts to victory.

Self-revelation lies, after all, at the center of not screenwriting alone but all creative expression. How can self-protection—that is, avoiding what is personal—serve any purpose other than to suppress, stifle, and suffocate the emotion that resides at the center of all worthy art?

Principle 9: Screenwriters must embrace authentic self-disclosure, no matter how painful, as the organizing principle of their movies.

Writing that is guarded, barren of feeling, evenhanded, objective, and dispassionate might be proper in a corporate prospectus. It might serve adequately for instructions regarding the assembly of a backyard barbecue grill.

As for screenwriting, however, such expression violates that most fundamental artistic principle of all: It's boring.

The Integrated Screenplay

Integration is an essential, elusive quality informing all creative expression. Integration transcends mere parts: tale, character, dialogue, and all the rest. Instead it embraces the whole picture.

What precisely is integration?

Integration is every bit as easy to understand as it is difficult to achieve. The integrated screenplay is one whose every aspect—each bit of action, every line of dialogue—accomplishes simultaneously the twin tasks of (1) advancing plot and (2) expanding character. Perhaps this is just another way of saying that each piece of information needs to tell the audience something new.

Call integration screenwriting's great equalizer. If in an identifiable, measurable, palpable way the material simultaneously advances story and character, all rules are off, all prohibitions are null and void. Integrate your whole picture and you can write anything at all.

Indeed, if from beginning to end a screenplay is genuinely integrated, the writer can successfully do even nothing at all. If that sounds crazy, remember that to no small extent crazy is precisely what art is.

Let us demonstrate.

As a screenwriting educator I preach that scenes in restaurants, for example, are to be avoided. Turn on the TV right now, go to a movie theater, or slap a DVD in the player. Soon enough, indeed too soon, you're likely to encounter actors sitting around tables in restaurants, not acting out the tale but narrating it as they engage in action that is not action at all: sawing away at their meal with silverware.

Lazy writers all too often have their characters narrate the tale while they engage in bogus "action": wielding knives and forks, sipping water and wine, blotting lips with napkins, sprinkling pepper and salt, and, most regrettably, flapping their jaws.

Still worse, such scenes inevitably begin too early, long before the true Aristotelian beginning, that is to say, the point before which nothing is needed. In the rare instance that a writer absolutely must place a scene in a restaurant, he certainly does not need to start with the characters entering the establishment, being greeted by the greeter, seated by the seater, and introduced to the busboys and kitchen staff. One certainly need not have the waiter describe today's specials; indeed, there's no need whatever to have the folks order their food at all. A writer should cut directly to the meat of the scene.

Best of all, again, writers should avoid scenes in restaurants altogether.

Unless they're integrated.

In John Patrick Shanley's *Moonstruck*, the character portrayed by Cher sits opposite a man at a table in a restaurant. The waiter arrives to take their order. Cher's companion wants fish. Paraphrasing, Cher says, "Fish? You're eating fish?"

"Why not fish?"

"Because you're going to be fourteen hours on a plane to Sicily. That fish will sit in your stomach and rot. You'll turn green."

"I don't want fish?"

"No."

"So what do I want?"

Cher prescribes precisely what he should order. "You want a light angel-hair pasta primavera. It'll sit gently in your tummy and digest. You'll be able to sleep on the plane and when you arrive at your destination you'll be rested and alert and ready to go about your sorry task."

Her dining partner nods to the waiter, confirming that this is his order. He turns to Cher. "You're an old-fashioned kind of woman," he says. "You really know how to take care of a man. You're exactly the kind of woman I need. Marry me."

"You call that a proposal?" she protests.

"Yeah, sure. Why not? You want me to get down on my knees?"

"Considering it's a proposal of marriage, down on your knees would be nice."

He shrugs, rises from his chair, then drops to his knees and proposes marriage.

She accepts.

Even though the setting is a restaurant, the characters are not exclusively eating and talking but also taking action. Right there, smack in the middle of the restaurant, amid the astonished diners, the suitor gets down on his knees and proposes marriage.

This is no car chase. This is no saloon brawl. Haven't we had enough—indeed too many—of those in too many movies?

Notwithstanding its restraint, it represents exciting dramatic action. Something is happening, something that is visual. It is so much more than merely a discussion among actors, a recitation disclosing data. It is a scene to be seen, not one only to be heard. It constitutes activity instead of passivity. In many ways, because it is subtle, because it is something small—ordering dinner—that sheds light on something big—the protagonist's character—it represents the most exquisite sort of movie action.

How do we judge it to be integrated?

First, it advances the story. *Moonstruck* is the tale of a woman who falls in love with her fiancé's brother. In order to have a fiancé she must become engaged.

Beyond the scene's lame venue—the restaurant—there is also the forbidden ordering of food. Does the discussion regarding entrees constitute dialogue that is integrated? Yes, because it expands our appreciation of Cher's character. At this early juncture in the picture she is something of an Earth Mother, a woman who knows how to nourish a man in the most traditional, maternal way.

The dialogue regarding the food establishes this nurturing aspect of her character. Indeed, she is a woman who holds romance to be a hoax. She need look no further than her own parents' wretched marriage to know that love is just a joke.

Eventually, of course, she becomes quite another woman. She realizes that a woman is entitled to passion, to steamy, seamy, searing, soaring romance. She'll discover that love is no mere trick, not a trap, not a burden but timeless and eternal joy. Love, Cher's Loretta will eventually determine, is the only reason we are here. Better to burn in hell for eternity than to endure a loveless, empty existence on earth.

In this fashion the characters are rendered fleshy and real. Instead of remaining static they develop, they expand. When Loretta tells her date how to order dinner, instead of lying there like lox the tale moves forward.

Thanks to integration, what is usually prohibited is legitimate. The restaurant setting and the ordering of the meal deliver story and character freight previously unavailable to the reader of the script and the audience in the theater. A scene that offers new information draws the audience closer to the screen very much in the manner of a primitive shaman drawing his tribal brothers and sisters more closely around the fire.

Integration, as I have already asserted, is so powerful an aspect of the well-crafted script that in the truly integrated movie it is possible to do absolutely nothing at all and still advance story and expand character.

How can a scene in which nothing happens advance story and character? Consider *About Schmidt* (Alexander Payne, Jim Taylor, adapting the Louis Begley novel). The movie opens with Schmidt, portrayed by Jack Nicholson, sitting stock-still alone in his office. There is absolutely no motion except for the sweep hand of the clock ticking off the seconds one by one. The time: perhaps a half minute before five P.M. The desk is devoid of clutter. The shelves are empty. The walls are bare; all the pictures have been removed.

In one corner of the chamber is a pile of neatly stacked boxes that can only contain the stuff removed from the desk and shelves and walls. Scoping out the office tells the viewer that Schmidt is retiring.

When it is precisely five o'clock, not a second sooner, Schmidt rises and exits. Presumably his stuff will be sent to him later.

With virtually nothing happening in the scene, without a single line of dialogue, the writers communicate a bounty of story and character information. We learn, as already stated, that after a long career Schmidt is finally retiring. We learn also that he is a stickler for detail; surely no one would have noticed, much less cared, if he had departed earlier in the day. Perhaps the reason he remains until the very last second reflects his reluctance to retire.

Since the scene is integrated, with all of the imagery advancing story and character, it works perfectly well. Indeed, for its economy and efficiency it is masterful.

Another splendid example of integration allowing screenwriters to write dialogue and action that should otherwise be discouraged is found in the made-for-television movie *A Woman Called Golda* (Harold Gast, Steve Gethers). Ingrid Bergman, in the final performance of her career, portrays the late prime minister of Israel. In one scene the chairman of the United States Senate's Armed Services Committee visits her. His mission: to inform her that he can sell only military weaponry that does not measure up to Israeli security requirements.

The senator arrives at the modest official residence in Jerusalem to find himself completely alone with the prime minister—no aides or assistants or secretaries. Her very first act—on its face nothing more than a quick and apparently inconsequential bit of dialogue—seems to violate one of our most stringent screenwriting prohibitions: She offers him a cup of coffee.

Collectively, in terms of person-hours, I do not doubt that fourteen trillion eons have been consumed by audiences across the globe watching actors in films and on television talk about, pour, and drink oceans of coffee. Acres of rain forest have fallen to provide the paper upon which unimaginative screenwriters have inscribed time-squandering, wheel-spinning dialogue surrounding the beverage.

Decaf or regular? Sugar and/or cream? Dairy substitute and/or artificial sweetener? Half-and-half instead of cream? Milk instead of half-and-half? If milk, whole? Skim? Condensed? Powdered? Boxed? Canned? Soy? Extra-rich? Low-fat?

Inevitably it's an unsubtle attempt by a movie writer to stall, to stretch, to fill, to pad, to bloat with air. Or it's an act of desperation by an out-of-ideas writer hoping to kill time until the next commercial.

Principle 10: In life we kill time; in movies time kills us.

Thanks, however, to the writers' skill, in *A Woman Called Golda* even the coffee is integrated and, therefore, justified.

How can the offer of a cup of coffee be integrated?

When the senator accepts the prime minister's offer of coffee, she goes to fetch it, leaving him all alone in the diminutive apartment's cramped living room. He sits on the couch and waits. He waits. He waits. He waits. Perhaps twenty seconds elapse—an eternity on film—in which absolutely nothing happens.

From the audience's perspective those twenty seconds feel like a year or two.

A wonderful tension builds both for the character—the senator—and also for the audience. At long last the senator rises and sets out to find the prime minister. He discovers her in the kitchen. She is just now setting his coffee on the table, along with a plate of pastry. She pulls out a chair, beckoning him to sit.

Even before a line is spoken we receive a lot of information. Subtextually we see that Israel, for all its strategic importance, for all of the attention it receives, is but a speck of a nation, a land so modest, so humble that its prime minister all by herself prepares coffee for high-level official visitors in her downscale one-bedroom government digs.

If that were the end of it, the business of the coffee would be justified because it is integrated; character and story advance some measurable distance. It is not the end, however; it is merely the beginning.

The senator settles in at the kitchen table and begins to consume both the coffee and a slice of the prime minister's home-baked strudel. He mentions the inferior military equipment his government is willing to sell. Golda expresses her dismay. From the mouth of the most unlikely person—an elderly Jewish lady, a former Milwaukee schoolteacher—there now spills military jargon as sophisticated and informed as would flow from a four-star general. She comments upon retrofitting bomb racks with titanium struts, speaks of explosive tonnage, cites statistics relating to radar range and weapons and ordnance and kill ratios, and a host of similar high-tech considerations.

The senator is awestruck. In shorter order he is converted to her cause. Why wouldn't he be? Madam Prime Minister is, after all, a mother. Perhaps still more to the point, she is a Jewish mother. She's got her prey exactly where she wants him: at her kitchen table.

He hasn't a chance!

Thanks to integration, nothing is turned into something. Something trivial is transformed into something profound. A character sits on a couch in a living room engaged in absolutely no activity beyond breathing. Yet the writer wields this apparent inaction so splendidly that the story relentlessly advances. The otherwise mundane pouring of a cup of coffee does not stifle the tale but intensifies it.

It's almost always a mistake to generalize, but here nonetheless is a broad, sweeping principle that is true in all cases:

Principle 11: If a screenplay is personal and integrated it does not matter what it's about.

Movies contain, after all is said and done, only two kinds of information: sight and sound. If each sight and every sound genuinely advances the story and enhances the audience's appreciation of the characters, and if the tale represents the intimate, personal sensibilities of the writer, audiences will be enthralled by it, regardless of its subject or setting.

Integration extends not only to story and character but to every other aspect of a screenplay. Worthy writers wisely choose actions and settings, for example, that synchronize with the rest of the film.

In *The Godfather* (Mario Puzo, Francis Ford Coppola, adapting Puzo's novel) a rich man defies the mob. How shall they punish him? Burn down his house? Break a knee? Implant an ice pick in his temple? All of the above? Perhaps these are workable after a fashion, but are they truly integrated? Are they fresh? Are they special to this character in this setting?

Definitely not. Instead, hooking into the previously established fact that the character boasts about a champion racehorse he owns, the writer has the man awake in his sumptuous silk-sheeted bed to discover his prize steed's severed head beside him.

In *Atlantic City* John Guare writes a scene in which a beautiful young woman stands in her kitchen stripped to the waist, massaging fresh lemon juice into her breasts. I acknowledge I don't mind one bit viewing such a scene even merely for its own sake; as discussed in a later chapter on conflict, eroticism has been a central component of drama since its earliest days on the ancient Greek stage, even if in those years the actors kept their clothes on.

The question arises, however: Is this scene appropriate to this film?

The answer: Yes, absolutely. The same woman has been seen earlier holding a crummy job serving fried fish at a fast-food counter. The fish odor permeates her every pore, serving as a metaphor for her disenchantment with her life, her frustration and self-contempt. The lemon juice treatment offers a humble opportunity temporarily to cleanse herself of this rancid reminder of her sorry station. Sure, it's erotic, but it's also much more than that. It properly integrates the movie's diverse scenes and actions. It isn't merely added on; it is woven elegantly into the film's fabric.

The challenge, then, in choosing actions and settings that are truly exquisite instead of merely serviceable, is for writers to look to the rest of their film. In story, character, theme, within the whole body of collective actions they should seek clues to direct them toward invention that is different and fresh compared to the usual material we see in movie after movie.

If action defines character, then character defines action. To determine what action a character should take and in what setting, the writer should study the character. Action and character, combined with dialogue and placed in the properly integrated setting, add up to screenwriting's single most important element: story.

Even though we're talking about disparate elements among the challenges confronting screenwriters, the unifying principle is, again, integration. When writers endeavor perpetually to expand character and story, they end up embracing the "write" thing: integration.

Example #1: A Jail Tale

Some years ago I received a letter from a prisoner in a California penal institution. He had heard me discuss screenwriting issues on a San Francisco radio talk show.

"During the past few years," he wrote, "I have devoted a great deal of energy to learning the craft of screenwriting, and I have completed four scripts."

This statement all by itself impressed me most favorably. Writers have to write a bundle of scripts just in order to become familiar with the form and the craft, and to find their own voice. That this writer had four scripts under his belt seemed to bode well.

"I write very much from my life's experiences," the letter continued, "based upon my rather intimate knowledge of cops and cons and the things men do in the dark."

If it's not quite poetry from Shakespeare, it is nevertheless nifty, dazzling, sparkling stuff. It's punchy and to the point; it feels personal and original. With few words it communicates a lot.

My correspondent went on to explain that he would have loved to attend the screenwriting seminar I was offering in the Bay Area just a few days hence. However, he wrote, upon checking his calendar he'd discovered that on that particular weekend he would once again be a guest of the state at the same luxury facility, exactly as he had been and would be for weeks and months and years to come.

That he could be good-naturedly self-deprecating about his incarceration impressed me even further; writers who take themselves too seriously are the most difficult among a group of naturally difficult creatures.

He asked for permission to send one of his scripts.

That he did not simply enclose the script but sought my permission to send it demonstrated that he was a writer who understood the etiquette regarding screenplay submissions. Despite what one hears regarding "connections," a truly smart query letter will win the approval of most any agent. The smartly shaped query is the way a writer turns an unsolicited script into one that is solicited.

I granted our prisoner permission to mail me the script.

It arrived, accompanied by a brief cover letter. The letter thanked me for my consideration and went on to discuss the subject of writing in a number of gorgeously crafted sentences.

He wrote:

> *This work gives me a new life, or a new sense of life in a way that has been, for me, most remarkable.*
>
> *I have come to believe that any person of talent, any person involved in the great task of bringing that talent to form and life in any worthy piece of work, brings at the same time life and form to his own soul.*

The poetic purity of his language left me thinking: Next to this guy I'm just a typist.

His letter continued:

> *When I write I stand with my future behind me and my past stretches out before me as far as my mind can see.*

I could not figure out precisely what he meant but, all the same, the language struck me as transforming.

What followed, however, was the most beautiful part of all.

> *And all the characters I have known, all the lovers and warriors and barkers and painters and scene-shifters and criminals, come round. And as I look back, I am coming to the conclusion that the rather bitter dispute I've had with the world was never more than a simple lovers' quarrel.*

I eagerly awaited receipt of this screenplay. When it arrived at my office, however, my anticipation turned to dismay. The script's length alone—one hundred seventy-four pages—offered ample evidence of its amateurism. Sight unseen, I already knew the writer needed to lose sixty-five pages or more.

Clearly I was under no obligation to read this convicted felon's work. Nevertheless, to ignore so hapless a soul seemed more loathsome than to offer at least a token response. I sat down one night just before bedtime, anticipating that three minutes was about two minutes more than I would spend with the script. I would glance at the first few pages, jump to the middle, scan the conclusion.

Then I would dictate a quick letter saluting the writer's talent and discipline. I would refer specifically to one or two points in the script so that he'd get the impression I had read it more carefully than I actually had. I would advise him that before showing it to potential representatives or purchasers he would need to trim it. Finally, I would wish him well.

Under the circumstances, I mused, surely God in heaven would credit my Good Works merit badge account.

Instead I was up half the night, biting my nails in terror, feeling compassion for the characters, sensing their horror, glory, desperation, courage, greed, selflessness, rage, and love. What appeared at first to be a loss-of-innocence story turned out instead to be a tale of innocence regained.

In the opening, Nasty, a veteran con in his forties, receives a new cell mate, a youngster of nineteen, Richie. Nasty takes a liking to the youth and hopes to educate him in prison etiquette, expecting to spare him at least some of the darkness that can befall a prisoner and cost him not only his soul but his life. All the same, Richie succumbs to dope and gangs. However futile his struggle to save Richie, Nasty learns important life lessons.

At one critical point Nasty receives a letter from his sister notifying him that a year earlier their mother died. Upon learning of his mother's death, Nasty grieves. What's more, his grief is exacerbated by the realization that he has fallen so low as not even to learn of his mother's death until a year after the fact.

Still worse is his sister's accusation that he killed their mother as surely as if he had plunged a knife into her heart. "It was your disgrace," the sister writes, "that destroyed her. Your outlaw life shamed her and brought misery and ruination upon her days."

Nasty goes crazy with grief and rage, torching his cell and earning himself a stint in solitary confinement—the hole. His only warm-blooded company is a rat, with whom he shares his paltry meals.

A confederate working the food detail, delivering the standard bread-and-water ration, whispers to Nasty through the grate, "Hey, Nasty, could you use some dope?"

"I would die for a taste," Nasty responds.

Prison policy routinely grants requests, even from cons in solitary confinement, to attend chapel on Sunday. If he will sit in the chapel's back row, Nasty is told, someone will pass him a package.

Nasty goes to chapel, but before anybody slips him any contraband he becomes mesmerized by the sermon, delivered by an evangelical Christian preacher, a visiting pastor from the local community. She is herself the victim of a rape that occurred years earlier, and has never recovered from the degradation and despair that has enveloped her existence ever since. In an attempt to move on with her life, she has sought refuge in Christ. She ministers to the sorts of souls who victimized her. Perhaps if she can teach violent criminals to seek peace and forgiveness, she, too, can finally achieve closure.

The young woman's sermon—its eloquence, its poetic lilt—rocks Nasty's tormented soul. Then and there, in response to her testimony, he forever renounces drugs and all manner of evil. He pleads with God for forgiveness.

He is converted to the faith.

At this point I experienced dismay. Savvy felons appreciate that religious conversion plays well with parole boards. I worried that the writer was falsely posturing in a sophisticated attempt to win early release, and that I was myself being exploited in a probation scam. Certainly it could not harm a prisoner's cause to have in his corner a university professor available perhaps to write a letter on his behalf or even to testify in person before the parole board in support of clemency and early release.

From a strictly creative standpoint, as a writing educator I feared that the script would become now merely a religious tract that, even if sincere, would be limited by a narrowness of purpose.

The narrative promptly disabused me of this notion. At this precise point the tale moves from Christian faith to Islam. This transition occurs through the good offices of another character—a convicted serial murderer—who has found serenity and liberation through his devotion to Allah. In this manner, by moving from one faith to another, the tale transcends any particular creed and becomes instead a story of faith itself.

Eventually a full-scale riot breaks out, in which our evangelist is taken hostage only to be rescued by a reborn Nasty, who has discarded his prison name and reclaimed his Christian one: Peter.

The change of name offers a poignant example of the power of integration. Normally it is foolhardy to change a character's name in the middle of a script. What can the writer achieve except confusion among his readers?

Yet here the name change expands the character and the story. It is appropriate that at the time of his conversion Nasty discard his prison moniker and reclaim his Christian name. Again, what is otherwise prohibited becomes licensed by integration.

Eventually the writer was able to trim the draft to presentable size and to win representation. Now long out of stir, he enjoys a successful career as a writer. All of this derives from two items: (1) the tale's personal nature and (2) its author's ability to write dialogue and action that is perpetually integrated, consistently advancing story and character.

Example #2: Death by AIDS—a Laff Riot

Another example of a script that appeared at first likely to be unworthy was written not in prison but in another well-regulated institution: the graduate screenwriting program at UCLA.

Our advanced screenplay workshops are the meat and potatoes of our Master of Fine Arts program. Each section enrolls only eight writers and, over our ten-week quarter, convenes once weekly for three hours. There are no assigned readings, no exams. There is but a single paper: a professional-quality feature-length screenplay.

At the first session each quarter far too many writers attempt to enroll. In order to choose the class members, I hear each applicant's story proposal. Based partly upon my assessment of the tale, I decide whom to admit.

I recall one such class in particular. As usual, we went around the classroom from student to student, listening to approximately three dozen writers pitch their notions. In due course we came to a writer who appeared grim. He had hobbled into the classroom on crutches; his skin appeared pasty and pale. On his face were telltale splotches, the discolorations typical of Kaposi's sarcoma, a form of skin cancer common among people with AIDS.

His story told of a closeted gay man who, upon learning of his HIV-positive diagnosis, decides at long last to come out and openly confront his sexuality and his mortality.

"Sounds good," I said, contemplatively stroking my scratchy professorial beard, nodding sagely, before moving on to the next writer.

In fact I lied.

I dreaded yet another tale depicting gay coming-out, all the more so one combined with AIDS. There resides, of course, exquisite drama in such a story. My only gripe was that in the past years there had been so many such stories. Here was yet another. It struck me as redundant.

I thought to myself: Does the world really need yet another AIDS/gay coming-out tale? Had not the subject been wrung dry?

Nevertheless, given this writer's medical condition, I simply did not have the heart to exclude him from the class. There was no way I could tell someone in such condition that he was not welcome in my course.

Reluctantly, I enrolled him.

When the script was handed to me at the end of the quarter, I put off reading it until I had evaluated all the others. Finally, I opened the screenplay.

What I read astounded me.

First, the story was told with great humor; in fact, it was an unabashed comedy. As I read it, I laughed out loud.

Comedy is, after all, not a lower but a higher form of dramatic narrative, not the least but the most demanding form. Compared with action/adventure or melodrama, for example, it is simply intolerant of any wobbling. With comedy, you're on the bus or off the bus. Comedy is funny or it is not. People laugh or they do not.

This script was funny indeed. It told of a narcissistic, primping gay man who logs lots of time peering at himself in the mirror. Only in his thirties, he already worries about wrinkles.

Upon his HIV diagnosis, however, he comes to worry not about getting wrinkles but about not getting wrinkles. He no longer worries about growing old; he worries about not growing old.

The script was splendid in almost every way.

The only problem was the unsympathetic treatment of the protagonist's brother. He was portrayed as a Christian fundamentalist zealot who believed that AIDS was merely Satan's handiwork, God's retribution for sinful behavior. In the brother's view, if the protagonist would only deliver himself to the Lord and beg forgiveness, his AIDS would flake away like so much dandruff. The writer felt, understandably, that his brother's attitude trivialized his medical issues and, more grievously, denied his identity.

I argued that all characters in a screenplay—including even the most heinous villain—should be rendered somehow human. Unreconstructed monsters from Jupiter are a lot less dramatic than flesh-and-blood human beings right here on earth who remind us not of aliens but of ourselves.

I suggested to the writer that he soften the brother's attitude.

"But that's based upon my own real brother," he insisted, "and that's the way he really is."

"I don't care how your brother really is," I said as gently as I could. "I care only about what is most dramatic, what is best for your movie. You want your brother to love and forgive you; will you love and forgive him? He did not spring whole in a religious vision from the head of Zeus. Like all of us, he carries the intellectual, emotional, ethical, and psychological baggage that was handed to him. You want your brother to understand you, but will you understand him? What's it like for him to deal with his own kid brother having a fatal disease, in particular AIDS?"

After mulling it over, the writer revised the brother's role, producing a far more sympathetic portrait, a more fully realized character who was palpably human and humane instead of stereotypical, predictable, flat.

The new version won not only an A from this instructor, it also won first prize in a prestigious screenwriting competition. Additionally, it won the writer representation at a leading literary agency. By every measure, a promising screenwriting career was launched.

Alas, however, soon thereafter the writer did something profoundly inconsiderate: He died.

At the funeral I was touched to see so many of his classmates from our UCLA screenwriting program. Many offered eloquent testimonials in his memory.

Eventually there arose a man whom I had never met, clearly a member of the writer's family. In his stumbling but loving way he spoke of the writer, expressing his grief but citing also the joy he had experienced in the last months, during which he had come to know and love him in a whole new way. This could only be the older brother. The process of writing the script had provided spiritual healing for both him and his sibling.

Principle 12: Movies heal.

As surely as our flesh and blood and muscle and bone become distended and misshapen from insufficient nourishment normally provided by vitamins and minerals and protein, so also do our spirits and souls warp when they are starved of creative expression.

This is no mere metaphor.

My onetime UCLA colleague, the late and legendary political journalist Norman Cousins, defied his doctors' grim prognosis of imminent death. He rented screwball comedies such as those of the Marx Brothers and Charlie Chaplin and Billy Wilder and literally laughed his way back to health, winning for himself extra years of life that his doctors had told him were simply not available.

Example #3: Middle Eastern Adultery

Some years ago I conducted a screenwriting master class for professional writers in the Middle East. The best among their stories was called "The New Room." In it, a woman in a suburb of Haifa bids good-bye to her husband as he departs their home for an extended business trip. "When you return one month from now," she tells him, "there will be a surprise for you: a new room."

"You studied construction at the University Extension and now you believe you can build an addition to the house?" he asks. "Such projects require substantial labor. In Israel construction is typically performed by Arabs. You are a woman, an Israeli, a Jew. Arab laborers will not take orders from you."

"I will engage an Arab contractor," she said. "He will hire and supervise the workers."

The husband cannot persuade his wife to give up her foolish scheme. "Promise me that whatever else you do," he cautions, "you won't let them use the bathroom. If they need to use the bathroom, they can go to the pub down the street."

At this moment the couple's young child toddles up to his father, who takes him into his arms for a farewell embrace. Before he can quite hug the kid, however, he is repelled by the stench of a badly soiled diaper. He wrinkles his nose and hands his son abruptly to the mother.

Father leaves. A bearded, disheveled, scruffy but affable and capable Arab contractor is engaged. He hires laborers and work commences on the new room. It proceeds apace. Midway through the job, however, at the conclusion of one particular day's toil, the contractor knocks on the door seeking permission to use the bathroom.

Face-to-face with the contractor who has shown himself to be reliable, respectable, and responsible, the wife cannot find it in her heart to refuse him and, reluctantly, she grants his request.

He enters the bathroom. A minute goes by. Two. Ten. Twenty. The Israeli woman wonders what in the world is going on inside the bathroom, and she regrets having broken her promise to her husband. It is perhaps a half hour before our contractor emerges.

He is unrecognizable.

Combed, scrubbed, clean shaven, now sporting a suit and tie, he is handsome beyond description. Next to this guy, Omar Sharif looks like Danny DeVito. "Forgive me," he apologizes to his employer, who stands there dumbstruck, eyes agape. "I have abused your generous offer to utilize the bath. My cousin, you see, is getting married in a village a mile from here and I needed to wash up and change my clothes for the wedding."

The woman stands there, drinking in the vision of the man, as if meeting him for the first time. At this moment the child toddles up to him and latches onto his trouser leg. The Arab moves to hoist the boy into the air for a cuddle.

"No!" cautions the mother. "His diaper is soiled. I was just about to change it. He reeks!"

She reaches to reclaim the child, but the contractor hangs on tight. "Please, madam," he protests, deeply inhaling the dreadful fumes. "This smell I love like life itself! Why not? Life itself is exactly what it is, no?" He waxes enthusiastic on the subject of children, procreation, the generations, and love. Our housewife is enormously taken with this alluring soul, who presents a stark contrast to her clinical, sanitized, Saran-wrapped, all-business husband.

Soon enough a sensual, erotic, and illicit love story emerges.

The script is truly a feast of human interaction of the most fundamental nature. When I met with the writer in order to discuss it, I started off with casual chitchat. Did she live here in Tel Aviv, where we happened to be holding the master class? She told me that she lived in Haifa, where the story is set.

"Central Haifa?"

"Actually a suburb."

"In an apartment?"

"No."

"Your home is a detached structure, a house?"

"Yes," she told me. She seemed to grow uncomfortable with my questions. What she told me of her life was, of course, fully consistent with the details of the script.

"Has a new room been added to the house since you moved in?"

"What's the difference?" she asked me, clearly annoyed. "Yes. A new room has been added to the house. So what?"

I could not resist asking: "Did you design the room yourself and hire a contractor?"

"Enough questions!" she snapped. "I refuse to be interrogated! Can we talk about the script?"

The script, of course, was precisely what we were talking about. It was, indeed, no mere screenplay but—like every worthy script—a depiction of the writer's own life, in more ways than the writer herself had even realized.

I do not doubt for a moment that our Middle Eastern writer truly believed she wrote fiction, and to some extent she was correct; surely she had taken liberties with the facts, with the data, as every writer must, reorganizing them into a better-fitting order, eliminating some real-life situations altogether while inventing others that never actually occurred.

Most likely there were just enough changes from reality that she was able to write her own personal tale without fully realizing she was doing so. Such is the nature of all estimable dramatic narrative. One writer from America's midsection states it this way: "We write our own lives; and then we write our own obituaries."

If a writer fails to personalize her story, if she fails to make it her own unique tale, regardless of how well turned it may be it will nonetheless also be flat, hollow, heatless, heartless, pale, frail, upholstered, laminated, and not wholly human.

Each and every movie explores only one and the same theme. Whatever else writers may think they're writing about, in fact we all treat but a single subject: ourselves. And that is why it does not matter what particular configuration of incidents and anecdotes roil a screenplay's vapors as long as the picture is whole and as long as it is informed by a vision and a voice every bit as singular as the author who creates it.

> *Principle 13: Even if you do not know that you are writing*
> *your own personal story, that is what you are writing.*
> *Your own heart and your own hand make every*
> *script you write only that: your own.*

Conclusion

A script may be an assignment from a studio based upon somebody else's idea. It may be the commissioned adaptation of a novel by a different author. In all cases if the screenwriter is capable, the script nonetheless will be personal.

This has to be due to the fact that Aristotelian narrative structure models the shape of an idealized, romanticized human life. Narrative's power resides in its ability to replicate the shape of life itself. Beginnings, middles, and ends do just that; they model the human agenda. The healthy, integrated screenplay, like the healthy, integrated life, contains a beginning (childhood) that is relatively short, a middle (adulthood) that occupies the vast majority of an individual's days, and a quick, snappy conclusion. Who among us seeks a long, slow, drawn-out end with intravenous tubes jammed in our veins and huffing, wheezing resuscitators stuffed down our throats? In good lives and good movies alike, ends come quickly; they're short, abrupt, and to the point.

The experience is inextricably linked with a sweet and healthy narcissism. I referred earlier to the movie screen as a window through which we spy on the lives of others. More precisely, however, I regard it not so much as a window as a mirror, in which we view reflections not of others' lives but our own.

Principle 14: The movie screen is not a window but a mirror.

Do I mean to argue that *Star Wars*, for example, is more than merely a skillful sci-fi romp? Does *Star Wars* represent George Lucas's own personal identity tale?

The short answer: Yes.

Note first that the protagonist in *Star Wars* is named Luke. Can anyone doubt that George Lucas—who calls his company Lucasfilm, and whose headquarters are on Lucas Valley Road—named the protagonist Luke purely by chance?

Likewise, can anyone imagine that the *Star Wars* trilogy does not represent George Lucas's particular and wondrous worldview, most especially his innocent, affectionately loopy notions regarding good and evil?

The antagonist, Darth Vader, is a man whose last name sounds awfully like "father." *Vater* in German means "father." Who is Darth Vader revealed to be at the end of the film?

Luke's father.

George Lucas is widely known to have had a strained relationship with his own father. Clearly, there is much in *Star Wars*, perhaps even more than its creator realizes, that is profoundly personal.

Write a science fiction picture if it suits you. Or write a goofy screwball comedy. Write a heartbreaking tearjerker. Write a macho, hair-on-your-chest, blood-and-guts action/adventure prison picture. Write a gay coming-of-age story or a tale about a woman who builds an addition to her house. No matter what you write, if it is integrated and personal, it treats one and the same subject: the writer who wrote it.

Weave a crafty tale that is thoroughly integrated and personal; you'll win audiences regardless of the picture's context. You'll succeed, too, in saying to audiences something that is worth their time, attention, and consideration.

Chapter 4

Creative Choices: Idea, Story, Theme, and Identity

A rt is choice.
   A painter may work in oil or tempera, watercolor or acrylic. She may choose a single hue or several dozen. She may apply the pigment to canvas or cardboard, to leather, plywood, or glass. She may smear it on thick or thin, with brushes that are fat or frail, with a pallet knife, a toothpick, a pipe cleaner, a finger, or directly from the tube.

The completed painting may be square, round, a cameo, a mural, a panel, a triptych. It could be abstract, surreal, or representational; a portrait, a landscape, a still life. However it turns out in the end, all paintings represent one and the same thing: a record of the artist's choices.

If choice making lies at the heart of all creative expression, it is especially true for film, as film's creators confront by far the greatest number of possible artistic choices. This is because movies by their very nature integrate both light and language, information that is not only visual but also aural. In addition, a movie is presented not in a single flash but over an extended period of time. Moreover, all the imagery and all the sound mean nothing unless they are deployed inside the collection of choices that come ultimately to constitute context and narrative.

Theme: The So-What Test

Somewhere deep inside every worthy screen story, binding the characters, shaping the dialogue, integrating all the scenes, lies a unifying thread that succinctly answers the question: So what?

This is the movie's theme. After a film's final frame there ought to be some clear sense of purpose, a reason for all the fuss and bother, a semblance of overall meaning.

A student in a screenwriting class at UCLA once suggested that while she wasn't yet sure what her story would be, she knew it would take a firm stand against pollution. I called for a show of hands among the students to determine how many people in the class favored pollution.

There were no volunteers.

Of course it is commendable (if not exactly courageous) to oppose pollution. That said, the task of a script is not to take a stance on some issue, however noble. A script's purpose is to tell a story.

Story and theme do not exist independently. Each is a function of the other. Solid stories naturally and unavoidably contain themes. Story's nature is such that beneath it lies a single organizing principle, a basic premise: the theme. Unwieldy, preachy, theme-first scripts flogging issues where everybody agrees contribute nothing to film besides boredom.

Movies without themes sometimes offer fast, fleeting fun, but they do not stick to the ribs. *Outrageous Fortune* (Leslie Dixon) momentarily diverts us but soon fades from memory. *Tootsie* (Don McGuire, Larry Gelbart, Murray Schisgal), on the other hand, remains forever etched on our cortex. The latter is about something; the former is not. The first is but a catalogue of zany antics; the second has something to say about important human issues: gender and identity.

If theme follows story, writers follow theme. Until his script is well under way, the theme is largely unknown even to the writer. Sophocles struggling with *Oedipus Rex* could not have been trying to teach the world a timeless lesson about the nature of man and woman. Working writers understand he was merely scrambling to get the pages finished by deadline. That *Oedipus Rex* became a classic offers testimony to one thing only: its author's genius. He wasn't operating differently from other writers; he was merely more talented and better disciplined.

The late playwright Arthur Miller reported that when he was approximately two-thirds of the way through a play its theme suddenly became clear to him. He then wrote the theme—just a handful of words—on an index card and pinned it to the wall above his typewriter. That guided the rest of his writing; it helped him determine what belonged in the play and what did not.

There is an ancient principle embraced by Zen archers: You cannot hit a target by aiming at it. Success here depends not upon seeing but feeling. Striking the target is more a product of heart than eye. Similarly, good writers do not make important statements by trying to do so. Worthy writers make important statements only by trying to tell worthy stories.

Diverse pictures often share common themes. They are treated over and over by all kinds of writers in all kinds of ways. The adolescent coming-of-age motif is an example. Just because it is tackled successfully in, say, *American Graffiti* (George Lucas, Gloria Katz, Willard Huyck) does not mean it can't be addressed again in *Diner* (Barry Levinson) or *Fast Times at Ridgemont High* (Cameron Crowe) or *Thirteen* (Catherine Hardwicke, Nikki Reed) or any of a host of narratives.

The challenge in confronting theme is to take a fresh tack. The theme may be similar to that of many other pictures. All the same, the story should be unique.

A curious quality of theme is that when it is spelled out in uncomplicated terms it appears trite and banal. What, for example, is the theme of *Star Wars*? Good triumphs over evil; love is stronger than hate.

What is the theme of *E.T.*? Love thy neighbor. *E.T.* argues thematically that we should not fear the unknown. That which is different, which frightens us, which appears ugly may eventually come to appear cute and cuddly and warm. More important, it may one day nourish and sustain us and deliver us from evil. Surely writer Melissa Mathison did not set out to say all that. Her assignment was simply to extend the tale of *Close Encounters of the Third Kind* (Steven Spielberg), to build a story around the notion that the departing spacecraft at the end of that movie leaves behind a child alien.

What is the theme of *Citizen Kane* (Herman J. Mankiewicz, Orson Welles)? You can't buy love. A man who has it all—wealth, women, power—is nonetheless unhappy and unfulfilled. Power plus wealth does not add up to happiness.

Tootsie? Living as a woman transforms a man into a better man. *Kramer vs. Kramer* (Robert Benton, adapting the Avery Corman novel)? Commitment is freedom; forming close bonds with others does not limit but expands the human experience, does not entrap souls but liberates them.

What is *The Godfather* all about? Family and fate. On the surface it

tells of gangsters and their crimes but beneath that it explores the relationships among brothers, the ways they get along, the ways they don't get
along. It demonstrates that no one can escape his fate. Michael never intended to become the don; nevertheless, he assumes that role because to
do so is his fate.

Herein lies yet another important aspect of theme. No matter how
alien to our own experiences movie characters may appear, in fact they
are only reflections of ourselves. We are not separate from them but connected.

What is the theme of *Terminator 2* (James Cameron, William Wisher)?
Might makes right? Guess again. Justice triumphs? Not at all. At the
end of the film, the Terminator starts to become human. How do we
know he's becoming human? He acquires a human trait: the ability to
feel. What does he feel? Pain. Hence the film's theme: To feel pain is to be
human.

Reiterating, theme is created subconsciously. A writer observes something. For reasons he does not understand he finds himself thinking about
what he has witnessed. If it haunts him for a sufficient time he may attach
to it events of his own creation. Eventually there emerges a story.

The screenwriter's choices are clearly limitless. What happens next?
What is the next line of dialogue? What is the next sentence? What is the
next word?

Making these choices expands rather than reduces the universe of
possibilities. New choices, rather than removing themselves from the
overall body of alternatives, create still newer choices. The universe of
choices expands exactly as does the universe in which we live. The choices
available to writers, therefore, are infinite.

There is, however, only one theme.

Principle 15: All movies treat the same theme: identity.

Grasping this principle completely requires us to embrace theme as
working writers do, not with our intellect but with our hands and hearts.
This is because film, as I argue repeatedly, is not about understanding but
feeling. To engage theme in their screenplays, writers need more than
merely to know their theme; they must own it. To accomplish this, they
need to grasp theme's relation to idea and story, for it is idea and story that
establish theme.

A Case Study: *Who's the Boss?*

To explore theme in a practical way, let us walk through an episode of a half-hour television situation comedy scripted by a writer who happened to be a UCLA screenwriting student at the time. It demonstrates that even as writers write about every imaginable subject, in fact all treat but a single theme: identity. Each work is merely another articulation of that singular theme, the writer's own identity. This theme has arrested the attention of every writer and every viewer since the invention of written dramatic narrative nearly three thousand years ago.

First, let's review briefly how the writer of the sitcom episode won the assignment in the first place. It demonstrates a fairly typical path TV writing careers follow, especially sitcom careers. To be sure, traditionally scripted broadcast TV sitcoms and dramas have been in decline now for a number of years. This has to be due in large part to competition from the surfeit of reality-based programming, plus cable and new media, not to mention video games and the Internet.

That said, there continue to be successful dramatic series and sitcoms. Additionally, there has arisen a substantial number of new dramatic and sitcom series on cable. When you add cable to the continuing—however diminished—success of some broadcast shows, overall opportunities for writers expand.

Our writer had originally written a spec episode of *Cheers* not expecting to sell it to *Cheers* but to use as a sample, a showcase script that demonstrates that a writer can write. It was designed as a calling card to be used in the campaign for future paid assignments.

Speculating—writing without any guarantee of eventual compensation—is the activity that occupies not only theatrical feature film writers but also writers struggling to break into episodic TV. The writer was able to find an agent willing to read the spec episode. This agent submitted it to *Who's the Boss?* (Martin Cohan, Blake Hunter) as a sample of the writer's work.

This is standard practice in TV. Write a spec episode in a particular genre—here the thirty-minute, three-camera, taped-before-a-live-audience situation comedy—and it may be used to win assignments on other shows within that genre.

The *Who's the Boss?* staff invited the writer to meet with them to pitch proposals for episodes. At the meeting, the staff listened to all the proposals and purchased none.

Devastated, the writer prepared to leave but, surprisingly, was instructed to remain. As is routine in episodic TV the staff had compiled a comprehensive list of their own ideas, for which freelancers would be hired to do the actual scripting.

They assigned one such idea to this writer.

For the benefit of those who may be so culturally impoverished as never to have been exposed to *Who's the Boss?* its protagonist is Tony, a man in his midthirties who, in exchange for room and board for himself and his early-adolescent daughter, keeps house for an attractive and prospering businesswoman.

American television seems to love last year's—or last decade's—controversy. Even with the modern women's movement well under way, television found it provocative, indeed downright hilarious, for a woman to be boss over a man rather than the other way around, particularly where the man's chores were domestic: laundering, vacuuming, ironing, cooking. Can't you see the network meeting where the proposal was originally pitched? "Tony vacuuming! Check it out! Vacuuming! Tony! Vacuuming! I'm gonna have a heart attack! Tony vacuuming!"

The episode our writer ended up scripting was based wholly on the following idea: Tony has a friend who's a priest. That is the sum total of what was provided to the writer.

The episode opens with Tony's young daughter angrily returning toys to her pal, the girl next door. They've suffered a spat and vowed to return each other's dollies and dishes, borrowed over the years; never again will they have anything to do with one another.

"That's a mistake," Tony advises his daughter. Friendship, he explains, is all that really counts in life. It is true that from time to time friends argue, Tony explains, but they also make peace. Forgiveness is the name of the game. He pleads with the girl to reconcile with her friend.

"Never!" the daughter responds.

Tony pleads with her to reconsider. He recalls a disagreement of his own with a pal from his old neighborhood. The two were fast friends until one day they argued over something—he doesn't even remember what—and went their separate ways, never again to have any contact.

"It is already ten years since that happened," Tony laments, "and not one day has passed, not an hour, that I have not felt diminished by my ruptured relationship with this once beloved friend."

Tony asserts that his daughter will be committing a profound error if she fails to heal the rift with the neighbor.

If friendship is so important, the daughter counters, why doesn't Tony make peace with his old pal from all those years ago?

Because, Tony explains, it's been so long since they've had anything to do with each other that he wouldn't even know how to find the guy.

Nonsense, the daughter protests; one or two or three phone calls will easily track down his lost friend. If Tony's not just blowing air, she goes on, if he truly means what he says, if he's not merely handing down the standard parental hypocrisy, he ought to reconcile with his buddy. If Tony will set that example, the daughter promises, she will make peace with her own friend next door.

In this way Tony's daughter shames him into seeking his long-lost pal. The mechanics of his tracking down the friend are not presented in the show. All that matters is that a reunion is arranged. A lesser writer would have squandered a substantial amount of time and language cataloguing Tony's activities locating his friend.

When the friend actually appears on-screen for the first time, it is a wonderful surprise to see that he wears the collar of a Roman Catholic priest.

Note the writer's finesse here. Even within the limited context of a TV screen, particularly the small screen of the *Who's the Boss?* era, there is nevertheless a great deal that a writer can communicate graphically. Here, for example, upon first sight of the old pal, we recognize his stature: priest. The former street thug is now a deeply spiritual man of the cloth. To learn this we need see only his priest's collar. It is a splendid bit of action that is visual instead of talky.

Principle 16: A movie is not a radio show.

Another trap this writer avoided was tipping his hand. A less skillful writer would have had some character say, "I hear Callahan became a priest." Where's the purpose in prematurely exposing such information except to blunt the thrust—to debauch the dramatic impact—experienced upon visually encountering the friend dressed in his collar when we first meet him?

In his *Poetics*, Aristotle urges the poet—surely he meant the screenwriter—to find the true beginning not only in a play but even in a part of a play. Not only whole plays but even mere parts of plays have their own beginnings, middles, and ends. The beginning, he tells us, is the part before which we need nothing.

We need nothing here before the two reunited pals, already reconciled, quaff coffee in the kitchen, exchanging old neighborhood lore, and in doing so revitalize their previously dormant relationship. A less adept writer would have wasted a good deal of time and language detailing the early moments of the reconciliation. Our writer, however, places the characters smack-dab in the middle of their rapprochement.

Tony and Father Callahan, at the kitchen table, swap fond memories—pranks played on one another and on mutual pals—laughing and enjoying each other's company as if nothing had ever separated them, as if over all these years not even a moment has been lost.

Now, however, Tony recalls a particularly mean-spirited prank he perpetrated years earlier at the expense of young Callahan. Upon hearing the ancient prank recounted, the priest's demeanor abruptly transforms.

"You're the guy who did that?" the priest asks Tony, incredulous, still clearly hurt even after all the years. "That was you?"

"Of course it was me," Tony boasts. "You didn't know that?"

Callahan acknowledges that indeed he did not know. "It was really you? That really hurt me a lot."

Tony smiles broadly and nods proudly, a Cheshire-cat grin smeared across his self-satisfied face.

Callahan coldcocks Tony, delivering a roundhouse punch to the jaw that sends him sprawling.

No one is more horrified than Callahan himself. He apologizes profusely, saying that he now realizes he's never lost his street-tough soul, that he has no business posturing as a servant of the Lord. He'd thought that when God called him to His service he had surrendered that gritty, aggressive aspect of his soul. Now he sees that it is all a pathetic joke.

Not to worry, Tony reassures him, rubbing his jaw, picking himself up off the floor. "I had it coming."

The priest tears off his collar. "I am leaving the Church," he announces. "I have no right to represent myself as representing God."

Nonsense, Tony argues. In the eyes of the Lord, he insists, all men and women—even priests—are sinners. To be saved, a man needs only to ask forgiveness.

Callahan will have none of this. He storms out of the house, his collar abandoned on the floor beside the table, his life as a priest now ended. Tony is mortified. He feels responsible for the turmoil he has caused. For one thing, Callahan was supposed to serve a spaghetti dinner at the local senior citizens' center, as he does every Thursday night. Now nobody will be there for the old folks. The least Tony can do is to go to the seniors' center and provide the dinner he feels responsible for having ruined.

Tony and his family show up at the center, spaghetti dinner at the ready. Where's Callahan? the elderly folks want to know.

Tony creates lame excuses.

Now, suddenly, Callahan appears.

The collar is gone; he wears civilian clothes. He announces that he is leaving the priesthood, and that he feels obligated to explain personally to the seniors that he will no longer be providing Thursday night spaghetti dinners.

Everyone pleads with him to reconsider, but he resists. "If God wants me to return to His service, let Him show me a sign."

At that precise moment there is a sharp knock at the door. A man enters who happens to be delivering a huge sign that has been ordered. It reads: SENIOR CITIZENS' CENTER—BINGO WEDNESDAY NIGHTS.

"There!" everyone observes. "A sign!"

"That's not what I meant," Callahan protests.

"You said 'a sign.'"

There is quite a lot of fun in the dialogue here revolving around the word "sign." "I didn't mean a 'sign' sign. I meant 'a sign.'"

"A sign is a sign."

"I meant a biblical sign," Callahan explains. "An earthquake. The Red Sea parting. At the very least thunder and lightning."

"You asked God for a sign and He gives you a sign and you're still not satisfied?"

Tony asks, "You think the all-powerful, all-knowing ruler of the universe has no sense of humor?"

At last Callahan is persuaded to return to the priesthood.

The last thing that happens in the episode, of course, is that Tony's daughter reconciles with the girl next door.

Right there, in a humble TV episode of a so-so series, is a perfect example of, among other things, Aristotelian story structure: beginning, middle, end. The end of the beginning is the point at which Tony is shamed into seeking a reunion with the priest. The middle ends with the appearance of the sign. The end, of course, is all that follows.

The episode also offers a perfect example of a fundamental screenwriting trinity: idea, story, theme.

Again, the idea: Tony has a friend who's a priest.

What value in that? Precious little. Indeed, all by itself it is virtually worthless. This fact allows us to underscore a screenwriting precept: The least important, most overappreciated element in screenwriting is the idea. What truly counts is not the idea for the story but the story itself, the sustained, integrated enterprise that combines character and tale and dialogue and all of the other elements collectively constituting the whole picture.

It is, however, neither idea nor story but theme upon which we focus here. What is the theme that underlies this tale? What is its overarching principle?

Simply this: Faith untested is no faith at all. Challenge offers the opportunity to renew and revitalize faith.

Moreover, the greater the challenge to faith, the greater its growth. Exactly as pressing five pounds will not bring much benefit to a weight lifter, so also will a weak-kneed challenge to faith fail to strengthen that faith. To build muscles one needs to press substantial weight; the greater the struggle, the stronger the muscle.

To be sure, critics, pundits, and educators hold no high expectations regarding sitcom episodes offered up on mainstream, commercial television. Nevertheless, the night this particular *Who's the Boss?* episode aired, millions of people were exposed to a profound lesson in faith and healing.

Millions of everyday folk learned that when they experience a crisis of faith, instead of succumbing to dread and fear they should rejoice in the opportunity it provides to forge an even greater faith.

All of this in an ordinary episode of a wearisomely familiar TV series, with prearranged characters in preordained situations. Here is testimony aplenty to the power of narrative and to the preeminence of story.

*Principle 17: Theme is expressed not in the idea
but in the story.*

In sum, a lame television episode with a facile, shallow idea, in the hands of a talented, disciplined writer, wields considerable power. An audience is confronted with penetrating questions about the very nature of life itself. That audience is provided with insights into religion, theology, clergy, family, friendship, loyalty, disloyalty, and more.

Note finally that the theme was a surprise even to the writer. The writer did not consciously acknowledge that the tale revealed the writer's own view of faith, or the role faith plays in defining identity.

The producers sought only a story built around the notion that "Tony has a friend who's a priest." Certainly they did not ask for philosophical commentary regarding the nature of faith. If that's where the tale eventually ended up, it was as much a surprise to them as to the writer. Indeed, theme is in its nature a surprise to all parties.

The lesson? It is possible to start with a narrow, slight, pale idea and end up with a theme that is hefty, deep, profound. Start with the theme, however, and no matter how profound it may be, all that is guaranteed is a script that is self-conscious, self-important, heavy-handed, and unworthy of the time, attention, and consideration of any audience.

*Principle 18: The theme of a worthy screenplay is inevitably
a surprise to the writer.*

Identity: The Only Theme

Like a river carving out a canyon, the route of any story seems to meander. Yet the underlying force sculpting that canyon is the same for all courses: gravity. The course may twist this way and that, widen here, narrow there, but its overall track is predetermined—and precisely so—by the forces of nature.

As surely as gravity steers the water, so does identity steer every screenplay. Where does it steer it? Right back to the writer who created it.

This can be illustrated by considering, of all things, the trial of Charles Manson. At one point the district attorney routinely asked a witness to state his name for the record.

"Objection!" barked Manson's lawyer.

"You object to the witness stating his name?" the judge asked.

"Absolutely right."

"Upon what grounds do you base your objection?"

"Hearsay."

Hearsay refers, of course, to testimony that is second- or thirdhand. Under American evidentiary principles testimony is permitted only if it is firsthand. Witnesses can report what they themselves actually heard or observed but not what others say they heard or observed.

The lawyer continued, "How does the witness know his name except for the fact that it was told to him by others, namely his parents?"

Naturally, the objection was promptly overruled.

Nevertheless, outside the courtroom the lawyer's point is profound. How do we know who we are? How do we know even our names? How do we know who we are other than by information reported to us by others?

Consider dreams.

Who among us does not dream? Who among us does not from time to time experience a dream so vivid, so seemingly real that upon wakening we are relieved to realize it was just that: merely a dream?

The question inevitably arises: How do I know that what I see as my real, true life is not a dream? How do I know I will not, only a minute from now, awaken to discover I am actually the Prince of Wales, or a jackrabbit in Nebraska?

I was an undergraduate in October 1962, the time of the Cuban missile crisis. We believed on that perilous Monday night that the world might very well end in nuclear conflagration the following morning. In the midst of all the turmoil surrounding such an event, I could consider only one issue: If tomorrow we were all to die in atomic hellfire and brimstone, why was I studying for the sociology midterm scheduled later in the week?

As in the best dramatic expression, there was at that moment a splendid mixture of the profound and the petty, the weighty and the mundane.

As with dreams, films mirror images of ourselves that are at once recognizable and at the same time alien. They help us tolerate life's mysteries.

There is in every woman and man a schizophrenic sense of who we are. One half derives from our own substance, the meaty, hairy, bloody, bony stuff of our physical being. The other half is reflected back to us by family, friends, associates, and even strangers.

I propose that we go to movies to figure out just what and who we are. That is why all movies at their core treat nothing but identity. Who am I? How do I know what's real and what's not? Why should I stop at the red lights? Why should I pay my taxes? Why should I put up with the bumps and bruises that afflict all of us every day of our lives?

That's the reason a personal film's subject matters not a whit as, once again, all movies are merely different treatments of the same subject: the writers who write them.

A wonderful example resides in the underappreciated *Dave* (Gary Ross). A humble, easygoing guy has a new identity suddenly thrust upon him: president of the United States. At first he resists. Soon enough, however, he embraces that identity. He becomes what his oppressors forced upon him but never in a million years wanted him actually to become.

Another splendid example is the masterful biopic *Malcolm X* (Arnold Perl, Spike Lee, adapting Alex Haley and Malcolm X's book). Here the thematic question is addressed in the very title. What does "X" mean except: Who am I?

The question relates directly to the unique experience of African Americans. Slavery resulted in, among other degradations, the theft of a people's history. Stolen from slaves among other things were their very names.

Malcolm X was born Malcolm Little, but from where does "Little" derive? It belonged to some long-dead white guy who raped Malcolm's great-grandmother. Why would Malcolm want to bear the label of this slavemaster rapist/oppressor?

Malcolm needed to reclaim his name.

What precisely was Malcolm's true name? Thanks to slavery, that has been lost to Malcolm and to history. Malcolm chose, therefore, the designation "X" to indicate that he does not know who he is.

Ultimately, as with all good stories, the film's impact resides in the way the story transcends its immediate arena and speaks to the hearts and spirits of not African Americans alone but all of humanity. Not only Malcolm but all women and men are, in a sense, forever strangers to themselves. This enables all viewers to regard the film's characters not as

Chapter 5

· · · · · · · · ·

Conflict: Violence and Sex

Must movies marinate in sex? Must they wallow in violence?

No, but many, probably most—including some of the finest films ever made—are positively saturated with sensuality and eroticism. Likewise, worthy movies must forever be violent.

If you prefer, you may think of violence as conflict or tension or stress. Screenwriters are urgently advised to consider the general disquietude essential to film as full-tilt, mean-spirited, straight-ahead violence. I urge them also to remember that enlightened, reasonable, rational discourse and courtesy, consideration, and consensus occupy an important place in our lives. In movies, however, they're boring.

I don't suggest that movie armies must perpetually beat out each other's brains, nor that all good films must provide an endless succession of looting, shooting, and rape. Neither do I hold that all movies must be greasy, oily sex orgies. All the same, however, emotional unrest must be integrated into each and every frame of each and every scene of each and every movie.

In HBO's timeless *The Sopranos* (created by David Chase) there is an erotic nude scene in which Carmela, protagonist Tony Soprano's wife, has sex with a man who is not Tony. Though the scene is titillating all by itself, it is not all by itself. Rather, it is part of the whole picture. The whole picture reveals Tony to be a throwback Neanderthal of a husband, a man who cavalierly cheats on his wife with his mistress du jour and armies of prostitutes. Carmela knows that she cannot change his behavior, but she can compel him to have a vasectomy so that there is no chance for the complications wrought by the issue of "illegitimate" offspring.

Carmela's own sex scene expands her character and enhances the story. By including the sex scene, *The Sopranos* writers demonstrate that Carmela is hardly a stereotype; she's no quietly suffering Mafia wife. If she cannot stop Tony from having relations with other women, if she cannot change his retrograde views regarding marriage, she can nevertheless assert her own power and reclaim her own dignity. By engaging in activities that are otherwise prohibited she carves out her own identity and establishes her own sense of righteous womanhood.

Movies typically allow husbands to cheat, and then to apologize and receive full forgiveness. A married woman, however, is rarely allowed to consummate a sexual relationship with a man who is not her husband. For that there is no forgiveness. Carmela, however, in engaging in the adulterous relationship accomplishes much more than merely "getting even." The sexual affair buttresses and underscores her sharply drawn self-respect.

Similarly, in *A Walk on the Moon* (Pamela Gray) Diane Lane's character, Pearl, betrays her marriage in an erotic sex scene with a romantic blouse merchant. It is not enough for Pearl merely to be attracted to her lover. For the movie to have any substance the adultery must occur.

Likewise, in *Unfaithful* (Claude Chabrol, Alvin Sargent, William Broyles Jr.) Connie Sumner, the character played by Diane Lane (again!), must actually engage in sexual betrayal so as to motivate the rage and sorrow belonging to her husband. Another example resides in *Under the Tuscan Sun* (Audrey Wells, adapting the Frances Mayes book). Frances, portrayed by Diane Lane (yet again!) needs not only contemplate but actually engage in sexual union with her Mediterranean lover in order to restore the balance that has been lost since the collapse of her marriage, which has been ruptured by her husband's philandering.

Can't a screenplay ever pause, rest, seize a quiet moment for philosophical reflection and tranquil contemplation? It cannot. Screenwriters merit the attention of audiences largely through the skillful shaping and wielding of violence and sex. There's more to movies than that, but first of all there is that. Moreover, all the other stuff pales by comparison.

Is this a dark view? Not at all. It is simply a practical, bare-knuckles approach to the practical, bare-knuckles enterprise that is dramatic expression.

Film's roots are firmly embedded in theater, an art form with thousands of years of tradition from which screenwriters may profit. Consider for example *Oedipus Rex*.

What's the play all about?

Some say fate, others faith. Still others wax philosophic regarding the nature of the human condition, the properties of the universe.

They're not wrong.

First and foremost, however, *Oedipus* is a story about a man who kills his father and beds his mother. It is the story of a fellow who, on different occasions during his lifetime, journeys in both directions through the same birth canal.

If that makes you queasy and uneasy, if you find that upsetting, that's exactly what Sophocles intended. Every worthy writer of dramatic narratives seeks to upset, disturb, and provoke audiences.

Still more, as if Sophocles feared audiences might find patricide and incest a tad too tame, he orders his protagonist, upon discovering the sorry truth about his life, not to sigh or weep or bite his nails or tear his hair or, in a stammering, sobbing soliloquy, bemoan his fate. Instead, with rusty metal stakes Oedipus pokes out his eyes. He exiles himself from his land, the land where he is king, to wander in darkness and dishonor the rest of his wretched days.

What a perverse view, scholars and critics might well protest, of so soaring, so timeless a classic. Doesn't *Oedipus* contain profound insights into the nature of man and woman, parent and child? Doesn't it abound with poetic lessons regarding fate and faith and life and death and more? Why obsess about the play's murderous and sexually perverse aspects?

The answer lies in the fact that whatever other issues *Oedipus* treats, first and foremost it tells the story of a fellow who slays his father and has intercourse with his mother. These features can hardly be characterized as merely incidental.

Likewise *Hamlet*, for all its poetry and grace, its rich characters and expertly crafted story, is a tale of sex, greed, murder, and revenge. By final curtain the stage is awash with blood, littered with no fewer than nine corpses. Bodies are run through on swords, others poisoned.

Next to *Medea*, however, these two tales are *Mary Poppins* (Bill Walsh, Don DaGradi, adapting the P. L. Travers books).

Medea, in a jealous rage provoked by her husband's womanizing, murders her children.

Imagine pitching such a project to the story department of a movie studio. "Disgusting!" the executive vice presidents might exclaim. "We'll have every parent group in the country picketing our offices, burning down our theaters. Senate committees will audit our books. Bloodthirsty mobs will lynch our projectionists."

Let me concede again eagerly, even gratefully, that violence in movies does not need to be blood-and-guts gore on the order of *Oedipus* and *Medea*. Still, among the best-loved classics it is almost invariably that.

What, then, of artists' social responsibility?

To be sure, responsible movies and television should ultimately promote nourishing, constructive behavior. Attempting from the start to serve lofty moral and social purposes, however, is a recipe for failure. It leads film and television artists to succeed not in achieving their noble objectives but only in boring their audiences. Years ago a warm and fuzzy, well-intentioned film, *Amazing Grace and Chuck,* attempted from the first frame to alert audiences to the threat of nuclear annihilation and the need for people to oppose war. Its writer, David Field, said in an interview that there were plenty of films about making war, and that the time had come, finally, to create a film about making peace.

These are uplifting, honorable intentions to be sure, but can peace or any other worthwhile cause be advanced by a boring movie? In all history there is not a single instance in which tedium is known to have solved any problem. Screenwriters serve society best by providing audiences with worthwhile movies.

The question is often asked: Do not socio- and psychopaths find inspiration in the violence they view on-screen? Common sense might suggest as much, but common sense tells us the sun revolves around the earth.

Contrary to the assertions of well-funded propaganda campaigns from blue-nosed, blue-haired pro-censorship groups with lofty titles on the order of Parents Television Council and League for Decency, there is little reliable scientific evidence that movie and TV mayhem provokes violence in real life. Studies establishing a causal relationship between media and violence win grants from publicity-seeking foundations but tend to be flawed.

There are university studies that demonstrate a close relationship between the amount of television children watch and the violence they commit. When children's television viewing gets up into five hours daily and more, there is a clear correlation with violent antisocial behavior. But isn't this actually a measure of neglect? Children watching TV five and six and more hours a day are suffering not so much from material on television screens as from a paucity of parental supervision.

In the past forty years, with sex and violence becoming increasingly explicit in media, violent crime has not risen but declined. Indeed, it has declined sharply.

If film and TV and video games are responsible for so much violence in our society, why does Canada, which experiences the same media as the United States, have a far lower violent crime rate? Why does Japan, whose media is far more violent than our own, have a significantly lower violent crime rate?

Screenwriters have to face the fact that violence is a natural and inevitable component of dramatic expression. To take film and television to task for violence is like criticizing rivers for flowing downstream.

The violent nature of film can be appreciated, deplored, addressed, or ignored, but it is inevitable and unavoidable in drama. Every worthy play, film, and television program is permeated by expression that at the very least wallows in conflict, and is often violent.

Consider *Bambi* (Felix Salten, Perce Pearce, Vernon Stallings). Is it not a tranquil, life-affirming, uplifting film you can safely screen for your kids?

Think about it.

Is *Bambi* really so serene? It tells the story of a gentle, adorable fawn—is there any other kind?—who witnesses its own doe-eyed mother shot to death by hunters. Bambi flees a raging forest fire, to this day one of the most stressful, frightening scenes I have ever seen. Orphaned, cringing in terror, he wanders the forest bereft and alone.

Reiterating, violence—call it conflict—is a natural and integral component of film and TV narratives. Notwithstanding this, however, film violence need not be physical at all. It is wholly acceptable for conflict to be psychological, spiritual, or emotional. By that measure, the Oscar-winning *Kramer vs. Kramer* is among the most violent films of the past half century, even if it lacks even a single shooting, stabbing, strangling, beating, or car crash.

The most grievous physical trauma in *Kramer vs. Kramer* occurs mid-picture, when the young son falls to the pavement from the monkey bars in the playground. Cradling the boy in his arms, Dustin Hoffman, playing Ted Kramer, sprints a block or two to the emergency room where, happily, the injury turns out to be superficial.

Nevertheless, *Kramer vs. Kramer* is an extraordinarily violent film, entirely inappropriate for children. What could be more violent than a mother and father battling for the custody of their own flesh-and-blood offspring? What could be more heartbreaking than two parents, who must have loved each other however briefly, battling for custody of the living, breathing issue of their loins?

Every scene, every moment in every movie thirsts for identifiable conflict. A responsible screenwriter should be able to point to any section of his script and answer the question: Where is the conflict?

The best intentions of the highest-minded practitioners aside, violence and sex are whole, natural, necessary ingredients in television and film. No screenwriter has to apologize for soaking his script with toe-to-toe, eyeball-to-eyeball conflict—social, emotional, spiritual, cultural, psychological, and yes, also physical conflict—page for page, scene for scene.

Airplanes that land safely do not make the news.

Families where everybody gets along splendidly with everybody are no subject for movies.

No audience wants to see *The Village of the Happy Nice People*.

Chapter 6
· · · · · · · · · ·

Illusion: Real versus Reel

M ovies are fake.

For one thing, they don't even move. A typical feature-length film is actually some hundred and fifty thousand individual still photographs projected in rapid succession upon a blank screen. Since there are twenty-four such frames per second, it seems sensible to calculate that each frame plays on the screen for one twenty-fourth portion of a second.

Yet even this is not true.

The engineers who designed motion-picture projectors integrated into the mechanism a shutter that revolves once each cycle in order to block the light during pull-down, masking the film's mechanical motion through the gate. Between every single projected transparency, therefore, sharing the cycle with the exposed frame is a period of total darkness. The darkness between frames consumes a shade more time than the frame itself. In other words, projected film consists mainly of blackness. During a typical feature running a hundred minutes, the shutter is closed cumulatively for an entire hour.

The mechanics of motion-picture projection underscore a fundamental screenwriting principle:

Principle 19: Life is real; film is contrivance.

As I mentioned in chapter 1, film is as contrived an enterprise as is possible for the human mind to imagine.

A preposterous exaggeration?

Exaggeration for effect is a legitimate writing tool. Nevertheless, I exaggerate here not in the least. Time, space, story, and characters are configured and reconfigured at the writer's will. Actors well-known to audiences as the people they truly are pretend to be characters they clearly are not. They strut about in situations that are manipulated and arranged right down to details such as makeup, hair, wardrobe, and more.

These actors recite memorized dialogue acknowledged to have been written by writers. Yet, if the actors are capable and the writing good, they deliver the lines in such a manner as to convey the notion that they thought the words up all by themselves, that the ideas just happened to occur to them at the moment they spoke them. Similarly, the actors move about the frame as if, without plan or prearrangement, they stumbled naturally into the circumstances depicted on the screen. What is carefully staged and rehearsed is presented as if it were spontaneous.

Moreover, as any student of film craft appreciates, scenes in films do not unfold on-screen in the order they are photographed. Some scenes, photographed earlier, appear later. Others, filmed later, play earlier. Even some substantial portion of the dialogue is likely to have been recorded—and rerecorded—in disparate places at separate times.

View a film, therefore, and you look at a broken-up, disjointed, disconnected assemblage of bits and pieces of scattered shots. The miracle is that they seem to flow smoothly and in an orderly fashion, permitting us to believe that we peer into real people's real lives, although we know precisely the opposite is the case, that the entire construction is an elaborate pretense.

Aristotle advises the dramatist to favor the plausible impossibility over the implausible possibility. What in the world can that mean?

Simply stated: Lie through your teeth. Just because something is actually true doesn't mean that it will appear so on-screen. It may well be quite the opposite. Movies are not about fact but fantasy.

Conversely, just because something's untrue does not mean that it will appear so on-screen. In the film *Don't Tell Her It's Me* (Sarah Bird), for example, Steve Guttenberg portrays a formerly gawky nerd who has a fantasy life as a heartthrob. In one scene, when he's in his "handsome mode," he rides his manly fire-breathing Harley into a gas station. An attractive young woman, dispensing gas to her car, catches sight of him. She is so taken with him, so distracted by his virile good looks that she neglects to release the pump handle when the tank is filled. Consequently it gushes fuel all over the place.

Now, anyone who has ever dispensed self-service gas knows that the pump clicks off automatically once the tank is full. Yet audiences have no problem whatever with this conceit, even as it plays fast and loose with reality.

Since there's a marquee over the entrance to the theater, since they bought tickets, since they're chomping popcorn and Milk Duds, somewhere inside their subconscious the audience must realize the whole enterprise of any movie is one extensive, elaborate, splendid shuck-and-jive.

Surely the last thing they desire or deserve is the truth. Truth is available in the street outside the theater for free.

Principle 20: It is not truth but sweet, seductive falsehood that audiences crave.

Bluntly stated, the screenwriter's mission is skillfully and lovingly to lie. Yet among screenwriters, especially among inexperienced screenwriters, there is a self-defeating compulsion to be truthful. I propose that this has to do with the most fundamental nature of film itself, its technology, its tradition.

When Thomas Edison invented the kinetoscope, where did he train its lens? On anything that moved. Do you invent a motion-picture machine to record objects standing still?

Edison's first films depict nothing besides motion—carriages, streetcars, pedestrians striding down the street outside his Orange, New Jersey, workshop/studio. Soon enough legions of early cinematographers were capturing images in motion: trains barreling down the track; waterfalls roaring over cliffs; indigenous peoples inhabiting their natural climes; prominent personalities cutting ribbons, launching ships, even delivering speeches in total silence. For years, mere motion was enough to fascinate audiences until, just past the turn of the last century, filmmakers for the first time found it necessary to synthesize actions and events, to arrange incidents and anecdotes into some semblance of order so as to hold an audience's attention.

In other words, audiences now required narrative.

At this moment screenwriting was born.

It has to be film's early roots recording reality, combined with the

camera's portability—its capacity to re-create scenes in their natural locations instead of on stages as in theater—that to no small extent explain
movie writers' obsession with verisimilitude.

Granted, much of moviemaking occurs today not on location but at
studios on soundstages, but no one who ever wandered through a dressed
set has failed to be struck by the faith with which reality is faked. A Har-
lem street on a back lot, populated by extras wearing appropriate wardrobe, appears to be the real thing. A middle-American home looks like a
middle-American home. A medieval castle looks like a medieval castle.
And if the set, the props, the people seem so real up close, consider how
vastly enhanced is that authenticity when removed one generation via
cinematography. In testimony to the miraculous nature of film, the camera creates representations of things that appear somehow even more real
than those things they represent.

It is not reality but this facsimile of reality to which screenwriters
must aspire.

Principle 21: Writers should prefer what appears to be true—even if it is not—over that which is actually, verifiably true.

Real, true stories with real, true characters are generally boring. Truth,
it is frequently asserted, is stranger than fiction. Undoubtedly, once in a
while this is actually the case. Far more often, however, truth is relentlessly, numbingly dull. It is the day-to-day annoyances, errands, chores
we all face. While audiences' lives outside the movie theater may from
time to time be rife with astonishment, much more often they swarm with
petty details: taxes, sniffles, rashes, squabbles, bruises, broken shoelaces,
a host of entities and experiences we would gladly forgo.

Whose life is perpetually inspiring, invigorating, exciting, expanding,
eye-opening? Nobody's. Even the president of the United States goes to
the bathroom, argues with his wife, reads lengthy reports rampant with
details he could just as well live without.

Life is in its nature positively saturated with tedium.

Thank goodness for that.

Without it, there would be no need for art, for creative expression of
any kind, including movies. That would be a terrible pity, since good films
offer expansive, life-affirming experiences that explain to us where, who,

and why we are. When they become preoccupied with ill-considered devotion to figures and facts, they betray their true calling.

Beware, therefore, of movies that purport to tell the truth.

Philosophers, intellectuals, artists, poets, and scientists have argued for millennia about the nature of truth. It is reasonable, therefore, to be skeptical of anyone who claims finally to have it all figured out.

Principle 22: Truth is always sought but never known.

Victor Weisskopf, a prominent physicist, has suggested there are two kinds of truth: superficial truth and profound truth. The first is truth the opposite of which is untrue. The latter is truth the opposite of which is somehow also true. Such is the truth we seek in art.

Truth of this order involves knowing more than precisely how many beans are in the jar. Historical, factual, scientific research has its place in our world for sure, but it is no replacement for writing. It is easier to spend hours and months and even years combing through books and journals, conducting interviews, compiling data, and recording footnotes than to sit alone in a room with blank paper or glowing computer screen, employing only thought and language, struggling to construct from thin air a tale with rich, ripe characters speaking naturalistic yet poetic dialogue worthy of engaging some assembled mass of people.

Principle 23: The challenge for screenwriters is not to look it up but to make it up.

Chapter 7

. . . .

Story: Tale Assembly

S tory is to movies as melody is to music.

To be sure, there is more to music than melody. Rhythm, tempo, texture, and tone are among a host of elements. But first comes melody. Melody is the most elusive, the most difficult component to capture. It is easier to devise an engaging beat, for example, or a unique texture, or an affecting tone, than to construct a melodic line starting somewhere, naturally and inevitably flowing somewhere else, pausing here to breathe, moving now to the next station on its own seductive, hypnotic continuum, finally arriving somewhere the listener acknowledges in his heart is the one place it positively must go.

A tale, likely apocryphal, is told of the young Mozart. As is common among teenagers of every generation, he liked to sleep late. Like most teenagers' mothers, Frau Mozart forever nagged him to arise. On a particular day when he was especially reluctant to stir, instead of poking his ribs and scolding, she hurried downstairs to the harpsichord and played an incomplete scale: do, re, mi, fa, sol, la, ti . . .

Ti . . . ?

The sequence hung motionless in the air, aching to be resolved. The tension had to be relieved, the score settled, the octave struck. Anybody with ears would have sought resolution of the incomplete scale, but for one so keenly attuned to music as Wolfgang it constituted an authentic agony.

He leaped from bed, took the stairs four at a time, and struck the final, calming "do," no doubt sighing with relief.

Story craft is no different. Something happens; instead of a note call it an anecdote, incident, or event. Its immediate result is a sweet sense of stress, which in turn compels something else—another incident or event—to follow. This tension/relief Ping-Pong game operates at the heart of story craft.

Many inexperienced screenwriters labor under a destructive illusion. Denigrating story, believing they possess instead a special knack for, say, creating fascinating characters, they convince themselves that to launch a script they need merely recall their creaking, cranky third-grade teacher, their crazy prankster pal from the old neighborhood, their quirky, affectionate mother, their high school swim coach, or their high school swim coach's quirky, affectionate mother. They expect the other details of the script somehow to sort themselves out.

Still other new writers believe that while they may not have a particular lock on character, they are God's gift to dialogue. They own an uncanny ear with a penchant for the natural, gritty, rhythmic, punchy, peppy, authentic poetry spoken by authentic people in authentic situations. They do not doubt for a second that rich settings populated with fascinating characters expressing cool, crisp, nifty dialogue will carry a movie.

Few writers, however, boast of a solid story sense. None—among them the world's most experienced, successful practitioners—maintain that story comes smoothly, effortlessly, without struggle.

In the recent past, story came to be characterized—to no small extent like writing itself—as retrograde, outmoded, linear, constricting. Narrative, we heard repeatedly from every quarter, stifles true creativity and suffocates effective character. Story was the moldering artifact of the ages, the detritus of dead old white guys like Homer, Sophocles, Shakespeare, and others.

Untested writers, and no small number of pop theoreticians, insisted that story is no more than a mail-order catalogue of incidents: this happens; that happens; something else happens after that. Liberated writers were encouraged to dispense with story altogether. They had merely to patch together a clutch of kooky characters, plop them in exotic, original settings, stick bright, brittle banter in their collective craw, and story would somehow shape itself.

The reality is, however, that stories do not shape themselves. Writers shape stories. It is no accident that the motion-picture studio office dealing with writers is not called the idea department nor the theme department nor the dialogue department nor the character department nor even the writing department. It is called the story department.

While all the elements of a screenplay are important, and none exists independently of any other, the most important component of all, and the most difficult to craft, is story.

Aristotle's so-called theory regarding story structure is no theory at all. It merely represents his observations of specific traits shared by the classical plays performed during his lifetime but written centuries earlier. His *Poetics* simply catalogues the characteristics he believed account for the works' longevity. He hoped to enable writers of any era to identify the fundamental techniques that drive dramatic narrative, much like the tales from ancient Greece, which hold audiences' attention millennia after their creation.

As my longtime UCLA colleague and sidekick Professor Emeritus Lew Hunter points out, the off-campus gang of screenwriting coaches has a vested interest in mystifying this creature called "story structure." If a particular instructor can convince writers he alone holds the magic formula for success, he can sell more copies of his books and more tickets to his seminars.

At UCLA we desire not to mystify but instead to demystify the process.

There's nothing the least bit mysterious about Aristotle's model. Every story, he tells us, has a beginning, a middle, and an end. The beginning is the part before which there is nothing. The middle is preceded by the beginning and followed by the end. The end is that part after which there is nothing.

This may seem so obvious as to appear useless. The fact is, however, that one of the most common mistakes among the thousands of screenplays I have seen over the decades is that they start not at but before the beginning.

Furthermore, they end not at but after the end.

Spike Lee is an example of an adept screenwriter who simply cannot end at the end. In his bright and flashy and in almost every other way splendid *Do the Right Thing*, for instance, the action culminates in the burning and looting of the pizza store and much of the rest of the neighborhood. What is "the right thing" for protagonist Mookie under such circumstances? Should he protect his employer's business from destruction by the mob or should he join his brothers in trashing the joint?

Mookie contemplates his dilemma, then hurls a trash can through the plate-glass window, clearly affirming the righteousness of violence. This action, Lee seems to say, is the right thing for Mookie to do.

Or perhaps he means to assert that it is the wrong thing.

Lee argues he is intentionally ambiguous here. He does not believe the artist's role is to dispense neat, pat, clean, approved, authorized, sanitized solutions to society's most difficult challenges. He demands instead that each member of the audience decide the issue for himself.

Some viewers will endorse Mookie's action; others will protest it. But surely every viewer can welcome the invitation the film provides for debate.

Moral ambiguity aside, however, all can agree on at least this much: When Mookie trashes the pizza palace the movie is complete. This moment clearly constitutes the ideal Aristotelian ending, the point after which there need be nothing. Indeed, the screen fades to black. There is every expectation that we are about to witness the tail credits scrolling across the screen.

Instead, the image fades back in and we are treated to a vision of actor Danny Aiello, who portrays the pizza store owner, and Spike Lee, as Mookie, discussing the issues. It seems likely that at any moment Larry King will drop in from the sky to moderate the exchange. The debate drags on with no effect other than to dissipate the movie's power. What does it add to the picture besides time? Is the tale advanced in any identifiable way? Are the characters expanded?

Not a bit.

The artist tells us only what he has already told us. He acts like the little kid at a family party whose parents importune him to play the violin for the relatives. The child balks and protests and resists but finally, reluctantly, consents. After he has mauled, say, a Dvořák *Humoresque*, it's time to assemble around the dinner table to chow down, but by now the kid is fully into his fiddle and won't quit. Soon enough family members are pleading with him to call it a day.

The beginning/middle/end construct applies not just to the whole picture but also to its parts. Each and every scene has its own beginning, middle, and end. Even parts of parts—for example, lines of dialogue—have a beginning, a middle, and an end.

Reasonable educators differ on how mastery of Aristotelian structure can be attained. Yet all agree that whatever approach is taken, the primary focus should be the story. There is more to screenwriting than that alone, of course, but first of all there is that.

All worthy stories are supported by something you can call a structure.

It is especially difficult for the layperson—indeed, for many experienced writers—to comprehend precisely what structure signifies when applied to story. The structure of a house is easy enough. There are a whole host of elements embodied in a house, but the basic structure includes three items: floor, walls, roof.

A story, on the other hand, upon first glance appears nothing at all like a house. A house is a tangible, measurable entity. You can stand beside it; you can stand within it; you can stand upon it. You can run your hand over portions of it, stroll through and around it, regard it from any number of angles.

Story, however, is a phenomenon whose nature is internal, intellectual, emotional, ethereal. It is supported not by beams but thoughts, built not of bricks but words. It can be read aloud so that one may hear it. It cannot, however, be seen, except inside one's own head until, of course, it illuminates a movie screen.

Still, while a story is in so many ways different from a house, like a house it has a structure whose basic components are threefold.

Aristotle's *Poetics*, if you take the time to read it (as I vigorously recommend), ought to be embraced as the classical equivalent of *How to Clean the Fuel Injector of Your Honda Civic*. Consider it history's first self-help, how-to, user's guide for dramatic narrative. It deserves, more particularly it requires, the most painstaking, step-by-step consideration. It need not be interpreted at all but merely obeyed.

A good place to start is the beginning. In my experience reading thousands of screenplays by amateurs and professionals alike, perhaps the single most common error is screenwriters' failure to begin at the beginning. All too typically screenplays commence not at but before the beginning.

Kramer vs. Kramer is an example of a film that begins at its proper Aristotelian beginning. It opens with Mrs. Kramer, portrayed by Meryl Streep, standing in the doorway, bags packed, trying to impress upon her husband that she is leaving their marriage.

A less skillful screenwriter might well have started earlier. He might have gone back to the couple's college days, their meeting, courting, and marriage. There would follow details of the relationship's decline. He squeezes the toothpaste in the middle of the tube; it enrages her. She wrings out her panties in the sink and leaves them draped over the porcelain lip; it disgusts him. His career soars and he's out late servicing his accounts; she grows morose whiling away the lonely hours watching soaps, neglecting their child, snorting whiskey and cocaine. Eventually, perhaps by the end of act 2, some seventy or eighty pages into the script, an hour and a quarter into the picture, they are at each other's throats. She weeps over his lack of affection. He gripes about her lack of support. She threatens to leave. He calls her bluff. At long last her bags are packed; she's out the door.

Screenwriter/adapter Robert Benton knew, however, that the tale is not one of husband and wife but of father and son; it is a story not of separation (man/spouse) but of reconciliation (parent/child).

The boy and man start out as virtual strangers, isolated from each other by the father's narcissistic preoccupation with career. The script is properly launched, therefore, with mother, bags packed, standing in the doorway. What went sour in the marriage is not pertinent. This is not to suggest that a rocky marriage could not be the subject of a film; it is merely not this film.

In *Kramer vs. Kramer* the end of the marriage is the beginning of the picture. Recognizing this, commencing at the authentic beginning, not a frame is wasted. Mom is jettisoned right at the start; father and son are promptly, properly hurled together at the absolute beginning, the point before which there is nothing.

Writers are well advised constantly to ask of the beginning of their tale: Is this the true beginning? Is this the point before which there is nothing? What would be lost if I started on page eight? Or eleven? Twenty-two? If nothing would be lost by starting on page eleven, start there. If starting on page twenty-two would merely cause some scattered but crucial information to be lost, perhaps that data can be inserted strategically somewhere into the succeeding pages, in the context of a particular character's speech or a definitive action by one or another player. Conveying some random information does not justify beginning a story twenty-two pages before its proper beginning.

As stated earlier, the question—Is this the true beginning?—can be applied not only to a script but even more precisely to a particular scene, or more narrowly still, to a single line of dialogue.

If a scene has to take place in a restaurant, for example, one need not show the principals arriving, being greeted, being seated. No audience need observe the distribution of the menus.

Since movies can cut right to the middle (from the Aristotelian standpoint the beginning) of an action or event, they must do precisely that— skip the menus, cocktails, wine, and leap directly to the main course, the meat of the scene. If one absolutely cannot avoid setting a scene in a restaurant, then the scene ought to open with the characters already present, seated, and served, and get right down to the pertinent, story-moving, character-advancing business at hand.

Structure is not limited merely to broad questions concerning story. Even a single line of dialogue is worthy of examination in order to determine whether it begins at the beginning. As discussed later, in the chapter treating dialogue, one need never open a line with "Look," or "Listen," or "Well," for no matter what follows it's already past the point before which nothing is needed. Is there any worthy difference between "Look, I love you" and "I love you" except that the former is thirty-three percent longer than the latter?

Granted, widely scattered instances of "Look," "Listen," or "Say," won't all by themselves wreck a script, but collectively they take the edge off the tale's thrust, blunt its momentum. Subliminally, they signal to both the script's readers and the film's viewers that this writer does not observe rigorous economy, that he does not value their time. A failure to observe economy in one area inevitably manifests itself in every other corner of his screenplay. The script brimming with unnecessary introductions and interjections invariably also contains lines and even whole scenes that can be excised.

Responsible creative expression requires that anything that can be excised must be excised. If it is not truly needed, why squander an audience's time?

This view of story structure replicates a scientific view of nothing less than the universe itself. Shatter an object into its smallest parts. Those fragments bear an uncanny resemblance to the overarching grand scheme. The infinitesimally small atom, with its electrons orbiting its nucleus, resembles the structure of the solar system, with the planets orbiting the sun.

Consider the hologram. Unlike the standard photographic negative, the hologram's "negative," when cut in half, continues somehow to contain the whole picture. This is because even just a fraction of the whole contains the entire interference pattern—holography's basis—for the complete original image.

This is merely another way of saying that little things look like big things.

Writers should note that residing within the smallest part of any one movie is a reflection of the whole picture, exactly as every cell in our bodies contains in its DNA all the genetic information necessary to reproduce the entire body. To state it more simply, as whole movies have structures encompassing beginnings, middles, and ends, so also do parts of movies—scenes, actions, and dialogue.

This is not just loose philosophical rambling, but a pragmatic strategy for improving scenes, actions, dialogue, and entire screenplays. It can go a long way toward helping a writer identify his movie's structure, and it can alert him to irrelevant parts that must be discarded. Any part of a movie without purpose has no purpose being in the movie.

Writers who grasp this principle can devise structural strategies to help shake loose the barnacles from their screenplays. A wholly integrated beginning/middle/end mind-set vastly economizes screenwriting, from dialogue through scenes to stories.

It is worthwhile, therefore, to review some specific rules pertinent to the three-part model of tale assembly.

First (appropriately), beginnings.

Beginnings

A proper beginning for a screenplay is easy compared to middles and ends. People tell me all the time about what they believe would be a great opening for a screenplay, even though the middle and end remain to be thought up, not to mention written down. I have yet to hear from a single person, however, who has no beginning but has a great middle and end for a one-day-to-be-written film. It is easier to spin the various threads belonging to a particular tale than to weave those same strands into an exquisitely integrated knot of an ending.

The key to beginnings, again, is to start as Aristotle prescribes, at that point before which nothing is required. *Citizen Kane* starts at what appears to be the end, Kane's death, but this is promptly seen to be the genuine beginning, as the biographical tale now flashes back to his earliest childhood, that same childhood reflected in the snowy crystal ball that opens the film. In *The Grapes of Wrath* (Nunnally Johnson, adapting the John Steinbeck novel) the beginning occurs with Tom Joad's return from prison to the abandoned family homestead. We don't need to see him in jail; we don't even need to know why he was incarcerated in the first place. We need merely to realize he has come home only to discover he has no home.

Story structure is not a formula. As indicated earlier, to integrate the scattered elements of a screen story into a coherent narrative is not the same thing as assembling a child's tricycle from its shipping crate. There is more to writing a screenplay than fastening flange A to tab B and securing strut C with wing nut D. While script structure adheres to immutable narrative laws, miraculously enough, screenplays are at the same time as individual as the writers who write them.

Primary among these laws is that the three basic parts—beginning, middle, end—are not equal in size. Beginnings and ends are shorter than middles.

In the beginning of any screenplay certain obvious tasks need to be addressed. They are addressed, however, not because writers consciously resolve to address them. Instead, they are irrevocably integrated into the nature of beginnings.

Tone

Primary among these tasks are establishing the movie's tone, introducing the protagonist, presenting necessary exposition, and possibly creating some sort of time lock. The most important aspect of tone is that whatever it is—comedic, tragic, melodramatic—it needs to be consistent.

More often than not, when differing tones seep into each other's territories, it is testimony to the writer's failure to resolve the challenge of structure. A film that has, for example, a serious tone—gritty, earthy—ought not suddenly dissolve into silliness. Audiences don't tolerate a failure of story craft, an inability to shape a well-rounded tale, suddenly turning everything into a joke. It is the equivalent of setting up some impossible situation and then paying it off by having the protagonist wake up to discover it was all a dream.

Stylistic or tonal crossover requires the genius of writers like Stanley Kubrick, Terry Southern, and Peter George, the creative powers behind *Dr. Strangelove*. It requires also no small quantity of luck. In *Dr. Strangelove* we have an absurd, slapstick comedy defiantly integrated with a terrifyingly credible military adventure.

Note, however, that *Dr. Strangelove* is exceptional. More commonly, tone requires quite the opposite: rock-steady evenhandedness, consistency from start to finish.

Even though a film's tone needs to be established at its beginning, it is nevertheless a mistake for writers to decide in advance precisely what the tone will be. Tone emerges in the context of working on a particular script. Should the writer have a vague notion to write an action/adventure script, for example, only to discover it is turning comedic, it's a mistake to drag it back to its originally intended tone. To do so is to imprison the tale in a stylistic straitjacket.

Writers should not write a lot about tone, as it is something that tends to establish itself. In *Hamlet* and *Macbeth*, for example, Shakespeare never describes the tone. He does not need to. A ghost at night on the parapet, likewise witches on the sulfurous heath, establish the tone without any extra language from the writer.

The important thing to remember is that once a writer finds his story's tone, whatever it may be, surprising as it may prove even to the writer himself, that tone needs to remain consistent.

Introducing the Protagonist

It might appear that the proper place to discuss the protagonist is in the chapter on character rather than story. In fact, however, when we talk about a tale's protagonist, we treat not just another character, nor even merely the film's central player.

We treat, instead, a basic tenet of story structure.

The clearer the protagonist, the stronger the film. Sometimes the role of protagonist is shared by two characters, for example, in *Romeo and Juliet* or *Thelma and Louise* (Callie Khoury). The wider the sharing, however, the softer the focus of the film.

Collective protagonists are hazardous to solid story structure. *The Big Chill* (Lawrence Kasdan, Barbara Benedek) provides an example. The focus of this tale is so democratic, spread so evenly over the half dozen collected central characters, that the story moves indiscriminately from one player to the next. The writers seem to be saying, "We don't discriminate here; we treat *everybody* badly." This is true, alas, for any movie without a clearly delineated central protagonist.

In fact writers must discriminate. As surely as a bus driver's job is to drive a bus, the writer's job is to discriminate. To discriminate is to choose. Creative choice-making is art's nature. With screenwriting, the choices are word for word, scene after scene. From this succession of hard choices springs a script's characters and dialogue and all its other aspects.

It is not impossible to craft an effective ensemble piece, one treating an apparently collective group of protagonists, and still somehow eventually identify a clear, central, single protagonist. *American Graffiti* provides an example. Here the writers succeed in establishing four central figures who are treated in what appears for the most part to be an evenhanded fashion. Yet long before the film's end it is quite clear that the character portrayed by Richard Dreyfuss is the film's center.

For its failure to manifest the same clear choice, *The Big Chill* spreads itself too thin. As soon as we begin to learn of a particular character's desires and disappointments we are whisked away to another player, without a chance fully to consider the first. Would not *The Big Chill* have worked more effectively had the writer chosen one or another member for the central role? It could have been the young dancer, the girlfriend of the deceased. This would have permitted the old college chums to be viewed from a singular vantage; it would have allowed for the kind of counterpoint— youngster against oldsters or sixties culture versus eighties culture—that delineates and defines both characters and stories.

Another tactic would have been to assign the role of protagonist to the couple—portrayed by Glenn Close and Kevin Kline—at whose house the action plays out. Or, since spreading the protagonist over even only two characters diffuses the focus, it could have been Glenn Close herself. In either instance the very nature of relationship itself could have been examined.

Then again, the role of protagonist could as easily have resided in the figure portrayed by William Hurt. The film comes fully to life only at that point at the dinner table when Hurt protests that the group's bond is a sham, a shared narcissistic illusion. He insists that, far from lifetime friends, they are in fact strangers who once, many years in the past, knew one another briefly. Here, at last, arrives an opportunity to confront loyalty, disloyalty, the quality of alliances.

Instead, in yet another attempt to service every player fairly, the narrative moves on to the next character, allotting him his own five minutes as "guest" protagonist before the joint is passed once again to yet another equally deserving figure. Everybody gets treated fairly, except for the audience.

Babel (Guillermo Arriaga) is an example of an otherwise splendid film that suffers for its lack of a clear protagonist. *Babel* overflows with engaging story strands and rich, bounteous characters. It never becomes clear, however, precisely whose tale this is. Compare that to the CBS sitcom *How I Met Your Mother* (Carter Bays, Craig Thomas). Notwithstanding its ensemble cast, a single character, Ted, presides at its center. All the other characters and actions filter through him. This grounds the story and provides it with a core.

All movies require a protagonist with clear needs, and also hurdles obstructing his efforts to satisfy those needs. That character, those needs, those hurdles, and that tone must be asserted in the film's beginning. This is the opening gambit that enables writers to capture the attention of audiences.

Time Lock

Often, usually early in a script, a clever screenwriter plants a time lock, a device requiring some specific event to occur, or a particular problem to be resolved, within a clearly predetermined period of time. This increases the story's tension.

In *The Bridge on the River Kwai* (Michael Wilson, Carl Foreman, based upon the Pierre Boulle novel) it is established early that the bridge needs not only to be constructed but also completed by a particular date. This hurries the film's conclusion. Under any circumstances the bridge's destruction is a splendid climax. The time lock, however, increases the tension not only at the end but throughout. It is just that much more delicious to have the bridge finished in the nick of time for the train's arrival, and just in time also for the explosion that sends bridge and train crashing into the river below.

In the underappreciated 1965 film *36 Hours* (George Seaton, Carl K. Hittleman, Luis H. Vance, adapting a Roald Dahl story), the time lock is still more inextricably integrated into the tale's structure. The invasion of Europe is but days away; the Nazis have precious little time to extract from the American military officer played by James Garner its schedule and location. To be sure, even without the time lock the methods for seducing Garner into revealing the information would play quite well, but the lock expands the picture's tension.

Not all stories lend themselves to time locks, but the resourceful writer digs deeply to locate a way to craft one into a script.

Exposition

"Exposition" derives from "expose." This involves revealing information already present but not yet available to viewers.

Too often exposition entails one version or another of a man with a pointer standing before a map delivering a speech on the order of: "We have three divisions to complete three missions in three days; the Japanese emplacements are here; our troops are here. The aircraft will strafe here. Landing craft will hit the shore here."

Even the most mundane film wants more invention and imagination than that.

Exposition is necessary at the start of virtually every film. The rules: Keep it short, present it in a fresh manner, and avoid making more of it than it is worth.

Often the best way to handle exposition is to spit it out, get it over with, and move along with your tale.

In *Stand by Me* (Raynold Gideon, Bruce A. Evans, adapting the Stephen King novella *The Body*) the exposition is handled somewhat self-consciously via a heavily pensive, ever-so-serious Richard Dreyfuss portraying the Writer. In a voice-of-doom narration he spells out for the audience events that transpired years ago. He prepares the viewers (as if it were necessary to do so) for the film to follow.

In *American Graffiti* the exposition is far more efficiently addressed. It is launched with little more than a dully lighted radio dial and music.

In a flash, the time and place and circumstances are set. Soon, in a hand-ful of quick exchanges, we learn that the characters portrayed by Ron Howard and Richard Dreyfuss are planning to leave town in the morning.

An especially inventive "man-with-a-pointer" bit of exposition is found in the charming Scottish film *Local Hero* (Bill Forsyth), in which an industrial executive addresses a group of bigwigs in a corporate board-room. Standing before the map of a sleepy little seaport, he wields the proverbial pointer, describing this aspect and that aspect of the coast's topography and the plans to construct a factory. What is different about this scene? The biggest of the wigs, a captain of industry portrayed by Burt Lancaster, is fast asleep. What is more, none of the sycophantic un-derlings dares rouse him. The scene is played out, therefore, with all the characters whispering their dialogue. It lends a cocky edge to the scene and renders what might otherwise be deadly dull fresh and funny.

A similarly clever twist on an otherwise weary film conceit is employed in the little-seen *Silver Bears* (Peter Stone, adapting the Paul Erdman novel) starring Michael Caine. A group of aging Mafiosi strip naked, don plush bathrobes, and march down a penthouse corridor high above Las Vegas. They enter a vast, round, steaming, bubbling therapy pool, discard their robes, and—with foot-long cigars clamped between their teeth—settle into the water.

There now unfolds what otherwise would be the all too familiar and obligatory Mafia boardroom scene. Moving it from a paneled corporate boardroom, or the back room of a strip club, to a tiled, steamy hot tub and turning the players into fat old naked men make it different from all the other films burdened with their own version of this same scene.

However it is accomplished, once the exposition is exposed, and once an audience appreciates a film's environment and tone, and once an ob-stacle is thrown rudely into the protagonist's path, we are ready to take a sharp turn toward the Middle.

Middles

Some theoreticians cite endings as the hardest part of three-component story structure. They are wrong. The hardest part of a screenplay is the middle.

For one thing, the middle is the longest of the three parts, constituting the tale's true bulk; it is several times larger than the beginning and the end combined.

Length is not the only reason the middle is hardest. I have suggested earlier that, relative to the other aspects of structure, beginnings are easy. Every writer, by the time he has outlined his story and sits down to write the whole script, knows how it begins. Additionally, he likely has a clear notion as to how it ends.

At the end of the beginning, just before the middle, stories typically seem smooth, uncomplicated. In *Citizen Kane* the reporters agree that "Rosebud" is the key to Kane's life; they'll conduct interviews and figure it all out. In *The Grapes of Wrath* Tom Joad catches up with his family, they resolve to seek a new life in California, and all will be hunky-dory. British officer Alec Guinness in *The Bridge on the River Kwai* wins his point with the Japanese prison camp commandant. The commandant will respect the officer's rank; the officer will have his men build a bridge across the River Kwai. In *Borat: Cultural Learnings of America for Make Benefit Glorious Nation of Kazakhstan* (Sacha Baron Cohen, Anthony Hines, Peter Baynham, Dan Mazer, Todd Phillips), the protagonist will return to his native land with a more realistic and less idealized sense of life, love, and innocence. In *American Graffiti*, Richard Dreyfuss and Ron Howard will enjoy a final, riotous, fun-filled night of debauchery in their hometown and then move on together to glory and adventure in the big city.

Audiences are not fools. They know the movie can't end after only ten or twelve minutes. That fact alone ought to signal clearly enough that complications are in store for both the characters and the audience alike. If the beginning launches the tale, the middle thickens the plot. Obstacles arise. Indeed, some commentators assert that the way to create a taut yarn is for the writer to place the protagonist here, his goal there, and then to litter his path with every obstacle imaginable.

Inevitably, toward the conclusion of the beginning, everything seems neatly, grandly easy. There is that moment where audiences are inclined to relax and hope against hope that everything will work out fine. Everything working out fine is great in life, of course, but in film it is boring.

At that very last moment, where it appears events will proceed smoothly, an event occurs that blows complacency sky-high. It may be as subtle as in *American Graffiti* when the Richard Dreyfuss character is merely smiled upon by the mystical girl in the phantom T-Bird; he will search for her throughout the rest of the film and, indeed, the rest of his life. Or it may be as broad as the blood-soaked murder in *The Godfather: Part II* (Francis Ford Coppola, Mario Puzo), of young Vito Corleone's mother before the boy's very eyes.

Invariably, beginnings end this way. All seems right and well and fit. Then, in a flash, all is wrong and nothing at all fits. It is in the middle that the complications play out.

Wrinkles and Reversals

If at the end of the beginning a complication arises that launches the tale's fundamental conflict, throughout the middle the plot thickens. The elements that thicken plot consist of wrinkles and reversals, obstacles and complications.

Through the middle of *American Graffiti*, for example, Richard Dreyfuss strides a perilous path strewn with impediments: Gang members from another town try to do him in, and he and his buddy experience a profound loss of faith, particularly as it relates to the pal's relationship with his girlfriend and the effect that has upon the boys' own bond. He attempts futilely—or at least that's the way it seems—to reach the apparently unreachable disc jockey at the radio station. All of these, of course, are obstacles—barriers tossed in the road before him. They are also wrinkles where the plot twists, knots, and turns upon itself.

Wrinkles, obstacles, impediments, complications all clearly relate to one another. Each interferes with the protagonist's forward motion; each requires him to take a step sideways, up, over, or even momentarily backward in order to arrive at that place where it was determined at the beginning of the tale he should go.

Because these related phenomena require a protagonist sometimes temporarily to retreat, it can be useful to consider them as reversals. In the skillfully wrought tale they foil the forward thrust; they require diversion and a host of shaping devices. Regardless of how one designates them, by obstructing the straight and narrow path they lend the tale dimension, which is a vital and elusive quality in story. The straight line is too direct to contain the desirable strangeness and fun viewers rightly crave. A no-detours story compares unfavorably to the sculpted curves, whorls, burls, eddies, and abrasions created by a strong writer's well-stocked arsenal of reversals.

Reversals also go a long way toward helping writers confront the twin-edged sword of predictability.

Predictability

Clearly, screen stories should not be too predictable; at the same time a dollop of predictability is desirable.

How much predictability constitutes a dollop?

If this were an easily answered question, screenplays would be easy to write. Obviously, audiences love surprises. Just as clearly, predictability can go a long way toward spoiling the excitement derived from unexpected twists and turns of the plot. If absolutely no predictability could be tolerated in a screenplay, we could watch every movie—even the finest—one time only. Once we know the way it comes out, that particular tale is totally and eternally predictable. Once we know "Rosebud" is the sled, we forever know "Rosebud" is the sled. Once we know that Jocasta is Oedipus's mother, can the revelation ever again surprise us? Once we have learned that Norman Bates of *Psycho* (screenplay by Joseph Stefano from the Robert Bloch novel) is his own mother, that stunning surprise ought to be rendered forever dull.

Yet, like children, we love to hear the best-told tales endlessly repeated. If in one or another retelling, just for variety, the tale is altered in even the tiniest way, our listener rudely summons us back to the original. If we view a print of *Psycho* and observe that this time Janet Leigh, playing Marion Crane, takes her shower at the Bates Motel, dries herself off, and climbs into bed for a good night's snooze, we will inspect the projector, the projectionist, our own eyes, and the medication in our I.V. drip in an attempt to figure out what went wrong. We would feel not only surprised but also cheated.

While smart writers don't want to telegraph events before they occur, a certain predictability is nevertheless useful—even necessary—in moving an audience through a tale.

If early in *Gremlins* (Chris Columbus) the elderly Chinese shopkeeper tells us that under no circumstances should the little critters come into contact with water, you can predict with certainty that they are going to be moistened before the last reel. It is not unlike Shakespeare opening *Macbeth* with witches spelling out—albeit in riddles—precisely what is to occur within the tale. We can be damned certain Macbeth will be king, and that, somehow or other, Birnam Wood to Dunsinane will move.

A desirable predictability in movies compares effectively to the children's game of Boo! What's more frightening—to walk down a corridor absolutely unaware that someone is going to jump out of a doorway, or knowing for certain that somebody is going to do just that?

On the surface it might seem the former is more unsettling, as the victim has no time to prepare. The truth, however, is quite the opposite. Knowing someone is hiding behind that pillar or in that alcove or under that bed causes the victim to tighten, to tense, to flex every muscle in dreadful anticipation of what is to come. When it arrives, for all its predictability the effect is all the more shattering.

When a script is criticized as predictable, what the critic truly means is not that it is predictable but that it is too predictable.

Coincidence

Screen stories are from time to time, sometimes justifiably, accused also of having too many coincidences. Can a good writer include in his story a glaring, convenient coincidence? Yes, but only one per script.

Surely it has more than a little to do with the fact that life itself is riddled with coincidence. Indeed, an extraordinary coincidence in everyone's life—a special sperm conjoining with a particular egg—is the reason each of us is here.

Still, life is life and film is film. For their money audiences rightly expect movies to be well worked out, the events skillfully woven. A respectable movie tale may be launched or resolved by a coincidence. Beyond that, however, people are entitled to a story that is exquisitely crafted. They resent dependence upon coincidence since they see it for what it is: lazy writing.

If audiences will tolerate a single coincidence, screenwriters ought to make it an important one. They can have it launch the tale's fundamental action or they can provide it later in the story as a device to undergird the resolution.

Preston Sturges's *Christmas in July* is an example of the latter. Well-meaning friends deceive a pal into believing he has won a contest. In the end he actually does win. Why do audiences tolerate the coincidence? Partly because it's the only such coincidence in the tale.

In *The China Syndrome* (Mike Gray, T. S. Cook, James Bridges), a television reporter in the company of a news cameraman films a story at a nuclear power plant when, by perfectly acceptable coincidence, the reactor happens to malfunction. Imagine if later in the picture, by some combination of twists and turns, the photographic footage of the event becomes lost or destroyed. Imagine, also, that the news team responds by returning to the plant to shoot more footage and, while they are filming, another such accident takes place.

Audiences would react with outrage, and rightly so. They would know the later accident occurs only because it suits the writer's convenience. Movie story structure—like movies themselves—is created to serve not the writer's but the audience's convenience. What is less convenient than writing a movie story?

Coincidences appear almost invariably early in stories. Occasionally, however, they occur later in the narrative. In either case, wherever that coincidence occurs, it is essential that it be the only coincidence in the script.

The Big Gloom

It is no coincidence, and also perfectly predictable, that by the end of the middle virtually every screenplay runs headlong into a formidable barrier. It is as if audiences by nature start fidgeting, stretching, yawning at this particular juncture in the narrative. Too often this is exacerbated by the fact that scripts lacking shape tend to sprint from the very beginning. Like marathoners who fail to pace themselves, roughly four-fifths of the way through the tale screenplays also tend to lose their wind.

Baseball addresses this issue with a well-respected convention: the seventh-inning stretch. You cannot stop a movie, however, an hour and twenty minutes into it and invite everybody to stand and flex and kibitz for a few moments and sing of peanuts and Cracker Jack.

Perhaps oddly, at this particular juncture the writer needs to craft a low point among low points, a deeply disturbing, horrible, dreadful moment when all appears forever and irretrievably lost.

Naturally this cannot be some artificial appendage invented at the last moment; it must derive naturally from an already well-structured story.

If this grim moment—not to be confused with the climax—occurs too early, at the conclusion of, say, the beginning, the entire script will run out of steam just at that point when the proper Big Gloom ought to descend.

In *American Graffiti* it is Dreyfuss's phone conversation with the phantom girl in the T-Bird when he learns once and for all that they will never, ever meet. This moment is darker and more frightening even than the flaming car wreck that soon follows and constitutes the climax. He realizes he will never find what he seeks, never truly fulfill his destiny, as long as he hangs around with his old buddies in his safe, familiar, stultifying hometown.

In *Terms of Endearment* (James L. Brooks, adapting the Larry McMurtry novel) it is the moment in the hospital when we learn of the impending demise of the young mother. In *About Last Night . . .* (Tim Kazurinsky, Denise DeClue, based on a David Mamet play) it is the overly convenient montage in which a "liberated" character played by Rob Lowe suffers miserably for the loss of commitment to a woman only a moment earlier he was so eager to shed.

The Big Gloom is that moment, occurring just before the beginning of the end, approximately eighty minutes into the film, where the protagonist is furthest from achieving his goal.

Ends

Place a white rat in a Skinner box—a cage with a trigger-controlled feed chute—and reward it with a pellet of rat food not whenever he presses the lever but the first time he presses it after a particular interval of time.

With just a bit of experience the rat soon learns that pressing the lever does not always result in a reward. Unsophisticated as an albino rat must be, he quickly gets the idea that rewards come only within a particular time frame. A graph of lever-pressing reveals a flat, seemingly random number of pressings over a period, rising suddenly as the prearranged time interval approaches. Clearly, the rat "learns" that the end is in sight, as is evidenced in the increased frequency with which he presses the bar as the moment approaches.

Some will protest that it is not fair to compare humans and rats. But rats and humans share at least this single characteristic, which is

pertinent to the art and the craft of screenwriting: When the end is in
sight they sprint like crazy.

There is an old directors' and editors' trick for handling love stories.
When after a long separation the lovers are finally reunited, they are seen
first to gaze longingly at each other from opposite ends of the big screen.
Then, slowly, each takes a step toward the other, and then another step,
and another. As the steps increase, so also does the pace. Finally, music
swelling, the boy and girl rush breathlessly toward each other in such a
manner as to establish a new Olympic record for the quarter mile.

Writers also tend to sprint when the end of their screenplay is at hand.
This, however, can be a serious mistake.

Ideally, of course, a script's conclusion is foretold in its opening. Once
the tension is properly set, its resolution can be taken for granted, even if
the required writing craft cannot. When the boys learn at the beginning
of *Stand by Me* that there is a body in the woods, and that the bad guys,
the older boys, also will be attempting to locate that body, we can accept
as given that the young boys will find the body and that they will accomplish this feat before their antagonists do.

This has to be so because the purpose of endings is to resolve and balance beginnings and middles. Natural as this process is, it can be achieved
only methodically, through the most painstaking deliberation. Scrambling madly just to get the pages finished is a recipe for disaster. Writers
need to resist the urge to hurry as the conclusion of their script approaches.

Once the end arrives, and once it has fled, and once the final credits
crawl across the screen and the curtains close and the houselights come
up, the audience should feel not uplifted, not superior, not virtuous, but
humbled. Each viewer should be left with a sense of his status as one more
wretched sinner. Each should be reminded of his own humanity. There
should arise within each member of the audience a sense that what has
transpired on the screen is really about him.

Ambiguity

Can a screen story be ambiguous?

Yes and no.

Art's worthy mission is not to achieve pat and pretty solutions to the existential problems dominating human intellect since the dawn of thought. Surely no mere movie can provide easy answers to questions that are by their nature unanswerable.

Principle 24: Art seeks not answers but questions.

The worthy film refines and articulates important inquiries. Perhaps this explains why a film's end ought to be every bit as unsettling as settling. While the burden is upon the writer to provide the audience a worthy tale populated by worthy characters, it is all right also to require the audience to work just a little.

An example is found in *The Revolutionary* (Hans Koningsberger, adapting his own novel), a film made at the end of a lamentable late sixties trend, when Hollywood attempted futilely and repeatedly to cash in on "revolution" as if it were Baskin-Robbins's flavor of the month. *The Revolutionary* went largely unnoticed, although it is arguably the best movie in that sorry group, or perhaps merely the least dreadful. Jon Voight portrays a protagonist who is at first totally self-involved, uncommitted, unprincipled. Through the body of the film, however, he is rendered caring, moral, ethical. In the course of the film he must decide whether it is right or wrong to resort to violence in order to seek a redress of grievances.

By film's end Voight's character arrives at something like a decision: He will hurl an incendiary device. Or will he?

As the movie trudges relentlessly toward its conclusion, just before the moment he is supposed to throw the bomb, the image freezes and the film fades out. The final credits roll. The audience is asked in effect to provide its own solution to this philosophical quandary.

Another poignant example of a splendidly written film with a justifiably ambiguous ending is the screen adaptation of the John le Carré thriller *The Spy Who Came In from the Cold* (Paul Dehn, Guy Trosper). Richard Burton plays a secret agent caught up in a richly convoluted plot involving spies, counterspies, counter-counterspies, and counter-counter-counterspies. Double agents? Forget them; le Carré provides triple, quadruple, quintuple agents. By film's end it is virtually impossible to determine who's on whose side. At the final fade Burton finds himself perched high atop the Berlin Wall with everybody shooting at him.

Whither shelter? On whose side will he ultimately settle?

Refusing to decide, the film leaves him lost in the netherworld of ambiguity. This drives home the film's theme, which has nothing to do with right versus wrong or right versus left but with the nature of loyalty and disloyalty. The ambiguity, therefore, is integrated into the fabric of the entire film.

Ambiguity occupies a rightful place in many movies, especially as it relates to their endings.

The Sopranos concludes its years-long run with an ending that is apparently ambiguous. The family is seated at dinner, in a diner, when mysterious figures enter. Suddenly there is only silence and darkness. Some say that the show's creator, David Chase, wants audiences to decide for themselves precisely what happens. I believe that what he intends is that Tony—perhaps also his wife and son—is assassinated. Why else the silence? Every previous episode ends with music over the tail credits. Darkness and silence represent the point of view of the dead. That, however, is just one more view among the many that have been offered regarding the meaning of Chase's ending. That the arguments are so vigorous tells us that there is no right or wrong to these guesses. There is only a welcome, provocative ambiguity that serves to keep us wondering about the narrative and its unforgettable characters.

Positive and Negative Space

The graphic-arts notion of positive and negative space can be useful to writers.

The positive space in, say, a portrait is that area of the canvas occupied by the subject itself. The surrounding area—call it the background—represents the negative space. Movies, as well as individual scenes within movies, also can be thought of as possessing positive and negative space.

Consider the entire script by itself, from beginning to end, with all the characters, dialogue, and action, as constituting the positive space. It is everything occurring within the film; it is everything viewed on-screen.

Even before the beginning of a script, however, there is implied backstory. Characters do not spring full-blown from the first frame. They must have lived before we met them, exactly like anybody in real life whom we meet for the first time. Similarly, once the film is over and the houselights go up, in the minds of both writer and audience the tale continues.

When *The Godfather: Part II* fades to its somber conclusion, with

Michael alone, isolated from friends and family, staring off into space, we can imagine that his life nevertheless continues, however sorrowfully.

Likewise, the first images we see at the opening of *WarGames* (Lawrence Lasker, Walter F. Parkes) involve military preparations to respond to a purported or simulated or actual nuclear attack—we don't know which. We can be certain, however, that these characters must have lived prior to these scenes, that the entire underground missile silo complex did not just arise in a flash but was there for some time. There is, in fact, no limit to the reach of negative space.

It is this limitlessness that differentiates negative from positive story space; the latter is finite, the former not. Some may consider negative and positive space as story versus plot, plot being that part of the story in the script, and story the boundless extent of the tale, forward and back.

The writer's first task in confronting story craft is to mark that precise point within the negative space where the positive space commences. Call it the beginning. Similarly, seizing the precise moment to call it quits is to define the final boundary between positive and negative space. That point is, of course, the end.

Defining the borders between one kind of space and another may appear a worthless exercise. In fact, however, it can be enormously useful in helping a writer determine precisely where the true beginning begins, i.e., that place before which nothing else is needed. In the same way it can help determine the end.

Writing for the screen requires the artist constantly to make hard choices. Anything that facilitates that choice making is to be welcomed.

Gravity—Cause and Effect

Stories move by a kind of gravity.

After Newton and until Einstein, gravity could be thought of as an invisible string tugging all objects toward the center of the earth. After relativity, gravity became a more grandiose phenomenon. It can be thought of as an object's reluctance to remain wherever it happens to be.

Such tension permeates stories. A well-crafted story does not want to rest; it wants desperately to keep moving.

Indeed, nowhere in nature is there anything like true stasis. Were an object somehow to succeed in making its way to the center of the earth, for example, it would not remain there. It would move with the earth it-self, revolving on its axis, traveling in its orbit around the sun, flowing with the solar system and the galaxy through space.

All any object really "wants" is to travel to its next station on the space-time continuum. Gravity can be thought of as an object's "discomfort" at being forced to stand still.

However far-fetched this all may appear, for writers to view story this way is in fact broadly and practically useful. Something happens, and another event is caused to succeed it, and something else is compelled to follow that—not just anything else but something that fits, something synchronous with the previous events. This is the way story advances. From time to time it may seem to rest, but rest is something it can never really do.

Movies ought to move. They should move audiences and they should move story and character. When even so successful a film as *Butch Cassidy and the Sundance Kid* (William Goldman) abruptly halts its forward motion, requiring the audience to suffer smiling actors riding tricycles up and back across the screen to the insufferable accompaniment of "Raindrops Keep Fallin' on My Head," the tale goes cold.

Writers must forever dodge the temptation to stand still, to regroup. Movie stories crank relentlessly forward at twenty-four frames per second. Like gravity, they grind ever onward, seeking resolution but never truly finding it.

Leave 'em Wanting More

Question: When should a film end?

Answer: (a) too soon, (b) too late, or (c) at exactly the right moment.

The correct answer is (a) too soon. Clearly, (b) too late is incorrect. For a film to drag on past that point after which nothing is needed is to squander an audience's attention.

Why not (c)?

Human beings simply do not possess the capability to determine with authority "exactly the right moment," nor indeed, exactly the right anything. God alone is perfect; the rest of humanity, screenwriters included, are all wretched sinners.

Again, the correct answer is (a) too soon, for "too soon" in movies is exactly the right moment.

Perhaps this is merely a fancy way of reciting the weary old show business rule: Leave 'em wanting more. Instead of relief, the audience ought to feel just a little disappointed that the film ends. This propels the viewer past the ending into the implied negative space, the phantom on-screen tale existing after the tale.

The rule for beginnings and endings: Start late, finish early.

Chapter 8

· · · · · · · · ·

Character

There are three basic rules for creating audience-worthy movie characters.

First: No stereotypes.

Second: Render everybody, even the foulest, most evil villain somehow sympathetic.

Third: Instead of having them lie there on a slab, static and stale, require your characters throughout the tale to evolve.

Development

If many screenwriters grudgingly acknowledge their deficiencies in plot craft, they insist they know how to paint rich, broad, wacky, sensitive, insightful, touching, colorful characters.

They have merely to call upon memories of colorful characters they have known. Doesn't every family possess at least one dark sheep, invariably an uncle, who hasn't held a job since he got out of the navy? Does not every college dormitory hold a jokester who, underneath his clownish facade, is a deeply sensitive poet? Did not every writer once work as a waiter or cabbie or bartender and meet a host of colorful characters, each one of whom would provide a fabulous portrait for a movie?

These may seem on the surface to provide some promise for conflict, but in fact they are for the most part too familiar. Even in the best of circumstances, regardless of how arresting they may appear upon introduction, if screen characters remain exactly the same throughout a tale, if they do not change, grow, develop—or, at the very least if they are not challenged to do so—the audience will grow for them, and what the audience will grow is bored.

Characters who from the first minute on-screen tell you everything there is to know about them are no different from real people who on first encounter regale you with every detail of their lives. Anyone stuck on an overseas flight seated beside such a character is all too familiar with the truth of this proposition. Audiences are entitled to a bit of a tease, a seduction, so that as a film develops, surfaces are stripped away and new layers of identity revealed.

Truly memorable screen characters start somewhere and end up somewhere else.

Dustin Hoffman as Ted Kramer in *Kramer vs. Kramer* starts out selfish, insensitive, narcissistic; he ends up expanded, connected, fulfilled.

Midnight Cowboy's (Waldo Salt, adapting the James Leo Herlihy novel) Ratso, another Hoffman portrayal, is introduced as a thieving, lying, rancid, scuzzy maggot; he finishes the film caring, considerate, and honest, if also dead.

Michael Corleone at the start of *The Godfather* is innocent, moral, principled; by tale's end he's bereaved, bereft, heartless, soulless, a power-mongering murderer of, among countless other victims, his own brother.

In *The Reader* (David Hare, adapting the Bernhard Schlink novel) Hanna and Michael are at the end of the movie vastly different from the characters we met at the beginning. Michael has grown to his mature manhood. Hanna, now literate instead of illiterate, appears to accept responsibility for her actions during the war.

It's hard enough to create a character who, even at first glance, is special enough to merit an audience's attention. Once that is accomplished, however, the real work remains: expanding and enhancing the character's humanity throughout the film.

Can't a character ever remain the same?

Sometimes. Patton is still Patton at the end of *Patton* (Francis Ford Coppola, Edmund H. North, from books by Ladislas Farago and Omar N. Bradley), every bit the inspired and inspiring, megalomaniacal warrior he always was. In the course of the movie, however, his character has been challenged, articulated, and rearticulated in such a manner as to provide a glimpse into why he is who he is. Even if we don't exactly like him, he fascinates us. Passing two hours with him in a movie theater proves a worthy expenditure of our time.

Sympathy

Complicated characters, rounded and whole, are infinitely more fun than folks whose entire book can be read in a flash. Nothing renders characters fleshy and full—even lying, scheming, conniving fiends—like a pinch of sympathetic human understanding.

Right here is the appropriate moment to consider the Prudent Person Principle.

Principle 25: Audiences will tolerate characters on-screen getting into situations where they would never find themselves, as long as the characters in the movie react the way the audience members themselves would react under those same circumstances.

Sympathy for one's characters raises a tale above the mindless equation in which everything—both evil and good—is perfectly so and, therefore, also perfectly boring.

Years ago, in the days before home air-conditioning, just to get out of the summer heat, my parents took me to my first film, the Disney live-action classic *Treasure Island* (Lawrence Edward Watkin, adapting the Robert Louis Stevenson book). There is no forgetting, in particular, Robert Newton's performance as the antagonist, crusty old peg-legged Long John Silver, a scoundrel among scoundrels. He torments young Jim Hawkins—Newton deliciously pronounces it 'Arkins—separates him from his beloved comrades, holds him hostage, threatens his life, renders his frail subsistence just generally miserable until, at last, on the beach, at film's end, the British sailors close in upon him, certain to liberate the youngster and deliver Silver to the law.

At the shore, the waves licking at his one good foot, Long John struggles futilely to free the lonely little skiff from the sand in which it is mired. In all of God's creation was there ever a more pathetic, more desperate figure than Silver at this moment? His wooden leg repeatedly slips in the sand, making it impossible for him to launch the dinghy. The wicked old buccaneer resembles an overturned turtle struggling hopelessly to right itself.

No human with a heart could fail to pity him.

At the last moment, with the British troops now sprinting into view on the ribbon of beach at jungle's edge, young 'Arkins leaps unexpectedly into action, surprising perhaps even himself. Urgently he collaborates with his oppressor, setting his shoulder against the vessel's gunwale, joining forces with Silver in a final, desperate attempt to save the old curmudgeon.

As the boat now slips past the breakers, carrying the pirate beyond the reach of his pursuers, we share both Hawkins's and Silver's pleasure at the escape. Despite his bloody record and evil heart, there is some shred of humanity in him; we rejoice in his redemption.

It provides audiences with a glimmer of hope for our own undeserved salvation.

J. R. Ewing of television's *Dallas* (created by David Jacobs) is an unreconstructed sleazebag who is nevertheless somehow deeply sympathetic. J.R. lies and cheats his reckless way to the top of the Texas oil world. He is faithless to his wife, to his friends, to his business associates, to his own brother and sister, even to his children. In one episode, through a shady deal involving the illegal export of fuel to Cuba, he betrays even his country.

Nevertheless, through it all there is something undeniably likable about the guy. His fragile, false smile and nervous, calculated twinkle endear him to us. Beneath all the synthetic Texas good-old-boy bluster, we see nobody other than a lonely, left-out little lad trying to win his daddy's attention and approval. (This continues to be the case even though—in the series' later seasons—Daddy is long dead.)

Do not all real-life human relationships transcend even the physical presence of the principals long after they are gone? Who among us in our hearts does not mourn daily the failed gesture, the lost courtesy we might once have offered a friend or sibling or parent who is now gone forever? Who can say with serene confidence he has won the unconditional validation of his mother and father?

When J.R. misbehaves, therefore, we see nothing but the naughty little boy with his hand in the cookie jar, hoping yet again for that reassuring, affectionate nod from his long-lost daddy. Instead of wanting to knock him to the ground and grind his face beneath our heel, we are moved to cuddle and comfort, to stroke and protect the wounded, trembling little fawn. His heartache is our own. We feel connected to our own humanity, our own pain, our own disappointment and shortcomings.

Tony Soprano is a crime boss and brutal murderer. He gives new meaning to the term "blood relative." Nevertheless, he is also a teddy bear of a guy, cozy and cuddly, with a twinkling eye and a warm smile. As different as he is from his audience, he is also just what they are: a spouse, a parent, a sibling. The conflicts he has with his wife are like the conflicts that inevitably arise among all spouses. His confrontations with his own adolescent kids are like the confrontations every father has with his adolescent kids. Instead of feeling different from so monstrous a personage, we feel connected to him. In the end, *The Sopranos* is not so much about a crime family as about a family.

Such complex characterizations have been at the heart of dramatic writing since its inception during the ancient Greek era.

Oedipus kills his father. Still worse, he violates the ultimate taboo: incest. Our hero, the king, regularly engages in sexual intercourse with his mother.

Consider the lengths to which Sophocles goes to maintain the audience's sympathy for such a character. The playwright fully appreciates that without sympathy there is no play but at best only a dark and evil sketch. He constructs a plot that prevents Oedipus from knowing the facts of his origins until it is too late.

Who could forgive a protagonist who knowingly copulates with his own mother?

Finally, upon learning the sorry truth of his situation, Oedipus is sincerely remorseful. This, along with the other devices, enables us to sympathize with the hero despite his unspeakable actions.

Television's Archie Bunker, in Norman Lear's *All in the Family*, is a bigot and, like most bigots, not especially bright. Still, the question needs to be asked: Who among us possesses no trace of prejudice? Archie may be stubborn beyond reason, blind to his own emotional and intellectual handicaps, but he is also unmistakably human. We learn to love the bigot even as we revile the bigotry. Our exposure to Archie enables us to examine our own biases. Perhaps the experience renders us a tad less judgmental. Our capacity for tolerance is expanded.

An illustration of sympathy's critical role is found in a comparison between two films: *Z* (Jorge Semprún, adapting the Vassili Vassilikos novel) and *The Battle of Algiers* (Gillo Pontecorvo, Franco Solinas). The latter is the superior of the two. To no small extent this is due to the fact that in *Z* the villains are wholly unsympathetic. The Greek generals who collectively represent the antagonist are portrayed as plundering, anti-democratic buffoons, greedy, selfish slimeballs who stage the military coup that oppresses their nation for more than a decade. They are depicted as unprincipled fools without a shred of humanity. In real life it may be true that they were precisely that. Movies, however, ought concern themselves not with historical accuracy but with superior drama.

Such treatment reduces *Z* to shallow good-guys-versus-bad-guys; hiss the black hats, cheer the white hats. Whatever tension and excitement are created by skillful cinematography, editing, and a thundering musical score are mitigated by characters who appear grossly to be contrived.

In *The Battle of Algiers*, however, even as the writers pull no punches regarding the side they favor (the Algerian independence fighters), they treat the enemy (the imperial French establishment and, especially, its military governors) with a cautious but palpable dignity. That the bad guys are not born evil, are not naturally bent on destruction, makes them no less horrifying but, quite the contrary, all the more so. They are, like all of us, the product of their heritage, the collective beliefs and biases imparted to them by the culture that reared them.

Miraculously, instead of excusing the French generals, instead of expiating their guilt, this evenhanded treatment renders them all the more culpable. Moreover, the native-born Algerian terrorists, clearly the heroes of the film, are depicted also as murderers of innocent children. The French militarists, even as they are unabashedly antagonistic, are depicted as clinging to their view of whatever constitutes safe and sane social order. The acts they commit are the same that members of the audience would commit if they lived inside the skins of these individuals.

The Japanese commander of the jungle prison camp in *The Bridge on the River Kwai* is one more example of an unrepentant tyrant whose humanity is nevertheless ultimately revealed, vastly enhancing not only the characterization but the entire film. He violates the international conventions pertaining to the treatment of prisoners of war. He locks his wards in hot boxes, humiliates, mistreats, degrades, and even tortures them. Yet the writers allow the audience to see him also as merely another unfortunate wretch caught up in circumstances that are larger than he, one more poor slob just doing his sorry, dreadful duty in a world he did not make.

We are permitted even to see him weep.

It is a far stronger, more memorable portrait than a run-of-the-mill bad guy.

Clearly, fine films abound with potentially unredeemable figures who are ultimately redeemed. A stunning example of this appears in *The Grapes of Wrath* when a bulldozer, a growling, fire-breathing dragon made of steel, arrives to raze the neighbors' farm where the Joads are staying since losing their own spread.

The farmers stand firm, shotguns at the ready. They notify the driver that in order to save their home they are willing to blow him right out of his cockpit. The driver, his eyes concealed behind smoky goggles, his nose and mouth swathed in a bandana to ward off the dust, appears very much like an alien from Jupiter. When he brakes the bulldozer, however, and lifts the goggles and unwraps the bandana, we recognize that he is merely a kid from the neighborhood. His own family has lost its farm, too. His good luck is to have found this job working for the bank, clearing out the structures on foreclosed farms. That he is in fact no monster but merely another human, indeed, a neighbor and friend, makes his task more painful, and the audience's emotion that much stronger.

Human treatment of human characters inevitably provides for heightened drama.

Stereotypes

Mainstream filmmaking suffers from a plague of typecasting. This pertains not exclusively to actors but to virtually all other film artists, including writers.

A writer, if he's lucky enough to become known at all, likely becomes known as a comedy writer or an action/adventure writer, a melodrama writer, a television writer, a woman's writer, a man's writer. Sadly, writers themselves frequently contribute to this obsession by populating their scripts with hordes of ready-made, all too familiar characterizations, more caricature than character.

There are in fact just two kinds of writers: good writers and bad writers. And good writers avoid types altogether in their scripts.

It is so much easier to jam a type into a script—the hard-hearted businessman, the good-hearted Irish priest, the beer-swilling hard hat, the by-the-books cop, the dumb blonde, the prostitute with a heart of gold—than to create fresh, original characters whom audiences will remember for their uniqueness, their differences instead of their similarities, the special qualities that render them not like but unlike everybody else.

There are two good reasons to avoid types.

First, such thinking not only degrades the human spirit, it also makes for rotten movies. If writers don't battle to consign bigotry to its rest, who shall assume the task? Certainly screenwriters have no stake in perpetuating racial, ethnic, sexist, or cultural typing.

That said, there is an even better reason to avoid writing such types into movies.

They're boring.

How could they be anything else? The reason weak, inexperienced writers include types instead of characters in their scripts is also the reason to avoid them. In movies as in life, characters immediately recognizable because we've seen them before are neither interesting nor memorable. Folks who upon first glance are already fully known to us are not worth getting to know in the first place.

How does a writer create worthwhile characters? First, by making them different from—not the same as—everybody else we see in movies. One useful technique is simply to imagine the most familiar stereotype and then present its exact opposite.

Consider the Oscar-winning *In the Heat of the Night* (Stirling Silliphant, adapting the John Ball novel). The portrait of a backward, backwoods, redneck sheriff represents Oscar-winning writing, and yet, without in any way criticizing Rod Steiger's Oscar-winning performance, the role is something of a stereotype. A truly great character would be a rural southern sheriff who is a faithful and devoted servant of justice, a man brimming with dignity and intelligence, imbued with an abiding reverence for truth.

The fact that in *Fargo* (Joel Coen, Ethan Coen) the sheriff is not only a woman but also pregnant, renders an otherwise stale, familiar character into someone human and fresh. It's no familiar convention but something new, something audiences haven't seen before.

Some years ago, with a major convention coming to the city, a New

York journalist overheard some cabdrivers salivating over the prospect of scamming swarms of naïve out-of-towners hailing cabs. He set out to write an exposé of crooked cab drivers. Dressed in a European-cut suit, affecting a phony European accent, and carrying foreign currency, he attempted to entice taxi operators into cheating him. He set himself up as the perfect pigeon, virtually pleading with cabbies to take advantage of him. To his astonishment and joy he was unable to entrap a single driver into cheating him. Indeed, the cabbies took care to drive him around the city expeditiously and economically.

It's one more monument to the wrong-headedness of generalizing about any group—even New York City taxi drivers. In real life it makes for poor relations; in movies it makes for flat characters.

The lesson: Avoid, lose, and eschew types. Instead, turn them upside down.

Descriptions

Screenplays are supposed to capture for the reader the experience of the viewer seated in a theater watching the movie unfold on the screen. For this reason, characters should be introduced in the script exactly as they are revealed to the audience. The proper place, therefore, to describe characters is where they first appear in the script.

These descriptions, along with everything else in a screenplay, should be brief and to the point. Basically just two bits of information are needed at the outset: gender and age.

Long, convoluted descriptions of a particular character's peculiar physical attributes, his past, his pets, the car he drives (even though he doesn't drive a car in this picture), the musical instrument he would play, if he played a musical instrument, are to be avoided. It would be bad enough if such descriptions were merely useless. In fact, they are worse than useless, as they make the script harder to read. They betray the writer's inexperience, his unfamiliarity with the form.

It is much easier to describe a character's rich, broad traits than actually to create such a character the way characters must be created: through their action and dialogue.

Specifications as to weight, height, coloring—if they are not integrated directly into the tale—serve only to restrict not only character but also casting. Don't say the hero is a redhead unless it is required by some specific plot point that he be a redhead. In *Basic Instinct*, for example, screen-writer Joe Eszterhas properly identifies the murderer as blond. This is not mere window dressing but an important part of the story. The blond hair is eventually revealed to be a wig.

Don't specify that a character is fat unless it is somehow a part of the story. The producer and director will either obey the writer (highly unlikely) and eliminate a perfectly good actor who happens to be thin, or, more likely, they will ignore the writer altogether.

In the television series *In Treatment* (Hagai Levi) the son of a divorcing couple is overweight. His weight issues are an integrated part of the story. Stress over his parents' failing marriage causes him to overeat, which in turn causes his schoolmates to poke fun at him. All this is presented as part of the suffering he endures in the context of his family's breakup.

Characters' actions and dialogue define who they are. The activities they engage in and the words they speak constitute their character.

Names

I overheard an expectant mother at a Hollywood party discussing baby names. She was considering Robin, Pat, Leslie, Chris, Ronnie, and Lee. "That's smart," I told her, even though I didn't really think so. "You avoid having to come up with two separate sets, one for girls, another for boys."

"That's not it," she said. "I just don't want to lay a gender trip on the kid."

I excused myself, went to the bar, and chugged my third and fourth Evians.

Life is life; art is art. In the latter, regarding character, I plead that you lay a gender trip on your characters, unless there's an integrated reason not to do so, unless not doing so advances the story. From a character's appearance on-screen an audience immediately recognizes the gender and age. On the page, however, this purpose is accomplished by ink alone.

Isn't writing hard enough? Give yourself a break by giving your readers a break. Except in those rare instances where, for integration's sake, the story requires otherwise, assign your characters names that are gender specific.

An example of necessary ambiguity is found in, for example, Julia

Sweeney's recurring *Saturday Night Live* personality Pat. If the character were named Patricia or Patrick, the entire sketch would be over before it began since the character's androgyny is the whole point.

Avoid assigning characters names that even merely sound alike, since it can cause confusion. Don't have a Harry and a Larry and a Barry in the same picture. It'll be clear enough on-screen who's who, but on the page it's another matter. Avoid having characters whose names even merely share the same initial. If you've got a Linda in your script why in the world would you include also a Lisa?

Conclusion

Don't describe all your women as beautiful and all your men as handsome. Language is the writer's stock in trade, and he ought to exploit it. If a screenwriter is sufficiently economical in his descriptions, there is room left over for a dollop of insight that can render a character special. There is space to provide an extra giggle that can coax readers into wanting to know more.

While it is true, as Aristotle asserts, that not character but story is the first principle of solid dramatic craft, it is film's characters who remain vivid long after their stories grow fuzzy in viewers' recollections.

Charles Foster Kane stays with us even as the convoluted twists and turns of *Citizen Kane* are forgotten. Don Corleone is with us always and forever even though he occupies a relatively abbreviated portion of the film. J. R. Ewing's precise shenanigans are lost in the fog of too many seasons over too many years, but J.R. himself is forever etched sharply into our minds.

Screenwriters need to render every character human. Their sweet sorrow must touch our hearts. Their joy should spark our own. Movie characters' imperfections should expand our own toleration of the humanity that surrounds us all.

Chapter 9

· · · · · · · · ·

Dialogue

Years ago, sometime during the middle 1950s, producer Mike Todd introduced an artistic and technological innovation that for several minutes promised to change the entire face—or at least the nose—of motion pictures. It was designated, perhaps more appropriately than intended, Smell-O-Vision.

A tale, probably apocryphal, is told of its public debut.

The first—and only—movie, a western, utilizing this process opened with a scene in an evergreen Sierra setting. Simultaneously, atomized Pine-Sol was sprayed into the auditorium. There soon rode across the screen a lone cowboy who set up camp and lit a crackling fire. On cue, an aroma of smoldering mesquite chips was released through the theater's air-conditioning ducts.

This latter effect promptly ran amok. The theater filled with smoke, and there arose among the audience a chorus of coughing. Obscured by thickening haze, the image on-screen grew dim. In the lobby, a customer stocking up on Jujubes at the candy counter caught a whiff of the fumes and yanked the fire alarm. Projection was halted and the hall cleared of patrons and smoke.

Had Smell-O-Vision come to enjoy the success of earlier technical advances—sound, for example—screenwriters today would have to worry about three basic elements in their scripts: sight, sound, and smell.

Instead they need concern themselves exclusively with two.

Since screenplays are in essence merely elaborate catalogues of details—character, plot, dialogue, action, setting, and more—it is easy to forget that all this information is conveyed solely via two distinct classes of data: sight and sound. Moreover, in a medium called moving pictures the emphasis should fall heavily upon the former.

This may appear to be a contradiction. At any given cocktail party, when profound insights run dry after the first quarter hour, and with everybody in the universe an expert on movies, inevitably someone pronounces the weary cliché that film is a visual medium.

Certainly it is true that moving pictures are first and foremost just that: pictures. When I was a film student at the University of Southern California in the sixties, sound movies had finally come to exist for a period merely equal to that of silent film. Writers of such films required no extraordinary insight to appreciate that audiences were not in the theater to read endless series of projected cards smeared with speeches, no matter how elegant the calligraphy or the language. Like today's audiences, they demanded physical, visual, dramatic action.

Still, a quick look at even a worthy screenplay reveals that what screenwriters write is for the most part talk.

There is, of course, a monumental difference between a talking and a talky picture. But the fact remains: Open a modern screenplay and you're looking mainly at dialogue. Given the notoriously feeble attention span belonging to too many readers, visual detail in a script—character and scene descriptions, bits of dramatic action—is commonly referred to as "the black stuff," because on the page it appears to be precisely that: random smatterings of ink grouped into bulky rectangular blocks separating the dialogue.

Painful to relate, a large number of producers and agents read only dialogue. If the writer is lucky, or expensive, the visual descriptions might be lightly skimmed. Here is ample cause for screenwriters to weave dialogue that is special, sparkling, pleasurable, painful, punchy, poetic, every word worthy, every line crackling. Also, it never hurts to be funny.

Each speech, however brief, must be worth hearing. Along with every other aspect of screenwriting, dialogue must perpetually expand our knowledge of the characters at the same time as it advances their story.

It's one more reason to keep scripts lean, neat, spare, devoid of detail and dialogue that are not absolutely essential. Movies projected onto the screen are, of course, fecund with detail, but with precious exceptions these details are not written but photographed. In a single frame's flash the camera tells more of a kiss or a sunset than the cumulative wordage of all the writers who have ever written.

But do not movie sound tracks contain components besides dialogue?

Yes.

How many such components?

Two.

What are they?

Music and effects.

What advice can we offer the screenwriter relative to music and sound effects in his script? Leave them out.

The test is always the same: integration. Is the particular music or effect linked to other aspects of the script? Is it necessary to the tale? Does it advance the plot? Does it move the characters?

There are, of course, exceptions. Consider the true story of the celebrated film music composer, my film school classmate and neighbor, the late Basil Poledouris. In his scuffling days he lived in the Echo Park section of Los Angeles, a hilly area that for a gruesome interval served as the drop-off point for victims of a serial murderer known as the Hollywood Strangler, a Glendale auto upholsterer whose hobby was murdering prostitutes and hitchhikers.

Like so many musicians, our film scorer worked only at night, because only at night is there sufficient silence to summon the tranquil Zen oneness so vital to composing jingles for underarm deodorant spray.

One such night, in the detached garage he had converted into his studio, he toiled to construct a musical motif appropriate to enhancing televised images of a client's brand of floor wax. Jammed among his keyboards and synthesizers, his half dozen dogs asleep at his feet, he slowly wrote and rewrote an arresting, original, irresistible six-note figure. He played the figure and played it again, adjusting it here, there, readjusting until, after eight hundred tries, he had it nearly half right.

Suddenly and abruptly, the dogs all awoke and went crazy. Collectively their eyes popped open, their heads jerked high, and they commenced a frenzied chorus of yapping and howling.

Their master himself came alive, scolding the pups, cajoling, now imploring them to silence. They would not quit.

Over their din the composer now made out other sounds—a car door slam, footsteps in the thicket, snapping twigs, rustling dry grass, a swishing of branches. Soon enough the car door slammed once more. This was immediately followed by the high-pitched yip of tires turning too quickly and the obligatory roar of an automobile engine.

Finally, silence was restored.

The dogs settled back into their snooze.

Near dawn, his assignment at last concluded, the composer himself sank into deep slumber exactly where he sat. He was awakened two hours later by the sound of sirens, helicopters, and policemen rapping at his door. They were full of questions. Had he been here all night? Had he heard anything unusual?

He related the disturbance involving the dogs, the car, the sounds in the bushes.

Why, he inquired, were they asking?

Because the Hollywood Strangler had dropped off a body not ten yards away amid the tall grass and tangled brush on the vacant hillside across the street. As part of their investigation, the police were eager to pinpoint the hour. Given his experience, Basil was able to help them out on that score.

That's the end of the true story.

It's not exactly Academy Award time, but it offers pertinent examples of plot-advancing sound effects—car doors, tires, motor, snapping twigs, rustling bushes—all of which would be wholly appropriate to include in such a screenplay because they are integrated into the tale.

Let us now take the tale another step; let's invent.

The police depart and the composer retires to his bed. He rises at two in the afternoon—a civilized hour for a musician—and drives into Hollywood to drop off last night's charts with his copyist. By now it's three o'clock, which for musicians constitutes time for breakfast. He enters a greasy-spoon diner. He peacefully quaffs java, leafs through the recording industry trade rags, and hardly notices the café's only other customer, a lanky, scrawny, wasted middle-aged guy, down at the far end of the counter, smoking a cigarette and reading the newspaper's account of the latest strangling.

Unconsciously, the stranger puckers his lips to whistle. The melody that emerges is arresting, original, irresistible. It's a mere motif, a simple little six-note ditty, but to the composer it is eerie, chilling, frightening, horrifying beyond measure. Worst of all, it is uncannily familiar. It stops him cold and sends shivers up his spine.

It's the jingle he wrote last night.

Who beyond our composer could know this tune? Can the fellow at the end of the counter be anybody but the Strangler?

If that's a responsible wrinkle for a story, we once again thank integration. One event is connected to another. Note, also, that the invented portion of the tale is much more fun than the actual facts. Here is one more example of the necessity to avoid telling the truth if you want to be a successful movie writer.

I create this fragment of a tale in order to provide a rare example of music meriting mention in a script. If the music in your script is as inextricably bound up in character and story, by all means describe it in the wide margins—the black stuff—of your script.

Otherwise leave it out.

What about background music?

At the opening of *The Big Chill* the principal players are seen in various locations packing their respective bags for a journey. In the background plays Marvin Gaye's "I Heard It Through the Grapevine." Perhaps the music is provided in order to set the period. The recording was, after all, popular during the characters' college days. Like so many golden oldies, however, it's probably playing at this very minute on a hundred random radio stations across America. Its ability to clue the audience as to period, therefore, is imperfect.

Beyond period, however, it can be argued the featured players have all learned "through the grapevine" of their mutual pal's suicide, the bit of story stuff that serves as the plot's engine.

Is it appropriate for the writer to specify the tune in the script? Unequivocally and without hesitation, the answer is: Perhaps. The question can be answered only with another question: Is it integrated? You cannot whimsically toss tunes into screenplays simply because you sense a sudden hankering for a taste of Marvin Gaye. The tunes, like everything else in a screenplay, have to be connected to the story.

The most important principle regarding sound, be it dialogue or music or effects, is that in movies, as in life, actions speak louder—and more eloquently—than words. Accordingly, screenwriters should favor the visual over the conversational. The last thing an audience wants is for characters to lecture them.

All that aside, however, and as we've noted, film scripts are mainly dialogue.

More than half a century ago, twenty years into the sound era, a film was produced without a single line of dialogue. *The Thief* (Clarence Greene, Russell Rouse) represented a bold experiment. Like most experiments, it failed. The writers' courage aside, all we learned from the film was how vital a role dialogue plays in well-written movies.

Dialogue has to be worth listening to all by itself. It has to have a quirky, rhythmic, engaging lilt. Of course nothing is all by itself in a movie. Everything in a movie is part of the whole picture. To that extent dialogue also has to move story and expand character. Since screenwriters are now and forever stuck with creating dialogue, let us consider common tricks and traps.

Dos

Economize

Economy in expression challenges all artists to say a lot with a little, not the other way around. Just like every bit of physical action, every line of dialogue needs a clear purpose.

Ideally, dialogue must in a single stroke accomplish two goals: expand characters and advance plot. In *Escape from Alcatraz* (Richard Tuggle, adapting the J. Campbell Bruce book), a prison psychologist inquires of the protagonist, portrayed by Clint Eastwood, "What was your childhood like?" Eastwood's reply: "Short."

Principle 26: Screenwriters are not paid by the word.

With a single word this character tells us more of his hard-knocks upbringing, his deprived, disadvantaged, loveless roots, than thousands of pages of speeches on rough times, our crazy cockeyed world, the grim and gritty neighborhood where he was raised, the mean kids who beat him daily, his cynical teachers' humiliation and abuse, his wicked dope-dealing stepmother, his absentee father, his cute, fluffy, floppy-eared little puppy who got run over by a garbage truck.

Of every bit of dialogue the writer must ask himself: Does this line move the tale? Does it tell us something new about the characters? Even if it does, is there a faster, fresher, more efficient way to accomplish this purpose?

Text and Subtext

Writers may repeat only if it's not repetitive. They may repeat when the dialogue is not text but subtext.

Text is what is said; subtext is what is meant.

Consider the Japanese masterpiece *Rashomon* (Akira Kurosawa, Shinobu Hashimoto, adapting two stories by Ryunosuke Akutagawa). Four observers tell the same story four times. Yet each participant's version is somehow unique. Eventually a lesson emerges involving the nature of perception and truth itself.

In *Terminator 2* Arnold Schwarzenegger appears at the beginning of the picture thrown to earth naked on the pavement in front of a mean and gritty bikers' bar out along some lonely highway. He walks into the bar and electronically sizes everyone up, measuring their size and shape with robotic precision. The bearded, leather-clad outlaws all stare in disbelief at the unclothed Austrian. He spots a biker shooting pool who is exactly his own size. The Terminator approaches and recites mechanically and unemotionally, "Give me your clothes and your motorcycle."

The biker might well be expected to respond with language on the order of: "No way. Are you crazy? You think I'm gonna give up my bike and strip off my clothes just because some mad-as-a-hatter buck-naked pretty boy asks me?" That would have been too textual and insufficiently subtextual. It would have been too on the nose, too much what it is. The audience would hear the line but not engage it.

The biker responds instead with a sarcastic smile and the line "You forgot to say please."

The text here asserts that if the Terminator had only said "please" the biker would have promptly surrendered his clothes and the key to his motorcycle. The subtext says something quite different. It says, "You're out of your mind. You're in major trouble, too. How dare you ask such a thing? My buddies and me, we're gonna teach you a lesson about biker etiquette."

Get to the Point

In the chapter on story structure, I argued that inexperienced writers often start their tale before its natural beginning, that is, before the point where nothing is needed. Many writers make the same mistake with dialogue.

It's like watching TV on a slow newsday when, in one of those pointless man-in-the-street interviews, a reporter encounters some hapless soul waiting in line for a bus and posits a profound query on the order of "What do you think about taxes?"

Invariably Joe Citizen responds: "Taxes? Me? You want to know what I think? About taxes? Me? Taxes? Well, since you asked, I'll tell you. If you're seriously interested in knowing what I really, truly think about taxes, believe me, I'm happy to relate it to you since you have, after all, inquired. Now, remember, this is just my opinion, I'm speaking only for myself, not for any other guy, not for my wife, not for my church, not for my dog, not for my kid, not for anybody besides myself. You really want to know? Do you? Okay, I'll tell you. Frankly stated, to put it candidly, to say it bluntly, to pronounce it directly and without hedging, in my own personal view, myself, personally, I think taxes suck."

I exaggerate a tad here for effect, but it pales beside the mountains of unnecessary verbiage common to too many speeches in too many screenplays.

The point is: Get to the point.

There is no excuse for having a character begin a line of dialogue with "I think." We can take it as given that anything any character says he also thinks. No line of dialogue that begins with "I think" cannot be improved by lopping off those first two words.

Another common problem is the vocalized pause, "Well."

Rich Little, an impressionist with wonderful skills for impersonating celebrities, once described how he worked out his Ronald Reagan impression. Reagan, he explained, began virtually every single utterance with "Well." Little, having performed at Reagan's inauguration, eventually received a letter from the White House expressing the president's appreciation. The comedian noted that even the telegram opened with "Well."

"You know" is another major problem both in speech and writing. In my view, any screenwriter who uses the phrase "you know" should be summarily drummed out of the Writers Guild.

Real-life conversations overflow with these blunted openings and nervous, useless interjections. There's no excuse for them in movie scripts. Conversations created by artists require choice, discrimination, selection, culling, sorting. Writers need to decide precisely what shall be included in a line of dialogue. Every bit as important—perhaps more important— they need to decide what shall be excluded.

Dialogue Not Dialect

Dialogue and dialect are separate enterprises.

Throughout his career, John Wayne refused to read screenplays containing slangy, twangy, lazy, yawning, shucks, gee-whiz, gosh-all-mighty jargon transliterated by writers seeking to impress him. By "transliterate" I mean spelling out the way words are pronounced or mis-pronounced.

These writers impressed him, all right, but not in the way they intended. Wayne didn't need writers to drop his *g*'s for him. He did not appreciate a writer substituting, say, "drivin'" for "driving." He told writers, "Write the script in English. If I choose to play the role, I'll play it like John Wayne."

Writers most commonly fall into the dialect trap when crafting foreign, ethnic, and racial roles. In real life, for example, middle-class white Americans commonly pronounce "going" and "coming" as "goin'" and "comin'," yet screenwriters typically drop the *g*'s in their scripts exclusively for impoverished folks, particularly disadvantaged Latinos and African Americans.

Does this not smack of bigotry?

Filmmaking, as I argue repeatedly, represents above all collaboration among the participating artists. Instead of resisting that, screenwriters ought to embrace it. Let the actors and the director seek the most effective way to deliver their dialogue. Write "Badges? We don't need no stinking badges," and leave it to the actor to pronounce it "Botches? We doh nee no steenkeen botches."

True, there is always the possibility the collaborators will botch it, but far more likely they will make it even better than the writer imagined it could be. In any case, the writer's choice is severely limited in the matter. By attempting to direct the entire film from behind the keys of his laptop, he can only limit his script's chances to soar.

The Rhythm Method

Material written to be read aloud is vastly different from material written merely to be read.

Some years ago I had dinner with some old film school pals and our spouses. Happily, the members of the group had by then already established themselves as respectable film professionals. Before dinner we all sat around in the living room guzzling wine and nibbling cheese, chit-chatting away with a distinct tilt toward film-phony showbiz babble. How's Bruce's project at Fox? Did Gary close his deal at CBS? Does Paul have final cut on his picture for Lorimar? Has Steve changed agents for the third time this month?

The hosts' daughter was then not quite two years old. During the cock-tail conversation, the mother trotted out the child, set her in the center of the rug amid the group, and retreated to the kitchen. After the obligatory chorus of oohs and aahs, the conversation drifted back to the standard, hollow, upscale patter. All the while the child, now largely unnoticed, stared with soft, dark, wide eyes at the circle of adults, scanning, tracking them with her gaze like radar. Perhaps some twenty minutes later Mom reappeared, plucked the child from the carpet, and took her away to her crib.

Moments later, the group was summoned to dinner. Thanks to the wine, I was motivated to visit the powder room before taking my seat at the table. Moving down the hall, I happened to pass the open door of the little girl's room. The sound emanating from that room stopped me cold, filling me with wonder and awe.

It was not much more than a quiet yammering, a bubbling, gurgling chant, a child's preverbal mantra. Yet it was also a fully faithful playback of the entire conversation that had just transpired in the other room. The girl could only imitate language in a crude, primitive manner, trafficking essentially in echolalia, the unstructured, wordless babble of babies. Nevertheless, unerringly she captured the overall effect, the gestalt, most especially the rhythm of the adults' chatter. Without a word of actual language, here were all the rising and falling inflections, the anxious, soaring interrogatories, the grunting, assertive affirmations, hedging vocalized pauses, queries and responses, couched denials, declarations and rejoinders, all the gags and giggles that had occurred in the living room only minutes earlier.

It told more of the basic nature of verbal interchange than any fifty screenwriting texts. It is impossible to reproduce the sound in print but it was one hundred percent rhythm: Dit dit dah? Dah *dah*! Dit dah? Dah! Dah dah *dah*.

That's what movie dialogue is: not real speech but reel speech, the overall effect of actual conversation.

As indicated in an earlier chapter, real speech is available free of charge in the streets. Dialogue, on the other hand, is worth waiting in line for. It needs to be special. Unless it writhes and wriggles, glows and glistens, it is unworthy of any audience.

Remember that all language is a kind of song with words and music, sentences hooking into each other with beats and pauses that follow lyrically. Tension constantly needs to be created and then promptly resolved.

Argue

Even if you can avoid having your script become a catalogue of bulky, blocky speeches, it is still not sufficient merely to have characters trade quips, no matter how clever and crisp and brittle the banter.

Instead, let your characters argue. Let each line challenge the next.

Don't let anybody agree with anybody else. As soon as there is agreement there is boredom. There is, of course, a difference between toe-to-toe, eyeball-to-eyeball argument and mere bickering. If your characters perpetually oppose one another through argument, however, the script will forever contain conflict without ever truly achieving resolution until the one and only place within a screenplay where resolution is sought: the end.

The MGM classic *Edison, the Man* (Hugo Butler, Bradbury Foote, Talbot Jennings, Dore Schary) provides an excellent example. Spencer Tracy, portraying the young inventor, is dressing for a meeting with the board of directors of the New York Stock Exchange in order to sell them the patent on his latest creation: the stock ticker. His wife fixes his tie as they discuss the price he should seek.

Paraphrasing, "Five hundred dollars?" his wife asks. "So much money? They'll laugh you out of the office."

"How much is reasonable?"

"Two, three hundred, tops."

"If I ask for five hundred maybe they'll counter with, say, two or two-fifty or even three hundred dollars."

The scene continues, with the couple quibbling over the issue. They're not scratching each other's eyes out. They're not chasing each other around the room. Still, however civilized, however polite, their disagreement lends tension to the scene, rendering it engaging, even compelling.

Principle 27: Consensus and agreement have an important place in life but not in art.

A writer crafting dialogue could do a lot worse than to imagine himself in a public place—for example, a park or restaurant—in close proximity to a couple of strangers who are in the midst of conversation. If they're peaceful, agreeable, if their affect is flat, there is no inclination to eavesdrop. Should the exchange turn argumentative, however, people will strain to overhear.

Writers are well advised to view their entire screenplay from start to finish as one extensive argument.

Don'ts

Reality

The grittiest, most naturalistic, most authentic movie is nevertheless a fantasy. The writer's charge is to present not reality but a thoroughly credible facsimile of reality. Inexperienced writers commonly create dialogue replete with "y'know," "hey," "look," "listen," and vocalized pauses on the order of "um," "uh," and "er," along with a host of other hedges and thrust-blunting interjections. When confronted, the new writer typically responds: "That's the way people really talk." The way people really talk, however, is available in the streets for free.

The way people really talk is boring.

The way people really talk is to bob and weave, to wander, meander, tack, equivocate, beat around the bush. The way people really talk is to pass time. In movies, however, the way people talk must be pointed, purposeful. Each and every line must deliver story and character freight.

The astute screenwriter provides only the full, spelled-out English words. The actors accomplish the hemming, hawing, and hesitating through their tone and inflection and intonation, wherever it is appropriate to the drama. The writer's challenge is not merely to tolerate that but to encourage it by leaving it out of the script.

Repeats

Unless it is for emphasis or irony, or an attempt to link lines so that they flow more rhythmically, don't have characters tell us what they already told us.

Far from underscoring any point, it blunts it.

In *Yentl* (Jack Rosenthal, Barbra Streisand, adapting an Isaac Bashevis Singer story) a prologue is superimposed on-screen informing us that in historical eastern Europe, education was available only to men. The handful of women who managed to achieve literacy were restricted to superficial romances. Scholarly works were reserved for men alone.

Just to be certain nobody in the audience misses the point, no sooner does the prologue fade out than a bookseller rides his cart across the screen hollering, "Books for sale! Scholarly books for men! Trivial romantic novels for women!" To drive home the point, he repeats it perhaps a dozen times.

Yentl makes her way to town, where the bookseller has set up shop. She sneaks over to his cart and picks up a scholarly tome. The bookseller spots her, seizes the book, and reminds both Yentl and the audience yet again—perhaps in the half minute that has elapsed they have forgotten—that scholarly books are exclusively for men and that she, a woman, is limited to frivolous, superficial tales of romance.

Audience members must surely sense they are regarded as imbeciles. In this covert testimony to the writers' disdain for them, an otherwise courageous, splendid film distances itself from its viewers. Why give audiences information they already possess? This is a mistake we see in TV show after TV show and movie after movie. It calls for a special screen-writing principle.

> **Principle 28: Don't have one character tell another character what you have already told the audience.**

In the vastly overpraised (in my view) *Scent of a Woman* (Bo Goldman, adapting a Giovanni Arpino novel), the blind character portrayed by Al Pacino sits on a plane beside his youthful caretaker while the latter describes in substantial detail a prank played upon his prep school headmaster. What in the world for? The audience has already viewed that prank. There is no excuse for a character telling another character information already known to the real-life characters who populate the audience. These living, breathing, ticket-purchasing beings are the true creditors in the movie equation.

Even in so worthy a film as *The Crying Game* (Neil Jordan) there is at least one such instance of the squandering of ink and light and time. Near the end of the film the Irish terrorist, now in prison, delivers a lengthy speech in which he describes to his girlfriend the manner in which the hostage he had guarded came to die.

What useful purpose is served by doing so? We already viewed that earlier in the film.

Can it be that the writer wants to expose the girlfriend's reaction to the news? If that is the case, one must weigh this benefit against the deficit of repetition. Again, the girlfriend is merely a creation of the writer; the audience, on the other hand, truly exists.

My vote is to exclude the repetition. Writers ought always err—since, as imperfect humans, from time to time inevitably they will err—in favor of brevity. Too little information is not as harmful as too much information. The former may engender a certain confusion, it is true. That is not as debilitating, however, as the boredom that accrues upon presentation of data that has already been presented.

Indeed, a certain confusion can even serve as an asset, since it draws audiences closer to the screen; it enhances their attention. Conversely, data that is repetitive causes them to turn away, to pay less attention. Once the writer loses an audience's attention it is a daunting task to recapture it.

Nothing in any film should be merely repetitive without advancing tale and expanding character.

Chitchat

Life is positively rancid with prattle.

Hi, how are you? Fine, thanks. Yourself? Not bad, thanks. The family? Just great, though the baby has a rash. You? Excellent. Say, would you like a cup of coffee? Sounds great. How do you take it? Sugar? Cream? Milk? Low-fat? Skim? Black, thanks. Have you any Sweet'n Low? No, but I have Equal. This is some beautiful day, isn't it? Sure is, but they said on the radio that it might rain.

This is the kind of dialogue that, when contained in a film, causes audiences to storm the booth and hang the projectionist with a celluloid noose. It is certainly natural, but what's so great about natural? Arsenic is natural. Botulism is natural. Influenza is natural. Boredom is natural.

What audiences crave and deserve is not what is natural but only that which appears to be natural. Economical is more important than natural. Dialogue that does not advance the plot or expand our appreciation of the characters may be natural, but ought all the same be banished from screenplays.

Bad movies and television are, of course, riddled with such trifling talk. One can only attribute its abundance to writers' laziness. It is, after all, far easier to spin time-passing, page-adding blather than to craft succinct, pointed, purposeful, confrontational language that excites and moves an assembled mass of people at the same time as it delivers story and character freight.

Chitchat has a place in screenplays only when it expands beyond its own immediate realm and attaches itself thematically to a film's central thrust. See, for example, the discussion regarding the film *A Woman Called Golda* in the chapter treating integration and gender, in which the otherwise mundane and time-wasting act of offering a visitor a cup of coffee is wielded as a powerful, plot-expanding, character-enhancing enterprise.

In *12 Angry Men* (Reginald Rose), on the steps outside the courthouse at the conclusion of the trial, one of the jurors says to another: "I never caught your name." The two exchange standard introductions and then bid casual good-byes, going their separate ways.

Here the apparent chitchat carries a profound subtext. The tale is an homage to the beauty of American jurisprudence, albeit idealized and romanticized, wherein common, everyday folk gather for no lesser purpose than the pursuit of justice and truth. The modest and proper pinch of chitchat at story's end underscores the miraculous nature of so humble yet noble an undertaking. It celebrates the fact that justice can be administered by total strangers gathering together in a jury room, ignorant even of one another's names.

The late British writer Harold Pinter often utilized in his dramas, with uneven success, seemingly inconsequential small talk in a way that mirrored the subsurface battles raging among his characters. In his movies and plays, the typical chitchat around the breakfast table became a metaphor for the despair of people too close to each other for too many years. The polite, chirping, cheery-sounding jousting was presented not as a way people engaged one another but quite the opposite, a method people used to build walls around themselves in order to protect and isolate themselves from others.

If a writer wishes to utilize chitchat in this manner he'll require brilliance on the order of Pinter. What's more, as noted, even Pinter occasionally overreaches.

A charming adolescent coming-of-age screenplay written by a student at UCLA was in its earliest draft saturated with polite, impact-squandering courtesies, pointless greetings, salutations. Virtually every scene started with choruses of "Hi, Debbie," answered with "Hi, Tom" and "Hi, Pete" and "Hi, Holly" before any scene ever got started, before any authentic drama was truly joined.

If the inconsequential greetings were removed, the entire script would shrink by twenty pages. When I suggested that the chitchat be excised in favor of meaningful dialogue, the writer responded, "That's the way teens talk, it's the way they measure each other, it's the way they chart their personal and emotional territory."

I never argue with writers. Any suggestion I make is just that: a suggestion. Any advice I give is just that: advice. It is not a command, demand, instruction, or requirement. Writers have every right to write as badly as they want.

Nevertheless, just before completing the final draft, the writer attempted to find some alternative language. At one particular scene's opening, instead of "Hi, Debbie," "Hi, Tom," he had Tom lead off with, "Sexy dress!"

Debbie's response: "Like it?"

Tom: "Love it!"

I don't claim that this exchange represents poetry rivaling Shakespeare, but surely it beats an endless tattoo of Hi-Debbie-Hi-Tom-Hi-Marci-Hi-Ted. It is subtly provocative, somewhat erotic, a much better measuring among adolescents than any chitchatty exchange of limp, listless greetings.

Liberated from chitchat, the writer returned to the script's beginning, located each "Hi" opening, and sharpened the entire screenplay. This resulted in a far stronger script.

Underscore

Inexperienced writers, overly anxious to communicate their dialogue's subtlety, tend to underscore speech, instructing the actors to emphasize this or that word. Sometimes almost whole speeches, even entire scenes, are underscored.

A well-crafted line of dialogue, however, ought to contain within its own context the natural locations for emphasis. "You talking to me?" as spoken by protagonist Travis Bickle in *Taxi Driver* is all screenwriter Paul Schrader had to write; he did not need to write: "You talking to *me*?"

Unless it is critical to the plot, unless there is some precise, integrated justification, writers should avoid underscoring. They should grant actors and directors full freedom to find the most effective, appropriate locations for emphasis.

Where did Shakespeare underscore?

Nowhere.

Does this limit an actor's ability to play a Shakespearean role? Of course not. Centuries of arguments regarding locations for emphasis testify not to the bard's weakness but his strength. "*That* is the question." "That *is* the question." "That is *the* question." "That is the *question*." Don't worry about these issues. Don't merely tolerate your actors' and director's various interpretations; encourage them.

When writers indiscriminately underscore, instead of punching, highlighting, or emphasizing a word or a line, they squander its impact and blunt the usefulness of underscoring in those rare instances when it has value.

Ellipses . . .

As frequently as writers wrongheadedly underscore portions of their dialogue, a still worse offense throughout a script is an unbridled scattering of ellipses.

An ellipsis is a series of three dots intended to represent dialogue trailing off before the end of a sentence. One such occurrence is an ellipsis; two are ellipses; three are three more ellipses than required.

Over his career, in addition to being a hugely successful comedy writer and director, Mel Brooks also has logged much experience as a producer. Many scripts, therefore, have been sent to him over the years. He once said that he was so weary of seeing ellipses in screenplays that in one of his pictures he was actually going to have a character speak the ellipses. Sure enough, in his gross, and grossly underrated, *History of the World: Part I*, a Roman centurion makes his way up a hill, proclaiming something on the order of "I, dot, dot, dot, I, dot, dot, dot, don't know, dot, dot, dot, what to say, dot, dot, dot, dot."

There are probably two reasons why inexperienced screenwriters are so fond of ellipses. First, too many screenwriters are control freaks. Rather than rejoicing in the opportunity film offers to be part of a creative family of artists and craftspeople, they want to dictate every detail: not dialogue and action alone but also acting, wardrobe, cinematography, makeup, hair, editing, and more. They seek not merely to write but to direct the entire film from their computer. In doing so writers often wish to compel actors to pause or hesitate wherever the writer deems appropriate. Yet effectively written dialogue conveys such pauses naturally.

Crafty dialogue invites actors to discover for themselves the nuances of delivery. Yes, there's a chance they'll wreck the writer's intent, but far more likely they'll invent something superior to what the writer has provided. A heartfelt confession, for example, might most effectively be spoken simply, quietly, in a straightforward fashion, without a lot of histrionic mumbling and bumbling and stumbling through a minefield of dots.

The second reason screenwriters use ellipses too frequently is because we are cowards. Rather than assert ourselves by purposefully and deliberately finishing a sentence with a good old-fashioned period, many prefer to trail off, to let a line deflate like a leaky tire.

I have read entire screenplays in which not a single speech ended with a period.

As argued earlier, to write a screenplay is to play God. Each writer creates the universe of Her screenplay. Does the all-knowing, all-powerful Ruler of the Universe hedge Her bets? Of course not. Does She equivocate? Never.

Neither should you.

Is there any place at all where ellipses may legitimately be used?

Yes.

When one character starts a sentence that another finishes, as if the latter were attempting to head off an unpleasant truth he expects the former to reveal, ellipses connecting the two incomplete lines—ending the first, beginning the second—are perfectly legitimate.

For example:

> HARRY
> Sarah's age? Why, she's . . .

> SARAH
> . . . thirty-nine.

Parenthetical Directions

Parenthetical directions are those little squibs enclosed in parentheses directly below a character's name and immediately above the dialogue. They usually contain information about the dialogue's delivery.

For example:

> HARRY
> Sarah's age? Why, she's . . .

> SARAH
> (interrupting)
> . . . thirty-nine.

Usually, as above, the parenthetical direction is unnecessary. It adds no new information. Remember, a good script is good characters in a good story, conveyed through sight and sound. When writers gratuitously provide a catalogue of parenthetical instructions regarding the manner in which dialogue should be read, it is not merely unappreciated but resented. The extra verbiage makes the script harder to read. The parentheticals also

intrude upon other artists' territories, inhibiting their ability to collaborate productively.

Another common mistake writers make with parenthetical directions
involves the description of action and other visual business.

> WILLIAM
> (picking up the gun,
> mopping his brow with
> his handkerchief, gesturing
> toward the door)
> Let's get out of here.

Readers, actors, and audiences ought to be seduced by a tale via a
writer's skill, the finesse demonstrated with people and plot. Instead of
brazenly asserting, resourceful writers should imply. In this way they
require readers to participate actively, to use their own heads to draw
themselves closer to the tale. Spoon-feeding, spelling out every nuance,
distances the reader rather than attracts her.

The first thing actors do when they receive a script from a movie
or television producer is cross out their character's parenthetical directions. In many screenplays that is quite a task, as there are scripts where
every single line is accompanied by such a prescription. The writer com-
mands one line's delivery be "joyful," the next "happy," the one after that
"gleeful."

Inventing a good story with good characters is hard enough work
without struggling to find synonyms that never needed to be written in
the first place. The situation, the context, the scene itself should compel
the line's emotion. What's more, it's good, creative fun to explore different
deliveries of lines.

In *Play Misty for Me* (Jo Heims, Dean Riesner) a deranged fan relentlessly stalks a disc jockey. At one point she confronts him in his convert-
ible, yanking his keys from the ignition and then retreating just a few
steps beyond his reach. With cars stacking up behind him, he requests
return of the keys. Dangling them in the air, the woman's response is
(paraphrasing): "You want them? Here they are. Come and get them."

Hovering above this line on the page is the parenthetical direction
"(livid with rage)." But with what else can one be livid if not rage? Halvah?

Borscht? "Livid," all by itself, is more than sufficient since rage is implicit in the word. Yet even when we exclude "with rage" the parenthetical direction remains worse than useless.

On-screen, the performer chooses to read the line in a wholly different manner. Instead of foaming at the mouth with fury, grunting and growling and grimacing like the Satan-possessed Regan in *The Exorcist* (William Peter Blatty), she speaks the words brightly, perkily, all gosh-all-golly good-girlish, almost as if coaxing a puppy to beg for a biscuit. That the line is spoken so matter-of-factly, so downright cheerily, provides a grim counterpoint to the character's rage and reveals the wacko she truly is. Her unearthly calm betrays her rage. Her lethal obsession, implied instead of expressed, compels audiences to experience the rage for themselves. Engaging audiences in this manner renders the scene interactive.

> ### Principle 29: Not computer and video games alone but all art is interactive.

The writers of *Play Misty for Me* were fortunate to have had an actress sufficiently secure (full disclosure: it's my sister Jessica Walter) to ignore the script's parenthetical restrictions. If the writers' orders had been followed to the letter, the film would have been less effective. Actors are not automatons. They are collaborators among the family of souls who create a movie. Writers should not discourage but actively seek their participation in the process.

Shakespeare utilized parenthetical directions exactly nowhere throughout his three dozen plays. Far from constricting performance and interpretation, opportunities for both were vastly enhanced.

Like ellipses, parenthetical directions to the actors constitute a plague upon screenplays. Given inexperienced writers' penchant for littering their scripts with them, I must acknowledge, however reluctantly, that here and there legitimate occasions for their use do in fact exist. As ever, the test is integration. If the parenthetical instruction offers new and necessary information, writers ought to use it. A common instance involves scenes with several characters, where it is unclear on the page precisely who says what to whom. If William, Harriet, and Charles are deciding who will drive the getaway car in their bank heist, it might serve to direct the dialogue parenthetically. Otherwise, we don't know whom William addresses.

WILLIAM
(to Harry)
You drive the getaway car.

As with so many techniques, parenthetical directions can be of value, but only if used sparingly.

Funny*!! Punctuation!?!?

Take a look at the comics in today's newspaper (if your city still has a newspaper, and if that newspaper has comics). Virtually every line of dialogue that is not a question ends with an exclamation point. So, if you want your screenplay to look like a comic, recklessly spray exclamation points throughout its breadth and length.

Otherwise, leave them out.

As with underscoring and parenthetical directions, a line's meaning ought to emerge from the situation and the language. Limp lines can't be rendered perky with wild squiggles, dots, question marks, asterisks, exclamation points, pound signs, and slashes. This sort of punctuation gives a script too much of a wow! gee whiz! holy mackerel! effect.

Long, Blocky Speeches

In life people do not make speeches to each other. Neither should they in films.

Movies prefer natural-sounding, quick, short, to-the-point dialogue with lines that link, interlock, intertwine, and bounce up and back among the characters like a Ping-Pong ball. (See the section above: "The Rhythm Method.")

Respectable professional dialogue possesses a sense of give-and-take, questions and answers, hooks and eyes, a singsong flow, an underlying seductive lilt that is at once pleasing yet disquieting. Clearly, this is easier to demand than to create. How to achieve it?

Carefully.

Write, rewrite, rewrite again.

Then re-re-rewrite again.

Before reading a script, the vast preponderance of agents and producers give it to a professional analyst for a written summary and appraisal referred to as coverage. Before the reader studies the manuscript she riffles through it, performing what I call "the reader's backflip." Even this superficial skimming quickly reveals whether the screenplay is saturated with lengthy speeches. If, instead of talking, the characters lecture each other, if there are interchanges of soliloquies instead of dialogue that is effective, efficient, snappy, peppy, perky, and provocative, this becomes readily apparent.

There are, to be sure, exceptions. The opening speech in *Patton*, for example, represents a tour de force opportunity for an actor (George C. Scott won the Oscar for his performance here). Patton's opening speech, however, is not a lot of disconnected rambling, but delivers story and character freight every inch of the way. Likewise, to consider another example, Tom Joad's speech at the end of *The Grapes of Wrath* is at once tender yet forceful. It summarizes the film in a manner that can only be characterized as poetic.

Citizen Kane provides still another example of an exception. Mr. Bernstein's monologue (another Oscar-winning performance, this one by Everett Sloane), in which he waxes nostalgic regarding a young woman carrying a parasol, is there not merely for its own sake but for that of the story. It connects with the experience of each and every member of the audience. Everyone has "a girl with a parasol" in his life.

Reiterating, however: These are exceptional. If writers mistake the exception for the rule, they will fall on their face every time. Look once again, if you can stand to do so, at the previously examined scene from *Scent of a Woman*, in which the prep school student delivers a monologue to Al Pacino's character, recounting action from an earlier scene we have already viewed. It adds nothing to the story but length.

To ensure that your script will be instantaneously pegged as amateurish, be sure to cram it with long, ponderous, heavy-handed, self-conscious, self-important, blocky, interminable speeches.

Conclusion

Throughout this chapter purporting to treat dialogue, we've touched upon a whole host of assorted screenwriting subjects: story (the Strangler), conflict (argument), and others. This provides further testimony to the importance of integration. It tells us yet again that we can't discuss one aspect of screenwriting without connecting it to others. Once again we see that film's value resides not in its scattered elements but in the way the elements blend into the whole picture.

Among all these elements dialogue is critical. While story, theme, and character are more immediate considerations confronting screenwriters, the medium by which these primary elements are communicated to audiences is largely dialogue.

Skillfully crafted dialogue shouldn't show. That is to say, it must sound as if the actors thought it up all by themselves. Audiences know better, of course, but they are entitled to the illusion that somehow the characters knew just what to say and when to say it.

Screenwriters need also remember that the best dialogue is often no dialogue at all. In the first episode of *The Sopranos*, for example, Tony and Carmela, anticipating an imminent raid by a federal anticrime task force, stash ill-gotten gains—guns, drugs, cash, jewelry—in a hiding place: an air-conditioning duct accessible through a grate in their living room's ceiling. Tony stands on a ladder beneath the opening and Carmela passes the booty up to him. Soon she is removing her gold bracelets and diamond necklaces. At last, wearing only her wedding and engagement rings, she stops.

Tony stares at her. Paraphrasing, she says, "That's it, Anthony. That's everything." He continues to stare at her. "All I've got left is my engagement ring and my wedding ring. Those aren't stolen, right?" He stares at her. After a moment she sighs, removes the rings, and passes them up to him.

At a nickel a word, creator David Chase could have become still richer by stuffing words into Tony's mouth. "I'm sorry, Carmela, but the truth is that both your wedding ring and engagement ring are indeed stolen property. I'm frankly ashamed to let you know this, but I'll make it up to you. I'll buy you legitimate jewelry that is truly your own. I hope one day you can forgive me." He might also add, "Blah, blah, blah, blah, blah." Not to mention, "Yadda yadda yadda."

Clearly his silence is far more eloquent than any mere dialogue. The silence causes the drama to play out where all good art belongs: inside the head of the viewer. Screenwriters are wise to consider that for its first thirty years—the silent era—film contained precious little dialogue, if any. Writers of that day appreciated that audiences hardly wanted to come to the theater only to read long speeches printed on cards and projected onto the screen.

When I read talk-dependent scenes I often advise the writer to imagine that she is writing her movie for the silent screen; that she should struggle to figure out how to use the minimum amount of dialogue, since, more often than not, the best oral communication is not dialogue but silence.

Chapter 10

· · · · · · · · ·

Action and Setting

The word "drama" derives from the Greek term meaning "to do; to act."

Principle 30: Drama is action.

Drama is not a bunch of characters sitting around talking, twiddling their thumbs, flapping their jaws, doing nothing. Screenwriters are required, therefore, to determine for each scene the action that most effectively advances the story and expands the characters and also to craft the ideal setting for that action.

Principle 31: Any action is better than no action; integrated action is best of all.

Years ago the master American playwright Tennessee Williams addressed our dramatic writing students at UCLA's School of Theater, Film and Television. For writers, having an encounter with Tennessee Williams is like enrolling in a religious seminary and having a Q&A with God. Regarding characters, Williams pleaded, "Have them stand on their heads. Have them pull down their pants. Have them do something—anything!—instead of nothing."

All the same, imaginative action that is not merely random but appropriate to the scene, that complements its diverse elements and furthers its purpose, is the most desirable action.

Action in screenplays can be broad and it can also be discreet.

Among film's most powerful characteristics is its ability to depict experiences and settings of such sweep as to defy representation in any other medium. A skyscraper afire in a film appears very much to be a skyscraper afire; on the theatrical stage it can be merely suggested. An ocean liner crashing into an iceberg on film looks just like an ocean liner crashing into an iceberg at sea; onstage it can be represented only through an inventory of clues.

What film does best, however, is not render that which is big still bigger; more important, it makes that which is little seem big. It makes the personal, intimate moment available to masses of viewers. Moreover, it accomplishes this with a facility that is not available to purveyors of theatrical drama or expression in any other format.

During the 1960s some of the most humane, most courageous films emerged out of Czechoslovakia. Tragically, this creative flurry was abruptly stifled by the Soviet invasion and occupation of August 1968. Among the more outstanding of these movies is *Loves of a Blonde* (Milos Forman, Jaroslav Papousek, Ivan Passer, Václav Sasek), a film containing one scene in particular that is at once painful and hilarious.

Two separate groups of laborers—one male, the other female—at work on a project in a remote section of the Carpathian foothills are brought together to dine in a common hall. Like overage adolescents, the men-starved women and the women-starved men are all excruciatingly nervous about meeting one another.

The camera closes in on one man in particular, who fusses distractedly with his wedding ring. Unexpectedly, it slips from his finger, landing on the floor with a loud clang. Was he mindlessly fidgeting, or did he subconsciously intend to remove the ring to conceal from the women the fact that he is married?

He drops to the floor in pursuit of the ring, and the camera drops with him, following him beneath the table, past row after row of knees, chasing the elusive rolling band. Soon, unbeknownst to him, the knees are no longer those of men but of women. When at last he emerges from beneath the tables triumphantly holding aloft the ring, to his chagrin he finds himself standing among the very group of people from whom he was trying to conceal his marital status—the women.

Here is a physically small, emotionally huge, logistically precise event capable of depiction on film alone; onstage it could no more easily be conveyed than a plague of locusts.

This is something film treats to full and brilliant effect. The screenwriter who creates such a scene exploits film's richest capabilities. He is inventive and fresh in the way that is required of all screenwriters.

Ironically, this also confronts writers with an apparent inconsistency. Detailed visual action, if not altogether skipped by producers and readers, is often merely skimmed. That is no reason, however, to favor talky scripts over pictures that are really pictures, that is, not radio shows but visual entities crammed full of action. The trick is first of all to select delicate, fine details appropriate to the film's story, and then to describe these details economically, without wasting a lot of language.

Static Situations

Settings, along with every other aspect of screenplays, should be integrated and fluid; they should be fresh and unexpected instead of familiar; and they should be conducive to the action taking place within them. Set a scene at an Internal Revenue Service tax audit, in a church confessional, at a gymnasium. Avoid settings that attempt to conceal the fact that the dialogue is not complementary to, but instead of, action. If the scene's import can be gleaned with the projector's bulb burned out, the writer requires greater invention and imagination. Restaurants, bars, cafés, cars, and dinner tables are all settings that writers are wise to avoid unless, again, they are truly integrated into the action.

Telephones

Screenwriters use the telephone entirely too much.

They use it in movie after movie wherein characters narrate the tale via telephone conversations rather than act it out. Writers need instead to invent action to carry the main burden of tale assembly. That's why the players are called "actors" and not "talkers." When a director is ready to shoot a scene, does she cry, "Lights, camera, talk"? She does not. She calls not for talk but "Action!"

Writers hurrying, bereft of energy and imagination, seize upon the telephone as a quick, cheap way to have actors tell the tale through talk instead of acting it out through action.

An actress of substantial experience, much of it in television, commented that the greatest breakthrough for performers was not Stanislav-ski but the touch-tone telephone. She swears the index finger of her right hand has grown measurably shorter as a result of dialing so many rotary phones in so many drab, unimaginative scenes. The advent of touch-tone dialing enables her at least to get the dialing done much more quickly, and it saves her a fortune in manicures.

If you positively must have a scene on the phone, make it special; see that it is integrated, as in *Atlantic City*. Here, a figure slinks into a telephone booth, pretends to dial but quickly hangs up, runs his hands atop the phone, locates a mysterious package, tucks it under his arm, and hastily departs. Almost immediately thereafter a second figure appears in the booth. He, too, feels around as if for a package and appears dismayed to discover there is none.

Here is a phone scene with no dialogue at all! Much story and character freight is transported solely via visual imagery and physical action. It sure beats having to watch actors read lines into a telephone.

If for some reason characters absolutely must speak on the phone, make it special. There is a scene, for example, in the comedy *My Favorite Year* (Dennis Palumbo, Norman Steinberg) in which the youthful protagonist telephones his home in Brooklyn to announce that he is bringing a world-famous movie star to have dinner with the family. The excited shenanigans in the background are grand fun. An aunt, for instance, wanting to wear her fanciest garment, puts on nothing less than her wedding dress. The call's craziness is not only funny, although that alone would warrant its place in the film. (My favorite line from *My Favorite Year*: "In this business you don't cut funny.") More important, it advances the story and expands the audience's understanding of the characters.

In *Hook* (James V. Hart, Nick Castle, Malia Scotch Marmo, based in part upon J. M. Barrie's *Peter Pan*), a mature Peter Pan has become prisoner to the telephone. Any action he engages in, any person's company, plays second fiddle to an incoming telephone call. At one moment the phone is ripped from him and tossed out the window into the snow. The phone is not used here to have actors narrate the action but instead it is itself a central part of the action.

In the pilot episode of a short-lived TV series starring Mary Tyler Moore, wherein Mary seeks a job as a reporter for a tabloid, during her interview she is frequently interrupted by a ringing telephone, which is promptly answered by the editor interviewing her. On the fourth or fifth such instance she runs out of patience, seizes the phone, and tosses it into the trash. She turns to leave but the editor tells her to stay. He is so impressed with her initiative and fortitude that he hires her on the spot. Here again we see the telephone used not as an alternative to the action but very much as a crucial part of the action. It advances the story—Mary gets hired—and it expands our appreciation of the protagonist—she is clearly a woman who has standards regarding the respect she is afforded.

Cars

So many movies have so many scenes in which characters endlessly drive around in cars that I have often wondered why the motion-sickness remedy Dramamine isn't sold alongside the popcorn and Milk Duds at movie theater candy counters.

A scene in a car, like any other scene, is tolerable if it is also integrated, that is, if it moves not only passengers but also story and character. Not surprisingly, most often it's merely one more cheap, easy way to have the tale told via talk instead of action, with scenery streaming by at roadside substituting for genuine action.

Smart writers avoid having characters drive around, chatting up the tale. Instead, they integrate it into the story, as in the scene from *Close Encounters of the Third Kind*, where the character portrayed by Richard Dreyfuss stops his truck to check the map, only to have the lights of a UFO appear behind him. Clearly believing it is merely another automobile, he signals for it to pass, which it does, directly over the roof of his pickup.

Restaurants and Bars

In a preceding section urging writers to avoid static settings, I've already cited bars and restaurants. For the same reason films are phone-crazy and car-crazy, they are also saturated with drab scenes set in restaurants and bars. Such settings may offer facile ways to provide actors with physical business—mixing drinks, wielding knives and forks—but after all is said and done such scenes tell the tale not through action but through dialogue.

The same actress who hailed the touch-tone telephone as a breakthrough for performers complains also that in her considerable career she has by now mixed tens of thousands of gallons of martinis. Once again, such activity is not action at all but a pale facsimile thereof. Such business is at best rarely integrated into story and character. It is a transparent attempt to mask the fact that the tale is being revealed not through action but dialogue.

An example is found in the movie *Running on Empty* (Naomi Foner). A former student radical, who has been in hiding for many years, arranges a clandestine meeting with her father. Where do they meet? In a restaurant. There they swap dialogue while the audience takes a nap. Wouldn't it have been more imaginative and action-oriented to have the father drive to, say, a carwash, where the daughter appears suddenly as, for example, an overalls-clad employee drying his windshield?

If a writer must have a scene in a restaurant, let it be like that in *The Idolmaker*. Here writer Edward Di Lorenzo gives us a brother, brilliantly portrayed by Ray Sharkey, reluctant to accept from his hoodlum father money intended for launching a new business venture. The confrontation is held in a restaurant, but it is not just any restaurant. Indeed, it is the restaurant owned by the younger brother, the "good" brother. The father provided this brother with the financial stake that enabled him to open his restaurant. What's more, the Sharkey character has been shown at picture's opening working as a waiter at the same restaurant, providing still further justification for the setting's integration.

Sharkey and the audience, viewing the father's abuse of the younger brother, come to appreciate the protagonist's tension should he, too, consent to his father's support. Character and tale are expanded in a single stroke.

About Last Night . . . has a scene set in a diner. The diner is run-down, decrepit. Later on in the tale the protagonist takes over the diner, restores it, and turns it into a thriving business. It becomes the vehicle of his liberation. It is a metaphor for his seizing control of his life. It is perfectly justifiable, therefore, to play out certain scenes in such a setting because, again, these scenes, like the diner itself, are integrated into the tale, advancing the audience's appreciation of the characters.

In *Big Night* (Joseph Tropiano, Stanley Tucci) two brothers open a restaurant. Here, as in *Moonstruck*, the writers demonstrate that in

skillful writers' hands restaurants can serve not only as integrated settings for character and action but even the usually mundane ordering of
the meal can be wielded as a central aspect of the drama.

The older brother manages the restaurant; the younger brother serves
as chef. In the otherwise deserted establishment, a couple orders their
meal. The woman insists on spaghetti with risotto. The Tucci character
discourages her. That's two starch dishes, he explains. It's like ordering
split pea soup and chicken noodle soup. Nevertheless, she is adamant. He
presents the order to his younger brother, the chef, who refuses to serve
her the two starches. The two then argue the issue. It all provides a splendid metaphor representing the confrontation between commerce and
art. The restaurant setting and the ordering of the food, therefore, are
integrated because they contain conflict at the same time as they expand
character and story.

That's a far cry from cheap excuses for providing actors with mundane
business—wielding knives and forks—to cover the fact that all they're
really doing is talking. Once again we see the power of integration. There's
really no setting you can't use, as long as character and story advance in
a palpable, measurable, identifiable way.

Hotels, Apartments, and Offices

There is in movies a lamentable glut of hotels, apartments, and offices.
Surely, sometimes such settings are justified. Television series set in the
home will invariably play out—where else?—in the home. As with all aspects of screenwriting, however, writers should impart to such settings a
measure of integration. They should render them not merely as the place
where the story unfolds but as an agent of the unfolding.

One UCLA writer's police action melodrama contained a scene in
which the protagonist, a lieutenant on the force, confronts his captain. In
the first draft, the scene played out in the captain's office. I asked the
writer to come up with a list of alternative locations. She came up with
perhaps a dozen, one of which happened to be a swimming pool.

Certainly a swimming pool is a more interesting setting than yet another office. Still, even the pool isn't all that special if it's merely a pretty
setting where the actors narrate the action. The setting must somehow
also drive tale and character. While a swimming pool represents a more

interesting image than an office, it ought to be still more than merely a new setting for an old scene.

It should expand the scene.

The selection of the new setting provoked the writer to think back into the lives of her characters. She decided that the captain, on orders from his physician to exercise, has taken to swimming at lunchtime. The scene now plays out at poolside, with the captain swimming up and back as the lieutenant walks alongside on the pool's deck, the two of them shouting their conversation.

Still more to the point, the lieutenant is a policeman who, writing in his spare time during his early years on the force, has produced a best-selling novel. He can afford to quit his day job and write full-time but desires instead to remain on the force. It's the source of material for his books.

The captain, however, wants him to resign. The author's success has provided him with independence. He has all the money he needs. He has the attention of the media. It's harder for the superior officer to control him.

As he walks alongside the pool, his antagonist beside and below him swimming his laps, he constantly has to wipe off his six-hundred-dollar Bally alligator loafers from the splash of the heavily chlorinated pool water. This gives the actor something to do. It's not just anything to do but something integrated. Here, on one hand, is a bestselling author who claims he's really just a regular cop. On the other hand, he can afford six-hundred-dollar Bally alligator loafers, which are surely beyond the economic reach of any mere cop.

The scene playing out at poolside provides a whole lot more fun than can be found sitting around yet another office. Far more than just plain fun, it also underscores the captain's competitive nature, seen through his humiliation of the lieutenant by requiring him to tolerate the eccentricities allowed him due to his superior rank. Similarly, it underscores the lieutenant's having to go along in order to get along. Dialogue, action, and setting are united into a single entity that inexorably moves all of the film's elements in tandem. Disparate fragments all blend into a single, unified entity, which is what a worthy film should be.

Giving the Actors Something to Do

Setting the scene with the captain and lieutenant at poolside does more than merely open it up. It provides the actors with physical business. The captain swims up and back, gasping, wheezing his dialogue. The lieutenant at poolside has far richer opportunities to flesh out his character, shouting at the captain in order to be heard above the din, dodging the splashes and puddles, slipping and sliding on the shiny, hard tiles.

All by itself this will not make a lousy movie good, but it will make an okay movie better. Broad, fertile environments are available to writers if only they will reach, stretch, invent, instead of rehashing the same old familiar, weary and wearying settings.

Earlier I invoked the name of the master American dramatist Tennessee Williams. In his classic *The Rose Tattoo* (Hal Kanter and Williams, adapting the latter's play) a scene is set in a hotel room in which the character portrayed by Anna Magnani confronts her lover, played by Burt Lancaster. The room is not just any hotel room, however. It is a seedy, seamy hellhole with a tiny in-room sink against one wall.

Magnani rinses out her stockings in the sink. She wrings them dry as only an Italian could wring them, with aching Mediterranean angst. The action symbolizes the relationship, which is wrung every bit as dry. Now she strings a cord across the room and hangs the stockings to dry. The scene, which might otherwise consist solely of two actors swapping lines in a dull, depressing setting, becomes instead a feast of sight and sound and action, all of it integrated into character and story.

On an episode of the incomparable eighties TV series *St. Elsewhere* (created by Joshua Brand and John Falsey) three members of the cast find themselves riding an elevator. They try on one another's glasses and comment upon their respective myopia as well as the cosmetic appearance of the various frames. All of this is small business rendered huge. Significantly, the particular episode in which this scene appears addresses issues of vision and blindness, further evidence of the writers' ability to master the art of integration.

Another splendid example of little things made big is found in *Kramer vs. Kramer*. Hard upon Mrs. Kramer's exit, with morning arriving and no sign of Mom, for once in his life Dad has to prepare breakfast for his kid. No big deal, right? Women make such a federal case out of these petty domestic chores. Dad can easily enough cook up a respectable breakfast for his son as effectively as Mom ever did. And never mind cornflakes in a bowl with milk. The kid can have whatever he wants.

What does he want?

French toast.

No problem. But no sooner does Dad stride into the kitchen than he discovers he's as lost there as in the jungles of Borneo. Where are the bowls? Where are the eggs?

Where's the bread, the butter, the sugar, the milk? Where's a proper whisk to fluff the stuff? Instead of an appropriate mixing bowl, Dad prepares the concoction in a tall tumbler, a drinking glass.

Naturally, this wrecks the bread.

In his own kitchen, Kramer is a stranger in a strange land. The writer invests with monumental tension the normally mundane act of cooking French toast. It illuminates the protagonist's characteristics far more eloquently than the sharpest, snappiest dialogue.

At film's end, when Kramer once again prepares French toast, we see that he now knows precisely how to do so. He whisks the eggs with the proper whisk, in the proper stainless steel bowl. He wields pots and pans with the elegance and finesse of a master chef. The everyday act of preparing his young son's breakfast demonstrates a midlife coming-of-age. The way Kramer prepares French toast tells us that he is now truly a man and truly a father.

In an episode of *In Treatment*, Walter, a former CEO involuntarily hospitalized following a suicide attempt, complains to his therapist about the institution where he is held. He tosses onto the table a handmade pot holder. It is the sort of item a kindergartner might make during arts-and-crafts hour.

Walter has produced his pot holder in "occupational therapy." It's a diminutive concrete item that translates big in meaning and emotion. It is a concrete representation of the degradation and humiliation he suffers as an inmate in a psych ward. The object and action collectively carry character and story freight most effectively.

In *Inglourious Basterds* (Quentin Tarantino) the Nazi officer hunting for Jews in occupied France sits at the table of a farmer, essentially interviewing him. The scene is rendered infinitely more engaging, however, by the officer's activity filling his fountain pen. This relatively petty action, demonstrating elegance and finesse, provides stark contrast to the hate-crazed task of capturing and murdering innocent people.

Trivial, ordinary, everyday objects and actions magnify films, expand them, enable them satisfyingly to fill a broad screen in a vast theater. Writers need vigorously and imaginatively to seek out and integrate such details, little and large, in order to tell their tales effectively and to paint full portraits of the characters who inhabit them.

Chapter 11

. . . .

Format

Compared to crafting a solid story filled with worthy characters speaking crisp, tale-wagging dialogue, setting a screenplay in proper, professional format is easier than tying your shoes.

Nevertheless, format is critically important. This is true first of all because it establishes a writer's professionalism.

Principle 32: If you want to be treated as a professional you must treat yourself as a professional.

Second, proper format serves also as a tool for rendering screenplays readable. And readability can be an elusive quality in screenplays. (Many of the items in this chapter are more easily understood by referring now and again to the sample screenplay page at the chapter's end.)

As asserted earlier, for all its complexity a screenplay is merely an elaborate list of two—and only two—kinds of information: (1) what is seen and (2) what is heard. All aspects of a screenplay—story, character, action, setting, and everything else—derive from sight and sound.

This requires that screenwriters work backward. After conjuring up images in his mind, the writer puts words on paper in such a manner as to cause the reader to see in his own mind something closely resembling the writer's vision. This is no mean feat. Its success depends upon the writer utilizing his imagination and discipline skillfully, so that from sight and sound alone characters' thoughts and emotions are revealed to a viewing, listening audience.

In a celebrated scene from Ernest Lehman's screenplay for *North by*

Northwest, Cary Grant, standing innocently in the United Nations lobby, suddenly finds collapsed in his arms the limp body of a stranger who, moments earlier, stood beside him. Grant, discovering a knife handle protruding from his late neighbor's back, reflexively withdraws it, at which point, naturally, news photographers' bulbs flash.

The image, soon to appear on front pages across the nation, of Grant, holding the knife over the victim's bloody back, makes him look very much like the murderer. A novelist could simply write that the character realizes he appears very much to be the culprit. In film, however, this information can be made manifest only through a combination of images and sounds: events, action, expressions on characters' faces, lines of dialogue, sound effects.

Format, then, is in fact no more complicated than placing the sound—mainly dialogue—in one place and the sight—action, settings—in another. In professional screenplay format the former occupies narrow margins forming a column down the center of the page; the latter is assigned wider margins, border to border nearly the breadth of the page.

The limitations of sight and sound require that a screenwriter never write what a character "thinks," "realizes," "recalls," or "remembers," nor what he "figures" or "calculates," for these are in their nature internal, mental processes, which in screenplays can be communicated by sight and sound alone.

The requirement to present such information visually is one reason that, compared to novels, screenplays represent for writers the more daunting challenge. Interestingly, many screenwriters—and no small number of other film professionals—reject this notion. This testifies to Hollywood's long-standing inferiority complex where among forms of creative expression the screenplay is viewed as a lower species. A novel's readers control the pace at which the material is absorbed. They can pick it up and put it down at will. They can skim this part or that part, or even skip it altogether. They can reread that other part forty times if it suits them. Movies, however, crank at twenty-four frames per second for everybody. For this reason it is wholly intolerant of inefficiency, totally unforgiving of poor economy.

Happily, if screenwriters are faithful to the limitations of sight and sound they can get away with paying almost no attention to format whatever; they can write their scripts any which way and then hire typists to set them in the proper margins, or use any of the widely available formatting software. In fact, costly software is not at all necessary. Screenwriters can write their script using the standard word-processing program Microsoft Word, for example, and create a couple of macros: one for wide margin (the visual action) and the other for the narrow (dialogue). To change the margins each time the script switches from action to dialogue is impractical, as in MS Word and many other programs perhaps thirty or forty or even fifty key strokes are required to reset the margins.

There is not and never has been an official, authorized screenplay format. Formats vary among production styles: standard theatrical feature film, three-camera taped television, and documentary. They vary also within forms; writers utilize format creatively to assert their personal style and taste.

As a writer and educator and long-standing member of the Writers Guild of America, West, I am occasionally approached by people seeking to codify the screenplay format, to determine once and for all precisely what the margin and tab settings should be, what terms should be uppercase and lower, where if anywhere to place "continued," whether to number the scenes, where and when to specify camera angles, plus other considerations.

Later I discuss the issue of authority wherein I reject the notion that my position confers upon me any such power. Writers ought to be free to manipulate format in any way that enhances their script's clarity. There is no good purpose in restricting screenwriters' capacity to invent, to be original, and for that matter to fall flat on their faces, even regarding mere format.

All of the rules and examples that follow, therefore, should be taken with not merely a grain but a truckload of salt. I urge writers to reject them freely, to run roughshod over them, to take responsibility for their own writing, to modify screenplay format in as many ways as they see fit in the effort to make their scripts readable.

Appearance

Cover

Script reproduction services frequently offer their customers screenplay covers that are laminated silver-flecked leatherette and bear the title in gold embossed lettering.

Turn them down.

A fancy cover looks bad. Illustrated covers are worse. It's what's be-tween the covers that counts.

Years ago, working on a project in New York and represented by the veteran agent Knox Burger, I wondered aloud whether a particular draft was in acceptable physical shape to submit to my producer. "It should look like a writer wrote it," Knox responded.

A draft of a screenplay should look like a draft of a screenplay. It should be legible, properly formatted, and not much more than that. Most cer-tainly it should not look like an item from a vanity press, a self-published document intended for mass distribution as literature. Too elaborate a cover all by itself suggests the writer is not confident of his script's content.

What should appear on the cover? Essentially two items: title and au-thor. If the script is not yet represented by an agency there ought also to be basic contact info as well: a postal mail address, an e-mail address, and one phone number. Since the writer's name is already under the title there is no reason to repeat it above the contact info.

I urge writers, in the pages below, to leave out any information regard-ing dates and drafts. I urge them now further to exclude all information regarding Writers Guild of America registration. Please do not misunder-stand: I most definitely recommend registering the script with the Guild. There is, however, no reason in the world to write on the cover that a writer has done so, much less to provide the particular registration number.

At the time of this writing the cost to register a script with the WGA is what it's been for decades: ten dollars for members and twenty dollars for nonmembers. Information regarding methods for script registration are located elsewhere in this book and can be found, also, by going to the Guild's website—www.wga.org—and clicking on "Registration." As with almost everything else in our society, it is now possible to register the script and pay the fee online.

Producers will assume that the script is registered. Expressing the fact on a script's cover and, as so many writers do, including also the registra-tion number suggests the writer is inexperienced and the script bush-league.

The writer of an original screenplay need not assert its originality on the cover or anywhere else in the script. Writers do not, for that matter, need to say that their script is a screenplay at all. A reader sees it's a screenplay—it's got description and dialogue, right? What purpose in printing beneath the title "an original screenplay by"? If the writer does not say it is a screenplay, will the reader think it's a chicken salad sandwich? If beneath the title there is no indication that the script is adapted from another medium then the reader will assume that it is original.

Economy counts, therefore, even on a screenplay's cover. Subliminally, a cluttered cover page, with date, draft, registration numbers, and the writer's address and phone number(s), constitutes inefficiency. There is something pure and pristine about a clean page with only title and author. You do not need to have "written by" or even merely "by." If there is a title with a name beneath it, give the reader credit for being able to figure out the connection on his own.

This may seem a petty consideration, which all by itself it surely is. In a screenplay, however, nothing is all by itself. Everything is part of the whole picture. Leaving unnecessary language off the cover page goes hand in hand with leaving unnecessary scenes and unnecessary lines of dialogue and even unnecessary characters out of the script.

Here follow two examples of title pages: a good one and a bad one.

BOTTOM DOLLAR
Ike Warshaw

<u>THE VILLAGE OF THE HAPPY NICE PEOPLE</u>
a satirical parody farce
a screenplay written by
Ike Warshaw

—based partly on part of a partly true story—
(© 2009 Ike Warshaw—all
rights reserved; no portion of this
screenplay may be copied or reproduced
or even merely talked about without
the express, written consent of
the author or his assignees)

Fourth Rough Re-revised Draft
July 11, 2009, 4:32 PM

Ike Warshaw
123456 E. Buffalo Speedway
Third Floor—Apartment 333
Houston, Texas 56789-3001
United States of America
iwarshaw@authorsemail.net

land line (666) 688-6688
office phone (888) 666-8888
cell phone (999) 888-6666
mother's phone (688) 666-8886
mother's cell phone (677) 999-6666
mother@mothersemail.net

Registered: Writers Guild
of America, West, Inc.
#987654321

Numbers: Pages, Drafts, Dates, Scenes

Naturally, a screenwriter ought to number the pages in his script. He should not, however, number his drafts or his scenes, nor should he include any reference—on the cover, the title page, or elsewhere—to the date of the writing.

1) Pages

First, regarding pages, the total number should fall within professional limits. Though there are variations, a typical screenplay page translates into approximately a minute of screen time. In the golden age of Hollywood—the 1930s and 1940s—when the typical movie fare included newsreels, short subjects, cartoons, previews of coming attractions, and not one but two full features, feature films generally had shorter running times than they do today. Many ran not much more than an hour; seventy-five or eighty minutes was plenty of movie.

These days there are no newsreels, nor are there shorts and cartoons. Also, double features are unusual. Accordingly, films have grown longer. A hundred or a hundred and ten minutes should be about right. Alas, however, too many films are far longer than they need to be. *The Curious Case of Benjamin Button* (Eric Roth, Robin Swicord) runs nearly three hours. One could read the original F. Scott Fitzgerald story several times during the same period. Likewise, *Inglourious Basterds* would be a finer film if it were an hour shorter than its running time of two and a half hours.

If the ideal length is about a hundred minutes, the screenplay should run about a hundred pages.

Generally, all artists need to be economical; their challenge is to say a lot with a little. Today I'm encouraged to see full-length scripts with page counts in the midnineties and even in the high eighties. The latter is unusual, however. A script much shorter than that is likely to be regarded as unprofessional.

The notion that proper screenplay length is one hundred twenty pages has been around for a number of years now, but knowledgeable people consider this too long. A hundred-and-twenty-page script seems bloated. When pages reach a hundred thirty pages and more, the script is likely out of hand and should be trimmed with a machete before being offered to agents and producers. It's true I've read worthy scripts longer than that, but they are the exception. As we've observed earlier, to confuse the exception for the rule is to fall on your face.

Compared to loftier considerations such as story, character, dialogue, and theme, all this talk about page counts may seem trivial. What, however, is a screenplay if not pages? Too many pages, or too few, suggest a basic lack of soundness, an inability to understand the limits and requirements of the movie experience.

Writers often approach me seeking a review of their screenplay. I never turn anybody down. The first question I ask is: How many pages? One caller reported that his script was three hundred and forty pages; another said thirty-five. Such page counts immediately clue any reader to the overwhelming likelihood the scripts are amateurish. No agent or producer will seriously consider any such screenplay.

Cruel as it may appear, aberrant page count alone imparts to a script an aura of amateurism. Of course, the number of pages cannot itself determine whether a script is any good; but it can easily reveal the distinct probability it is bad.

A professional reader at a studio or agency who synopsizes and analyzes scripts most certainly prefers a screenplay of a hundred and five pages to one running a hundred forty. If a script is relatively short, even before reading it he is its fan; of course, upon actually reading the script he may quickly change his mind, sometimes even as soon as one-third of the way down the first page.

But at least he starts out liking the script.

Conversely, the same reader hates the hundred-forty-page script before he cracks page one. He sees such a screenplay as the barrier between himself and lunch. Indeed, writers can do a lot worse than to view their task simply as keeping the reader's mind off that pastrami sandwich awaiting him at the studio commissary.

A good writer makes his reader forget lunch.

There are exceptions. A friend and former student, writer/director Alex Cox (*Repo Man*, *Sid and Nancy*), in his earliest days at UCLA handed me a script running a hundred and seventy-nine pages. Before reading any of it, I waxed reprimandingly about the need for economy and efficiency not in film alone but in all creative expression. I pointed out to Alex that he was asking me to do his work for him, that he shouldn't hand a script of such length even merely to his teacher.

He pleaded that he had no idea where to cut.

I carried his screenplay around with me for perhaps two weeks. Finally, on a day when I had meetings scheduled all around town, I planned to tackle it in fragments among the various appointments. After the first meeting, however, upon reading the first several pages, I became so caught up in the story's intricate, spellbinding plot—quite uncharacteristic of the disjointed, quirky style for which Alex became celebrated—I found myself so eager to find out what happened in this breathtaking tale that I canceled the rest of my meetings.

In the end I was in solid agreement with the writer that there was no earthly way to trim even a single scene from the script.

However, any writer who bases his style and working methodology on so anomalous an example asks for trouble; he isolates himself from ninety-nine percent of agents and producers. Let such a script be not his first but his second project after he is the world-famous creator of megahits and has acquired thereby the clout to do whatever he chooses, including overwriting.

It is pertinent to note that now, decades after the fact and notwithstanding Alex's international acclaim, that hundred-seventy-nine-page script remains unsold and unproduced.

2) Drafts

No matter how many drafts of a script you write, consider every draft to be a first draft.

A script may represent a commissioned assignment from a producer, studio, or network, in which a particular draft conforms to a specific contractual stipulation—say, that by a certain date a rewrite or polish is due. In such instances the date should certainly be stated on the cover. When writing speculatively, however, regardless of how many drafts and rewrites and polishes and repolishes, consider every script to be the first draft.

Inevitably, of course, several drafts will be written. We'll discuss this more in a later chapter, but for now let me assure you that no writer should ever sit down expecting to imbue the script with perfection in the first draft. It never happens. As surely as no woman should expect to give birth to an adult, no writer should expect a first draft to emerge sufficiently mature as to be ready for submission to agents and producers.

Once a draft is offered, no matter how kindly the reader reports his reaction, if it is negative he will not be interested in later drafts. Writers should understand that no first draft is filmed exactly as written. This means that even if the draft is good enough to buy, there will be changes. Upon rejection, writers need to learn how to say: "Thank you for your consideration and attention." It's a self-defeating proposition to launch into paroxysms of: "I'm planning to change this and that; this is a metaphor for that; that is a metaphor for this. In this present draft I was really just sort of sketching out the basic ideas. May I ask you to take a second look after it's rewritten?"

If the script is going to be rewritten, it should have been rewritten before it was offered to readers. A reader has every right to ask: "If you plan to rewrite this, why'd you take up my time with it now?" He'll think twice before he reads another script by that particular writer.

UCLA film school alum and superstar screenwriter/director David Koepp (*Spider-Man*, *Jurassic Park*, *War of the Worlds*) attributes his success to his ability to slog through no fewer than seventeen drafts. Rewriting, then, is the name of the game. Nowhere on a script, however, should there be any indication that a particular draft—even the seventeenth—is anything besides the first. The best way to abide by this rule is not to write First Draft or Rough Draft or First Rough Draft or Revised First Rough Draft or Re-revised Rough First Draft on the cover.

Leave out draft numbers altogether.

3) Dates

Should a writer put the date of completion on his draft?

No.

Again, this may not hold for a commissioned assignment in which a writer fulfills the precise stipulations of a contract. In any other instance, however, unless he wants the script to grow old instantly, a writer should leave out the date.

Some writers believe that unless they put the little copyright squiggle accompanied by the year, the script is not legally protected. This is simply not true. What many writers consider to be the copyrighting of a script is merely the registration of the copyright. The copyright itself is created as the script is written. What is more, and contrary to myth, plagiarism is not much of a problem in the movie business. Of course sometimes it occurs, but it is most exceptional. Creating worthy characters, crafting razor-sharp dialogue, constructing compelling stories—those are the problems.

A date on a draft simply dates it. That's why the year of copyright printed by the studio onto the finished film itself is commonly rendered in Roman numerals. It makes it harder to figure precisely how old a film is. Studios want their movies to seem fresh; writers should feel the same way about their scripts.

Just because a script is old doesn't mean it won't sell. Movies like *Unforgiven* (David Webb Peoples) and *In the Line of Fire* (Jeff Maguire), both with an Oscar-nominated screenplay, are but a few among many to be based upon scripts that were written years, even decades, before being produced. That aside, however, there is in Hollywood a prejudice against material that is not brand-new. Agents, producers, and their readers vastly prefer a new script to one that has made the rounds. Remember, even a script that is merely a few months old will be suspected of having traveled from agency to agency or producer to producer. Still, every writer wants every producer to think his script is being offered to him before anybody else in the universe. Why would a writer want to announce to prospective producers that others have already declined the opportunity to acquire his screenplay?

Unless you want your script to age right before your eyes—and the eyes of the entire film and television community—put no date on it.

4) Scenes

Should a writer number his screenplay's scenes? Again, no.

This may seem confusing to new writers who have located existing scripts to read, as in so many the scenes are numbered. Scripts change form as a project develops: Scenes are not numbered until the script is sold and turned into a shooting draft, that is, the final draft before the screenplay is actually filmed. The draft of a published script, or one discovered online or in a library or bookshop or located through a script service, may not be the original, master-scene script but the shooting script. (I'll have more to say on this in the section "Master Scenes Only," later in the chapter.) Numbering the scenes is easy; a secretary can do it after the script's written. Script formatting software can be enabled to address the task. I suspect the reason so many novice writers number their scenes is the same reason they include angles, lenses, close-ups, pans, tilts, and zooms—they believe it lends their script an aura of professionalism.

Ironically, it has precisely the opposite effect: It makes their scripts appear amateurish.

With word processors and screenwriting software now ubiquitous, many writers blame their software for numbering the scenes. Such writers need to be reminded that the software is supposed to work for them, and not the other way around (see principle 37). If necessary, writers should make it a point to customize their program, which is to say, disable the software's scene-numbering capability.

Font

Computers have provided a bounty of conveniences for screenwriters, and also whole new ways for us to embarrass ourselves. One surefire formula for an amateurish look is to use fancy and outlandish fonts. The industry standard is Courier New, 12 point.

I once received a script that had a different font for every single page. When I inquired of the writer why she had done that she told me that these fonts didn't represent even one-tenth of the fonts available on her software.

Reading that script I worried I would develop a brain tumor.

I also received a script that was printed in coordinated colors; that is, each character had a particular color, so also did his dialogue and action. If sent through a paper shredder and poured into a bowl the script could have passed for a serving of Kellogg's Froot Loops.

Color is fine on-screen but not on the page.

Artwork and Illustrations

From time to time a screenplay crosses my desk that contains graphic illustrations. This is a mistake. Don't decorate the script; merely write it. To include illustrations is to suggest that mere language isn't enough for this script; it needs help.

I read a script that told the story of a particular American artist. It was a fine script but handicapped, in my view, because there were color illustrations of the protagonist's paintings. I told the writer they were beautiful but had to go, as they represented flashing neon lights blinking: "Amateur! Amateur! Amateur!"

The writer insisted the graphics absolutely had to be in the script. I never argue with a writer.

> **Principle 33: "Author" derives from "authority"; every writer has to be his own authority.**

This writer, like every writer, has the right to make his script look as unprofessional as he wants it to look.

Binding

I apologize to no one for discussing matters so seemingly trivial as a screenplay's binding. A properly bound script may lack an engaging story, it may be populated by flat characters speaking limp, lame dialogue, but its amateurish nature won't emerge until somebody actually reads it. An unconventionally bound script, however, immediately flaunts its amateurishness to readers even without their opening it.

The professional standard requires brass brads, those round-headed fasteners with two flat tails, one slightly longer than the other. Use two brads—push them through two of the holes drilled through the script, and spread their tails apart so they hold.

Make sure the brads are the right size. It astonishes me to contemplate how many scripts I receive that have flimsy, wimpy brads that fall out of the script if I'm so foolish as to bother to read it. What is the likelihood that the writer will have successfully addressed the central issues such as story, character, and dialogue but be unable to provide the right-size brads? If you can't get the easy stuff, how will you get the hard?

As with so many other screenwriting issues, what is significant about bindings is not so much what to do as what not to do. Anything about binding that is quirky suggests that the writer is inexperienced. I tell my screenwriting students that appearances are not important. That is to say, appearances are not merely important, they are the most fundamental aspect of the enterprise. The impression a writer makes is everything.

What kind of impression does a writer make upon a reader who, even before viewing the first word on the first page, realizes the script is unwieldy even in the physical sense, that it's a challenge just to hold it in his hands, that the pages are difficult to turn? Is a reader likely to expect that the writer got everything right except that?

A producer told me that if she had two scripts to read but time enough for only one, and if one of those scripts had three brads and the other two, she would read the one with two brads. Two holes, not three, represent the professional standard.

Is this consideration not petty in the extreme?

Absolutely.

The principle is nevertheless worth repeating: No aspect of a script—not its font, not the material on its cover and the material of which the cover is made, not even the brass brads binding it—are separate from the professionalism—or lack thereof—it exudes.

Spelling and Punctuation

In my fourth decade at a world center of higher learning, I acknowledge that I'm something of an old schoolmarm.

After all is said and done, language alone is all that is available to writers to ply their trade. There is nothing the least bit trivial, therefore, about punctuation, grammar, and spelling.

Typographical errors, rotten spelling, lousy punctuation, lazy word choice, and sloppy grammar attest only to carelessness and imprecision, mortal enemies of worthy art and craft. I've never seen a script that had an engaging story populated by memorable characters speaking sparkling dialogue that also just happened to overflow with bad spelling, punctuation, grammar, and unprofessional format. These items are all a measure of the dedication that goes—or does not go—into the writing.

Reiterating, if a writer can't get the easy stuff, how will he get the hard?

A confession: I am myself the world's worst speller. Yet my scripts are (damned near) perfectly spelled.

What can account for this? My software's spell-check program?

In fact I avoid spell-correcting software altogether. I still plow through old-fashioned, analog, printed-on-paper dictionaries, not only seeking correct spellings but also to learn new words as I go. Spell-check programs deny writers the opportunity to expand their vocabularies.

Additionally, many typos are misread by editing software as correct. No software will be able to tell you that you meant "rent" when you typed "rant" or "cold" when you typed "bold."

Proofing, therefore, with a dictionary at your side, serves the double purpose of correcting errors and broadening your first and most powerful tool: vocabulary.

Uppercase and Lower

How does a screenwriter decide what names and terms to capitalize?

There are well-established rules. When each character is introduced for the first time in the screenplay, his name should be entirely uppercase. Whenever his name appears above a line of his dialogue, again, caps all the way. When a reader comes upon a name in a screenplay she knows immediately from the typeface whether this is a new character or someone she has met earlier in the script.

There is a technical reason for this, too. It involves the production manager.

Screenplay format has a lot to do with supporting a production manager in his effort to turn a script into a nuts-and-bolts production plan, including a shooting schedule. He needs to break down a movie in terms of budget, actors, props, costumes, sound effects, and all the other details that constitute any film.

That's why, for example, integrated sound effects are also written uppercase. If, for example, a GUNSHOT is indicated in a scene, the production manager will need to alert the sound editor to create that cue or to locate it in a sound-effects library. Placing it in caps, therefore, is a way of making sure he sees all the details for which he needs to make arrangements.

We write, of course, not for production managers but for readers. Still, the same rules apply. The subtle nuances of image and sound come fully to exist only when the film is finally shot and edited. Prior to that, in order to provide the reader a thorough understanding of the imagined film, it is helpful to get those salient facts to stand out from the general descriptions.

Uppercase letters help accomplish that.

A reader scans a scene and quickly sees what characters are in it, as well as the essential props and necessary sound effects, all of which, if truly integrated, should go a long way toward explaining the essential action. If there are important, integrated, character-advancing, plot-advancing sound effects, these are indicated in capital letters, not simply because it's easier for the production manager to spot them, but because the reader can see them, too.

Sloppy format makes it difficult for a production manager to determine what is concretely needed, and upon readers it presents an impression of amateurism. It makes it difficult for readers to figure out the who, what, where, when, and why of a screenplay. It makes it unlikely that a screenplay will ever get as far as a production manager's office.

Within different format approaches there is plenty of leeway. Writers should read as many scripts as they can so as to see the various techniques. And then they should choose their own style, integrating techniques that appeal to them and seem to promise to help them tell their tale in the clearest manner possible.

Electronic Submission

As I've said previously, writers across the nation and around the globe send me screenplays. This is not a burden but a blessing. To interact with creative, courageous film artists is a gift. I require that writers send their scripts as hard copy via old-fashioned snail mail.

To send a script to an agent or producer electronically constitutes a presumption. The writer presumes that the recipient is willing to read it on the computer screen or print it out himself. That said, it appears that electronic submissions are becoming increasingly routine. Before transmitting via the Internet, however, I would seek the permission of the party to whom I'm sending it.

Bear in mind also that a script sent electronically still needs to have the proper formatting. Sometimes these transmissions get compressed, and the documents might be stripped of their formatting as they make their way through the ether. That can result in making the script appear to be amateurish. To avoid this, send the script as a PDF file rather than as a Word document.

Theatrical Films versus Television

There is no shortage of commentators asserting that certain kinds of screenplays are especially suited for theaters while others perfectly fit television.

Respectfully, I say "hogwash."

These same people would have sworn that a brawling, sprawling biblical epic on the order of *Masada* (Joel Oliansky, Ernest K. Gann), for example, could work only on the broad canvas of a football field–sized screen in an ornate movie palace. In fact, *Masada* worked perfectly well on the small screen, prior to the age of the oversized flat screen that is now so common in so many homes.

They also would have you believe that a close-focus, personal, emotional family drama along the lines of, say, *Kramer vs. Kramer* or *Terms of Endearment* would work well on television alone. Again, they would be wrong. Both play exceptionally well on the big screen.

It is worth remembering, therefore, that there are but two kinds of movies. These are not television movies and theatrical movies but good movies and bad movies. As noted elsewhere, every pseudointellectual believes he can secure his perch among the elite by "discovering" that television is mediocre. This is in fact rank snobbism. Television is more like other forms of creative expression than it is different from them. Like all art, most of it fails; some small portion of it is splendid. Indeed, in the new millennium it is sometimes said that more interesting work appears on TV than in theaters. For one thing, it seems major studio theatrical features offer diminishing originality. So many movies are mere elements of packages. This subject will be explored more comprehensively in part 3, treating the "business" side of screenwriting. For now, let's merely note that it appears every new movie upon release is already old: It's a prequel or a sequel or a remake or an adaptation from another medium. What other medium? Perhaps a novel but as of this writing now also an amusement park ride, a board game, a video or computer game, or a comic book.

There's no denying the successes of the *X-Men* (David Hayter, Tom DeSanto, Bryan Singer), *Pirates of the Caribbean* (Ted Elliott, Terry Rossio, Stuart Beattie, Jay Wolpert), and *Grand Theft Auto* (Rance Howard, Ron Howard) franchises. These appear to provide audiences with a sure thing. The customers' expectations are met. That said, I plead with writers to reach and stretch and take risks.

The challenge is not to meet but to exceed an audience's expectations. Instead of getting what I expect, I want to be surprised.

TV—in particular cable—seems to be originality's last stand. The last thing I would do, therefore, is to dissuade screenwriters from writing for television. That said, I urge these same writers to avoid indicating anywhere within their script that the project is intended for TV.

This may seem to be a contradiction, but it is not. A writer submitting feature-length material to an agent or a producer has no reason to differentiate between theater and TV. Both the theatrical feature and the movie for television run approximately the same number of minutes and pages. A reader considering a project apparently intended for the big screen can just as easily view it as something suited for television.

Happily, the reverse prejudice does not obtain. A script apparently written for theatrical release can be easily considered as appropriate for television. Therein lies all the reason required for a writer to avoid specifying one or the other. Let the reader think it's a theatrical feature since the form remains the Rolls-Royce of long-form narrative. Often the most successful television writers aver that they are merely slumming in TV until they can get into features. Writers are paid better, however, and generally treated better in television than they are in the world of theatrically released feature-length movies.

Content

Title

Never underestimate the importance of a screenplay's title.

There are those who maintain that if you don't know the title of your script before you start writing, it's too soon to start writing. I'm not entirely unsympathetic with this notion but I also feel that it takes the principle too far.

Still, the point is important. A proper title testifies to the writer's focus, to the overall cohesion of the myriad elements constituting the integrated screenplay. Nonetheless, from time to time writers may be ready to start writing without yet having discovered their script's title. It may emerge late within the work itself, perhaps in a good line of dialogue.

The best titles are abrupt, quick, and to the point. Quite often they are the name of the protagonist. Look for example at Shakespeare's titles: *King Lear, Julius Caesar, Macbeth, Richard III*. Look at the great Greek classics: *Agamemnon* (Aeschylus), *Medea* (Euripides), *Oedipus Rex* (Sophocles). Look also at films: *Batman* (Samm Hamm, Warren Skaaren, based on characters created by Bob Kane), *The Godfather, Patton, The Graduate* (Calder Willingham, Buck Henry, adapting the Charles Webb novel).

Two (in my view overrated) pictures that were hugely successful with critics had (again, in my view) hugely unsuccessful titles. *No Country for Old Men* (Joel Coen, Ethan Coen, adapting the Cormac McCarthy novel) and *There Will Be Blood* (Paul Thomas Anderson, adapting the Upton Sinclair novel) were referred to by one critic as *Something Something Old Men* and *Something Something Blood*.

A good title has to fit neatly into the open-ended sentence: "Hey, let's go see . . ."

This suggests that a title must not be spread out all over the place, not only in the marquee sense, but also emotionally and intellectually. As with so many other aspects of screenplay format, a good title is no substitute for pale characters residing within a frail story. As with the bulk of format questions, it's more a matter of harm avoided than quality added.

As frequently as titles leap clearly and succinctly to the mind of the writer, inventing a reasonable title can also be a question of darting about, trying one, then another, seeing how each feels, determining whether it fits. Fine titles are often discovered. It's as if they're already there, hovering, waiting to be plucked from the air, or from the pages of the script.

Character Lists, Bios, or Casting Suggestions

A dramatis personae at the beginning of a screenplay is a sure sign the writer is unfamiliar with the form. Even worse than a list of the characters are casting suggestions. Though a list of characters is appropriate to a stage play, even in a play it is no substitute for character development through action and dialogue.

No actor appreciates such "help" in getting to know a character. He expects the character to be defined by the action and sound in the script. The proper place for character description is that point at which we first meet the character in the script, exactly as the audience will meet him on-screen. And even then the description must be concise.

At several writers' conferences I have attended, an occasional writing coach or educator suggests that before starting a script writers should get to know their characters by creating biographies of them. What kind of tree would this character be if she were a tree? If she were a candy bar, what kind of candy bar would she be? What kind of music would she tune to on the radio? If she could live in any particular period in history, which would it be? Are her dreams in color or in black-and-white?

At such conferences, if I'm feeling polite, I'll lie and reluctantly allow that such exercises could be useful. In fact, I believe the opposite. They are the stuff of dilettantism. They're not useful but anti-useful. They encourage writers to believe that characters exist somewhere outside the context of story. I have already argued, however, that characters are created by their actions and dialogue.

Unarguably the richest, most complex character in all of English-language dramatic literature has to be Hamlet. What is the playwright's description of this character? Three words: (1) Prince (2) of (3) Denmark. There's not a word about melancholia. Where does this Hamlet fellow come from? He evolves out of what he says and what he does. So must all worthy characters.

Master Scenes Only

Even the briefest scene in a screenplay, when projected upon the screen, likely contains numerous separate shots.

Say a spy meets a confederate at a hot dog stand, and they exchange documents, cash, and quick conversation, then the spy departs. On-screen there might well appear a wide shot of the stand, a reverse angle on the approaching character, a closer shot of the contact, perhaps close-ups of the cash and the documents. Within the conversation there would likely be several two-shots containing both characters, plus various over-the-shoulder singles—close-up images of each character's face alone in the frame as seen from the other character's point of view—speaking, reacting.

Additionally, there would likely be cutaways to peripheral characters and sights: the vendor smearing mustard on a hot dog, the sizzling grill, pigeons pecking at crumbs, another customer downing a soft drink, a homeless lady poking through the garbage for bottles and cans.

These glances provide color, texture, and tone to a movie, but the screenwriter who indicates every one of these shots in his script becomes his own worst enemy. First, compared to one master scene, shattering the description into a blizzard of separate shots makes it difficult to read. Second, breaking up a scene, indeed an entire script, into all of its various shots, is the editor's task. The editor enjoys having the writer do his work for him about as much as the writer enjoys having the producer's manicurist's cousin's mailman's dentist "touch up" his dialogue.

Instead of a flurry of fragmented images, one broad, all-encompassing view of the setting—a master scene—is preferred. In our spy scene above, the writer needs merely to call the widest shot HOT DOG STAND and provide the handful of essential details: characters, basic action succinctly described, and the dialogue.

A note of caution: I constantly urge writers to read as many scripts as they can find. If they do this, however, they are likely to see scripts—among them some of the most splendid—that do not look anything at all like master-scene scripts. That's why writers need be aware that they may be looking at a shooting script, one that has been prepared immediately prior to production and is likely to have information that is not quite as essential.

The writer is not likely to be involved in the preparation of this final version. Whether he is or not, he needs to concentrate not upon the shooting script, but on the showcase script, the master-scene script, the early draft that clearly depicts the fundamental action and dialogue, with just enough ruffles and flourishes to allow him to establish his own style.

These days it is possible to obtain screenplays from a variety of sources. What's more, screenplays are being published in greater numbers. Readers need to be mindful, however, that published screenplays are frequently presented in incorrect format. William Goldman's *Adventures in the Screen Trade*, for example, contains his unconventionally formatted and overly descriptive script for *Butch Cassidy and the Sundance Kid*. A script by Goldman, bestselling novelist and longtime screenwriting superstar that he is, is likely to be read more carefully than one by the rest of us—he can get away with being a little loose. SUNY Buffalo professor Brian Henderson's *Five Screenplays by Preston Sturges* and *Four More Screenplays by Preston Sturges* present scripts exactly as they came out of Sturges's typewriter. These contain plentiful examples of professional formatting to regard as a model.

Technical Film Jargon

Compared to novels, compared to poems, even excellent screenplays can be a chore to read since, in the purest sense, screenplays are not meant to be read so much as they are intended to be filmed. Cutting up and back between snatches of dialogue, description, action, and business, the endless smattering of shots, angles, and set-ups inevitably renders even a good script rather a burden both to eye and to brain.

Every screenwriter should write in such a fashion as to make it possible for any intelligent reader to understand and, if at all possible, even enjoy his script. To this end, fancy film-tech jargon—lenses, angles, effects, tilts, pans, trucks, zooms, the entire array of camera moves—is to be avoided except in those rare instances when it is inextricably integrated into advancing both character and tale.

The purpose of a screenplay, simply stated, is to convey to readers the movie playing in the writer's head. The writer imagines a movie; he describes it in words on pages. The reader reads the pages. Ideally, from the words on the pages the reader sees in his own head a movie closely resembling the one playing inside that of the writer. That's the task, and it's not an easy one.

A common mistake is to assume that the greater the number of words, the clearer the meaning. In fact the opposite is true. As writers ramble on and on, endlessly detailing this item and that one, the swarming verbiage does not clarify but obscures the action. A sunset is a sunset.

On film it will be as plain or as beautiful as the one available on the day it is filmed. If in his script the writer describes a sunset that is "maroon, streaked with amber, with a lingering hint of cyan and the merest suggestion of magenta," the crew will not wait around for a sunset that fits the description on the page. They'll shoot the sunset God throws at them the day they set up to shoot it. Indeed, if it suits a production's schedule, they'll shoot the dawn, run it backward, and on-screen declare it to be sunset.

Writers who squander language not only make their scripts more difficult to read, they communicate that readers need not pay close attention to what is written, as it contains obvious conceits to be discarded upon production. If a writer wishes his script to be closely attended, he better be certain everything in it is worth attending.

Do not, therefore, write for the cinematographer or the editor or the chief electrician, gaffer, or first and second assistant director. Write instead for the reader and the audience.

Effects—Fades, Cuts, Dissolves

Writers should leave optical effects out of their scripts just as they should exclude superfluous sound effects. The test, as always, is integration. If the effect is genuinely needed, if absent the effect some identifiable, plot-enhancing, character-expanding facet is blurred or altogether lost, the writer may include it in his script. Otherwise he should leave it out.

Should writers write "CUT TO:" between scenes?

They should not.

What in the world does CUT TO add to a script besides words and, collectively, whole pages? I have read screenplays where if the CUT TOs were deleted, the script would shrink by ten pages.

If one scene follows another, and there is no CUT TO between them, will the reader expect the writer intended a ripple dissolve, in which the image shimmers, blurs, and appears to be submerged in liquid? Will the reader expect that the intent was for a spiral wipe, a spinning-headline effect whirling at the same time as it zooms in toward the lens?

Of course not. If no effect is indicated between scenes, the reader will assume the leading scene cuts to that which follows. He will rightly assume that the final frame of the preceding scene is butt-spliced to the leading frame of the new scene. No useful purpose is served, therefore, by throwing in CUT TO.

Integration, as I argue repeatedly, trumps everything else. From time to time within a script, after an integrated sequence of scenes in a single segment of time and a single locale, as the tale moves to a new time and new place, it can be helpful to provide a CUT TO in order to separate the end of one broad section from the next. It is a gentle way of saying: We're done with this business in this time and place; now we move to new business in a new time and place.

Remember, however, that this is relatively rare.

Fades and dissolves, like cuts, are self-explanatory. A FADE-IN finds a scene slowly composing itself on the screen, usually from darkness, although it is possible also to fade in from bright, pure, linen white. DISSOLVE describes an overlapping fade: One scene fades out at the same time that another fades in. In the early days of filmmaking this effect was sometimes referred to as a CROSS FADE.

On those rare occasions when there is sufficient justification to warrant indicating an effect, that effect is written entirely in uppercase letters.

Traditionally a dissolve, as opposed to a cut, indicates that between the shots some period of time has passed. Cuts, on the other hand, suggest one moment follows directly upon another. This was the case during film's classical period. In the past decades, with audiences now well familiar with film grammar, dissolves are rarely necessary. Generally these and all effects are aesthetic choices best left to the editor.

Fades—in or out—in the current film era are as unnecessary as dissolves. From time to time, instead of cutting, it may be pleasing and appropriate to fade in and out between scenes, but these are judgments best left to the writer's collaborators: the director and the editor.

Film characteristics that early audiences found terribly disruptive are nowadays perfectly acceptable. This is true even for jump cuts within scenes, when a piece of action seems somehow to be missing.

Audiences today need a lot less information than they used to. With film having a history now of over a hundred years, viewers tend to be far more cinema literate than they were during the pioneering stages of the art. They seem able to follow a tale's drift more effectively than in earlier times.

I strongly suspect this is due largely to more than a half century's exposure to television. Pundits love to denigrate television's influence, what they see as the numbing, bludgeoning effect of so much information sprayed upon so many people over so much time.

That said, watching television has helped audiences learn to absorb scattered information far more quickly than before. The typical television hour involves teasers, billboards (announcements of upcoming programming: "Film at eleven!"), and commercials, each in a sense a separate show all by itself, each with its own independent narrative including a beginning, middle, and end. There are announcements regarding future programs, plus bits of programs, constantly interrupted by still more sets of interruptions. Say what you will about TV's relentless blizzard of data, there is no denying that it has prepared audiences to follow stories that would have been confusing to earlier generations of viewers.

Screenwriters need, therefore, to limit their use of technical instructions.

Point of View (P.O.V.)

The telephoto binocular-matted shot of what a man sees, following the image of the man peering through binoculars, is an all too familiar example of a P.O.V. shot.

P.O.V. stands for point of view. On the page it looks like this:

EXT   THE ROAD   HARRY'S P.O.V.

The audience views the road from precisely the same perspective as Harry, as if the lens were Harry's eye.

A Raymond Chandler story, *Lady in the Lake*, was made into a film (adapted by Steve Fisher) that was one hundred percent P.O.V., as if viewed perpetually from one person's vantage. Predictably, while fun at first, the movie quickly grows tedious, as overuse of any technique or effect quickly devolves into gimmickry.

Avoid using P.O.V. when intending simply to describe the image on-screen. I once read a student's script in which a character was to sit in a chair. The shot called for:

MARVIN   P.O.V. CHAIR

It is amusing to contemplate what this shot would have looked like on-screen had the writer's instructions been followed. Since it's presumably the chair's point of view, there would have been a big bottom descending toward the lens, a vision of Marvin as seen by the chair, if chairs could see.

"We See" and "We Hear"

As already indicated, the stuff in the wide margins—description, action, business—is information intended to be communicated visually. That within the narrower margins—for the most part dialogue—is communicated via the sound track. For writers to specify "we see" or "we hear," therefore, is redundant. In a properly formatted script it ought to be clear precisely which is which.

In the case of sound effects, these need merely to be capitalized. For example: "There is the SOUND of a car's ENGINE STARTING." What purpose is served by saying "we hear"?

Present Tense

Quest for Fire (Gérard Brach, adapting the J. H. Rosny Sr. novel) is a film set tens of thousands of years in the past; *Star Wars* takes place in the distant future. Both films, however, play upon the screen now, today, this very minute. That's why screenwriters should tell their stories in the present tense regardless of the script's setting in time. As soon as a reader reads that something "happened" or "occurred," he appreciates the writer is not conversant with film's fundamental nature.

Screenwriter and educator Michael Colleary, while a student in an advanced UCLA screenwriting class, wrote a script involving terrorists who, at tale's opening, seize, blindfold, and abduct a journalist. There follows a host of other scenes involving other characters in scattered locales.

Then, at last, we meet up again with the hostage and his captors in their lair. The script at this point notes that the victim's "blindfold has been removed."

I chastised (ever so gently) the writer for using the past tense "has been," and insisted (more gently still) he say simply that the blindfold "is removed."

Michael hesitated. Wouldn't that suggest—even though this is not the writer's intent—that the audience sees the blindfold actively being removed?

I asked Michael, "What if they do? Isn't that preferable? Instead of starting off the scene with the blindfold already gone, why not open with the blindfold actively being removed? Doesn't that more effectively connect the scene to the earlier one? Doesn't that render the script more active and less passive?"

Thinking this way spurred the writer to conceive yet another idea. Why not show it from the prisoner's P.O.V.? That is, at scene's opening have the blindfold cover the camera lens and, as it is removed, the audience is provided a sense of the scene from the character's own perspective.

My view was that this takes the notion a trifle too far, lending the scene unnecessary clutter. Still, it represents the kind of creative, imaginative thinking that befits good writers and writing. From a petty prescription to write screenplays in the present tense there arose a rush of creative thinking, precisely the sort of mental process that encourages inventive, imaginative film stories.

Flashback

Clichés become clichés because they are so useful. This has to go a long way toward explaining the exploitation of flashbacks throughout movies to such an extent as to imbue scripts using them with a certain self-consciousness.

Still, the flashback has its place. If a writer wishes to utilize a flashback he should decide that it is the most efficient, most articulate way of advancing his tale at that particular point.

Ideally, once the decision has been made to use a flashback, it should be integrated into the format exactly as it will be revealed to the audience viewing it on-screen in a theater. There's no reason to write in the script "FLASHBACK." It should become apparent to the reader of the script at the same time and in the same way as it becomes apparent to the audience watching the film unfold on the screen of a movie theater.

In the golden olden days, flashbacks used to start with rippling shimmer dissolves, as if to clue the audience that we are now seeping, slipping, bleeding our way backward in time. But with today's movie-literate audiences, such devices are no longer necessary.

Ideally, again, the flashback should occur in the script exactly as it will appear on-screen. If it takes some measure of time for the audience to realize we have moved into the past, such uncertainty can be exploited by the writer as a tension-creating device.

The effect may be clearer on-screen, however, than on the page; the filmed, visual information is so much more lush than the black-and-white of the written script. This may justify overruling what I previously said about indicating flashbacks in the script. It may make it reasonable for the writer to indicate clearly on the page that the sequence is indeed a flashback. Such a shot might read:

EXT   THE BARN   FLASHBACK

The point, as always, is to help the reader follow the story as it will be followed on-screen. It's permissible for writers to do this as long as they remember that it's a bit of a cheat.

Cheating

Again, to label a flashback as a flashback represents a kind of cheat. In the purest sense, it ought to become clear within the story that a particular sequence is a flashback. Draping the page with little clues indicating "flashback," and attaching hints to the screen such as optical effects like a ripple dissolve, are heavy-handed methods that represent spoon-feeding. If the audience in the theater can live without the optical clues—for example, dissolves—as these days they generally can, cannot also readers be left to figure out for themselves that a flashback is a flashback?

The problem is, of course, that the screen provides information so much more plentifully than the page. That's why the reader sometimes needs a bit of help. In movies this kind of help is often characterized as a "cheat." And although in life to cheat is immoral and unethical, in films it is perfectly acceptable. Any film is in its essence, in a certain sense, from start to finish not much more than one elaborate cheat.

Sometimes, therefore, in helping the reader follow the tale as written on the page, here and there a writer may properly cheat. He may state, for example, that one character is another's employer. He may identify two women as sisters, a boy and a man as father and son, even if it's not yet precisely clear what the audience seated in the theater sees and hears that communicates this information to it.

Cheating is useful as long as it is not abused. Writers who cheat too broadly, too frequently, take readers for something they are not: fools. In such instances writers fool only themselves. The key is, naturally, to cheat with consummate skill and to do so sparingly.

Cheating is a phenomenon that occurs not only on the page but on the stage. A director will instruct an actor to "cheat" his look—focus his attention not on the face of the person to whom he speaks but to a spot several degrees east or west—as on camera it may more effectively fulfill editorial requirements.

Movies, ultimately, along with all artistic expression, should uncover the basic truths underlying the essential nature of man, woman, and the universe. Ironically, one way in which they honestly fulfill this holy calling is to cheat.

Gentle Reminders

One useful screenwriting cheat is occasionally to offer the reader gentle reminders of what she has already read.

This is cheating because, ideally, the information in the script should unfold precisely as it will on-screen. Difficulty derives, however, from the fact that the images projected upon the screen, combined with the actual sound track, provide far richer data. A character on the page, for example, is mere ink—not much more than a name plus the briefest description. On-screen, however, that same character, even before he speaks, even before he takes any action, may be instantaneously recognizable as a particular star. Should he appear briefly, then reappear later, nobody seated in the theater watching him on-screen needs to be reminded as to his identity.

On the page, however, the reader may very well need some assistance. Even an unknown actor provides more information to the theatrical audience than his part in the script offers the reader. An actress, even a complete unknown, on-screen possesses a certain look, speaks in a particular voice, stands with a specific slouch. Should she appear briefly in an early scene, and then reappear much later, the audience has a far better chance of remembering her than does the reader for whom she is merely a collection of inky squiggles printed on paper.

This is why it is justifiable now and again to remind the reader who is who and what is what. For example: "Jenny, the woman seen earlier wrecking the vending machine at the Laundromat . . ." If technically this is a violation, in the interest of readability such gentle reminders are licensed.

Montage

Montage, like flashback, long ago became something of a film cliché. And like flashback, if overuse has hurt montage, the reason it is used so much is that it frequently serves as an economical way to expose a great deal of information necessary to the story.

At the same time, however, montage is too often used to pad and pump a film that lacks sufficient weight. The otherwise charming *Elvira Madigan* (Bo Widerberg, Noelle Gilmour, Johan Lindström Saxon), for example, presents a host of montages in which the young lovers float in slow motion through fields of flowers, with lush Vivaldi playing in the background. Pretty as it is, since it lacks all sense of story and character development and advances the film's thrust not a bit it quickly grows boring. Instead of serving as an economizing device, it has the opposite effect. It stretches out the picture and causes the audience also to stretch, and to yawn.

Likewise, in the otherwise splendid *Play Misty for Me*, the movie suddenly grinds to a halt while Clint Eastwood, reconciling with his former girlfriend, traipses through fields of high grass waving languorously in the wind with cool jazz playing in the background. Even with the beautiful Donna Mills frolicking naked under a waterfall, this viewer struggled to stay awake. Eastwood, as director, in this section of the film celebrates his love of jazz. Alas, however, while it may be stimulating for him, since it has nothing to do with the story, it leaves audiences cold. Self-stimulation has its natural place in our lives, but it is not nearly so lofty and fulfilling an enterprise as making love.

Screenwriters considering montage should decide first of all to avoid it altogether if possible, as it has a way of reminding audiences that they are at the movies. What audiences want, of course, is not to remember but to forget. Even though they know better, they want to pretend they're watching real people in actual situations. Second, writers should utilize montage only as an economical method for depicting otherwise complex, unwieldy sequences.

A typical example is a car chase. The opening of *Beverly Hills Cop* (Daniel Petrie Jr., Danilo Bach) contains a breathtaking race through Detroit streets in which big-rig trailers chase each other and are themselves pursued by police vehicles. Described shot for shot, such a sequence might occupy several pages of script.

While viewing such a chase on-screen is fun, reading about it in a script is not. The reader wants to know the essential action and plot points. What is the basic nature of the chase? Does the prey escape or is he apprehended?

In such an instance, instead of describing this shot and that one, the trucks, the police cars, the writer is best off simply calling the shot CHASE, and then listing the salient features as they arise. In this manner a lot of pages are saved, as well as a lot of reading time.

Years ago I read the first draft of a comedy in which the cops chase not a truck but a paisley-emblazoned hippie-style souped-up school bus. The writer called virtually every shot. In the second draft he reduced it to a far simpler montage:

EXT   ROADS AND HIGHWAYS   THE CHASE

POLICE CARS with lights flashing and SIRENS SCREAMING pursue the speeding BUS.

—the bus departs the main road;
—a police car, following, runs into a ditch;
—a second police car crashes into the one in front of it;
—the bus sails off safely into the sunset.

In this fashion an unwieldy, marginally readable thirteen pages of chase were reduced to one-fifth of a page, without any necessary information being lost.

Sample Screenplay Page

I close this chapter on format by presenting an example of standard American screenplay format. "INT" stands for "interior" and signifies a scene set indoors; "EXT" means "exterior" and denotes a scene set outdoors.

Note tab settings: #1 business; #2 dialogue; #3 parentheticals; #4 character's name.

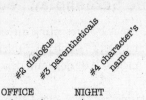

INT   OFFICE   NIGHT

MORRIS and HARRIET fuss about the place, preparing
to close up and head for the show.

TWO TEENAGERS enter.

TEENAGER #1

Can we have a Ping-Pong ball?

MORRIS

There's a thirty-dollar deposit.

TEENAGER #2

You're kidding.

MORRIS

You'd be surprised how many we
lose in just a single season.

As the teenagers fish through their pockets for the money, the
NAGHILAHS storm into the office.

MORRIS (cont.)
(to Mr. Naghilah)

You're in the casino. You went on
stage five minutes ago.

MR. NAGHILAH

We don't go on until we're paid.

MORRIS

What are you talking about? Jackie
already gave you the money.

Harriet sails in.

HARRIET

Oh, I'm so sorry. Jackie gave me
the money. Wait here. I'll go to my
room and get it.

She darts out of the office. The teenagers still anxiously fish
through their pockets, extracting a dollar at a time.

From Jackie Whitefish by Andrew Bergman and Richard Walter

All CAPS first time each character appears in a scene
All CAPS immediately preceding dialogue
Lower case subsequent time each character is mentioned

Chapter 12

. . . .

Feedback: Notes on Notes

Autumn always fills me with anticipation and excitement.

I am eager to greet our new crop of UCLA screenwriting commandos. If past is prologue, in a few years they'll own the film and television industry; in no time at all we professors will be pleading with them for operating funds, scholarships, and an endowed chair or two. We'll implore them to acknowledge the university in their Oscar acceptance speeches. Since so many among them become not only writers but also producers, we'll likely plead with them also for an occasional TV or movie assignment. Above all else, what thrills me about the new writers I meet both on and off campus is the expansive, open-minded manner in which they respond to criticism.

By "criticism" I do not mean pejorative nitpicking or cynical reprimand. I refer to creative analysis that is not patronizing or destructive but honest and candid and supportive, commentary offered in a spirit celebrating among other qualities the requisite courage writers need.

Unlike poets and painters, screenwriters do not operate in isolation. They are part of a vast family of contributors. Given film's collaborative nature, screenwriting involves more hemming and hawing, greater bobbing and weaving, enhanced give-and-take and flat-out compromise than one sees in any other format. It encourages me, therefore, to witness writers soliciting and welcoming sincere, supportive criticism and accepting it with gratitude and with dedication to improving their work.

Naturally, here and there is an exception. From time to time, upon citing even the slightest deficit, I have seen curtains draw shut behind a writer's eyes. The eyes are still open but the mind is closed. An attitude like this hurts not the teacher or producer or story editor but only the writer.

Writers should not, of course, mindlessly take notes on ruled yellow legal paper and then promptly execute any and all recommended changes, whether they come from their professor of their producer. Instead, they should weigh, consider, examine, evaluate, and reevaluate the suggestions offered. If they are like all the writers I've ever worked with, they'll agree with some reactions and disagree with others.

That is precisely as it ought to be because, after all, it is nobody else but the writer who bears responsibility for the script and who will carry whatever credit—or blame—that accrues.

Privately, I admit that from time to time I am dismayed by a writer's earliest draft. In such instances I mask my pessimism and attempt instead to identify and underscore whatever strengths—however limited—may also reside within those pages. Invariably, upon reading the revision some weeks later, I am both surprised and pleased by the improvements.

Something clicks inside the writer and she sees what she needs to see. The revised draft reverses my expectations. The uncanny ability of writers to improve their scripts through rewriting keeps me and my colleagues fresh and alert as we slog it out in the screenwriting education trenches.

My model among arts educators is the legendary twentieth-century cello virtuoso Pablo Casals, whose master classes I was privileged to observe when I was a teen during the late fifties. Don Pablo knew that before he could teach an artist he had to win her safety; that is to say, she had to feel secure under his mentorship.

Casals had no shingle outside his studio advertising "Music Lessons." Students had to be talented, disciplined players merely to win the right to study with him. To me, they all sounded like accomplished professionals even at their first session.

Predictably, students performing for him for the first time were nervous. As they played he would nod slowly, rhythmically, contemplatively. Upon their finishing he would sit quietly for a hefty moment, as if deep in thought. At last he would pronounce, in his richly European-accented voice, "Beautiful." He would nod his head slowly in apparent awe and say again, even more forcefully, "Beautiful!" He would watch from the corner of his eye as the player relaxed her shoulders in relief. At this precise moment an expression of excitement would take over his face. He would mutter, as if in afterthought, "Perhaps still more beautiful if you paid attention to the intonation and the phrasing and the tempo and the timbre and vibrato . . ."

The first time I saw this I thought it was spontaneous. After observing it time and again, however, I realized it was a conscious, deliberate strategy designed to win the artist's confidence. He knew that he could not teach the player until he had won from her a sense of safety under his tutelage.

This represents the organizing principle of our approach to teaching screenwriters at UCLA. We start with what is positive and work our way forward. Admittedly, in a worst-case scenario I feel very much like a plastic surgeon working with a burn victim, seeking just a few good cells from which to start a graft. Those cells are inevitably there, however, even if one has to dig for them.

This is a far cry from too much arts education, which consists of brutalizing the student's sensibility, trashing his efforts and expectations. There are arts educators, alas, who seem to thrive on tamping down their students' enthusiasm. They appear even jealous of their own students, despite the fact that the students' success testifies to their own expertise as teachers.

Decades of experience teaches me this much: An inept, all-over-the-place, unwieldy, unfocused early draft can, through the painful but unavoidable process of revision, be rendered worthy and whole.

Consults and Insults

Smart writers learn that true success—a career that is sustained over time—requires the ability to respond intelligently to criticism and to tolerate, as indicated above, seemingly endless rewrites. With this in mind, writers—from total amateurs to veteran superstars—turn increasingly to professional consultants, women and men who'll read and analyze a script prior to submission, who'll ask the hard questions before the prospective agent or producer or studio executive asks them.

Savvy Hollywood writers appreciate that as difficult as it is to sell an original script or to garner a commissioned assignment as part of what is known in the trade as a development deal, still far more difficult is it to get that script to the screen. Just because they paid for the script does not mean they'll shoot it.

I have trafficked in film education long enough to see writers flare brightly and burn out. I have known writers who were younger than I who are now older than I. I have witnessed writers win development deal after development deal over a couple of years, earning even seven figures in fees, who never had any of their scripts produced.

I have also known writers who have had their films produced but not released. In Hollywood, if you're successful, you merely move up to the next level of disappointment. You write the script but it doesn't sell. It sells but isn't produced. It's produced but isn't released. It's released but croaks with the critics and tanks at the box office.

Surely this is why, increasingly, writers are learning that the first film professional who views their script ought not be an agent or a producer but a consultant—that is, a capable script analyst.

This is true, as I have indicated, even for writers with commissioned development deals. Typically such an arrangement involves "a draft and a set." Everybody knows what a draft is. The set refers usually to two revised versions of the draft. The first is often called just that: a revised draft or a first revision. The second is often called a polish, presumably because by that stage the script needs merely a bit of last-minute shading and shaping, highlighting and fine-tuning.

Of course, I've never known a writer who was assigned to polish another writer's script who did not believe the job was actually a "page-one rewrite," i.e., a total overhaul amounting in the rewriter's eyes to an entirely original screenplay. Likewise, I've never known the writer of a first draft where another writer was hired to do a page-one rewrite who didn't consider it to be merely a minor brush-up, a subtle tweaking, in other words, a polish.

Often, among various phases of a development deal—perhaps between the first draft and the first revision, or perhaps between the first revision and the polish—prior to turning the script over to the producer the writer will engage a consultant to review it and to prepare notes, all the better to enhance the chances for the writer to stay with the project and for the movie to make it to the screen.

I have over the past number of years consulted in this fashion on no small number of screenplays. Sometimes I'm retained directly by the writer (an independent writer or a writer with a commissioned assignment), and sometimes it's the writer's employer (the studio or production company or network) who retains me.

Once I've decided that the script merits encouragement and that the writer is one with whom I want to work, I don't merely reread the script but study it, blue pencil at the ready, inscribing extensive notes in the margins as I go. It is a painstaking process. Few pages are likely to emerge unscathed. Some pages will have more of my own ink than the writer's.

I simply do not know how to work with a writer other than to offer criticism that is not generic but specific. I present concrete, discrete, particular questions regarding concrete, discrete, particular scripts. What use is it to a writer to be told to "punch it up" or "tone it down" or "lighten the love angle" or "beef up the antagonist" or "tweak the dialogue"?

When I get to the end of the script, I immediately write a broad overview of the whole picture. I try to identify those places where the protagonist is clearly articulated and where the script's major strengths lie. I endeavor also to determine precisely where the tale needs to be underscored and undergirded and just generally shored up. I try, likewise, to help the writer focus and refocus with regard to tale assembly and structure, character, dialogue, and anything else that is even remotely appropriate.

My commentary is handwritten in an impenetrable chicken-scrawl on the back of the last page and in the margins of the script. It is necessary for me to translate my commentary; I do so in a written report often running twenty to thirty single-spaced typed pages. There are two reasons this report is needed. First, there is the aforementioned illegibility (for which I blame Desdemona Pickerel, my fourth-grade teacher at P.S. 112 in Long Island City). Second, I have invented a homemade, freeze-dried shorthand, my own personal stenographic code. I have created this system not to be coy, cute, or cryptic, nor to befuddle, vex, or confuse writers, but simply because it helps me move more quickly.

What follows is an inventory of the kinds of notes that I inscribe upon scripts. It catalogues the notes I write and, therefore, the sorts of weaknesses—and strengths—I most commonly encounter.

Hwk? or See/Hear or Ink v. Light

"Hwk?" simply stands for "How [do] we know?" "See/hear" simply asks of the writer: "Precisely what do we see; specifically what do we hear?" "Ink v. light" means that information presented as light projected upon the screen may be perfectly clear to the viewer of the film in the theater, but the same material may appear dense and confusing to the reader when it exists merely as ink on the page.

Recently I analyzed a script containing a passage meriting the notation "hwk?" or "see/hear." The screenwriter had included the following description: "Charlene is wounded by this revelation; she is reminded of the many years of neglect—and even outright abuse—she suffered at the hands of her mother."

It is easy to impart such information to the reader of the script. But how in the world is the viewer of the film, seated in the theater, going to get that information? What will he see? What is seen and heard that makes this evident to the viewer?

Screenwriters need to remind themselves constantly that a screenplay represents only two kinds of information: sight and sound. All other aspects of a screenplay—story, character, and everything else—derive from these two categories of information alone.

This is one of those screenwriting facts that is so obvious that—like Edgar Allan Poe's purloined letter—it is all too easy to overlook. "Hwk" or "see/hear" may seem on the surface to indicate petty, technical criticism of a script, but in fact it indicates a fundamental misunderstanding of the art and craft of screenwriting.

Ess. Det. Only or SIFYN

"Ess. det. only" stands for "essential details only" and "SIFYN" means "save it for your novel." I read a screenplay containing a passage describing a delicatessen in which a particular scene plays out. All sorts of colorful but unnecessary details were included: the clanking of plates and silverware, the din of the dishwashers, waiters calling orders to the chefs, the harsh fluorescent lighting, the plate-glass window looking out onto the street.

Astonishingly enough, the writer provided even the following information: "The air is thick with the rich, sweet smell of pastrami."

This is a movie. It's true enough that movies do from time to time smell, but only metaphorically, and never of pastrami. The incorporation of all these details violates the requirement that all data must be essential. In addition, it violates the sight/sound principle.

A screenplay should contain no information that can be excised without materially affecting the reader's impression of what is on the screen and what is playing in the sound track. Tolerable details are integrated. They move the story forward and expand our appreciation of the characters. "Integrated" in this sense is synonymous with "essential."

I urge writers to embrace a rule belonging to the world of espionage. Spies operate on a "need-to-know" basis. They are given only as much information as is necessary to accomplish their task. If they are captured and subjected to torture, they cannot reveal information they do not have.

Writers ought to reveal only essential information because otherwise their readers will be tortured by having to endure too much data. Readers of such material quickly realize—sometimes consciously, often subliminally—that a writer who offers too much information does not need to be read too closely, since so much of the material is mere window dressing that fails to deliver story and character freight.

Imagine a screenplay that describes a scene at a vast country estate in the Hudson Valley of upstate New York. On a summer afternoon, an elegant banquet takes place on the grassy riverbank sloping down to the water's edge.

If writers were paid by the word, they could grow quite rich describing this scene. They could provide details regarding the weather, the way the puffy white clouds billow in the bright summer sky, the way the sun dapples the grass as it filters through the willows that shudder and tremble in the warm summer breeze. They could add to their fortune by squandering time—and ink—detailing the costumes of the guests and the staff, the cuisine, the festive decorations, the hairstyles.

Bash Hollywood all you like; isn't the mainstream commercial American film community everybody's favorite whipping boy? Nevertheless, everybody agrees that Hollywood is great with wardrobe, hair, lighting, set and scenic design, art direction, and more. If the screenwriter throws in all sorts of unnecessary information, he not only renders the script more difficult to read; still worse, he intrudes upon the territory of his various collaborators.

In our Hudson Valley tale, therefore, the writer can effectively condense the description to the following seven words: "A lavish lawn party is in progress."

Aren't these words enough to evoke the precise image that is desired?

A curious aspect of creative expression—especially in screenwriting—is that the fewer the words, the clearer the meaning. Less language allows for a greater appreciation of the scene, setting, story, and characters.

Principle 34: Less is more.

Drekt/Akt

"Drekt" and "akt" stand for "direct" and "act."

This designation is closely related to the previous one, as it concerns necessary details in a script. Specifically, it refers to extraneous directions and cues offered to the actors and/or the director. Usually these are instructions to "pause" or, worse, to "pause thoughtfully" or "meaningfully." A weak writer may offer: "Alice hesitates for a moment. She looks to the sea, then to the shore, then to the distant barn and the hayloft. She settles down onto the overturned wheelbarrow and contemplates her life."

I can't imagine an audience that would be excited by the image of an actor "contemplating" anything at all, much less her character's so-called life.

"Drekt" and "akt" simply advise the writer not to direct the picture or to act out the parts, but "merely" to write it. I place the word "merely" in quotation marks because that word has no place in the same sentence as—much less adjacent to—the word "write."

$?

A dollar sign residing next to a question mark often sits in the margin beside some petty, trivial, inconsequential action or dialogue. The everyday polite exchanges—greetings, salutations—that saturate life occupy a proper place in the real world but in the reel world they are boring.

The purpose here is to pose the question: Is this line of dialogue or bit of action sufficiently special as to warrant the audience's money, not to mention their time? It usually accompanies dialogue along the lines of: "Say, would you like a cup of coffee?" Or it may be placed in the margin alongside a bit of business such as: "Gladys enters the apartment, removes her hat and coat, and hangs them in the closet. She goes to the kitchen and boils a pot of water for tea."

Let the apartment teem with terrorists.

Let the closet conceal goblins and ghosts.

Let the water turn out to be industrial-strength hydrofluoric acid.

Let the screen broil with action that is saturated with conflict, that engenders tension and stress and action that is worth paying money to see.

S. or N.

"S. or n." stands for "something or nothing."

It suggests that if writers provide a character with a line to speak, it really ought to be a line to speak. In other words, no groans, no moans, no gasps, no wheezes, no mere sounds, no stammering or stuttering.

Typical places that might win the "s. or n." notation are lines of "dialogue" such as:

MARY

Arrrgghhhhhh!

I place the word "dialogue" between quotation marks because such a line is not dialogue at all. Such noises are going to be produced by the actors in the unique manner they produce them. They will grow out of the scene and setting and situation, not out of a last-minute decision by a writer to toss in some spelled-out intake of breath, cough, sniffle, or sneeze.

Another typical spot for the "s. or n." notation is in the margin beside a fragment of a line in which a character says, effectively, nothing.

For example:

MARY

But . . . I . . . I . . . only wanted to

see if . . . you . . .

"S. or n." simply means: Give an actor a line or don't give an actor a line. Don't give him a fragment of a line. Don't give him a mere noise to make.

3 Strikes

Baseball is tough, but screenwriting is tougher. In baseball you're allowed three strikes before you're out. In screenwriting, however, you need three hits before you get to first base.

What in the world can this mean?

Simply this: Not one or two but three questions regarding information in a screenplay—be it character, action, or dialogue—need affirmatively to be answered before that information can be tolerated in the script. The questions are: (1) Is there a purpose for including the information? (2) If so, is it a worthy purpose? And again, (3) if so, is this the best way to achieve that purpose?

This is just another way of underscoring the primacy of integration. All too frequently I encounter writers who, upon being asked to explain the purpose of a specific item in a script, respond that there was none. A writer may contend, for example, that there was an amorphous "feeling," a generalized sense that it would be nice, or cool, or charming or groovy, to include whatever it is that is included.

In fact, however, there can be only one legitimate purpose that justifies including anything at all in any script. Bits of description or dialogue are worthy if palpably and unmistakably they move the story forward and expand character. If the asserted "purpose" is merely to satisfy a whim on the part of the writer, that is no purpose at all. This sort of information ought to be promptly deleted.

Principle 35: A screenwriter's best friend is the delete key.

Even if there is, in fact, a purpose for the information, that does not necessarily justify its placement in the screenplay. Rather, it leads only to the second question: Is this a purpose that is truly worthy?

Once again, a purpose that is worthy is one that affects, steers, expands, and enhances both story and character.

For example, if a writer's purpose is to set the scene's mood, I stand against it.

Principle 36: Mood is "doom" spelled backward.

It's easy enough to smear oodles of moody descriptions upon a screenplay, but it is hardly any substitute for story and character. Setting the mood is in my own view not a legitimate purpose worthy of a writer's talent and toil nor of a reader's time.

A final way to make sure that the purpose for information is justified—strike three—is to ask the following: Is this particular line of dialogue or bit of action the best way to achieve that purpose?

At a crucial turn in *The Lion King* (Irene Mecchi, Jonathan Roberts, Linda Woolverton) Simba's father is killed, trampled to death by a stampede of rampaging wildebeests. Is there a purpose to the scene? Absolutely. The father needs to die so that, first of all, Simba can eventually assume his place. Every bit as pertinent, in keeping with antagonist Scar's scheme, Simba needs to be made to hold himself responsible— however falsely—for his father's death.

There is, therefore, not only a purpose but one that is clear and necessary. We still have to ask, however, is the stampede of wildebeests the best way to achieve that purpose?

Again, yes.

Surely we can concoct a host of other ways to kill the father. He could become ill; he could stumble into a deep excavation and become trapped; he could fall off a steep cliff. There is no end to the manner and method by which his demise could be contrived.

A stampede of wildebeests contains such exquisite drama, however, and it is splendidly in keeping with the setting, neatly integrated into Scar's sophisticated scheme, which entails not only the lion's death but the need to instill in Simba a sense of responsibility for his father's death.

Three hits.

The writer can go to first base.

The wildebeests can trample Simba's father into lion marmalade.

The important thing to remember about this particular rule is that if only one or even two of the criteria are met it is the same as if none have been. Only when all three questions are satisfactorily addressed is the material deemed worthy to reside in the screenplay.

In *Slumdog Millionaire* (Simon Beaufoy, adapting the Vikas Swarup novel) a Mumbai police sergeant and his superior officer detain and interrogate Jamal Malik, even going so far as to torture him in order to determine how someone so humble, so uneducated, is able to answer the seemingly unanswerable questions posed to him by the host of a television quiz show.

Does the torture pass the three-strike test?

It does.

First, there is a purpose: finding out if he is cheating. Second, is this a worthy purpose? Yes, because a most fundamental aspect of the plot is reconciling the protagonist's lowly stature and life of unspeakable deprivation with his uncanny ability to answer the questions correctly. Third, is this the best way to achieve this purpose? Again, yes. It not only satisfies the plot's requirement to get to the bottom of the cheating issue, but it also expands the cruelty and oppression Jamal experiences not only as a contestant on a television quiz show but also as a member of a desperate and impoverished society. Additionally, the torture serves the purpose of motivating Jamal to reveal the experiences in his life that provided him with the answers.

No Tt or DES

"No Tt" stands for "no Tarzan talk." I am indebted to my UCLA colleague Fred Rubin for stating it this way. "DES" stands for "declarative English sentences." It simply means that writers should stick to traditional sentence structure, with a subject and a predicate—a noun, a verb, and frequently an object—instead of writing sentence fragments. From time to time writers, perhaps believing that they serve economy in doing so, drop articles from the sentences constituting their description of action and scenes. They'll write something like: "Picks up gun. Goes to window. Loads. Aims."

This sounds too much like: "Me Tarzan; you Jane." Hence the "Tt" designation.

Sentence fragments can be sexy and nifty and alluring for a few pages, but after a short while they become numbing, wearing, wearying. The writer's best hope is ordinary, everyday language and sentence structure that describe extraordinary, alluring, exciting action and character.

Often plain, workmanlike, standard, schoolmarmish sentences form a quiet, solid field against which action and character can really shine. The contrast between the tone and style of the language and the excitement of action and character bring the latter two into relief and intensify the writing's impact.

Notnot

I am constantly bemused, not to mention befuddled, to read material in screenplays that instead of telling me what happens—what is seen and what is heard—informs me of what is not seen and what is not heard.

This most commonly occurs in language describing a character's failure to respond to a particular line of dialogue. Remember, no response is just another kind of response. It is often the most eloquent and articulate response of all.

Imagine that a character in a script is asked a question but fails or refuses to answer. Writers will too often write something on the order of: "Sharon does not answer."

Isn't it obvious that if Sharon answers, she answers? If she answers, that answer will constitute the next line of dialogue with Sharon's name above it. The "notnot" notation simply means that writers should write what happens and what is spoken, not what does not happen and what is not spoken.

I read a script years ago containing a scene in which one character grills another and the latter refuses to respond other than through silence.

The scene reads something like this:

> HARVEY
> Answer me!

> JACK
> No response.

> HARVEY
> I demand that you answer!

> JACK
> No response.

I asked the writer if he intended for the character named Jack actually to speak the words, "No response." He responded, of course, that this was not at all his intent. He simply meant to indicate that in the onslaught of Harvey's interrogation, Jack remains silent, refusing to answer the questions.

If Jack doesn't answer, I explained, then he doesn't answer. The writer simply gives him nothing to say; that is, he leaves the space blank.

"You mean the character's name with nothing under it?" the writer asked.

"No," I said. "No character's name, no dialogue."

"Then how does the reader know that Jack does not respond?" the writer asked.

"How does the reader know that Jack does not sprout wings and fly? How does he know that Jack does not on the spot have a sex-change operation and win an election as congressman from the Fourth District of Indiana and, on top of all that, just for fun, sing the chorus from Bizet's *Carmen*?"

The business between Harvey and Jack ought to appear on the page as follows:

HARVEY
Answer me! I demand that
you answer!

Note that no "beats" or "pauses" or parentheticals (for example, "angrily") or other directing and/or acting cues are necessary.

Simply stated, anything that is not in the script is not in the script—in other words, "notnot." Writers only need to provide information as to the dialogue that is spoken and the action that is taken, not what dialogue is not spoken and action not taken.

This may seem stunningly self-evident, yet it is, like so many other obvious matters, commonly overlooked.

It is a problem that affects not only dialogue but also action. For example, in the above-mentioned script, a writer may have the impulse to include a descriptive sentence like "Jack does nothing" or "Jack sits perfectly still." If Jack does something, tell us precisely what it is that he does. Do not tell us what it is precisely—or even generally—that Jack does not do.

Readers ought to be credited with the ability to understand that what's in the script is what's in the script. What's not in the script? All the rest of God's creation.

Too Straight-Line

Not long ago, when I was testifying in court as an expert witness in a case involving copyright infringement, the opposing attorney asked me what precisely I meant when I used the word "story."

Why, everybody knows what a story is, I responded. You don't need to be a senior, tenured professor at a world center of higher learning to know what "story" means, I told the court. This happens, that happens, something happens after that, and so on. That's the story.

Certainly there is no denying that the nature of story is one thing following another and another and another until the end. Of course, there is much more to story than simply that. Stories ideally want to appear shaped, sculpted, finessed, molded, and massaged. Their final shape should be not a plain and simple straight line but round.

Stories start to look like straight lines when effect follows too hard and too quickly upon cause, when dramatic tension is heightened and then immediately resolved, a question asked and promptly answered, stress achieved and instantaneously relieved.

Dave is a movie in which screenwriter Gary Ross avoids a too-straight-line look in a number of ways. There is a scene in the presidential limousine, for example, where Dave, attempting to pass as the president, enjoys a lustful glance at the first lady's thigh. Quite some time later in the picture she reveals to him that it was at that moment she realized he was not her husband but an imposter. Her husband, she explains, has not regarded her with lust in too long a time.

An effective technique to avoid the "too straight-line" designation is to connect one piece of plot to another by distancing them along the story line. A less skillful writer than Ross would have shown the first lady responding to Dave's glance in the very next scene, perhaps even in the very next moment, confronting him with the truth of the situation. "You regarded my thigh with lust," she might have said to him. "I know, therefore, that you are not who you claim to be."

There's drama there, to be sure. It's not dreadful, not wretched, not awful, but it's not nearly as good or as stirring as it potentially could be. By mixing and remixing the incidents and anecdotes that make up the tale, the writer can tease and seduce and engage the audience, while configuring and reconfiguring the arousals and resolutions.

Slumdog Millionaire avoids straight-line deficits by jumping up and back imaginatively in space and time. Instead of simply spelling out the events in the order in which they actually occurred, they are mixed and matched and whipped into a froth of enticement and fascination. The audience becomes a collaborator in patching together the bits and pieces and paraphernalia of the plot.

Checkerboarding

"Checkerboarding" is just another way of indicating that a script is "too straight-line" and needs more closely to resemble something like a checkerboard, which has a more rounded shape than, say, a Monopoly board. In the former, chessmen or checkers swarm and move up and back and across the field in various directions. In the latter, all the pieces move in the same direction and follow an identical path.

The well-turned plot starts somewhere, goes somewhere else and then somewhere else, before finally returning to a point along the path from which it earlier embarked. In other words, it doesn't look at all like a string of pearls.

L.f.

Baseball offers yet more language we can borrow (see, for example, the three-strike rule above).

"L.f." stands simply for "left field." The designation indicates that a tale has taken so rude a twist that it has turned into a movie entirely different from the one we'd been watching. A film producer told me once of an otherwise commendable script submitted to him telling the story of a young man's struggle against cruel disadvantage to win an advanced professional education. He overcomes various obstacles that are personal, emotional, social, and situational. Then, practically at the end of the script, he becomes involved, quite unexpectedly, in a dreadful automobile accident that leaves him paralyzed.

So highly charged and weighty an incident cannot be tacked onto the end of a tale like the cardboard appendage in Pin the Tail on the Donkey. All of a sudden, the film will seem to be some other film. Imagine, a movie in which an adopted daughter seeks her birth mother. At the last moment, an hour and a half into the picture, Martians land in her backyard and take her through a time warp to Brooklyn in October 1955, where Johnny Podres is shutting out the Yankees in the last game of the World Series.

I don't argue that you couldn't have a wonderful film depicting a woman kidnapped by Martians. That is one story; the adoption/search tale is another. Solidly crafted narratives seek a sense of connection, each event linked with everything else. Too much "l.f." material leads to stories with elbows sticking out at odd and awkward angles, in dark, confusing, lost corners.

In *Million Dollar Baby* (Paul Haggis, adapting stories by F. X. Toole) a boxer and her mentor struggle with issues relating to gender in her campaign to become a prizefighter. Suddenly, in the last twenty minutes or so, she becomes paralyzed. A whole new movie now unfolds regarding a whole new issue: euthanasia. Should the mentor collaborate with her by assisting her suicide?

Here are two potentially splendid movie stories, but they are also just that: two stories. Writers should choose one story per movie instead of choosing one story and then, as if out of nowhere, introduce from left field an entirely different story.

Conk

"Conk" stands for "concrete." Thomas S. Kane's *Oxford Guide to Writing* provides an enlightening appraisal of concreteness. Kane asserts that the best writing is not abstract or generic or general, but concrete.

Kane offers an example. "The lake was surrounded by structures." He compares this general and generally inferior description with the following, superior concrete one: "Surrounding the lake were a rickety clapboard boathouse, a dock and a log cabin." Surely the latter example for its concreteness is preferable to the former.

In screenwriting—as in all writing—concreteness is one of the most essential elements. For example, rather than setting a film, or a scene, in, say, "a Midwestern town," try "Springfield, Ohio." Writing generally about a vague town dilutes a screenplay's effect. Even if there is no such place as the writer presents, the reader senses that the opposite is the case, and enjoys the feeling that he is reading about something actual rather than invented.

Instead of saying that a character wears expensive clothes, identify the particular label. Or even create a label of your own. No one will ever challenge you. A depiction of a man wearing "a broad-breasted chocolate-brown Armani suit and alligator Magli loafers" is far more effective than the vague description of "contemporary, tasteful, costly clothes."

The trick is, of course, not to go too crazy smearing on extra language. The beauty of concreteness is that with precious few words writers can pack a lot of wallop and create descriptions that are fleshy and fulfilling.

This rule applies also to the description of actions performed by characters in the script. In a second-grade classroom, for example, instead of having the schoolchildren "engaged in various activities," have them "gluing Popsicle sticks, finger painting, cutting colored paper into magic lanterns."

Mstrso

"Mstrso" is short for "master scenes only."

If one reads a great many screenplays—as I urge writers to do—he ought to be aware that there is a substantial possibility that the script he is reading is in fact not an early draft but a shooting script. Shooting scripts are the ones distributed most widely, since numerous copies need to be made available to all the artists and craftsmen and the various studio departments: casting, props, editorial, sound, camera, advertising/promotion, and more. Once a film is released and exhibited and, eventually, consigned to foreign distribution, DVD release, cable, Internet, and the like, the production company will discard its scripts. Those that survive end up in bookshops and catalogues of mail-order script suppliers.

Keep in mind that there is a vast difference between a draft written for the purpose of selling and a final shooting draft. The latter inevitably contains information that may be necessary for the technicians—camera angles and other sorts of data—but that would only impede the pace at which the reader could absorb the tale.

When a film is actually produced, the typical scene is shot several ways at various angles with various numbers of players in each shot. Ultimately the editor arranges the images in a series of generally quick cuts with technical designations that are pertinent to the cinematographer, editor, script supervisor, and director but otherwise make for difficult reading.

If I see a lot of "two-shot" and "wide" and "close-up" in a script, I'm likely to scrawl "mstrso" in the margin in an attempt to encourage the writer to include only the overview, the broad image of the whole scene, without obscuring the essential issues.

Prez

This issue is discussed in another context in the previous chapter—"prez" stands for "present tense."

All action and description in screenplays must be told in the present tense, even if it's set in the past or in the future. For example, *2001: A*

Space Odyssey (Stanley Kubrick, Arthur C. Clarke, adapting Clarke's story "The Sentinel") starts thousands of years in the past and moves into the not too distant future. Nevertheless, the whole picture unfolds on the screen in the here and now.

The Curious Case of Benjamin Button plays fast and loose with time and space, yet the entire screenplay is told in the present tense. Writers should attempt not to describe what is about to happen or what has just happened but only what happens. This may strike some readers as a relatively minor consideration but, in fact, it represents a most fundamental screenwriting principle.

Some writers insist that there is no way to describe some particular facets of specific actions without utilizing the past tense. In *Dave*, for example, there is a scene where we return to a room that was previously jam-packed with characters but is now virtually empty. How do you describe the second leg of that pair without saying that "everyone has left the room," which is, of course, a past-tense construction?

Gary Ross, screenwriter for *Dave*, knows exactly how. Here, the antagonist, a political Svengali portrayed by Frank Langella, is an underhanded powermonger. He stands in a room filled with people, all of them watching Dave's speech on television. We cut away to Dave delivering the speech "live" before Congress. It becomes clear enough that he is blowing the whistle on Langella's power-broker character, exposing his misdeeds and crimes.

We cut back to this character. He is in the same setting but it is now completely deserted, except for Langella himself. The writer does not need to say, "Everyone has left the room." To state this in the present tense, Ross needs merely to write: "The room is empty," or "The character is alone." Instead of telling what has happened, we tell what happens. We do not whisper extra information in the reader's ear and in doing so betray the form in which we write. Instead, we do precisely what we must: tell the reader of the script precisely what it is that the viewer of the movie in the theater sees.

This kind of change, executed throughout the whole picture, represents not a petty but an enormous—and enormously beneficial—improvement. It brings the writing into closer focus and conveys to the reader the sense that he is in the hands of an experienced professional. Additionally, it picks up the narrative's pace.

Novry

This smashed-together mash of letters stands for "no 'very.'" It simply means that there is almost never an excuse for use of the word "very" in the descriptive passages of a screenplay. There may arise an occasion to use the word in dialogue, but even this is rare.

Almost any word when combined with "very" can become another, more appropriate word. If someone in a film runs, for example, "very fast," we can say instead that he sprints, hurries, rushes, scrambles, races, breezes. If someone is "very scared" we can say he is terrified, petrified, shaky, shaken, rattled, trembling, quaking, sweating, numb, paralyzed, fearful. If the weather is "very cold," then it is also freezing, frigid, and frosty.

And those are just the *f*'s.

Reiterating, occasionally "very" may appropriately be used in dialogue. I recall walking along West Seventieth Street in New York City some years ago, when a woman a half block away, headed toward me, lost control of her big, floppy poodle, who shed her collar and leash and bolted toward me. The dog raced right up to me, leaped up, placed her forepaws on my chest, and proceeded to lick my face. Unbeknownst to the woman, I am a dog nut, barking mad for pooches. I stroked the poodle and kibitzed with her until the owner caught up and replaced the loose leash.

"Friendly pooch," I remarked.

"Very," the owner replied, in a voice laced with embarrassment and contrition.

This exchange might win no Oscar, but in the right scene it represents reasonable dialogue. This, however, is the exception.

Mark Twain wrote that writers should replace every "very" with "damn." Since editors in his era would then have deleted every "damn," this was, of course, Twain's way of telling writers to eschew the use of "very." If he had owned a computer, Twain surely would have advised writers to enable global search and replace in order to delete every appearance of "very."

Punch

At a writing conference, purely as a courtesy, I attended the poetry workshop presented by a friend, University of Hawaii professor Steven Goldsberry. What did I need, I asked myself, with any kind of rinky-dink poetry workshop? In truth, under Steven's tutelage I learned timeless lessons about writing not only screenplays but any and every format. Perhaps the most useful advice Goldsberry gave was to encourage writers to consider every sentence to be a joke, and to remember that jokes end on the punch line.

This is useful to screenwriters struggling with issues regarding both dialogue and description. Don Corleone in *The Godfather* does not say: "He won't be able to refuse the offer I'm going to make him." The punch line in this sentence has to be "refuse." That's where the drama resides. That's the most powerful word, the one carrying the greatest stress. With the sentence ending on the punch line it becomes among the most timeless lines ever uttered in any movie: "I'm going to make him an offer he can't refuse."

Similarly, the unforgettable line from *Jerry Maguire* (Cameron Crowe) "You had me at 'hello'" works far better as written than, say, "When you said 'hello,' you had me." The power lives in "hello," which seems on the surface so inconsequential, so formal, so routine a word, and yet here is packed with romance. Likewise, "Show me the money," from the same film, works far more effectively than, for example, "The money is something I want you to show me." The punch line here is clearly "money."

Xpltlang

This may look like the name of a remote Chinese city but it actually stands for "exploit language." It simply means that writers should use every available tool to tell their tales, to depict their characters, to describe their actions—in short, to write their screenplay.

The first and last tool writers have is: language.

When I scrawl "xpltlang" in the margin I refer specifically to the selection of particular words. That is, writers ought to be selective about the words they write. I am fed up, for example, with the wretched abandon with which writers abuse and toss about the word "incredible." The weather is incredible, the scenery is incredible, the music is incredible, the heat is incredible, this is incredible, that is incredible, the other thing is incredible.

What is truly incredible is overuse of "incredible."

Why not astounding, amazing, preposterous, wonderful, wondrous, unbelievable, extraordinary, splendid, stunning, shocking, mesmerizing, profound, deep, marked, remarkable, just for openers? If we writers do not exploit the English language to its best effect, if we do not protect it, who will?

Drma/Do

As I've mentioned earlier, the word "drama" comes from the Greek word meaning "to do." It does not mean "to talk."

Turn on the TV, surf through the channels; in series episodes and televised feature films alike you are guaranteed to come upon too much talk.

Film is first of all a visual medium and it is far better, therefore, to show rather than tell. Writers need merely to get their characters out of the same, lame, drab locations—restaurants, bars, cars, living rooms, dining rooms—that are prone to recitation and conversation and to place them in newly invented settings that present opportunities for action.

In *Fargo*, for example, the protagonist, portrayed by William H. Macy, tries to arrange to have his own wife abducted and held for ransom. Early in the picture, when he meets with the criminals he hires for the purpose, the scene is set in a bar wherein the Macy character simply tells the prospective kidnappers-for-hire the purpose of his plan. Surely this could have been handled in a more inventive, imaginative, provocative, action-oriented setting and fashion. To rely upon mere dialogue to advance the tale is simply lazy.

This does not mean that all scenes must play out during earthquakes, in flaming skyscrapers, among squadrons of soldiers on battlefields, or amid legions of passengers on ocean liners plying iceberg-plagued seas; nor does it require that all action be heroic. Simple, ordinary, everyday actions, if wielded by writers with discipline and craft, work effectively.

A writer at UCLA created a short film that depicts the meeting, romance, and eventual marriage of two people who at the beginning of the story work together in the same office. In the original draft, the couple first encounter each other at the water cooler.

This struck me as a location likely to promote not action but dialogue. I asked the writer to come up with a list of alternative locations. Somewhere within the catalogue of places was a parking garage.

In the revised draft the woman is in the garage to get her car so as to drive to an important meeting. She discovers, however, that she has a flat tire. The man comes upon her as she struggles to change the tire. He offers to help. She finds his offer deeply offensive. Does he think that a woman cannot change a tire?

"Is that what the women's movement is all about?" he asks. "Have women struggled so that their sister, dressed to the nines in preparation for an important business meeting, can break her perfectly manicured nails and tear her hose in the service of removing lug nuts from the rear right wheel of her steel-blue Camaro?"

In what is otherwise an ordinary setting—a parking garage—actors do not merely talk out their conflicts and their emotions, but they play them out, act them out. They wrestle not only emotionally but also physically as together they jack up the vehicle, pry off the hubcap, struggle with the lug nuts, haul the spare from the trunk.

Can anyone fail to see how vastly superior a location the underground parking garage represents as compared to, say, the upstairs reception area or in front of the water cooler? The latter is a location that encourages talk; the former galvanizes action.

MoomPIX

This designation is closely related to the previous "drma/do."

Growing up in New York City, "moving pictures" was pronounced "moom pitches." For economy, I've shortened the "pitches" part to "PIX." It means simply that film is an enterprise requiring eyes more than ears. It suggests also that whatever those pictures are, they ought not be static but dynamic; instead of lying there still and flaccid, they ought to bounce, pop, sizzle, crackle, and roll right along.

In *Shoot the Moon* (Bo Goldman) we are treated to the image of an actor sitting quietly at the beach contemplating his fate. Audiences are entitled to something more exciting than watching a guy ruminate, even if the guy happens to be portrayed by so capable and distinguished an actor as Albert Finney.

In too many films we watch actors sit and talk and recite the tale. Fully realized movies, though, are meant to be looked at more than listened to. Moreover, the images that are looked at should be not static, still, limp, or wan but supercharged with action, tension, and the stress that should lie at the heart of dramatic expression.

That's what makes it dramatic.

There is an expression in theater: People do not exit a play whistling the scenery. Movie audiences do not exit the theater whistling the cinematography. Pretty pictures alone won't do. They need to be integrated with action and dialogue; like everything else in the movie, they must perpetually advance tale and character.

I love a good slide show as much as the next guy. A worthy movie, however, is no mere slide show.

Cue the Pigeon!

For all that movies have to do with dreams, fantasy, and imagination, they are in fact also a relentlessly practical enterprise. They need not only be dreamed up and written down but also physically crafted.

Legendary director Frank Capra, in his biography *The Name Above the Title*, tells of working as an assistant director during the silent era. His director demanded of a scene at the seashore that the sky be filled with birds. Cleverly scattering fishermen's bait on the sea, Capra was able to attract a flock of gulls.

He was proud of his achievement.

Nevertheless, this did not satisfy his boss, who, after peering through the viewfinder, demanded that the birds be brought in "one at a time."

It wasn't enough that Capra had figured out how to get birds in the sky, all by itself no small feat. He had to produce them single file.

The point is that everything in a screenplay must be capable of being filmed. Nothing should be included that is not truly expected to appear in the final film. The screenplay is not supposed to be a substitute for the movie but a practical guide to its realization on-screen.

I read a script once where, in a scene in a park, the writer designates that "a pigeon settles onto a bench." If this film is *The Attack of the Killer Pigeons*, a tale of terror involving a plague of rabid fowl bent on destroying civilization, then it is certainly appropriate to include special effects involving pigeons.

That said, a writer cannot just for fun throw a living pigeon into his film, any more than he can throw one into the washing machine along with his underwear and socks. You want a pigeon in your picture? You've got to have a pigeon wrangler to train and control the wee beastie, to get him to do the things he's supposed to do, and not do the things he's not supposed to do. Moreover, a representative of the Society for the Prevention of Cruelty to Animals must be present on the set.

This requires a lot of time.

It also costs a lot of money.

If, on the other hand, the writer's intent was to include the pigeon merely for effect, the effect may not be the one he intended. Readers of such a script might well conclude that they are dealing with a writer who is loose with details, who does not intend for all the paraphernalia in the script actually to appear in the film.

What possible result can this have other than to communicate to the reader that she need not pay close attention to what she reads? Is that the effect writers seek? Certainly not. Smart writers desire the contrary. They want the reader to believe that each and every item in the script is important, that it counts for something, that it moves tale and character and is also fast, funny, sad, and dazzling.

Writers should be certain that each and every detail occupying the script, each item of aural and visual information, is integrated. Taking this approach, writers can captivate the reader and create the impression that, in the long run, leads to representation, sale, and longevity of career.

Fmpmt!

This acronym may read like a stifled sneeze or an exhalation of disapproval, but in fact it represents the following: Find and make your point and move your tale!

This notation generally accompanies a lengthy description or block of dialogue that is overwritten and unwieldy and wants desperately to be pruned. For instance:

> LINDA
> I've been thinking about this for quite a long time,
> Harry, and it has finally occurred to me that in the
> end there's truly no hope for us. Why, all you ever
> do is think of yourself. You have no room in your
> life for any other person. How can you ever expect
> to be happy? I don't know how you can stand to
> look at your own face in the mirror each morning
> when you shave. All I know is that I'm sick to tears
> of this marriage and can't stand even another minute
> of it.

This speech just rambles on and on and on. The whole point seems to be contained in the final sentence: "I'm sick to tears of this marriage and can't stand even another minute of it."

The point is: The writer needs to find the point! She has to make the point and move the tale forward. She has to lose all the stuff that surrounds the point. Otherwise, good dialogue is smothered by unnecessary chatter. Cutting, excising, trimming, deleting are among the practices that enhance drama.

"Fmpmt!" applies not only to dialogue but also to descriptions of settings and actions. I frequently read material of this sort: "Harry places his hand on the doorknob, hesitates, now slowly turns it. He takes a deep breath, looks at Linda, now at the door as he pulls it slowly open. He steps through the portal first with his left foot, then his right. And now, with a ringing finality, gradually he pulls the door closed behind him, leaving Linda and the house and his past life where it belongs, in his own, personal history, in that special part of his former existence that exists for him and for all the people in his previous life no more."

The writer is using almost a hundred words to say what could easily be communicated through only two: (1) Harry (2) leaves.

It may not be necessary to say even that much. Errors that win screenwriters a "fmpmt!" in the margin are often associated with violations of the "drekt/akt" notation advising writers not to direct or act the picture but merely to write it.

Payoff? *and* Aha!

This particular note relates generally to questions involving integration. I have already asserted that the healthy screenplay is the integrated screenplay, where every item fits, where every element possesses a purpose.

That is why when I see a particular item of dialogue or description in a script, contained usually in the early pages, I will write beside it the first part of the above note: "payoff?" By this I simply mean to register the item and remind myself, and the writer, that eventually it needs to be touched upon again. Some meaning has to be made apparent so that it lies within the bounds of plot and character craft, since language in screenplays cannot exist for its own sake but only for the sake of story and character.

Writers need to make a special effort, therefore, to eliminate all superfluous, whimsical, unnecessary, word-squandering, attention-debauching language in the script.

When the item is in fact paid off—if indeed it is paid off at all—I will write "Aha!" in the margin, recognizing that the writer has managed to meet this requirement. It is hard enough to set up anything at all that is worthy, and harder still to keep track of it, and even more difficult to maintain it in one's own mind and in the mind of the reader or viewer.

At the beginning of the excellent screenplay *Phenomenon* (Gerald Di Pego), protagonist George, portrayed by John Travolta, rises from his bed early one morning and crashes into a handcrafted willow chair. We quickly see that his house is cluttered with an oversupply of such chairs.

This might very well call for a "payoff?" in the margin.

Later on, we will learn that a woman, Lace, whom George finds thoroughly attractive, manufactures the chairs and that George has covertly been purchasing them. This would win in the margins a bold "Aha!" The writer managed to set something up, then paid it off. Character expands; story advances.

Later in the film, while walking through a field George finds himself suddenly dizzy and queasy. The feeling quickly passes. Again, this would earn the writer a "payoff?" Later, Di Pego reveals that this ill feeling is associated with a seismic fault in the earth and reflects George's ability to predict earthquakes.

Therein lies another "Aha!" for the writer.

When the "payoff?" meets the "Aha!" not immediately but some distance down the line, the writer demonstrates an ability to "checkerboard," which also helps avoid writing material that is "too straight-line." Once again, we see that nothing stands alone but is instead part of the whole picture.

Clue/Hands

Writers just generally love to gripe, most especially regarding ways in which idiot story editors have screwed up their precious, poetic pages. In my own experience, however, I have enjoyed generous and attentive consideration from studio executives and story editors, with whom I have struggled in the service of good screenwriting.

At Warner Bros. many years ago, for example, I worked with a particular story editor on the screen adaptation of my first novel. From time to time I would write within the dialogue words like "anyway" or "besides" or "by the way."

Whenever I would do so, the story editor would reprimand me in the marginal notes with a jocular remark on the order of: "'Besides,' since Richie has apparently forgotten that we're paying him five thousand dollars a week to mold, shape, sculpt, plane, carve and whittle dialogue so that it flows naturally and is worth paying money to hear, he's going to fall down on the job and cop to crude locutions like 'anyway' or 'by the way' or 'besides.'"

When I see one of those words in the context of an otherwise worthy piece of dialogue, I inevitably scrawl "clue/hands" in the margin. This indicates that I have found evidence—a clue—to indicate that the writer is setting up a bit of necessary information and then smashing it together with another bit of information and connecting the two with a limp "besides" or "anyway" or similar bit of language. In other words, I see the writer's hands showing, steering, and forcing the dialogue into shape.

I have a writer pal with whom I go to the movies sometimes. Whenever he hears such dialogue he'll start to type in the air, as if to suggest that just beyond the frame he can actually hear the writer flailing away at his word processor.

Great film art and craft are supposed to be, from top to bottom, invisible. The dialogue should appear to have been created naturally and effortlessly. Moreover, it should appear also to have been created not months and years earlier by writers, but here and now by the characters in the movie as they recite the lines. When we hear "by the way" or "besides," we are reminded that the movie was written by a writer.

Too On-the-Nose

When something is too much what it is—too textual and insufficiently subtextual—it can be said to be "too on-the-nose." In other words, what is sought is not expression alone but implication.

In the vastly overpraised *Leaving Las Vegas* (Mike Figgis, adapting the John O'Brien novel), in order to convey that the protagonist, a disgraced and discredited—guess what?—screenwriter, suffers from alcoholism, he is shown prancing through a supermarket filling his cart with bottles of booze. Throughout the film he is seen repeatedly guzzling liquor straight from the bottle, puking his guts out, then collapsing unconscious. This represents business that is too on-the-nose. The organizing principle of the protagonist's character—his drunkenness—is revealed not subtly but brazenly, not subtextually but superficially.

Compare this with the superior treatment of alcoholism in the classic *Lost Weekend* (Charles Brackett, Billy Wilder, adapting the Charles R. Jackson novel), in which the protagonist's addiction is revealed not by Ray Milland's imbibing fluid from a hip flask but, instead, by his sneaking to the window, opening it, and pulling up a cord dangling from below, revealing, finally, a hidden booze bottle.

We do not even need to see him take a nip to realize that he is hopelessly alcoholic.

A splendid example of writing that is subtle, not too on-the-nose, lies in the script sent me by the incarcerated writer I mentioned earlier. At a point midway through the tale the protagonist flies into a rage, torches his cell, and is slammed into solitary confinement. In order to depict his loneliness after several weeks in the hole, the writer could have had him recite an eloquent soliloquy commenting upon his fragmented, disconnected existence. Alas, this would have been entirely too on-the-nose.

Instead, the writer crafts a scene in which the character befriends a rat. He rolls his crusts of bread into pea-size balls and tosses them to the rat. This is his only contact with another warm-blooded creature. Is that not a whole lot more articulate, more artistic, more emotional, more dramatic, than the guy delivering a speech, no matter how poetic, no matter how eloquent, regarding his sad and sorry plight?

Eventually another prisoner, serving on the food detail, delivers bread-and-water rations to the solitary-confinement cells. He rattles on the door and whispers through the grate, "Nasty, it's me, Noodles. You okay in there?" Nasty does not say that he is not okay, that he is in fact miserable. What he says instead is, "Sure, great. Never better. In here it's Club Med."

This represents understatement, overstatement, irony, and sarcasm all rolled into one. By stating not the case but in fact the polar opposite of the case, the character's loneliness is rendered poignant and palpable for both the reader of the screenplay and the viewer of the film.

It can't be said often enough: Writers are well advised to imply rather than express. What is expressed hangs there full and whole in front of the audience for their observation and comprehension. What is implied, how-ever, seduces and engages. It plays out where all worthy art ought to play: in the mind of the observer. That is the most effective form of creative expression because it involves the audience not as a dispassionate observer but as a willing participant, a collaborator.

4v.6

The numbers here represent approximations and the "v." stands for "versus."

As I review screenplays, I often find overwriting so egregious that in an attempt to illuminate the issue I'll number the words, with separate tallies for those that are necessary and those that are not, and then I'll express them in a kind of ratio separated by the *v*.

This can be applied both to dialogue and description.

In a preceding section, "Fmpmt!," I cited a bit of overly descriptive writing that employed no fewer than ninety-seven words but required only two. This could have been expressed as follows: 95v.2. It means we've squandered ninety-five words where we need only two.

This is, of course, an exaggerated example. Contemplate instead that merely four words were wasted out of a sentence of, say, ten. That would result in a notation of "4v.6." Some might protest that this is a relatively petty consideration. Four words have been wasted; so what? So this: At that rate of cutting, a script of one hundred ten pages will be reduced by fifty-six whole pages.

Once again we see that if all by itself a particular miscue in a screen-play appears to be petty, these errors are never alone but are part of the whole picture. A change of attitude regarding language can ease and sweeten the reading of a script, can help make it sizzle and dazzle.

NoFX

In technical movie talk "FX" stands for "effects."

Here, however, the designation refers not to film effects—shimmer dissolves, spiral wipes, morphing, green screen, and the like—but to computer/printer effects such as centering, right-margin justification, italics, boldface, and related word-processing capabilities. While the com-puter age offers a bounty of new capabilities for writers, it creates also vast new opportunities for errors and loss.

*Principle 37: Screenwriting software is supposed to serve
the writer; not the other way around.*

I recommend writers resist using all the bells and whistles provided by word-processing programs and screenwriting software. It may seem logical that right-margin justification—text printed with a neat and even right margin, such as you see in published typeset works—ought to present a neater, more orderly appearance and ought thereby to enhance readability.

In practice, however, the opposite is the case. Studies reveal that the same material written with right-margin justification reads more slowly than when presented ragged right.

That aside, there are far better reasons for writers to eschew any kind of printer effects. Their scripts should simply appear to have been typed on a typewriter. This does not mean that they must not use computers and the fanciest laser printers; it requires simply that the appearance of the script be calm and tame and professional.

Fancy computer graphics in a script—for example, using boldface for emphasis—carry the same burden as artwork. Again, as indicated in the chapter on format, I have viewed screenplays that were magnificently illustrated with full-color paintings, drawings, and photographs. Alas, for all of the gorgeous imagery, the net effect of the graphics is a sure sign that the writer is not an experienced professional.

Subliminally, perhaps also consciously, fancy graphics suggest to the reader that the words alone are somehow not enough to tell the story, depict the characters, and create the dialogue, and that they need extra attractions—the newest electronic doodads and add-ons—to expand and enhance their meaning.

Clok

Even if a motion picture has no motion, the clock still continues to move. "Clok?" (sometimes depicted as a little circle with a pair of hands in it and a question mark beside it) poses the question: How much time will this particular bit of business in the script actually occupy on-screen?

So many writers seem unaware of this most fundamental screenwriting principle. So many screenplays are replete with do-nothing, hang-around material in which people and events effectively just stand—or lie—there, apparently for their own purpose rather than to advance plot and expand character.

Principle 38: Movies move.

I have already described screenplay passages in which a woman enters her apartment, hangs up her coat, fixes herself a drink or prepares a pot of tea, changes into more comfortable shoes, and, at long, long last, dials someone on the phone.

Why include all this lame, lackluster material in the script? "I wanted to set the tone," a writer may explain. "I wanted to give the audience a breather."

Principle 39: Breathers are for after the movie. During the movie audiences seek not breathers but breathlessness.

In such instances I am certain to inquire: Precisely how much time will be expended to depict this so-called breather?

The writer will typically say something like, "Not long. Perhaps only a couple of minutes."

I'll invite the writer to sit quietly with me—not looking at a watch, not silently counting off the time—and experience the feeling of not two minutes but only one. In truth, we'll sit not even for a minute but only for half of one minute. It is, however, ample time to feel preposterously awkward. Writers will squirm and fidget, sweat and just generally die from the discomfort provoked by merely sitting quietly with absolutely nothing to do for even only thirty seconds.

When the half minute expires I'll ask, "Are you surprised to discover how heavily even a mere minute weighs in the absence of drama?" Inevitably, the writer is surprised to contemplate that a minute could last for so unendurable a period. When I tell him that the period was not a minute but merely a fraction of a minute, the writer realizes that time ought to be used more wisely.

100min18mos

Speaking of minutes, the ideal film occupies approximately one hundred of them.

From script to released picture eighteen months is just about the shortest amount of time in which a movie can be produced. In recent decades movies have come to run too, too long.

Too many long movies run well beyond two hours, never mind a hundred minutes. This is testimony to the (self-)destructive power of directors. Neither Scorsese nor Coppola nor Oliver Stone nor Paul Thomas Anderson nor the Coen lads nor Spike Lee, and certainly not Akira Kurosawa or Chen Kaige or Bernardo Bertolucci, is above making films that run way beyond their proper Aristotelian ending—that is, the point after which there is nothing.

In too many movies the director simply refuses to get off the stage.

Movies are often awash with inconsequential events that squander precious time but fail to exploit character and story. When an ending runs on too long, or when pointless, ordinary, everyday action occupies and preoccupies a script, I am likely to scrawl "100min18mos" beside it in the margin.

If the writer is the luckiest screen scribe who ever breathed, if his script wins representation the day after it is written, if a producer is so swept away that he produces the picture immediately, it may actually appear on screens eighteen months later. This represents, of course, the highest, most desirable, most favorable set of circumstances.

Call it a best-case scenario.

The obvious question, therefore, that the writer of every script must ask himself when writing every detail and line of dialogue is: If eighteen months from now I finally win a hundred minutes of an audience's time, is this how I want to spend even a fraction of one of those minutes? Do I want to have them view a woman getting into comfortable shoes after fixing herself a pot of tea? Do I want them to hear characters trading inconsequential chitchat?

Though fixing a pot of tea and hanging up a coat in a closet are, in their own way, "something," in dramatic terms they're nothing, since outside of integration with other aspects of the film, they pack no emotional wallop, expand no story, and advance no character.

Unless the teakettle boils over and severely scalds someone or the closet contains the rotting, flesh-shredded remains of a serial killer's latest victim, the action is merely a waste of time, effort, ink, and film.

Eye/Eye

This is sometimes inscribed as a crude graphic depiction of two eyeballs. It suggests to writers that at this point in the script they should be heightening a particular conflict, that the competing interests of the char-

acters in the scene need to be underscored or laced with sufficient inten-
sity to suggest that they stand eyeball to eyeball in conflict.

In Chazz Palminteri's *A Bronx Tale*, for example, a gang of motorcycle
hoodlums bursts rudely into a neighborhood bar that happens to serve as
the unofficial community social center. It happens also to be run by the
local crime boss, who politely requests that the bikers leave.

The lead biker responds without particular hostility that he and his
buddies merely seek a couple of beers, after which they'll happily depart.
Since his request has been made in a manner that is respectful, the don
acquiesces, instructing the bartender to serve the fellows.

If the scene went on much longer in this manner, I might have drawn
double eyeballs in the margin, suggesting that there's no fun in movies
where folks congenially achieve serene and reasonable agreement, and
that the writer would be better advised to craft some eyeball-to-eyeball
conflict into the moment.

Chazz Palminteri, however, is too skillful a writer to require any such
advice. In an instant he informs the setting with truly original physical
and emotional conflict, ending with the Hell's Angels being chastened and
chastised. Beer sprays, feet and fists fly, heads are bopped, and motorcycles
parked outside are reduced to scattered nuts and bolts and twisted metal.

The writer of another film could take a cue from Palminteri. In *Field
of Dreams*, writer Phil Alden Robinson (adapting the W. P. Kinsella novel
Shoeless Joe) has his protagonist, upon hearing mystic voices in his head,
decide to tear up the cornfield in front of his country home and build a
baseball stadium in its place. When he confronts his wife with his scheme,
she speaks dialogue that takes the following tack: "Honey, I know your
plan sounds crazy, but we love you, and we'll stand behind you whatever
you want, no matter how zany it seems."

That's precisely the kind of passage that would win from me an "eye/
eye." Would not the scene carry greater tension if the wife, instead of
blindly, blandly acquiescing, angrily protested? Would not that conflict
render the picture more dramatic?

Instead of her saying, "Hey, it sounds wacky, but if it's what you want
we'll support you," she might argue, "Are you out of your mind? You
dragged us from the big city to this lost, remote outpost, and we went
along with you. Now that our lives are finally beginning to settle in and
find balance you decide on a whim, thanks to some infantile, macho,

adolescent wet-dream fantasy about playing catch with your dad, to tear up not only the cornfield but our lives. Count us out! We won't stand for another moment of your egomaniacal, narcissistic selfishness."

I'm not about to argue that the suggested dialogue is ideal. But isn't the attitude likely to encourage greater dynamism and drama than the wife's original speech? A wife blithely consenting to her husband's wishes, deferring not to her own but to his dreams, may fulfill the male author's idealized, romanticized notion of what a marriage ought to be, but does it represent the highest, most effective drama?

I award Robinson a pair of eyeballs in the margins for the whole scene.

1 or o.

The marginal note "1 or o." stands for "one or the other." It usually applies to the tiniest fragment of a screenplay—for example, a line of dialogue—but in certain instances it can refer to an entire scene.

Let us say the dialogue is as follows: "No. Absolutely not." In the margin beside such a line I might very well write "1 or o." This means, of course, that either of those brief sentences is sufficient; why include both? Redundancy earns the writer only squandered time, wasted attention, spilled ink.

"No" means "absolutely not."

"Absolutely not" means "no."

Why in the world say the same thing twice or, worse, three times? Sometimes I see information repeated many more times than that. In such instances I may inscribe actual numbers beside each instance—l, 2, 3, 4, etc.—recording a tally in order to help the writer see precisely how many times he repeats himself.

As with virtually all criticism of screenplays, most writers are grateful to have such repetition pointed out to them. They would rather be alerted to deficits by their teacher, or by their fellow writers, than by agents or producers or executives they hope will facilitate the making of a deal and, God willing, a movie.

Nevertheless, from time to time a writer receiving a "1 or o." protests that the repetition was included in order to lend emphasis. "No, absolutely not," the writer may argue, is stronger, more vigorous, more adamant, than merely one or the other of those mini sentences.

The effect is, however, precisely the opposite. Repetition that fails si-multaneously to expand character and move story—repetition that merely replicates what has already been stated—does not add but diminishes dramatic impact.

I often compare the well-integrated screenplay to the intelligently de-signed automobile dashboard. Every switch, every knob, every lever has to fulfill a function. A switch performing no such purpose, a lever that is simply there for the look or the feel or the sound it produces—for exam-ple, a bright, crisp click—is evidence only of poor design.

Likewise, two switches performing the same function are just as bad as one switch performing no function. Senselessly duplicated controls represent poor design, since each renders the other pointless.

The same can be said for the abundant paraphernalia that constitute a screenplay, be it a line of dialogue or, as suggested above, an entire scene. This sort of repetition is all too common, not only in bad films but among worthy ones as well. Even the screenplay for so worthy a film as *Schindler's List* (Steven Zaillian, adapting the Thomas Keneally novel), for example, is not above rating in its margin "1 or o."

Schindler's has a scene wherein a young woman prisoner is executed with a shot to the head. It succinctly establishes the lethal nature of Nazi cruelty, perversion, and persecution. Not long after the scene, however, we are treated to the specter of the concentration camp's commandant wield-ing a rifle and, from his balcony overlooking the camp, gunning down prisoners for sport.

It is, of course, all by itself a horrible image and ought to evoke an emotional response from viewers. However, it is not all by itself; it is part of the whole picture. And when placed in the context of similar scenes that have imparted the same sort of information, scenes like this make a point that has already been made. Rather than sensitizing viewers it numbs them. The horror of Nazism is not that deranged maniacs murdered people but that otherwise sane, common, rational, ordinary citizens—millions of them—coolly, blithely tolerated it and, still worse, eagerly supported it.

The overlong and ponderous *Prince of Tides* (Pat Conroy, Becky John-ston, adapting Conroy's novel) gives us a scene early in the picture where a suicidal daughter witnesses the degrading spectacle of her father refus-ing to pause even briefly from his television show in order to acknowledge his child's birthday. The scene descends into substantial violence involving, among other things, a son blasting the TV with a shotgun.

In a later scene, the daughter is raped by a trio of marauding criminals.

Is the latter dramatic? All by itself it is very much so. In the broader context of similar scenes saying similar things, however, the impact is diffused and dissipated. Tension, instead of being heightened, is mitigated. Reduced tension, of course, is precisely the opposite of what we seek in the worthy, healthy, integrated screenplay.

As indicated earlier, there is simply no reason for a character in a movie to tell another character something that the writer has already communicated to the audience.

Choose one.

Or choose the other.

Don't choose both.

'Veen

"'Veen" is a crude abbreviation for "convenient."

I often read scripts in which one or another aspect of the plot occurs apparently for the convenience of the writer alone. Regardless of the often solitary nature of screenwriting, successful film writers are never alone; in a sense they collaborate not only with the other members of the creative family of artists and craftsmen who make the movie but also with the audience viewing the finished product. It is for the convenience not of the writer but this latter group that the movie is ultimately created.

In *Indecent Proposal* (Amy Holden Jones, adapting the Jack Engelhard novel) a husband desperate for money "rents" his bride to a wealthy man for the weekend. The bride falls in love with the fellow. Why? Because he is attractive? Because he's rich?

The only reason for her to fall in love is that the script says so. This serves the convenience of the writer, who, without this particular turn in the plot, would not have much of a story.

Keep in mind, however, that screenplays are written for the convenience not of the writer but the audience. Even if events do not flow smoothly, they must appear to do just that. The anecdotal, incidental material that constitutes the story cannot appear to have been set up like ducks in a row to suit the writer's purpose. They need to seem to unfold seamlessly, spontaneously, naturally.

This is true even if—upon close analysis and inspection—there is in fact nothing about movies that is seamless, spontaneous, or natural.

Bw! Cyc!

This unpronounceable designation stands for a line ranted by King Lear during a storm: "Blow, wind! Crack your cheeks!"

I write this in the margins next to dialogue that is lame, tame, flat, tepid, wan, pedestrian, or otherwise inconsequential. Frequently this is dialogue that is merely passing time, the sort of swapped courtesies and politenesses that saturate real life but have no place in movies: "Hi! How you doing?" "Pretty good, you?" "Great! How about a cup of coffee?"

Pedestrian passages may move a smidgen of data regarding the tale, but they fail to expand character. In dialogue such as this, writers have their characters narrate the story instead of acting it out. "I went to the parking lot to look for Janet but she wasn't there. I waited for a while, then walked around the neighborhood to see whether or not I might spot her. Finally I just gave up and went home."

Such a line merits a "Bw! Cyc!" beside it in the margin to indicate that even if the writer cannot equal Shakespeare, she ought to try. Loud, proud, poetic dialogue is preferred over that which lies there frail and flaccid like a slice of smoked salmon.

A simpler way to express this principle: Movie dialogue should be worth listening to. It should pop and sizzle and crackle and sparkle and dazzle, make us laugh, make us cry, scare us half to death, even repel and offend us, but never bore us.

Of course, it must also expand character and advance story. It is easy for a teacher or consultant or agent or producer to demand that dialogue meet these high standards and quite another for writers to achieve them. Nevertheless, that's what writers are paid to do.

2bxpo

Every screen story has what is called its backstory: information regarding the characters and their lives implied to have occurred prior to the commencement of the film itself. For example, the earliest images in the film *Midnight Cowboy* feature the Texas dishwasher Joe Buck shedding his apron and preparing to make his way by bus to mean old New York City.

Clearly Joe had a life before this point. He was born, he suffered whatever privations had led him to the lowly job of dishwasher, he might have received a stunted sort of education that convinced him that New York City throbs with sexually starved women eagerly craving a masculine, leather-clad dude like Joe for the purpose of copulation.

Sometimes it is necessary to reveal some of this information to the audience concretely; often it is not. In the former instance, it is wise to dispense with the facts quickly.

Even the immortal *Casablanca* (Julius G. Epstein, Phillip J. Epstein, Howard Koch, based on the play *Everybody Comes to Rick's* by Murray Burnett and Joan Alison) could stand to lose the little introduction—the too-brazen exposition at the front of the film—in which, just in case anybody failed to have heard of World War II, a short lecture summarizes the state of hostility among nations.

"2bxpo," therefore, stands for "too-brazen exposition." It can apply not only to backstory data revealed at the beginning of the movie but also to scenes occurring later.

Conclusion

Here follow the first few pages of the earliest draft of the screenplay that became *River's Edge*, written as an assignment in a UCLA screenwriting class. The notes are those I actually provided for the writer, Neal Jimenez. They provide a concrete example of notes in action and their place in the process of rewriting.

THE RIVER
Neal Jimenez

EXT   RIVER   BARELY DAWN

AKT/
DREKT

TIM, twelve, stands on a footbridge overlooking the river. braving the cold, dark morning. He holds a doll in his hand. [and stares at the water rushing by below him.] 9v.7

SIFYN!

The dim, lonely light of dawn casts a languid, dreamlike spell over the scene, further enhanced by Tim's icy stance.

He drops the doll off the bridge. and we see it slowly fall, fall through the air. We hear a distant, human sound over the

~~ambience of the rushing water, and~~ Tim casts his eyes to a faraway cliff at the river's edge.

Two <u>human</u> <u>forms</u> can be made out on the cliff, one lying, one sitting. The prone figure ~~appears to be~~ ^{is} nude. ~~Again we experience the languid spell, only this time it's caused by more than just the light. [time itself has been slowed,] obvious from the graceful flutter of the leaves on the trees and the hypnotic stirring of the dust.~~ The Seated Figure lets out a distant WHOOP. ~~which echoes and dissipates just as~~

PREZ.

THE DOLL hits the water with a ~~[very]~~ ~~pronounced~~ SPLASH. ~~which carries into~~ *now*

INT   KIM'S ROOM   EARLY DAWN

KIM, six, opens her eyes, as if awakened by the splash.~~ing sound. only half awake, and we see her room from within her lingering nightmare: dark spaces stretch infinitely, curtains hang ominously, shadows move with menace.~~

hwk?
see/hear?

A DARK FIGURE appears at the door. The Figure slowly approaches. ~~but~~ Kim ~~[cannot move, she's paralyzed.]~~ ~~She~~ screams ~~louder and louder~~ and the figure ~~keeps coming and~~ finally grabs her. ~~and we are snapped out of the nightmare because it's~~

MATT, Kim's 17-year-old "stoner" brother, comes to comfort her. ~~Were it not for the immediate calming effect he has on the hysterical Kim, we might be worried about his presence in her room. After a moment~~ <u>Madeleine</u>, Kim's 35-year-old mother, appears at the door, dressed in a tattered robe as faded as the light in her eyes.

MATT
Settle down, Kim, everything's okay.

KIM
She's dead, she's dead.

EXT   RIVER

THE DOLL floats downstream at normal speed and in the
background [~~we see~~] TIM climbs on his bike and rides off.

"merely"   ⌈ ~~The camera follows the doll in a closer shot for a ways~~
            ⌊ ~~before we~~

~~PAN~~ Up to the cliff, ~~seen earlier~~. SAMSON TOULETTE, a
everything large, muscular teenager, sits at cliff's edge, smoking a joint.
in the wide He lets out another WHOOP.
margins
"we see"   lies
           Behind him [~~we see~~] ˄ the NUDE FIGURE. She is dead and
           covered with handfuls of leaves and twigs and dirt. ~~Her eyes~~
           ~~open wide, she seems to stare at Samson as he finishes his~~
           ~~joint.~~

EXT   SACRAMENTO STREET

SAMSON cruises the barren streets in a dinosaur of a car.
Occasionally a nine-to-fiver flashes past him.

INT   7-ELEVEN

TIM plays a video game in the corner of the store.

SAMSON enters, pulls a single <u>beer</u> from the rack and sets it
on the counter. The two acknowledge each other with a
glance.

The CHECKER looks skeptically at Samson, then points to a
sign that says: IDENTIFICATION REQUIRED FOR
PURCHASE OF ALCOHOL.

                         SAMSON
              I left it at home.

                         CHECKER
              Sorry.

The checker ~~goes to~~ grabs the beer, but Samson has a hand on
it. ~~first.~~ Tim, ~~from the corner of the store, watches. the mild~~
~~conflict. He~~ moves to the drink section.

> CHECKER
> I'll take that, thank you.

> SAMSON
> Don't be tight.

> CHECKER
> Let go of the beer.

Tim pulls a second beer from the rack. At that moment he
~~[notices]~~ the STORE CAMERA ~~set just above him. He~~
looks into the lens and ~~[we see] him~~ staring straight out of the
MONITOR right over the checker's shoulder.

hwk? *(margin)*

AKT/DREKT "MERELY"

Tim's ~~looks to make sure he isn't being watched~~ his back is
now to us on the monitor. He puts the beer in his coat pocket
and walks out of the store.

~~Samson and the checker are still in a stand off. Finally~~
Samson ~~gives in and~~ turns to leave.

EXT   7-ELEVEN

TIM
~~TIM~~ waits by Samson's car. Samson comes out of the store
and climbs into his car, noticing immediately the beer sitting
on the passenger seat. ~~He looks to Tim.~~

AKT/DREKT "MERELY"

> TIM
> Don't mention it.

NOTNOT
Samson ~~doesn't mention it. He~~ opens the beer.

> TIM (CONT.)
> I saw you this morning.

> SAMSON
> Yeah?

~~He takes a swallow of the beer. There is a pause.~~ AKT/DREKT

> TIM
> Got any dope?

SAMSON

No.

SEE?HEAR? AKT/DREKT "MERELY"

~~Another pause. Tim is beginning to get uncomfortable. He is not impressing Samson, as he had hoped.~~ Samson reaches over and opens the passanger door.

SAMSON

~~Get in.~~ I know where to get some.

DREKT/AKT
                                              s
Tim ~~hesitates, then starts~~ loading his bike into the back seat.

INT   SAMSON'S CAR   MORNING

Samson   Tim
~~SAMSON~~ cruises the empty streets as ~~TIM~~ watches him drive. ~~a reverence in his gaze.~~ AKT/DREKT

PART II

· · · · · · · · · · ·

Craft

Chapter 13

. . . .

The Writing Habit

When asked to offer his single most important piece of advice for writers, author Tommy Thompson responded: Every day, no matter what else you do, get dressed. The most destructive mistake a writer can make, Thompson insisted, is to sit around the house all day in his bathrobe.

Thompson did not talk about inspiration. He did not mention grammar and spelling. Neither did he say anything about research techniques, or character, dialogue, or plot. This was not because he considered these items trivial. He understood that none of them matters if writers don't first master something else: the writing habit.

I have already stated that writers are for the most part a fussy, finicky lot. Likewise, I have asserted that not one of them truly likes to write.

It is not wise, therefore, to expect writers ever to want to write. Instead of wanting to write, writers simply write. For better or worse—perhaps a bit of both—writing must become an ingrained, routine procedure that cannot be shaken except by further writing. A confident grip on story structure, a thorough understanding of characterization, a brilliant ear for dialogue, and crafty entrepreneurial business savvy all amount to nothing absent the writing habit.

Ideas

Among writing's most overrated entities is the idea.

I rarely meet a soul who does not have a fabulous idea for a movie.

Worse, people seem forever eager to share these ideas with writers. Working writers don't need other people's ideas; they have plenty of their own. Ideas, even the best among them, are still mere ideas. All by themselves they are useless. Value resides in the idea that is worked out and written down, structured into a story with characters speaking nifty dialogue, all in the service of a tale meriting and sustaining an audience's attention for a hundred minutes.

The problem for a writer about to write a screenplay is not to find an idea but to discard all the other ideas he already has, arriving at that one to which he is willing to commit hundreds—maybe thousands—of hours struggling.

Ideas occur in odd places and at curious moments. A writer sees a flash of action in real life; it may be grandiose and spectacular—a house ablaze—but more likely it is mundane: a depositor quarreling with a bank teller, a nun at roadside changing a tire.

Whatever it is, the writer may find himself from time to time involuntarily thinking about the incident or the idea. It may remind him of something in his own life. He may fashion fictional incidents and anecdotes of his own invention and attach them to the notion. Eventually he may sense a three-act structure asserting itself.

E. L. Doctorow describes in an interview how he invented *Ragtime*. In a full-bore writer's depression, a total famine of inspiration, not a clue as to what he might write about, he paced aimlessly up and back in the study of his home in New Rochelle, New York.

After a long while he found himself pressing his face against the wall. In utter desperation, he decided to write about the wall.

He imagined the wall at the time of his writing, and the house to which it belonged, and then he worked his way back to when the house was built early in the twentieth century, and soon he was writing about New Rochelle at the turn of the past century, weaving an imaginative tale involving leading personalities and colorful events of that era. Before he knew what was happening, he was writing *Ragtime*.

With regard to original screenplays, many writers finally sit down to write a script once the idea has quietly percolated for a year or more. Almost any idea, even a bad one, can be turned into a good screenplay. Indeed, when I was just starting out as a screenwriter, while still enrolled as a student at the University of Southern California film school, I was now and again approached by producers who had ideas and sought to hire writers to turn them into screenplays. In such instances my greatest struggle was to remember not to tell the producer how terrific I thought the idea was until he actually told it to me.

As a starving student/fledgling writer I was not about to tell any producer eager to spend thousands of dollars on an unknown writer that his idea did not interest me. I acknowledge that sometimes I accepted ideas that I regarded poorly, or at least feigned more enthusiasm than I actually felt. From some fairly lackluster ideas I was able to coax solid screenplays satisfying not only my employers but even myself.

A former student of mine, Tom Musca, cowrote (with Ramón Menéndez) one of my favorite movies: *Stand and Deliver.* It tells the true story of the educator Jaime Escalante, who succeeded in teaching calculus to working-class and impoverished Latino high school students at Garfield High in East Los Angeles's barrio. The kids all passed the calculus exam administered by the Educational Testing Service of Princeton, New Jersey.

When the ETS administrators in Princeton saw that all these downtrodden Latino youths had passed the calculus test, they assumed that the only way this could have happened was through cheating. They insisted that the test be readministered. They sent teams of special proctors to oversee the exam and put each student in a separate room so as to be certain they could not cheat.

The results were the same: The kids passed the calculus exam with flying colors.

Tom said to me, "Imagine me pitching this project to Hollywood. The climax is that these kids take a math test." Then, after a pause, he added, "Twice."

Principle 40: A great idea for a movie is merely that—an idea.

If an idea is good, all that remains is the toil, the sweat, the invention, the characters, the settings, the dialogue, and everything else—in short, the writing.

Writer's Block

Once a writer has played with an idea in his mind for many months—sometimes even for years—he may decide it is time actually to put pencil to paper, or fingers to keys. He may also find that he is stuck, that he just can't seem to get started. Or a writer may be well into a script that has been flowing smoothly for many pages only to become blocked.

A writer who truly wants to start writing must first of all shed the naive need to enjoy himself. Enjoyment is for audiences. Enjoyment is for later. Fun is not for writing but for after writing.

Blocked writers who sit around idly waiting for inspiration, hoping against hope for some probing insight, are forever condemned to stagnation and self-contempt. The cure? Simply start writing. Never mind good, bad, indifferent. Just get words onto paper. And if a day passes where the writer stumbles clumsily through even only two, three, or four pages, and if out of all that there is but a page, or a page plus a fragment of another page, that is even remotely useful, a writer could at such a pace—even taking weekends off—write three to four respectable feature-length screenplays every year.

Principle 41: Writer's block is the natural state of writing.

Writer's block is a hoax. Blockage is writing's natural state. It derives from the immature notion that writing ought to be easy, ought to flow like Niagara or, if not quite Niagara, at least some reliable backcountry creek.

Over the years, working writers have suggested a broad menu of techniques to deal with writer's block: change locales, change working hours, switch from computer to felt-tipped markers and oversized spiral-bound artists' sketch pads.

The only remedy for writer's block is writing. The blocked writer's salvation lies in learning not to shun but to embrace the inevitable reluctance that accompanies all creative activity.

When new writers complain to me that they are frustrated, I tell them I am glad to hear it because it signals to me that they are having the sorts of real experiences belonging to real writers.

No writer has a right to expect to want to write. To dissolve the obstruction in his creativity a writer need merely plant his rear in his chair and his fingers on his keys, and keep it/them there for several hours each day.

Working Methods

Writing, solitary enterprise that it is, requires writers to find their own individual method, to create their own daily schedule and routine.

When I was just starting out, I looked outside myself to other writers for cues as to the right and wrong of it. Two of my USC film school classmates had already become quite a successful team, and for too many years I criticized myself for failing to follow the schedule they had devised for themselves. They were at the writing table by eight, worked without pause until precisely twelve thirty, took off exactly thirty minutes for lunch—always the same lunch: tuna fish, no mayonnaise, just a splash of lemon juice—then worked again all afternoon, no nonsense, writing relentlessly until five thirty.

As senility and decrepitude encroach ever more closely upon me, I now surrender more readily to my own quirks and instincts. Intellectually, I should prefer to be able to rise bright and early, plant myself immediately by the warm, glowing screen of my faithful word processor, boot up the cruise control, write productively, indeed inspirationally until noon or maybe even one thirty, and call it quits for the day. Instead, I rarely get to the screen until one or two, and every bit as rarely start any actual writing until a couple of hours later, working into the early and middle evening hours.

That's the way it is for me, that's the way it's always been, and if past is prologue, for me that's the way it's going to be. After so many years working in such a fashion, I finally surrender to the routine, and at long last realize that this is my own natural rhythm and there's no useful purpose in resisting.

Writers need to permit themselves to achieve in whatever manner serves. Some work slowly, steadily, all day, day after day. Others dawdle hour after hour until, with hardly any time left at the end of each day, they leap suddenly into an orgy of finger-flailing productivity.

Other writers start in the evening and work all night. Still others work in their heads for months, putting nothing on paper, then lock themselves in a garage or cabin or motel and write endlessly, around the clock, catnapping here and there, until their task is complete.

Some writers measure their output by hours, others by pages. For everything else writing is—story, language, inspiration, character, art, craft—first of all it is pages. When you get right down to it, there's page one, then comes two, which is followed by three, and all the rest after that. It may not be romantic to look upon it that way, but for working writers that's the way it truly is. It's the way we meet our deadlines.

Too many writers view their deadlines as their enemy.

Principle 42: The deadline is the writer's friend.

From time to time a writer in my UCLA class will approach me a week or two before her script is due at the end of our academic quarter, seeking an extension of the deadline. To meet the deadline, she explains, she'll have to scramble and stumble and sprint. I tell her: Scramble and stumble and sprint. Pressure makes diamonds. Scrambling and stumbling and sprinting has a way of shaking loose the barnacles and causing writers to economize in language and incident, resulting in a meaner, leaner screenplay.

Principle 43: Don't let excellent get in the way of good.

Deadlines are not to be dreaded but embraced. No script will ever be perfect. Dawdling has never been known to improve any script. Indeed, taking extra time often renders a script self-conscious and clunky. Given too much time, writers often overthink their story and lose their spontaneity and naturalism.

Generally, scripts take as long to write as the deadline—self-imposed or assigned by a producer—allows.

Writing habits and working methodologies are as personal and individual as writing itself, and each writer needs to find his own method, his own schedule, and not rely upon others to set some authorized standard. Instead of intellectualizing about how he ought to work, a writer should just work.

Writing Venue

Among the many myths about writing is that writers hate to be disturbed.

In truth, working writers live for disturbance. A writer who is not from time to time interrupted soon finds himself compiling lengthy shopping lists, cleaning his nails, rereading the lost-dog ads in the classifieds, tweeting, and surfing pornographic websites.

Myself, I phone to check Utah ski condition reports, even in August.

The lost little cabin in the woods—no neighbors for miles, no disruption save the chirping of birds and babbling of brooks—is the novice's dream but the working writer's nightmare. In such a setting a real writer soon goes mad.

A world-famous mathematical theoretician accomplishes his finest analyses in airport lounges. He goes to the airport even when he has no flight to catch, just to sit and scratch out his notes and formulae on odd slips of paper balanced precariously on his lap. He finds the anxious, swirling motion of dislocated people all about him somehow calming, as if the stress and disruption require him to concentrate.

In Los Angeles, writers are easily isolated. We work alone in our studies, sometimes never leaving the house for days or even weeks on end; we travel alone in our cars, all too rarely interacting with drama's most fundamental resource: people.

This is one more reason I rejoice to be part of the UCLA community, where people move about on foot and actually talk to each other, exchanging wonderfully inconsequential small talk mixed occasionally with the profound. The university setting provides a writer with a superstructure of support; it gives him a chance to practice such outlandish activities as greeting people. "Hello, how are you? Nice to see you. Myself? Just fine, thanks." That may not seem like a whole lot, but for writers, social cripples as we tend to be, it constitutes communion with humanity. Notably, I sometimes come upon some of my most prosperous former students hiding in library carrels at UCLA, or holed up in the campus latte emporium, even though they have fancy office suites at major studios and luxurious seaside retreats at Malibu.

Must one live in Los Angeles or New York in order to ply the screenwriting trade?

No.

As discussed later in chapter 17, "Script Sales Strategies," introductions to agents and producers are best achieved not by personal visits or even by telephone calls but by the United States Postal Service and e-mail. Writers, especially inexperienced writers, are best off not attempting to win commissioned assignments by orally pitching ideas to producers but by speculatively writing a feature-length screenplay, and then another and yet another.

A writer eager to work specifically in episodic television needs to be located in Los Angeles, it is true, as this happens to be where the business is. Situation comedies and dramatic series are more often than not written by staffs signed to the various shows, and these staffs have regular staff meetings. Additionally, such shows are sold on the basis of oral pitches, and writers have to be available locally to show up for the pitch meetings.

That said, however, I also know writers who live far from town and send in their episodes directly from their computers as PDF file attachments to e-mails. Where a writer writes counts less than what he writes.

Outline versus Treatment

Prior to jumping in and writing, in order to create a script that is integrated, sustained, and from start to finish worthy of an audience's consideration, a writer needs a plan.

One kind of plan is an outline.

An outline is not a treatment. Treatments are hardly worth treating since they are a form writers dread and rightly so. I never knew a single writer who dreamed of writing a treatment. Treatments take the fun out of screenwriting. A treatment is simply a description of a movie told, as with all screenplays, in the present tense. A treatment is an outline that has been fattened up and turned into something resembling formal prose.

When writers submit a treatment accompanying a script that has already been written, the treatment is read instead of the script. If writers, especially new writers, submit treatments for scripts that have yet to be written, the agent or producer is not likely to give it much attention, as no matter how brilliant it may be, it still provides no proof that the writer can write a screenplay. In rare instances where unknown writers actually succeed in selling treatments, better-known writers are often hired to write the screenplay.

Writers are best off forgetting treatments altogether and paying attention to screenplays. To that end it is worth reiterating that before writing a screenplay a writer needs to write an outline.

In many ways, it is harder to outline a screenplay than it is to write one, for if any part of writing can be said to be fun, it is that which follows the careful process of outlining. That's when the writer truly meets his characters for the first time, hears their dialogue, and now and again is surprised by the tricks they play on him. Moreover, each day as he writes his quota of pages and adds them to the pile, he derives satisfaction from knowing soon he'll have a draft, something he can hold in his hand and thump on the table. You can't thump an idea, a concept, a notion against any table. Only pages will do.

To create a useful outline, on the other hand, takes lots of time and results in precious few pages; the writer is denied the comforting vision of that ever-accumulating pile of pulp. Outlining is like trying to carry steam in a bucket. In outlines writers deal only with wisps of actions, ghosts of characters, translucent ideas, intangible quantities.

And from these ethereal ingredients they are required to fashion solid, shapely tales to entice, seduce, and enthrall audiences. Is it any wonder outlining is among writing's most daunting, frustrating experiences?

In many ways, however, it is among the most necessary.

A still-admired but largely burned-out American playwright not long ago revealed that whereas early in his career he carefully, painstakingly wrote detailed outlines, more recently—presumably because he is now so vastly experienced—he just sits down and writes his plays from scratch. Tragically, his current works appear to be written precisely that way. They are scattered, haphazard, disjointed, disorganized; the playwright clearly cares not as much as he used to about his plays, and neither do audiences.

Screenwriter Steven De Souza (creator of, among many other projects, the *Die Hard* franchise) told me that he likes to write what he calls an uncritical first draft. This is a draft he produces at lightning speed, with no attention to spelling, punctuation, or grammar. He attempts to get everything into it that he possibly can that relates in any way at all to the story.

Inevitably these drafts come in way too long: perhaps a hundred sixty pages or more. De Souza then places the script in a drawer and does not look at it for a period lasting perhaps a couple of months. Then he takes the script out of the drawer and reads it. Invariably, he sees half of it for what it is: trash. That thrills him, because he realizes he has half of a really promising script. He knows now also what the script is about, who the protagonist truly is, and the answers to a host of other questions.

If this works for De Souza it may work for you. The trick is to try it and try also other methods and find out.

Outlining is just what it implies: the construction of a broad overview of the story line; a list of scenes; a shapely catalogue of events, incidents, and anecdotes collectively constituting the tale's bones. Outlines need as much detail as necessary so that the writer—nobody else—may fully know his tale. It is possible to become so preoccupied with detail that the outline becomes a substitute for the script itself. In such an instance a screenplay risks appearing mechanical, cold, disconnected, aloof. It may all fit together neatly enough, but it will lack warmth and spirit.

The challenge of outlines is to fill them as richly as possible while at the same time leaving room for surprises. Outlines should contain little actual dialogue.

An outline ought to serve as a tentative guide. If in the midst of writing the actual script a better idea visits itself upon the writer, he ought to seize it.

During the process of outlining, a point arrives at which the writer may feel he's almost ready; and when he feels that way, he probably is ready. In writing, as in life, there is no such state as completely, perfectly ready.

Among the biggest mistakes writers can make is to rein in a script that strays from its outline.

Principle 44: The outline was then; the script is now.

Instead of restricting the imagination during scripting, writers should do just the opposite: set themselves and their narrative free. Roam widely and wildly and stay open to the surprises that inevitably arise. The tried and true is often trying and truly dull. Don't stifle your imagination by trying to haul a story that runs off the tracks back to some old and hoary previous intellectual notion. It is not the running off but the tracks that are the real problem.

Scene Cards

Another technique for planning a screenplay involves the use of scene cards. Scene cards and outlines are not mutually exclusive methodologies; writers can usefully integrate the two.

A scene card is just what it says: an index card containing a number relating to its position within the sequence of scenes throughout the film, the setting of the particular scene, the names of the major characters appearing in it, and a brief description—one or two sentences—of the action.

Many writers find scene cards far more useful, far easier to work with than the traditional outline with its numbered list of scenes. For one thing, with scene cards it's simpler to experiment, to switch scenes' order, to shuffle them around. Scene cards provide writers with a hands-on feel for their story.

Occasionally, a writer will know that a scene is needed in a particular place within a tale, but he may not be certain precisely how that scene should be mounted, what action it should contain, what characters ought to participate. With scene cards it's easy to sketch several such scenes and keep them handy until, in the broader context arrived at later, it becomes clear which scene serves best, and where precisely it may fit.

With scene cards, again it's easier to try things out, and trying things out is what screenwriting—especially tale assembly—is all about.

A typical movie contains perhaps sixty such scenes, although that depends upon what precisely the writer considers to be a scene. One writer's scene is another's sequence; one writer's sequence is another's shot. By my own estimation, a scene is a unified piece of action in a single setting with its own clear beginning, middle, and end. It can be as brief as in *The Godfather* where the man wakes up to discover his prize racehorse's bloody head in his bed: asleep, awake, horror. Or it can be as complex as the finish to *The Bridge on the River Kwai*, where Alec Guinness looks proudly to his completed bridge, then to the abandoned dynamite plunger, then to the train clattering toward the overpass. He races madly to the detonator and falls upon it, destroying his own creation, the bridge, which in a flash he has come now to regard as evil.

> **Principle 45: Every scene in every film is a mini movie all by itself, with its own beginning, middle, and end.**

Scene cards are particularly handy in helping writers maintain an overall sense of their tale. A writer needs to be able to skip over this part and that one when he is not quite certain, and keep on moving forward in order to find the key plot points and other pivotal moments. He needs to be able to live with a certain uncertainty.

Scene cards enable the writer to accomplish this in the same way film editors assemble an incomplete film, one for which certain scenes have not yet returned from the lab. They utilize a technique called slugging, that is, inserting a blank piece of film into a missing scene's place until the actual footage becomes available.

Writers working with scene cards can similarly slug scenes; they can insert a blank card, or one with merely some superficial suggestions. In this way they can move forward without becoming bogged down in the infinite minutiae at the heart of all filmmaking.

Writers, as indicated, can also integrate outlining and scene cards. A writer starts a script from a carefully constructed outline. Without preparing scene cards, he proceeds directly from the outline to write the first draft of the script. Then, upon running into trouble (as writers seem almost invariably to do around the end of the middle, approximately two-thirds of the way through), he returns to the beginning of the script and spends a morning, or a day, scene-carding his tale as if the story did not already exist, as if he were inventing it for the first time. He creates scene cards from as much of the script as is already written. The physical manipulation, the representation of the story on crisp, firm cards, can provide the momentum necessary to push the story's leading edge through the barrier that's got it blocked.

Rewriting

After all the planning, outlining, and scene-carding, after a first draft is written, at long last it can be rewritten.

What's more, after it has been rewritten it can be rewritten again.

Principle 46: Real writing, especially reel writing, is rewriting.

No writer ever sits down to start a new project without thinking, This time, at long last, I'm going to get it perfectly right the first time. Sure, I may go a little more slowly. Yes, I may move forward with just a tad more deliberation, but what I write will stay written exactly as it is written forever and a day.

This, however, never turns out to be the case.

Sometimes a student tells me he's keenly resistant to the process of outlining, that he prefers instead to write an unplanned, oversized, rambling, rumbling, overblown first draft. He acknowledges he's not sure precisely how the tale will unravel, but cannot figure out any way to get into it other than to get into it. If he feels strongly enough, I may encourage him to get started. If all he gets out of the experience is a sprawling, brawling, unwieldy, all-over-the-place rough draft, he can use it as an outline and through massive rewriting eventually sculpt the tale into its fullest form.

Whatever a writer's eccentricities, there is no escape from the need to rewrite. No matter what techniques a writer employs, eventually he ends up rewriting. Rewriting is so integral to writing's nature that writers find themselves rewriting their pictures in their minds years after they have been filmed, distributed, and exhibited.

So it is possible, therefore, to rewrite too much. A script can be written over and over until the life has been written out of it. More often than not, I suspect, this kind of manic rewriting owes something to a writer's reluctance to let go of his tale. For one thing, no one will criticize a script until the writer actually finishes it and gives it to somebody to read. Eventually a writer has to take a stand.

More narrowly, and every bit as problematic, is the tendency among many writers to rewrite each day all the pages from the very beginning. This can cause the front end of a script to become slick and brassy while the back end, instead of getting closer, seems to grow increasingly distant.

It's a wise writer who avoids going back to the beginning every day.

Francis Ford Coppola, widely celebrated for his directing, is also a first-rate writer. He has a hard rule about rewriting. Write page one, and then place it facedown. Write page two and put it facedown atop page one. In this way a writer should work his way through the entire script. In other words, according to Coppola, don't rewrite at all until you've got a complete first draft, no matter how awkward and unwieldy that draft may be.

Later, you'll rewrite.

To my own taste, and based on the habits of numerous working writers I have come to know, this rule strikes me as harsh. When many writers sit down to address their day's task, the first thing they do is rewrite the work they did the previous day. Wisely, however, they resist the urge to go farther back than that. With yesterday's pages rewritten, they can begin writing today's new pages. Tomorrow they will rewrite today's pages and write an equal number of new pages. In this manner writers can leapfrog their way through a respectable first draft.

Granted, it's hard—for many writers perhaps even impossible—to resist looking only at yesterday's work before going on to today's. Yet too much preoccupation with previously written pages can prevent writers from moving forward in their tale; it undermines momentum.

Perhaps the most difficult part of rewriting is fulfilling the specifications of a producer. Most writers are, after all, only too aware that though they may have been paid money for their script, there's no guarantee it will actually be filmed. Sometimes, therefore, they all too eagerly agree to any and all changes suggested by their producer in the wrongheaded notion that this will somehow enhance the script's chance for production.

To be sure, some producers are tremendously adept at helping writers find their way. Sadly, however, too many executives ask writers for specific changes that even they themselves—the producers who are asking for the changes—do not believe are worthy.

Writers should be mindful in this regard of a Hollywood phenomenon called "the hydrant effect." This means that every producer and every producer's assistant wants to pee on his script, that is, wants to put his mark on it, so as to be able to claim later that he was the one who suggested this, that, or the other thing that accounts for its success. That's why producers sometimes ask for changes they actually believe are unwise. Too often they fear that if they merely congratulate a writer on his performance, the producer will appear to be lacking insight and creativity. It requires a certain courage to read a draft and say: This is fine, let's shoot it.

Sometimes producers make up the suggestions as they go along. The script is basically fine but will be better if: all the characters are rewritten as Armenians; the tale is reset in the future (or past, or present); the locale is changed from Ohio to Latvia, or the seventh moon of Saturn.

Writers, ever eager to please, ever eager to see their script move from ink on the page to light on the screen, too hastily agree. Armenians? Of course the characters should be Armenians. I'll have them all Armenian for you by later this afternoon. The future? Sensational! Latvia? Perfect!

The problem here, of course, is not only that such acquiescence fails to enhance the chances the film will be shot. It actually militates against them. This is because producers subconsciously want their writers to defend the creative choices in their script. The producer paid the writer good money; he must be a good writer, he must have good reason for putting into the script whatever he has put into it. If a writer too willingly agrees completely and totally to amend those pages, where's his commitment to his work thus far? How soon will he abandon the writing he's embracing all so eagerly today? Is he a screenwriter or a stenographer?

The solution? I recommend writers adopt what I can only characterize as the yes-but approach. Yes, we can reset the tale in Latvia, but then we'll lose this, that, and the other thing. Yes, we can rewrite the characters as Armenians, but then how do we explain this turn, that turn, and the other turn over there? Sure, we can set the story in the past, or future, but then we have to change all these fundamental aspects relating to aspects we once admired.

While writers ought never be intransigent regarding script changes and rewrites, neither should they abandon backbone. Producers, aware of it or not, appreciate a writer who stands behind his writing.

That's why writers are wise to fall back upon what I call the old truth ploy. They serve themselves best by reacting to producers' questions and suggestions with honesty.

Experimentation

Writers can deal more easily with rewriting—indeed, with all aspects of creative expression—if they view a screenplay for what it truly is: an elaborate experiment.

Years ago I was writing a comedy for a studio. Having completed a first draft, I met with the director to discuss rewrites. After complimenting those aspects of the script he favored, he suggested areas that needed to be changed. As he went through the first of several such changes, I obediently checked off the sections that concerned him, eliminating passages he wished eliminated.

After a few moments he looked up and asked: "Aren't you going to argue with me?"

I told him that I would argue with him just as soon as I disagreed with him.

Principle 47: Maturing as a writer means more than merely learning to throw away; it means learning to love to throw away.

We continued reviewing the script and finally arrived at an area of disagreement where we nearly came to blows. Nevertheless, there blossomed a grudging mutual respect for each other. He didn't ask for changes just to ask for changes; I didn't pretend to agree with him when in fact I disagreed with him, nor did I defend passages I regarded as indefensible. As in any collaborative enterprise, the individual egos must become submerged in the collective ego that belongs to the whole project.

How does a writer determine once and for all whether a line, a character, a bit of action, or any other aspect of a script is worthy or worth discarding? There are often arguments on both sides.

As I argue repeatedly, the answer is always the same: integration. If the line, the character, or the action moves the story forward, it belongs in the script. What do writers do, though, when they are uncertain about whether or not the business is truly integrated?

A useful rule comes from, of all the unlikely places, the United States Department of Agriculture. What does a citizen do upon opening a jar of home-preserved food only to discover something suspicious such as bubbles, gas, discoloration, odor? In the case of salmonella, tasting even just the tiniest portion could cause a healthy adult to become seriously ill. With botulism, it could just as easily prove fatal.

The USDA came up with a rule that serves not only home-preservers of fruits and vegetables but also writers.

Principle 48: When in doubt, throw it out.

Clearly, there's no problem deciding whether or not to include in a screenplay material that is positively, absolutely vital to the tale, i.e., material that is integrated. Similarly, material that is obviously superfluous poses no problem; good writers simply throw it away. It's the in-between stuff that gets us into trouble. The USDA rule addresses this issue squarely: If there's any doubt at all as to whether or not to include a bit of business, lose that business.

Sometimes writers anguishing over a particular element's appropriateness in a script might do well to take a blank sheet of paper, draw a line down the center, and list all the affirmative reasons on one side, all the negatives on the other. Often a pattern emerges, clearly demonstrating to the writer the need to keep—or to lose—the bit.

There may be a host of reasons favoring inclusion. On the other side there may be but one lonely reason supporting exclusion. That single reason, however, may be important enough all by itself to warrant tossing the bit. For example, the one and only reason militating against a piece of business might be that it slows the story.

Anything that slows story belongs in the wastebasket.

A writer cannot stand outside his script, intellectualizing about it, trying to calculate in advance what will work and what will not. He's got to roll up his sleeves and try stuff out. If something ends up eliminated—a character, a scene, a line of dialogue—it does not mean the experiment was a failure.

Quite the contrary, discovering that something does not work represents just another kind of experimental success.

Experiments are performed to determine a specific result, to learn something, to discover some precise piece of information. Thomas Alva Edison tried all sorts of filaments for the lightbulb, from sewing thread to human hair, until he stumbled upon one that—inside an evacuated globe—worked quite well. Was the experiment with human hair a failure because it proved to be a poor filament? Quite the contrary, the experiment was a total success, because Edison found out what he needed to know, that human hair did not serve his purpose and he needed, therefore, to search further.

Screenwriting is no different. If a writer tries something out and ends up throwing it away, the experiment can nonetheless be considered a success. The writer has determined what he needed to determine.

Gratitude versus Attitude

This book argues that writing is a wondrous—if often painful—journey of self-discovery. Understanding the importance of identity is crucial for writers. As ultimately they write only of themselves, it follows that a clearer, stronger sense of self helps produce clearer, stronger screenplays.

However, writers need contemplate not one but two identities.

First, there is the artistic, creative self who writes the scripts and also "acts" in them, at least in his head, portraying not only the protagonist but all the other characters as well.

Second, there is the professional self. This is the writer/entrepreneur, the responsible working screenwriter who embraces the daunting, competitive dream-trafficking dodge with intelligence, circumspection, and tolerance. He confronts with serenity the maw and muck and mayhem marking the professional film and TV community.

Principle 49: A writer's job is to place himself in the minds and bodies of other people and think and act as they do.

This principle is true, of course, for every character in every script. It is also every bit as true for the professional writer dealing with the "characters" in the show business community: agents, managers, producers, story editors, development executives, attorneys, studio and network vice presidents.

Film is, as I argue repeatedly, not about fact but feeling. Writers, like all artists, are passionate souls who experience their emotions deeply. From time to time they soar and rejoice; every bit as often they wallow in depression and despair.

Frustration and disappointment come with the territory and have got to be accepted by every writer. More than that, they have to be exploited as part of a writer's arsenal for expression.

However, obsession with heartache and rage to the exclusion of affirmation and healing militates against an otherwise successful writing life. Indeed, it can bring a promising career to a grinding halt. Too often it causes writers to become their own worst enemies. Hollywood does not have to destroy writers; writers are perfectly capable of destroying themselves, and often with style and aplomb. This happens not only among inexperienced writers, but also among the highest-paid, most widely celebrated professionals.

Rather than squander the energy derived from the frustration that inevitably accompanies creative expression in any format, writers need to channel that power, to exploit it in the interest of charging their work with verve so that it dazzles and sparkles more powerfully than they ever imagined it might.

Save the Rage for the Page

At UCLA's film school and all around the world—at screenwriting seminars, conferences, lectures, panels, and workshops—I am asked every imaginable question regarding every screenwriting issue: story, character, dialogue, agents, packaging, contracts, commissions, options, and more.

Sometimes the queries address scripts I have read. Whatever the question I always try my best—with uneven success—to answer as precisely as I can.

There are two questions in particular, however, I steadfastly refuse to answer. In fact, they are broad and narrow versions of the same question:

1) Do I have what it takes to be a writer?
2) Is this particular script worth revising or should I just abandon it?

It is not up to anybody but the writer himself to decide whether or not he has what it takes to be a writer. I have met writers who showed no early promise but over time achieved a creative critical mass that blossomed into a stunning career.

Sometimes I read scripts that appear to be hopeless but upon revision suddenly crystallize and achieve vast success.

It is so easy for one writer (or writer/educator) to tell another that his script is going nowhere and ought to be abandoned. He might glibly advise: Why throw good effort after bad? Cut your losses and pull the plug. Chalk it up to drill; value it as experience.

A writer may, however, have some substantial amount of time, toil, and talent invested in a script, to say nothing of the soul and the spirit of the artist that resides in every work of creative expression. For all he or anyone else knows, it all may come together in that very next draft.

On the other hand, a writer may be wasting his time, poring over work that ought truly to be let go. It can be a mistake for a writer to keep rehashing the same old material. I know writers who've rewritten one script over and over again dozens of times over dozens of years.

Thus, as easy as it is for one writer to tell another to abandon a script, he can just as cavalierly tell him to stick with it. Moreover, advising him to stick with it might be every bit as faithless as telling him to quit.

Who's to decide?

Clearly, responsibility for such a choice rests solely on the shoulders of the one who bears the burden of its consequences: the writer. It is he, after all, who ends up doing the heavy lifting, the arduous rewriting of a script that ought to be cut loose or, with a heavy heart, cutting loose a script that might well benefit from yet one more rewrite. For the sake of success, not to mention sanity, writers need to learn not merely to tolerate but to embrace the struggle. I have met a handful who were so embittered, so rancid with rage, so bloated with pessimism and contempt for themselves and for everyone around them, that I strenuously had to resist advising them to sprint as far from the movie business as it is possible to travel.

I remember one writer who was where every new writer wishes to be. He had a respectable agent eager to represent a script he had written. The problem was that in its earliest version he had collaborated on the story with another writer. The two had had a falling-out; a residue of ill will remained between them. Moving ahead with this project required the consent of the other writer, as he still had legitimate claims to some portion of the copyright. "The greedy bastard wants twenty-five percent plus shared story credit," the writer complained to me.

I asked him what he thought was fair.

"I don't doubt he's entitled to shared story credit," he allowed, however reluctantly, "but as far as the points are concerned, I don't believe he ought to get more than fifteen."

"That's the dispute?" I asked. "You believe he should get fifteen and he wants twenty-five? Offer him twenty. It's in the vicinity of what you consider reasonable. Consider also that whatever his percentage turns out to be, there's every possibility that nothing will come of it anyway. It may well turn out to be twenty percent of nothing. In the meantime you've got an agent eager to circulate your script. Even if you don't sell it, you begin to create your reputation and launch a career."

The writer protested. "I'd rather have the whole project scuttled than see this guy get twenty-five percent."

As patiently as I could, I explained to him that he was not merely a fool but a damned fool. For disagreement over five phantom percentage points of a purported pact that didn't even exist, he preferred to ease comfortably into the warm, soothing marinade of outrage.

Anger has its place in our lives. There are excellent causes for anger; if we're never mad we're brain-dead. Even Mother Teresa sometimes got angry. Anger is a natural, wholly human, and in some instances even a useful, productive aspect of the human condition. It can motivate a writer to do what needs to be done. It can be part of the emotional engine that drives a screenplay. What anger must never be, however, is the organizing principle of a personality. That needs instead to derive—especially for artists—from quite the opposite: affirmation, healing, and love.

Writers need to save their passion for their scripts. Energy devoted to hating agents, reviling directors, loathing actors, producers, executives and every other manner of collaborator should instead be directed to tale and character and all the rest of the art, craft, and business of screenwriting.

I once recommended a truly excellent script to a producer who returned it to the writer with a basically benign rejection letter that included an innocuous and misguided comment characterizing some of the dialogue as "occasionally stilted."

Whether the producer was right or wrong is a matter of opinion. The producer had done what was important: He had given time, attention, and consideration to the writer and his work. The writer responded with an incendiary letter decrying the perceived insult, denouncing the commentary and its provider, assigning him and his company to one or another circle of hell.

What useful purpose is served by a tantrum? How does this writer expect to succeed in an arena as difficult and competitive as screenwriting if he assigns authority over his work and his self-perception to strangers?

I can tell you one result of the angry response: I never again recommended this writer to another producer. I saw that if he doesn't receive precisely the reaction he seeks, he flies into a rage and makes a dreadful impression. He reflects poorly not only upon himself but also upon me, a person merely trying, however feebly, to offer such support as I am able.

There is an ocean of difference between the merely solid spec writer—a writer capable of turning out a crafty original speculative script—and a writer who can work with producers. Distinctly not of the latter class is the writer who creates a promising script but then flies into paroxysms of vein-popping rage when someone suggests that the girl's dress should be green when the script indicates quite clearly that it is red.

A former student and current friend, screenwriter Gregory Widen, calls this "the red-dress/green-dress syndrome."

"Green? A green dress? Are you an idiot? That's the stupidest thing I ever heard of! Green! I wrote *red* dress! Quit tampering with my vision! Quit marching roughshod across the broad, shining terrain of my creativity with your mud-caked, blood-splotched jackboots!"

Writers like this burn themselves out before they have a chance to burn out everyone around them. They burn themselves out before they even catch fire in the first place. They cannot see beyond the horizon of their own frustration and heartache. They do not understand that the professional film and television community is actually quite small and that if you burn your bridges you burn also your britches.

From time to time I have worked in the capacity of producer, supervising the development of scripts for various production companies. I recall winning a generous development deal for the writer of a family comedy. The executives entrusted me to serve as the project's den mother, alternately coddling and scolding the writer as appropriate, generally shepherding the project through the development process.

The studio executives were ready to turn the writer loose to write a full draft—which was exactly his desire—except they needed, if only to satisfy their egos, to "approve" the outline. This way they could do what studio executives do: pretend to be creatively involved in ways that they are not. (See our earlier discussion regarding the hydrant effect.) It is common among experienced writers to collude with producers in this ruse, then down the line perhaps trade it in for a modicum of clout on a creative issue that concerns them.

The meeting opened with the usual banter and repartee—mindless sports chatter ("How about that game!") until at last the so-called discussion came around to the script. "Now remember," the executives said to the writer, "to make the protagonist strong."

Clearly they wanted a simple nod, a generic reassurance, and they would have then been happy to approve the writing of the draft. All the writer had to do was tilt his head forward and pretend to understand. One minute later these executives would not even remember that we'd had the meeting, much less what had been discussed.

Instead of nodding and making nice, however, instead of murmuring a benign and benevolent, inconsequential consent, with beads of sweat forming on his brow the writer squawked, "Strong? What do you mean?"

"You don't know what 'strong' means?" they asked him. "Forceful. Willful. Adamant. Firm. Uncompromising. Committed. A fellow with a point of view resonating with conviction. A man who doesn't waffle. A guy who's not easily swayed. A fellow who doesn't flit from this to that. Ballsy. Hairy-chested. Vigorous. Get it?"

Instead of nodding sagely and asserting that he got it, the writer stammered, "Not really."

The meeting dragged on, with the guys in suits growing nervous about the guy in jeans and his script. I practically had to carry him out of the room, promising to the executives that we'd be back for another meeting the following afternoon and pick up where we'd left off.

At the subsequent meeting we promptly won the go-ahead. This was because, under the threat of death, I'd compelled the writer to agree to nod and say yes whenever I looked at him, and otherwise not to speak at all, unless I tugged on my left earlobe.

Writer as Victim

Too many writers who win success in television or film come to believe they have a birthright to employment; they expect it to continue into eternity. They come to depend on guaranteed money, referred to as up-front money, and often cease doing what every writer must do: speculate, take chances, continue to create without guarantee of sale. Writers need to learn that when action (screenwriting) is married irrevocably to expected outcome (dollars) frustration and disappointment are the inevitable result.

I had a conversation with a writer of substantial repute. He is the author of one of the all-time box office blockbuster successes, a movie seen by more than a billion people around the world.

Nevertheless, for more decades since then he has not worked a lick. He confessed to me with rare and splendid candor about the two reasons his career had gone cold. First, after his monumental success, he got too big for his britches, fired the independent agent who had faithfully struggled for him during his scuffling days, and succumbed to the siren song of a star-studded megafirm, where promptly after signing him they put him on Ignore.

Beyond that, he lost the will to speculate. He had grown fat—metaphorically and literally—on TV deals, where money is always delivered up front, in advance of actual writing, and rich feature development deals, where a writer may win a sizable advance before he is required to apply butt to chair and fingers to keys.

A former student of mine who has achieved astonishing success with a wildly acclaimed comedy tells me that his greatest struggle now is to avoid the distractions—rich rewrite assignments and plush development deals that are not likely to lead to actual pictures—and churn out his goal of three daily pages of speculative draft.

This is precisely what all writers—experienced and not—must do. They must write scripts. Contract or not, writers write. They don't sit around and wait for somebody else to tell them what to do. They don't become slaves to studios or networks or even to universities. They assert themselves in their own lives as their own masters. The clearest way to do this is to continue to create material, no matter what. These are the writers who succeed and whose careers are characterized by longevity.

If you sit where I sit, you see too many writers flare brightly and then burn out. The ticket for sustaining a career is speculative, self-motivated writing.

When they're busy with their writing, there's no time to bemoan their fate, to feel sorry for themselves, to wallow in self-pity, to contemplate self-destruction, to contemplate destruction of studios and studio bosses and studio bosses' nannies.

A winning writer's winning attitude is Write On!

If a writer is fortunate enough to earn money in the screenplay dodge, he should save the bulk of that money to buy time against those periods that he is "between assignments."

He should use that time to do three things: write, write, and write.

He should be grateful for the privilege of being mistreated in this business. Far worse than mistreatment is no treatment at all: the gnawing, hollow horror of being ignored.

Satisfaction

Writers should never seek satisfaction.

Consider an incident reported in the *New York Times.* A vigorous elderly gent—with a shock of snow-white hair—entered the Museum of Modern Art carrying an attaché case. He rode the elevator to the second floor and made his way along the corridor until he stood before a vast abstract canvas, part of the museum's permanent collection, a work that had hung in that same spot for the better part of forty years.

He set his case upon the floor, snapped it open, and withdrew a vial of turpentine, another of linseed oil, various tubes of paint, several paintbrushes, and an artist's palette. From the tubes he squeezed upon the palette multicolored dollops of pigment.

By this time, of course, the museum's security officers had been summoned. Unobtrusively a pair of uniformed guards assembled behind the man at the rear of the gallery. Upon observing him lift a brush and poise it over the canvas, they sprang into action, slapping handcuffs on him. They informed him, first, that he was under arrest and, second, that he had the right to remain silent and, third, that if he should nonetheless choose to speak, anything he said could and would be used against him in a court of law.

All the while he protested, claiming to be the very same internationally renowned artist who scores of years earlier had painted the very same canvas hanging before them. Amid their prisoner's remonstrations, the security officers carted him away to the local precinct house, where after an hour or so he was able to summon an associate who could vouch for the fact that he was indeed the artist he claimed to be.

It seems he had visited the museum a week earlier, taken a look at his painting, and decided that it needed a bit of a brushup in one corner.

Here is the hallmark of a true artist!

Celebrated worldwide, wealthy beyond his wildest dreams, he is still not satisfied with his work. He still wants to rewrite—in this instance repaint—a renowned and respected work created almost half a lifetime earlier.

I met a prominent screenwriter at a conference who happened to be adapting for the screen the bestselling novel written by another writer attending the conference. The novelist lived in a remote part of the Northwest. The adapter told me he'd traveled to the author's home to spend a few days reviewing the book and discussing the adaptation.

He noticed on the author's desk a copy of the novel with handwritten notes inscribed in the margins. He asked the author if he was preparing a new edition. The author told him that he was not; the changes, he explained, were only for himself. He wanted to get the book—a triumphant bestseller that had won a lucrative film contract and would lead ultimately to the release of a successful film—just exactly right, even if only for himself.

Screenwriters, painters, and all purveyors of creative expression are well advised to quit seeking satisfaction. If they hope to maintain even a semblance of sanity, they need to learn how to live with dissonance, discord, and a generally unsettled opinion of themselves and their work.

Fall on your face if you must, but rejoice that it is your own face and nobody else's. Be grateful that you have the energy and spirit—not to mention the courage—to soar high enough to crash once again.

Chapter 14

. . . .

Emotion

Film is for feeling.

There's more to it than that, of course, but first and last there is that. Moreover, what audiences feel need not be pleasure. Frighten the folks, make them cry, make them angry; they will stand in line to see your movie. Human beings need regularly to experience strong emotions; it's how we know we are alive. As surely as muscles atrophy from disuse, so also do feelings.

Consider the movie theater a gymnasium for the senses. It is an arena not for serenity and logic, not for intellect and reason, but for passion.

In his insightful *Ascent of Man*, mathematician and philosopher Jacob Bronowski posits an insightful theory into film's nature and origin. The caves at Altamira, Spain, whose walls are emblazoned with primitive paintings, were not domiciles, Bronowski notes. The tribes did not live in these caves but retreated to them from time to time to celebrate the paintings.

The paintings' subject is the local fauna, in particular the bisonlike creatures that were the hunters' prey. The tribes' very survival depended upon success in the hunt. The animals' flesh provided protein; the skins supplied shelter and clothing.

The beasts, however, were far larger than any individual caveman. They also bore lethal racks of antlers with which to gore predators. They strode on hooves capable of trampling men. How could mere humans, Bronowski inquires, conquer animals stronger, larger, swifter than they?

The hunters' advantage was that special trait belonging to humans alone: the ability to cooperate intellectually and devise strategy. Stealthily they would approach the herd from downwind and then surround it. At precisely the proper moment, they would drive it in the direction of comrades lying in wait, armed with spears.

What would a man do, even one armed with a spear, when faced by a herd of charging buffalo? The natural reaction would be panic and flight.

The hunters needed to learn how to control and overcome that panic. They needed to train their emotions so that instead of fleeing they would collectively stand their ground. The caves provided a place for the hunters to rehearse their feelings. The chambers were a safe arena to experience intense, frightful emotions without risk.

The inner enclaves housing the paintings were accessible through twisting tunnels that rendered them opaque; light was provided by tallow-fueled torches. With the torches flickering somewhat in the manner of a movie projector, the images must have appeared to be in motion. Indeed, the bison on the walls were drawn with multiple sets of legs, as if to suggest motion.

These paintings are, in a sense, the precursor to the animated film, and the caves are the original movie theaters, minus popcorn and validated parking.

In the caves' security the hunters could allow their emotions to simulate those experienced in an actual hunt. Later, in the hunt, recalling the cave experience they could steel themselves against the natural, instinctual response: panic. The caves and their paintings provided them with the opportunity to simulate the panic so that they were familiar with it when it arose during the real hunt, and they could therefore stand their ground instead of dropping the spears and running away just as fast as they could.

Stampeding bison today pose no great danger to modern men and women. What authentic peril confronts us? Terrorism? Murder? In an everyday sense, the greatest immediate true hazard in our lives has to be the automobile. Since 1945 alone more than ten times as many Americans have died in car crashes as in all the collected battlegrounds of World War II.

Is it any wonder movies are replete with car crashes?

What else besides auto wrecks represents a threat to our lives and our serenity? Crime. Disease. War. Broken hearts. Broken families.

Are these not perpetually the stuff of films? Reiterating, the movie theater is the modern-day version of the primitives' cave. A film is a life simulator enabling modern men and women to rehearse their emotions, to experience desperate, painful sensations in an environment of total safety.

Movies, therefore, offer a lot more than mere fun, though the best of them provide that, too. Like the cave people, our very survival depends upon our ability to process intensely painful emotions. If movie art permits us to accomplish this, then film is as fundamental to our spirits and souls as food is to our flesh and bone. Cultures deprived of artistic expression warp and distort as surely as famine misshapes children's bodies.

The hard fact is that our daily lives are racked not so much with pain as with tedium. Our hours overflow with trivial chores. Sadly, the predominant feeling experienced by most people most of the time is no feeling at all but rather the absence of feeling: numbness, boredom. If art is first and foremost concerned with feeling, it should come as no surprise that artists are people who experience feelings intensely. When they feel bad they feel despondent, even suicidal. When they feel good they feel ecstatic.

Screenwriters should embrace screenwriting for what it is: the business of feeling.

Ego

As asserted in the introduction, writers hate to write; the prospect each day of addressing blank pages or glowing computer screens fills every one of us with dread. People who work alone, cooped up by themselves in their own little closet day after day, trafficking in their feelings, marketing their emotions, peddling their dreams, easily develop into obstinate, prickly creatures. Fantasizing as a profession is not without its hazards. Foremost among these is the ever-diminishing capacity to discriminate the real from the reel.

At a recent dinner party, while I was recounting some breathtakingly clever anecdote, my wife, privy to the actual events, interrupted, exclaiming, "But that's not how it really was."

Instead of overturning the table in rage precipitated by her stepping

on my punch line, in patient, measured tones I rejoined that selected embellishments help tell a tale better.

"There's a difference," she said, "between selected embellishments and
pure fantasy."

"Pure fantasy," I insisted, "is what I do for a living. It pays our rent. It's
my work."

"You're not at work now," she said. "You're having dinner with
friends."

Simmering in the sweet sauté of my superior intellectual juices, I silently contemplated what nonwriters can never understand: For a writer,
dinner with friends is work; lying in the sun is work; visiting the powder
room is work; sleeping and dreaming are work. William Faulkner is said
to have divorced his first wife because she failed to understand that when
he appeared to be staring idly out the window he was actually hard at
work.

Is it any wonder that people who embrace so grandiose a calling are
likely to be awkward when it comes to social skills?

This difficulty daily confronts all working writers. For screenwriters,
however, the problem is exponentially more troublesome. Novelists and
poets, for example, enjoy total control over their writing. Their work is
their work; nobody comes between artist and art, nobody "improves" it
or "tweaks" it except the writers themselves. Nobody is brought in to
"punch it up" or "tone it down." To them accrues all credit and blame. To
a somewhat more limited extent this is true also for playwrights, who,
unlike screenwriters, own the copyright to their scripts. They are consulted
on every script change. They are also present week after week during re-
hearsals.

Not a word in a play can be changed without the playwright's consent.
This is a far cry from the experience of screenwriters, who, on those rare
occasions when one of their scripts actually films, may even be banned
from visiting the production.

Hence, the riddle: What's the difference between a janitor and a
screenwriter? Answer: The janitor is allowed on the set.

Screenplays are rewritten mercilessly, perhaps dozens of times, even
when scripts are not filmed, often until the work is no longer recognizable.
Screenwriters have more than ample occasion to suffer, therefore. Such
working conditions are not likely to attract balanced, integrated, fulfilled
personalities.

Some years ago my longtime partner at UCLA, Professor Hal Ackerman, was introduced to master screenwriter Julius J. Epstein, whose credits include, among many others, *Casablanca*.

"Oh, Mr. Epstein," Hal gushed in breathy awe, "I am so thrilled to meet you. All I or any of my film-phony friends ever hope is that just once in our lives we might become associated as you have with something bigger than ourselves, something timeless, something celebrated into eternity like *Casablanca*."

Did Epstein say "Thank you very much," or "How kind of you to say so"?

He did not.

Instead he said, "*Casablanca Schmasablanca*. I'll tell you about *Casablanca*, since you brought it up. You know the part in the end where Claude Rains tells Bogart the thing about a beautiful friendship and all that? Originally it was supposed to be something else, a line was added that made the whole thing much more effective, something I had worked out at great length, in considerable detail, but no, Bogart had his own ideas—isn't that an actor for you?—and Curtiz, the director, he had some notion about some other thing—isn't that a director for you?—and even my own agent, in flagrant betrayal of his client—isn't that an agent for you?—conspired with the rest of them against me and I tell you the picture would have been so much better if they had left it exactly as my brother Philip and I had written it."

There's a working writer for you. Not only incapable of fielding a simple compliment, he sees in it instead an occasion for griping. Griping about what? About how the producers and agents and actors ruined his work scores of years ago. Precisely what work did they ruin? *Casablanca*.

Please, God, let somebody ruin my work like they ruined *Casablanca*.

William Goldman is another example of a rich, respected writer with vast acclaim in fiction, nonfiction, and film (*Butch Cassidy and the Sundance Kid*, *All the President's Men*, *Marathon Man*, *The Princess Bride*, and many others) who in print manages shamelessly to carp and complain about how miserably he has been mistreated on project after project.

Goldman's invaluable book *Adventures in the Screen Trade* eloquently articulates his experiences writing films. No screenwriter—veteran or rookie—should fail to own a copy. Still, for all its insights and contributions it is also replete with abuses and indignities heaped unceremoniously upon the beleaguered writer by folks famous and obscure. Dustin Hoffman was rude when they worked together on a couple of pictures. Worse still, Robert Redford wouldn't even give Goldman his home phone number.

Goldman laments that he couldn't just pick up the phone and call Redford directly; he had to go through Redford's secretary! Granted, to a literary lion like Goldman it might prove a tad off-putting, but does it truly merit such rage as to record in a memoir?

This is not to say, again, that ego does not occupy its right and righteous place in the making of worthy art.

Consider, for example, my late father, a musician who enjoyed an impressive career as a section member in major orchestras and also as a player on literally hundreds of recordings. Some years ago he put out a record of solo performances. A copy of the CD arrived at my house at precisely the same moment as my beloved but jaded uncle Morris, who spotted the album.

"Your father makes records?"

"But you know he's made hundreds of recordings," I said.

"Solo?"

"He's a bass player," I said, as if dear Morris didn't already know that. "He's a crusader, a warrior for bass and bassists. This record's part of his campaign to win respect for the instrument not merely as background but in its own right as a melodic instrument."

"He makes money on that record?"

"Money?" The record in question was in fact highly experimental, not at all geared for the mass market. "I doubt it shipped platinum," I said, borrowing record business jargon for a bestselling recording. "Maybe it breaks even, or perhaps he realizes some modest honorarium."

"I get it," Uncle Morris said, "it's just an ego trip."

I was taken somewhat aback; there seemed something so pejorative in the pronouncement. Then, in a flash I heard myself saying, "Yes. That's exactly what it is. An ego trip."

For the first time in my life it occurred to me how deeply integrated into art is ego. There is, of course, much more to art than ego alone, but there's no escaping the fact that creative expression entails—indeed requires—no small involvement with ego.

Some years ago, during contract negotiations, an actor friend participated in Screen Actors Guild meetings over the question of billing. Billing refers specifically to the manner in which screen credits are displayed on-screen: their relative size, the length of time during which they appear, whether a name stands alone or shares the screen with others.

After hours of wrangling, weighing, arguing, a member stood up abruptly and barked, "Billing! Ridiculous! Whose name goes where? Above the title or below the title? What size typeface? Absurd! This is nothing but ego!"

Another member arose from his chair.

"You bet your life it's ego," he said. "Why should I apologize for it?" He scanned the room. "Those are our faces up there, our flesh and blood. Those noises are our own and only voices. Why in the world ought we not accommodate our egos?"

In fact, for screenwriters and actors alike, screen credit involves much more than ego alone.

It involves money.

First, an artist's billing reflects his professional stature within the entertainment industry. For the most part, while audiences certainly care about actors, they care not a whit about who wrote a film, any more than they care who was the chief electrician, who was the key grip.

Still more directly, billing is contractually connected to writers' financial compensation. Even so small a consideration as the word "and" instead of an ampersand symbol ("&") between two names can result in differences of literally millions of dollars. Two writers connected by an ampersand, for example, are considered a team, a single unit, each person receiving only half as much profit as a single name separated from the others by the word "and."

The purpose here is not to nail down all nuances pertinent to billing. I intend simply to grant permission to screenwriters to flex their egos. Anyone who writes for the screen, who expects his fantasies to be worth sharing, who expects audiences to trade cash for the privilege of that sharing, had better be supplied in abundance with ego and self-esteem.

Criticism

Some years ago I collaborated with another writer on a comedy for a New York producer. Holed up in an apartment on the Upper West Side, we worked like slaves, writing and rewriting until at last we had a presentable draft. This was during the precomputer era, and our cut-and-paste was just that: pages literally chopped up into fragments and reassembled with glue into a coherent draft.

We took the one and only copy to a shop to be photocopied, but stopped off along the way to grab a bite at a Szechuan restaurant. After gorging on sweet-and-sour squid, we returned to the car only to discover it had been burglarized; the attaché case containing the script was gone.

"Let's not panic," I said, at which point we promptly panicked.

Searching blindly in every direction we dove through garbage bins, upended litter baskets, frantically combed the gutters in every direction in the hope that the culprit had abandoned the case and its contents nearby.

After a while I said, "Wait. We have to role-play."

"You think now's the time for West Coast flower-child Zen exercises? You've been baking your brains far too long in the California sun. We have to find the script," my New York pal remonstrated.

"No," I said. "We have to imagine we're a junkie in need of a fix. He passes the car and sees the attaché case. From his point of view it can only be crammed with jewelry and cash. He breaks the window and grabs the case. He doesn't look like the kind of guy to be carrying an attaché case, so he looks for some nearby alley to hide himself and examine the loot." I turned three hundred sixty degrees, scanning the area. "There!" I said, spotting an alley between two buildings a half block down the street. "The script is in that alley."

We made our way to the mouth of the alley.

Sure enough, away down at the end we spotted in the shadows a tossed-away attaché case with scattered pages flowing from its broken lid. While I waited on the sidewalk holding my breath, my collaborator walked the alley's length and emerged moments later, thumbing through the script.

"What do you know about that?" he said, peering closely at the pages. "The guy made comments on it." Squinting at phantom letters that weren't really there, he pretended to read aloud: "Lacks parallel structure. Dialogue stilted. Characterizations flat."

My collaborator was, of course, kidding. In fact, however, when it comes to movies, everybody's a critic.

It is a burden screenwriters must bear. More than merely bear it, they must come to welcome criticism, to seek and solicit it. Finally, and most important, they must learn how to turn criticism around, to transform what might at first appear negative and destructive into something useful. Criticism is part of screenwriting's routine; writers must remain available to it, must exploit it in the service of improving their writing, must use it to help sculpt and reshape their scripts.

In truth, all any writer wants to hear upon completing a draft is that it is perfect, brilliant, life-changing, eternal. Anything less engenders despair, a slashing of confidence and wrists.

To reiterate, screenwriting's purpose is first and foremost to provoke intense, passionate feelings. As already stated, people drawn to such an endeavor inevitably experience their emotions strongly. If civilians suffer injury when criticized, for writers the experience is excruciating.

Inexperienced writers typically figure—incorrectly—that once they mature as artists, upon achieving success criticism ends. Who dares criticize an established, respected writer?

The answer is, of course, everybody. The more successful a writer becomes, the more widely his work is distributed, and the broader target he presents for pundits to criticize.

Worse still, the greater a writer's success, the greater the jealousy engendered among both the public and his colleagues (and competitors) within the arts community.

What is important for writers handling criticism is not merely to be polite even when it is unsolicited, unsound, and downright stupid, but somehow to remain open to that odd, slim fragment that might prove useful.

To get the kinks out of my joints (and my mind) after a day's slaving at the computer, I swim. Recently, toweling off in the locker room, I was approached by a young fellow. "Enjoy your swim?" he said in a tone that seemed somehow fraught with anger.

"Yes, thanks," I muttered. As he continued to stare, I heard myself asking, "You?"

"Me?" he responded. "How can I swim? I'm the lifeguard. I have to sit there watching you. And you know what? I don't like what I see."

Instead of calling Campus Security to report this weirdo, I asked him, "What do you mean?"

"First, you're chopping your stroke, cutting it short, squandering its

full reach. Second, your head rides too low in the water. Third, . . ." Unsolicited, he continued to catalogue all the atrocities I commit while moist.
Notwithstanding his lack of social grace, there appeared a faint but certain
authority in his pronouncements.

The next day I tried out his suggestions in the pool.

I cannot say that it felt good; quite the contrary, changing my style
made me feel awkward. Nevertheless, when I was through, the clock revealed to me that I had substantially cut my time. Clearly my swimming
had improved. This provides further evidence of the fact that all people—
swimmers, writers—need stay open to criticism, no matter how unwel-
come, no matter how coarse, harsh, and even useless it may at first
appear.

Some years ago my agent at the time offered what struck me as a
uniquely worthless suggestion regarding a draft of a script I had just written. Instead of telling him that it was the dumbest notion I'd ever heard,
I stated in a perfectly civil tone that I'd certainly explore his thought, all
the while thinking how presumptuous he, a mere agent, had been to offer
any suggestion at all. I'm the writer, I thought but did not say. You're the
salesman.

For weeks I stewed quietly in the venom generated by this broker's
affront. Then, weeks later, rewriting the script, I suddenly came up with
what I took to be a brilliant and original notion, something that solved a
host of story problems. After basking in self-satisfaction, I was abruptly
humbled when all at once it occurred to me that I had merely incorpo-
rated the agent's suggestion. I did this not as a concession to him, but
purely in service to superior writing.

Writers need to respect criticism if not critics. Respecting does not
mean accepting. Remaining open to criticism is not the same thing as
indiscriminately agreeing to any and all suggestions.

Dumb, negative, jealous, destructive, backbiting criticism is by no
means the only problem writers face. Affirmation can be a problem, too.
For though approval is a lot more fun than scorn, it can be every bit as
deadly. It is a short walk from praise to patronization. Moreover, artists
are suckers for praise.

When my first novel was published, an undermining, crazy-making
colleague at the university constantly asked me for a copy. Clearly, he was
not willing actually to purchase the book. Insincerely I promised eventu-

ally to lend him a copy, but forever put off actually doing so. Finally, catching me unawares at my office one day, he spotted a copy of the book on a shelf, seized it, and fled.

I figured that was just one less copy of the book to offer some deserving soul.

The next day he was back in my office returning the book, which he had actually read. Lustily he sang its praises, complimenting "the broad, rich story, the flesh-and-blood characters, the sweet, punchy, yet poetic dialogue." I found myself figuring I had underestimated this fellow. He wasn't such a bad guy after all. Had I not misjudged his perception, his taste? In two seconds flat I was his servant simply because he claimed to have liked my book, and I'm his grateful admirer to this day.

Rejection and Heartache

Finishing a script generally brings screenwriters not so much joy as despair.

There are two reasons for this. First, day by day, hard at work upon a screenplay, a writer knows just what to do with himself: Write the script. On completion of the draft he is cast adrift. Often there sets in a quiet panic. Happily, that eventually gives way. Sadly, what it gives way to is a deep, dark disappointment and depression.

Second, as already discussed, until the script is complete there is no possibility of having it criticized and rejected. Even the finest scripts engender their fair share of negative commentary. No one has to wait in line for his ration of backbiting and nit-picking. Now that the period of grace is gone, we have a couple of remedies. Foremost among them, after taking the shortest breather, a writer should move right on to his next project. Writing is always the writer's best defense. Instead of sitting by the phone, eating out his heart with a knife and fork, forever awaiting an agent's or producer's reaction, a writer should be hard at work writing.

In addition, writers have to learn how to allow themselves to feel lousy for a while. To the writer's substantial advantage, he may endure scores of rejections, but he requires only a single acceptance. Tales abound of movies rejected everywhere, year after year, finally to be sold, filmed, and turned into critical and financial successes. Oliver Stone's highly lauded *Platoon* is an example. Stone, already a power to be reckoned with, peddled *Platoon* around Hollywood for a decade before getting it to the screen.

No writer, therefore, no matter how respected, no matter how success-ful, is above rejection. Instead of being "intelligent" about it, instead of being rational and enlightened, the writer needs to gnaw on his heart and his soul for perhaps a couple of days.

Upon encountering rejection, writers should not waste time and energy defending their work. A script is its own best argument for itself. When scripts are rejected, instead of engaging the rejecter in a shrill ex-change about how right the writer is and how wrong the reader, instead of discussing potential rewrites and revisions, writers should learn simply to recite: "Thank you for your time, attention, and consideration."

Then they should take their script elsewhere.

Years ago I wrote a script speculatively, only to have it rejected by the first agent to whom I offered it. When I inquired—foolishly—what pre-cisely it was that he had found lacking, he said that he had found its story thin, its characters shallow, its dialogue amateurish, its scenes and set-tings unimaginative, its theme bereft of merit, its incidents and anecdotes familiar and pedestrian.

With a perfectly straight face, I said to him, "So you're on the fence about it?"

"No," the humorless broker said. "I don't like the script at all. I think it's a really, really bad screenplay."

Oddly enough, I was starting to enjoy this exchange. I told him that he needn't spare my feelings, that if he took a dim view of the script he could say so; I assured him I could take it.

I am able to relate this experience with no small joy because I went directly across the street (Sunset Boulevard) and delivered the script to a rival agency where a representative promptly read it and phoned the next morning to say that he wanted to represent it. Only weeks later he secured a cash offer from a producer eager to option the rights.

Possibly, after a slew of rejections, and especially if the criticism seems to be generally consistent, a writer might want to hold on to a script for a while and restudy it with an eye toward rewriting. Or he may simply abandon a script. Every experienced writer has scripts he has written— among them ones that have sold, in some cases scripts that have even been filmed—that now he would never show. Writers need to learn how to let go of a script, how to focus not on the past but the present and the future. If a writer is successful, sometimes after he has let go of a script it may well come to be rewritten by one or several other writers.

In various places throughout this book we discuss at length the necessity for rewriting. The process can be arduous in the extreme. Rewriting one's own work is hard enough, but being rewritten by others can be more painful still. Nevertheless, it is part of screenwriting's nature, and writers need to learn how to accept it.

Many producers throw another writer, or team of writers, upon a script simply because they do not know what else to do. They may consider the original writer "written out," or they may see hiring and firing writers as their only function after assigning parking places.

In fact, pain aside, it is a privilege to be rewritten. When a studio hires writers to rewrite your work, while you may view it as testimony to their dissatisfaction with your effort, in fact it may mean just the opposite. Personally, I reject the notion—dear to the heart of many producers—that with screenwriting two heads, or three, or four or five, are better than one. That may be true for designing toasters, tires, or tea bags, but screenwriting is subjective. Objectivity is for other endeavors, not art.

Nevertheless, when a studio regards a project as hopeless, it cuts its losses and drops the script. When it hires additional writers, thereby committing additional money, this is evidence not of faithlessness but of faith.

There is at UCLA a professor of ceramics who requires beginning students, upon completing their first project and having it evaluated by their classmates and instructor, to smash the piece against the wall.

Principle 50: Art hurts.

The purpose here is to instill in the students a healthy respect for the distance artists are required to maintain between themselves and their work. An artist's art, like his child, is of him, from him, like him. It resembles him in so many ways. After all is said and done, however, the art is the art and the artist is the artist. The notion may appear obvious, but for artists it is a distinction that can be difficult to embrace.

If it is difficult for writers, consider actors. Writers may suffer when their scripts are rejected, but their scripts are still just that: their scripts.

When an actor is rejected it is his voice, his look, his posture, his walk, his flesh, his blood that are adjudged to be wanting.

> *Principle 51: The reason there are actors is so that there can*
> *be one group of artists that suffers more profoundly*
> *and is treated more shabbily than writers.*

Pain is a critically important—and unavoidable—aspect of creativity. Creative expression, as Bronowski asserts, is uniquely human. It derives from our facility to visualize the future, to anticipate it, to represent it in images we project in our head, or on the wall of a cave, or upon a movie screen.

Chapter 15

. . . .

Crazy Art

I am now in my fourth decade teaching.

Counting all the way back to kindergarten, however, I have still probably logged more time as a student than as an instructor.

I recall with uncanny clarity the very first hour, the inaugural morning of my formal education at P.S. 11 in Sunnyside, Queens. It was on that particular late-summer Monday in 1950 that I learned screenwriting's single most important lesson.

Our kindergarten teacher, the overfed, underloved Miss Crimmons, was every bit as decrepit as the Benjamin Harrison–era building in which she plied her trade. Scanning the roster, mispronouncing virtually every name, she asked each of the forty students to tell the class what his father did for a living.

There was not a modicum of interest, of course, in whatever anybody's mother might have done. Mothers during that period generally did not work outside the home. Accordingly, we reeled off fathers' professions. This provided the opportunity not only to learn about our classmates but also to consider appropriate subjects for further study. One kid's father, for example, was an electrician; this sparked a discussion regarding the miracle of electricity, that curious and splendid phenomenon that boils our oatmeal even as it freezes our Popsicles. Another pupil's father was a plumber, and from this there flowed conversation regarding water and waste in urban America.

At long last came my turn. I volunteered that my father was a musician.

"No, no," Miss Crimmons said somewhat too patiently, suppressing a grimace. "We're not talking about hobbies. We're not talking about what our fathers do for fun, for sport, for recreation in the evenings or on weekends. We're talking about professions. Do you understand what we mean when we say 'profession'?"

"It means you get paid," Arturo D'Agostino called out. He owned a perpetual off-kilter half-grin that would lead swiftly to his designation among his classmates as Crazy Art.

"No calling out!" Miss Crimmons called out. She asked me again, "Do you understand what we mean when we say 'profession'?"

"It means you get paid," I said.

"That's right," Miss Crimmons said, nodding approvingly. "So tell us what is your father's profession?"

"Musician," I responded again.

"He's paid money to play music?" she scoffed. No doubt she ruminated that there would always be students incapable of engaging certain fundamental principles no matter how painstakingly articulated; such was an educator's lot. "He's paid money to play music?" she asked me again.

"That's right."

Ever so feebly, enlightenment seemed to encroach upon her. "You mean a musician? A professional musician? Your dad performs at dances and weddings and bar mitzvahs?"

"He played those kinds of gigs when he was working his way through college," I allowed. Growing up in a musician's home I was conversant with the lingo, which I did not consider to be lingo at all but plain, everyday English.

"And what precisely does he do now?" Miss Crimmons asked, leaning far too heavily upon the "now," extruding it and then sectioning it into several distinct syllables.

"He performs with Arturo Toscanini and the NBC Symphony Orchestra."

Her eyes widened only slightly. "That is impressive," Miss Crimmons conceded, however grudgingly. Then and there, on my first day of kindergarten during a sultry midcentury New York City September, she posited the most profound interrogatory it has been my experience to hear.

Granted, on the surface it may not sound like a whole lot.

Her gaze narrowing, the teacher inquired: "What instrument does he play?"

"Bass," I answered.

"What?" she said, recoiling, squinting, her nose wrinkling as if someone had just cut a ripe, wet, buzzing, mustard-colored fart. "He plays what?"

"Bass," I said again.

"What's that? What in the world do you mean?"

"Bass," I said with a shrug. "Sometimes it's called string bass or contrabass, sometimes double bass. I've even heard it called bull fiddle. Musicians call it bass. It's like a great big violin. It's so big, in fact, that the player can't hope to tuck it under his chin like a violin. Instead it stands on the floor. The performer positions himself behind it." The reason I knew all this is not because I was precocious, though I may well have been that. I knew about it for the same reason the kid whose father was an electrician knew the difference between an ammeter and a voltmeter, and the kid whose father was a plumber knew the difference between a pipe wrench and a hex wrench.

"Now hold on just one moment, young man," Miss Crimmons said, brightening. "It's like a big violin?" In the air she created with her hands the shape of a phantom violin.

I nodded.

"And it stands on the floor?"

"Right."

"The musician behind it?"

"Correct."

Teacher seemed now to overflow with satisfaction. With serene conviction she announced, "That's called a cello." To be certain that I had it right, she repeated herself, enunciating each syllable as if it were a whole and separate word. "Chell," she said. After a decent interval she added, "Oh."

"It's like a cello," I acknowledged. "Certainly the bass is closer to the cello than it is to the violin," I said, nodding eagerly.

"Stands on the floor?" Miss Crimmons said.

"Yes."

"Musician behind it?"

"Right."

I could see the teacher's impatience dissolving now into anger. "That instrument," she pronounced ever so slowly, "is called a 'cello.'" Even a five-year-old could see that Truth and Reason were not likely to prevail on that particular Monday morning.

I chose a new tack. I said the smartest thing I have ever said in my entire life. Looking Miss Crimmons in the eye, I said, "Okay, it's a cello."

Never did I doubt that I was right and she was wrong. Never did I suspect that my own dear daddy was mistaken about his life's work. It simply did not occur to me that Colleen Crimmons alone knew the truth regarding the appropriate nomenclature for the several brownish red, curved, carved, sculpted wooden behemoths that graced nearly every corner of our already overcrowded apartment.

That day I learned a most fundamental principle regarding life, art, and screenwriting.

> **Principle 52: People in positions of authority do not know what they're talking about. Worse, they do not want to know.**

Offered the opportunity for expansion, given the chance to learn the truth, instead of welcoming enlightenment authorities are likely instead to reject it. If pressed on the matter, their scorn turns rapidly to anger.

How ironic it is, therefore, that notwithstanding my lifelong disdain for authority I have myself become over the years a figure cloaked in authority. People are afraid to tell me their opinion of a particular movie because they may get it "wrong," as if there were an approved, authorized list of good and bad movies by which audiences had to abide.

Remember always that an educated guess is still only a guess, and that an expert opinion is merely that: an opinion.

Horsehair, Sheep Gut, and Screenwriting

My father, I have said, was a musician who made his living playing the bass.

What precisely is a bass player's job? It entails entrails. Not just any entrails, but the intestines of sheep, for it is from sheep gut that bass strings are manufactured. Consider also that the bow is made of horsehair.

What the professional bassist does in the narrowest sense, therefore, is to pass his life dragging horsehair across sheep gut. Day after day, year after year, he saws the tail of a horse up and back across the intestines of a sheep.

By itself, such behavior sounds sufficiently bizarre as to warrant court-ordered psychiatric evaluation. Is it not on its face a ludicrous, indeed perverse, activity for any human being, no less for one calling himself an artist?

If that were the end of it we might on appearance alone consider the offender to be daft. But it's not the end; it's only the beginning. The player does not merely saw sheep gut with horsehair but, as one might expect, in doing so produces a sound. Contemplating the circumstances, it would seem a safe bet the sound should be grating and ugly.

What if the player were to claim that in the hands of a capable practitioner the sound is in fact so beautiful, so mellifluous, so engaging, so compelling as to cause people to line up four abreast around the block for days on end, tolerating snow, sleet, rain, hail, and panhandlers for the privilege of paying perhaps even hundreds of dollars in order to pass a couple of hours in a chamber listening to that sound? Would we not consider the claimant to be clinically deranged?

Yet that's precisely what the talented, disciplined, professional bassist does. He scrapes horsehair against sheep gut, causing the latter to vibrate. In exchange, listeners put money in his pocket and food in his children's mouths.

It's crazy.

So, too, is all creative expression.

> **Principle 53: Art's not smart. It's dumb. Creativity as a profession is not intelligent and reasonable; it's wacky and eccentric, mad as a hatter, jerky as sin.**

Creative expression is not logical, circumspect, intelligent, or responsible; it's illogical, unreasonable, manic, and irresponsible, especially as an activity preoccupying grown women and men.

Is screenwriting any different from the other arts? Yes.

It's crazier.

Recollections of dreams, and dreams themselves, provide interesting parallels to writing for the screen. Everyone dreams. From time to time each of us tells another about a particular dream we had.

Consider a friend who wishes to tell you his dream but, prior to relating it, insists upon two conditions. First, he requires that you pay attention not for several seconds or even a handful of minutes, but for two hours.

Would that not all by itself cause you to wonder about your pal's mental health?

What if prior to his description of the dream you were required also to remit, say, fifteen dollars for the privilege of hearing it?

Would you not laugh in his face?

Would you not summon paramedics?

Would you not crank up the lithium in his I.V. drip?

Yet that is what each and every screenwriter does with each and every screenplay. He orchestrates, choreographs, arranges, and rearranges his dreams. He expects audiences not only to tolerate those dreams but to give them their undivided attention.

And not a little bit of money.

Narrative expression is a bizarre activity, a uniquely human enterprise. As near as we can determine, not tigers, not toads, but human beings alone engage professionally in fantasy. No wonder such a life and such a living are so devoutly to be desired. What greater glory than to spin tales and in the bargain have folks pay your rent?

When it works, when it fulfills its purpose, screenwriting is a noble and nourishing and healing endeavor for creator and audience alike. However, it is anything but sensible. In fact, it is richly nonsensical. Perhaps the most destructive mistake any artist can make, therefore, is to plan, to calculate, to exercise reasonable caution, because reason and caution are for airplane pilots and civil engineers, not screenwriters.

Do You Believe in Magic?

Earlier we discussed musical instruments. Let us for a moment examine one such instrument, the Stradivarius violin.

Thanks to technological advances in medical imaging, it is now possible to clone a Strad. The wood from which violin bodies are constructed is, after all, organic matter. Using techniques such as magnetic resonance imaging plus positron-emission and computer-analyzed tomography, scientists are able to map precisely the inner and outer dimensions of the Strad, a heretofore impossible task to achieve without tearing the precious instrument apart.

These techniques allow scientists to extrapolate computer models, enabling them to duplicate the exact dimensions of the original. Moreover, the wood for the "new" Strads is itself salvaged from cabinetry of the period so that even the material used is in every respect identical. Thanks, furthermore, to spectrographic analysis, chemists are able precisely to replicate the glues and varnishes the Stradivarius brothers used in the crafting of their instruments all those years ago.

There is only one difference between the true Strad and the clone: The latter has an inferior tone.

What can account for this?

Clearly, in creating the clone, they left out the magic.

Principle 54: The most serious mistake an artist can make is to leave out the magic.

Good books on screenwriting, enlightened seminars, intelligently designed academic programs are useful to be sure. They are no replacement, however, for magic.

Writers can strategize and computerize, can plan and calculate and intellectualize, but in the end we need to let go of all that and just stumble around, plod on blindly, bounce and buffet and bump and bumble along.

That, too, is crazy art's way.

If from time to time we cannot find the magic, we need to set all the books and schemes and software aside. We need to apply our fingers ever more diligently to the keys.

We might just find that the magic finds us.

The Movie Theater as Church

Why are so many movies so bad?

First of all, as I argue elsewhere, they're not.

Movies are merely as bad—and as good—as any and all other forms of creative expression. If most films lack merit, the same can be said for most paintings, literature, sculpture, music, batik, macramé, papier-mâché, bread dough, chopped liver, and forms and formats yet to be created.

Even so, the question remains: Why is any movie ever bad? After all, a screenwriter can read all of the books treating the subject; he can attend a myriad of seminars now offered across the country and around the globe. One can enroll in master of fine arts screenwriting programs at numerous institutions of higher learning.

One can work with an experienced consultant, or two or three, or a veritable squadron of such consultants.

Notably, one can take all the time one wants. Writers can write and rewrite, and re-rewrite, and re-re-rewrite ad infinitum until the script is robust, ready, and right.

Still, the vast majority of movies fail to merit our time, our attention, or our consideration, to say nothing of our dollars.

The question: Why?

The answer: I don't know.

That is, of course, the one answer that is never permitted at institutions of advanced study. To admit that one does not have The Answer to virtually any question displeases the boards of directors of the corporations that fund research grants, to say nothing of the editorial boards who decide what to publish in scholarly journals. During all these years as a faculty member at a world-class academic institution, I have learned one thing above all others: It is not answers but questions that scholars and artists and audiences ultimately seek.

Principle 55: Smart questions produce not answers but further questions.

The question posed here—Why are so many movies so bad?—is especially intriguing.

For it is the very same question asked not of screenwriting educators but of God.

Why does an all-knowing, all-powerful ruler of the universe create this world, riddled as it is with famine, fire, flood, not to mention talk radio? In other words, why does a perfect God create an imperfect universe?

This question is by its nature religious. Why shouldn't it be? Movies are, after all, very much a religious enterprise. They take place in a theater that in many ways resembles a church, a mosque, an ashram, a temple, a synagogue. Audience members sit in ranked pews, chairs, or benches. They observe a smaller number of people philosophizing, pontificating, preaching, performing.

People go to movies for the same reason they attend church. We seek to explore the difficult questions that befuddle our existence. We seek to understand the mysteries and the myths, to solve the puzzles and riddles that surround, astound, and confound us.

Movies, therefore, are no mere frill but instead a fundamental component of contemporary human experience.

Our late UCLA colleague Dr. Norman Cousins was not the first person to understand that spirit and soul are closely connected to flesh, blood, and bone. This is no mere metaphor. Cousins, as discussed previously, having received from the medical community a terminal diagnosis, literally laughed himself back to health by watching zany comedies, in particular Marx Brothers classics. Instead of mere weeks or months he survived a substantial number of years beyond his doctors' prognosis. Given film and television's ability to reach billions of people all around the globe, more hearts are healed, more bodies mended by art than by legions of medical professionals.

As I mentioned earlier, creative expression—art—is something that is uniquely human. Beavers do not engage in it. Neither do termites, plankton, or krill.

Only humans.

Humans who fail to engage in creative expression—as creators, as observers—are not a whole lot different from walking, talking, breathing, sweating pieces of meat. They miss the opportunity to fulfill their nature. They deny themselves the chance to interact with the rest of the human family in the grand and glorious spirit of integration and cooperation that lies at the heart of creative expression.

They miss the whole picture.

PART III

· · · · · · · · · · · ·

Business

Chapter 16

· · · · · · · · ·

Cooperation and Collaboration

Except for seeing photographs proving it actually happened, I would expect I'd hallucinated the entire episode in a mescaline-addled late sixties flashback. The fact is, however, that in the fall of 1967, when I was a film student at the University of Southern California, I served as teaching assistant to the nuttiest professor of them all, Jerry Lewis.

He taught a course in directing.

The details of my warm and curious relationship with Jerry Lewis are sufficient to constitute a whole separate book. For our purposes here, let me say simply that after a couple of years he made me an offer I could not refuse: dialogue director on what would turn out to be his last big-studio picture.

Because Jerry Lewis enjoyed rubbing elbows with star athletes, he cast as actors in the picture several members of the Los Angeles Dodgers. Foremost among them was center fielder and team captain Willie Davis.

Davis was in the full flush of his prime. Twenty-nine years old, he had enjoyed the strongest season of his career and was arguably the best player on the team.

He was also a contract holdout.

This was the era before free agency, and players were severely limited in their options; they had largely to go along with whatever deal management offered. They could not jump to another team. Their sole bargaining chip was the threat to sit out the season.

Indeed, during the winter of the picture's production, that was precisely what Willie Davis threatened to do. One morning, while driving to the studio, I heard on the news that he had finally signed his contract with the Dodgers. When I encountered him on the set, I asked, "How much?"

He answered, "Fifty thousand dollars."

Even adjusted for inflation, this superstar and leading hitter and fielder for one of the most profitable franchises in baseball accepted compensation so paltry as to equal but a fraction of the commission paid to today's major player's agent.

The movie's property master took home that much in a year. By any measure, for a fellow at the top of his game in so brutally competitive an arena, here was compensation that was scandalously stingy.

It will be asserted by many, of course, that fifty thousand dollars is a lot of money just for playing ball. I disagree most vigorously. I have little patience for those critics who over the years have said that Johnny Carson, for example, was paid too much money for "merely" hosting a TV talk show.

That inconsequential little talk show earned hundreds upon hundreds of millions of dollars for the National Broadcasting Company. The total worldwide syndication value of its episodes surely reaches well into the billions.

Did Johnny Carson personally contribute to the show's phenomenal success? Certainly the folks at NBC thought so, as they eventually agreed contractually to marry Johnny's name to that of the show. It was no longer *The Tonight Show* starring Johnny Carson but *The Tonight Show Starring Johnny Carson.* Even when Johnny took a night off and a guest host (occasionally Jerry Lewis) replaced him for an evening or a week, it was still *The Tonight Show Starring Johnny Carson.*

Carson had become, in effect, not an employee of the network but a co-owner of the show, not a hired hand but a partner sharing appropriately in the profits. He no longer worked for "the Man" in exchange for wages, however generous; he was instead the Man himself.

The same applies to professional athletes.

Thanks to free agency, star athletes no longer toil as field hands for their masters; instead they subcontract their services and are paid not a salary but something much more closely resembling a portion of the proceeds they generate for the overall enterprise. At the outset owners complained that such arrangements would bankrupt the sport, and painful public battles have raged over this issue. In truth, however, team profits have generally soared. It has turned out to be an arrangement beneficial to all parties.

At this point, a reasonable reader may ask why in the world a book about screenwriting even merely touches upon this subject. The answer: It illustrates a healthy development not only in film but in television and new media in the new millennium.

Now well into that millennium, the boundaries between once clearly delineated adversaries blend, blur, overlap, and merge: tribe versus tribe, master versus slave, labor versus management, North versus South, East versus West, landlord versus tenant, women versus men, capitalism versus communism, commerce versus art. Formerly clear territories bleed around the edges, seep into one another's acreage, and eventually their borders altogether disappear.

Old, familiar, comfortable, trusted distinctions no longer obtain. They give way to a new singularity that finds its purest embodiment in the moving image.

Labor/Management

We have already seen that in professional sports there is a substantial erasure of the line dividing owner and player. This is increasingly true for corporations in general. Workers associated with various corporations are now characterized as worker-owners. Indeed, the notion of employees becoming shareholders in the company for which they work represents an expanding phenomenon.

An attorney does not merely work for the firm; if she passes muster after a decent interval she becomes a partner, with full rights and responsibilities. University professors do not simply work for the campus; once they survive the rigors of tenure review they participate actively in its governance, determining and executing its principles, policies, and procedures.

In no world is the marriage of labor and management more abundantly clear than in show business. For in movies—and in some ways even more so in television—labor is management. Increasingly, writers produce the shows they write.

A common misconception among writers—and among the general public—is that in order to protect their scripts, writers must also direct them. I have known a number of writers, however, who acquired sufficient clout to win the right to direct their own screenplays, only to have those scripts wrecked and devastated beyond description. Worst of all, with the writer at the helm of his own picture, there is no one else around to blame when schedules and budgets go awry.

The only thing worse than having some idiot director wreck your movie is wrecking your own movie.

Perhaps at long last the overappreciation of directing is diminishing. George Lucas, for example, after the original leg of the *Star Wars* films, did not direct again for more than twenty years. Who, however, can doubt that the projects he designed and produced bear his creative stamp, that they are unique to him and his singular aesthetic, his particular artistic sensibility and style?

I am asked from time to time whether I'm bothered by the high price— sometimes millions of dollars—paid to leading screenwriters for even just a single script. My answer is always: No. I am, after all, a writer and also a writing educator. Why would I object to writers receiving oodles of money for their services?

Others may ask: Does not all this attention to money obscure the basic principles that inspire writers to write in the first place? Does it not sully the bright spirit that lures audiences to movie theaters? What about art, creativity, dreams, invention, imagination, fascination, and fantasy? Doesn't all that get lost in the flurry of dollar signs?

I'll say it again: I'm not a bit bothered by writers getting paid lots of money. I firmly believe we ought to get as much as we can persuade—or compel—movie companies to pay us.

What I like best about the newly elevated compensation for writers is that it supports the proposition that it is not the director but the writer who is truly film's first artist. Writers, of course, have always known this. Over the past couple of decades writers have been paid nosebleed-high fees for their services. Money is, after all, a metaphor representing everything else. Moreover, money is a metaphor with numbers on it. In the present instance money is a metaphor for respect.

Issues regarding compensation, however, can become something of a distraction.

Principle 56: Screenwriting is not about the movie business; the movie business is about screenwriting.

The dollars proclaim that at long last even Hollywood gets the message: A movie can't make money without a solid story. Special effects won't do it; stars can't do it; neither lighting nor scenic design nor art direction nor wardrobe and makeup can do it. First and foremost success is achieved through story.

Story is the domain of the writer. Writers, therefore, instead of working for the producer find themselves to be not his hired hand but his partner.

Reality/Illusion

We live in an information hurricane. Symbols and signs rain down upon us, competing ceaselessly for our attention. A man in a public lavatory, for example, is likely to find himself staring at an advertisement positioned at eye level above the porcelain. Increasingly, instead of hard-copy ads there are digital screens. Likewise at the gas station's pump island. A fellow downing a pastrami sandwich at a deli is likely to be surrounded by flat screens running news, sports, political chatter, and more.

Sometimes it gets tricky trying to differentiate between the images themselves and what it is they purport to represent.

Consider that in Los Angeles it is illegal to possess a "look-alike" replica handgun. These are authentic in appearance but incapable of firing. Occasionally they are utilized in crimes. A victim confronted with a faithful model of a nine-millimeter Glock wisely assumes the weapon is real and cooperates with the felon wielding it.

Real guns, however, that can actually fire bullets and wound, maim, and kill, are legal. I cite this not as ammunition for the debate regarding gun control but merely as evidence of the increasing overlap between reality and illusion.

Because I interact daily with so many writers, agents, and producers, I have come to be both burdened and blessed with an informal first-look deal with America and the world. Writers regularly send me screenplays. Agents and producers constantly approach me seeking screenwriters and scripts.

Some years ago I received a call from the management team representing a major prizefighter. His boxing days waning, they sought for him a transition to acting. They asked me to keep an eye out for an action/adventure script suitable for launching his film career. They had one condition, however. In keeping with the fighter's desire to provide young

American males with an affirmative role model, he was unwilling to be depicted on-screen as causing anybody harm.

How does a boxer end up with a management team that can telephone a film professor for help in launching an acting career except for the fact that he punched real men's faces with his real fists in a sincere attempt to knock them unconscious? He draws the line, however, not at engaging in such activity but merely simulating it.

Free thought is married to free expression. Even totalitarian societies cannot prevent citizens from thinking whatever they choose to think. It is not thoughts but the expression of thoughts that can be controlled. Individuals seeking censorship will not parade in the streets bearing placards reading THOUGHT CONTROL NOW!!! They will call instead for "intelligent, reasonable, enlightened, expansive, responsible limitations upon only those sorts of expression 'proven' to be 'destructive.'"

Here is merely one more example of the blending of borders and boundaries residing at the heart of both film and society.

Cooperation/Collaboration/Competition

What often appears on the surface to be competition is actually just another version of cooperation and collaboration.

Consider the Olympic games.

Here is a universe of apparent confrontation. Are not the athletes of one side attempting to defeat the athletes of the other? Are there not in the end clear winners and losers?

A lopsided victory over an inept opponent is not admired as much as a close win over a capable competitor. Opposition makes us strong. Competing teams need each other. What separates them is petty compared to what they share.

Writers ought to view creative expression as, among other things, an athletic competition requiring a keen spirit, sharp reflexes, and a body strong enough and healthy enough to support the talent within it.

I am an addicted swimmer who cannot write—or sleep or breathe—without his daily freestyle fix. As such, of all the Olympic events I take the greatest interest in aquatics. While viewing the swimming competition during the 2008 summer games in Beijing it occurred to me that the event was not competition so much as cooperation and collaboration.

Consider that it requires a large number of individuals even merely to stage the Olympic games. A site has to be chosen. Facilities need to be constructed. Officials and judges and administrators, timers, coaches, referees, and assistants of every stripe have to be trained, recruited, and appointed, to say nothing of the athletes themselves.

Competition, again, can be seen as but another form of cooperation.

The End of Adversity

Film represents the noblest, most elegant model of affirmative, creative, cooperative competition.

Where else besides film does so diverse a family of artists and craftspeople—including "the suits": accountants, attorneys, executives, distributors, exhibitors—combine in great numbers to engage in a common creative purpose? Ideally, each participant rejoices not in his own but in the collective ego that represents the whole picture.

Simply stated, film is not an adversarial enterprise. Indeed, more than any other entity, it provides women and men with a vehicle emphasizing not separation but symbiosis, not drudgery but creativity.

What, in practical terms, does this mean for screenwriters?

It means that they should not act or direct or photograph or edit the movie. They should not art-direct it; they should not scenic-design it. They should not cast it.

They should just write it.

Writers ought not restrain but encourage the participation of their creative partners. True, the players may wreck the film. There's also every possibility, however, that they will cause it to soar beyond the writer's most rapturous expectations.

This leads us to yet another screenwriting rule.

Principle 57: Smart screenwriters show the way, then they get out of the way.

In my public lectures and in my classes at UCLA I extol the virtues of three provocative principles that are not what many people expect to hear from a senior, tenured professor at a world-class center of higher learning.

First, reach as many people as you can.

Films are not made so much for the artists who create them as for their audiences. They do not need to reach a blockbuster audience, though there is no scandal in doing so. To be certain, however, their audience must be larger than merely the writer's friends and family.

Second, accept that sex and violence occupy a proper place in film and television.

Like it or not, sex and violence have resided at the heart of dramatic expression since the earliest recorded drama thousands of years ago in ancient Greece.

Third, lie through your teeth. What matters is not the data but the emotion.

To these precepts I should now like to add two more.

Principle 58: Bourgeois, middle-class values are the hope of the world.

When people struggle for food, clothing, and shelter, there is no place for art. These basic commodities and conditions are required in order for art of every kind to flourish.

Principle 59: The wisest course, the most enlightened route for any person or people, is not separation but assimilation.

People complain that it is virtually impossible to buy, for example, a wholly American-made car. Each and every automobile contains components built in a host of countries on various continents.

Instead of lamenting this fact, people should welcome it. What's wrong with people all around the globe participating in enterprises that unite diverse souls in disparate places dedicated to the cause of producing a singular product and achieving a unified goal?

It's great to know your roots, but this cannot take the place of interacting with all the humanity around us. Current trends that compartmentalize the human experience, that lend currency to the discredited institution of segregation, that balkanize our existence, represent but a blip on the landscape. The whole picture of the future is the assimilation and, for better and for worse, the homogenization of world population, culture, and experience.

Is that wonderful or dreadful?

Yes, it is wonderful or dreadful, depending upon who views it, from where and at what time. To lose what is familiar can be sad. Uncharted territory is by nature frightening and sometimes also dangerous.

To study, to protect, and to preserve phenomena that constitute cherished components of a people's legacy is one thing. To turn history upside down and run it in reverse is quite another.

Marshall McLuhan, the brilliant Canadian visionary, proposed years ago that the invention of the printing press ultimately made possible the Industrial Revolution. The shattering of experience into bits and pieces and symbols, which is what the printing press does to language, eventually and inevitably brought us the assembly line and mass production. Printed books became the first mass-produced item.

There are echoes of this process in film. Film makes possible the worldwide sharing of experience that renders inevitable the resurrection of the global village. At the same time as film is the instrument of such change, it is also itself the embodiment of that change.

Nowhere else is there more collaboration among diverse parties in the creation of something whole, something wondrously common, than in the motion picture. Those among us lucky enough, crazy enough, to participate in devising the plan—that is to say, writing the screenplay—fulfill a charge placed upon us not by any mere studio chief but by the Force that is with us and that drives not only movies but life itself.

Chapter 17

. . . .

Script Sales Strategies

Teaching in a highly competitive program at an esteemed institution of higher learning brings me into close contact with many of screenwriting's sharpest, brightest students. They bring talent, discipline, and language skills—the whole array of writing strengths—and they also bring a single glaring weakness: too much show business savvy. One mistake that flows from this is their attempt to exploit the latest trend.

Avoid Trends

At the first meeting of an advanced screenwriting class at UCLA, each student briefly presents an overview of the screenplay she hopes to write. I shall never forget one such session. One student had a father-and-son story; another had a tale about a painter making his way west after the Civil War. Another's concept involved restless youths thumb-tripping their way through outer space. If some notions were more promising than others, not one was on its face unworkable.

Then, offering not a shred of story detail, a student blithely announced that it was his intention to write a tale that, as he put it, "closely synchronizes with the profile of product sought by the new administration at [a particular studio]." Sad to relate, the fellow was deadly serious. Like too many big-university, Hollywood-hip screenwriting students, he devoured the movie trade publications, websites, and blogs daily in an attempt to divine studio politics, personnel, and, worst of all, current trends.

If ever there were a recipe for failure, it is that; it's the reason I confiscate the trades whenever I catch my students reading them. Trade publications and websites have their proper place, to be sure, even though for the most part each constitutes little more than a catalogue of publicists' sweet lies, an inventory of who's pretending to work on what purported project.

Writers hoping to impress agents or executives by cashing in on current trends are already too late. Yesterday's trend is today's yawn. This season's fad, whatever it is, had to be in the pipeline two years ago.

Principle 60: It is too late to exploit the latest trend precisely because it is the latest trend.

The lovely irony is that even in wicked old Hollywood, the wisest tack a writer can take is foolishly, recklessly to follow his heart and tell his most personal story, the tale unique to his experience. Skittish writers seek refuge in trends no doubt because the tactic seems safe. In fact, however, there is nothing safe about writing.

Principle 61: The most hazardous strategy artists can follow is to play it safe. Instead of avoiding risk, smart writers embrace it.

To reach audiences, writers have to take chances. They must confront the awesome challenge inherent in peddling their fantasies. All writers, in particular new writers, face the overwhelming likelihood that what they write will come to no fruitful conclusion. As asserted above, instead of avoiding it, successful screenwriters fling themselves headlong into risk.

The well-written script, even unsold, serves a multitude of purposes. The writer can use it as a sample of his craft in order to seek representation. He can offer it to production companies in the hope of winning funds—through a development deal—to write yet another script based on yet another idea. He can hope to land an assignment to rewrite somebody else's script. A good script should enable the writer to support his writing habit and confront the awful risk yet again.

Principle 62: The smartest marketing strategy is good writing.

Representation

Every writer at least once in his life should visit a studio story department. Floor to ceiling, occupying every linear foot around the perimeter, stacked six to sixteen deep along the walls are scripts, thousands of scripts, scores of thousands of scripts. Fully ninety-nine percent of these screenplays remain unsold, and even among the precious few for which money has actually changed hands, the vast preponderance remain unproduced.

How does a writer get his script past that fortress of felled forests and into the hands of someone with the authority to film it? Must he seek an agent, or can he make direct submissions to production companies?

The answer is: Yes—he may seek an agent or he may make direct submissions to production companies.

Direct submissions to production companies, however, are almost always unwise. Generally, a script mailed unsolicited to a studio will be returned unopened and unread. Studios believe this protects them from nuisance plagiarism suits. Presumably, they cannot successfully be sued for stealing a script they have not read.

As already argued, writers have to place themselves in the role of their counterparts and see things from the opposite perspective. Imagine what it is like to be a producer who receives a script not from an agent but directly from the writer. What is he likely to think? Isn't he going to imagine that the writer likely tried to interest an agent or several agents in representing the script and that they must have turned him down? Why else would he be making the submissions himself? In such an instance, the script arrives with an aura of rejection and defeat looming over it even before it has been opened. This is all the more reason to find an agent to submit your script rather than submitting it on your own.

The roots of artists' representation lie in the ancient notion, partially justified and partially not, that creative souls—poets, painters, writers, composers—whose business is emotions are too sensitive to wallow in matters so mundane as money. They must avoid at all cost, the theory holds, bruising those delicate egos upon which their creativity depends.

In truth, however, writers should consider themselves working people, and working people need declare themselves masters of their own fate. Regardless of how high-hearted and sweet-minded a writer may be, it is a dreadful mistake for him to consider himself above the fray.

Notwithstanding any of this, in order that artists may on the one hand create their art, and on the other pay their rent, over the ages there has arisen a cadre of representatives. These are business-minded folk who, in exchange for a percentage of the sale, deal with merchandizing.

For one thing, at the same time as they attend to their art, working artists may well lack the time and spirit to wheel and deal in the professional arena. For another, presumably they do not possess the business acumen to appreciate the finer points of negotiation—rates, rights, revisions, reruns, residuals, and other complications. On its face, a professional arrangement to sell or develop a screenplay may seem simple enough: The producer agrees to pay the writer a certain amount of money in exchange for writing the screenplay.

How much, though, if any at all, is to be paid in advance? How much on conclusion? Is there a bonus on commencement of principal photography, that is, when cameras roll? What is the fair size of such a bonus? Must the writer first prepare an outline for the producer's approval? What about rewrites and revisions? Can the producer fire the writer midproject and hire someone else? If that's the case (as it too often is), who gets what kind of credit on-screen?

How much money for the writer if and when the film is shown on television or the Internet or distributed on DVD? What about the second time it is shown on television? For that matter, what about the three hundred and forty-seventh such telecast? What about foreign rights? What about sequels? What about the producer's right of first refusal on the writer's subsequent project(s)?

Clearly, writers require expert support in all these areas. Agents ought to be able to provide that.

Some years ago I made the mistake of reading one of my own contracts. I say "mistake" because reading a contract can wrongly lead the writer to think he actually understands it. To be sure, I own no such presumption. The contract could have been written in Navajo for all the sense it made to me.

A measure of the document's complexity and obscurity can be found in a note on page one. Beyond mere salary, my agent had negotiated some number of "points," a percentage of the film's net profit. Beside the phrase "net profit" was an asterisk. At the bottom of the page was another asterisk and the legend: "For definition of Net Profit see Appendix A."

Need I relate that Appendix A was all by itself several times longer than the entire contract?

To attain a sense (sometimes false) that one's rights are fully protected, relationships with agents—and possibly also lawyers and/or managers—are necessary.

Contacting a Representative

Writers, social cripples that we often are, must nevertheless learn some of the social etiquette that is useful not only professionally but also personally.

1) Mail Manners

Notwithstanding what I've said above, one independent screenwriting educator complains that to suggest that writers can win a representative's consideration simply by writing a smart query letter is absurd. He says that writers must nurture elaborate, sophisticated alliances, interlocking matrices of relationships developed by schmoozing it up at industry parties and panels and by hanging out in trendy showbiz restaurants and bars, getting to know the right people. He asserts that the reason I tell this dreadful lie is because it's what writers want to hear.

Ironically, the last thing writers want to hear is that it is easy to get an agent to consider a screenplay. It is far more soothing to contemplate that there is something wrong with the agent than to confront the sorry reality that likely something is wrong with the query letter or, worse, the script.

Instead of worrying about clever schemes for winning an agent's agreement to represent a screenplay, writers should worry about writing a screenplay that is genuinely worthy of a worthy agent's representation. In fact, agents eagerly and urgently seek scripts from new writers. My office at UCLA receives requests from agents for new material every week. Callers and correspondents actually get mad at me if I fail to supply them.

If agents are hard to reach, if they are reluctant to consider new writers, how can one account for all of the telephone traffic I get, the letters, faxes, e-mail, and now also tweets, plus Facebook and MySpace postings and even messengers showing up in the flesh, refusing to leave until they are handed a screenplay for delivery to their bosses?

On one occasion no fewer than six agents from what is arguably the most powerful and prestigious agency in town showed up in person at my office to stage a commando raid (I could have sworn I saw hand grenades strapped to their belts) demanding screenplays by new writers. I have seen agents appear uninvited at screenwriting award ceremonies, clipboards at the ready, signing new writers as they strut through the door.

What counts, again, is the writing. To reach an agent a writer need merely write a sharp, short, smart, savvy query letter. In an upcoming section I'll provide an example of such a letter, the actual query that won consideration for the then-unknown writer of a screenplay that became not merely a film but a franchise.

As demonstrated, if the query letter is properly written it will lead to an invitation to submit the screenplay. This is how an unsolicited script is turned into one that is solicited.

From time to time writers complain that they have tried this technique and failed. They assert that they sent query letters to any number of agents and received no invitation to submit their script; their requests were either outright refused or, far more typically, ignored.

When I hear such stories I invariably ask the writers to read me their query letter. In virtually every instance the problem becomes plain as day: The letter is a train wreck. More than likely it contains too much information about both the writer and, even more often, the script.

One of these writers, however, read me his letter and, frankly, it struck me as perfect. I could not for the life of me imagine how any agent—much less dozens upon dozens of agents—could have refused the opportunity to consider the script. After a long silence during which we collectively pondered his dilemma, the writer muttered under his breath, "Maybe it's the synopsis."

"The what?" I asked.

"The synopsis," he said again.

"You sent a synopsis along with your letter?" If a writer encloses a synopsis in his letter, that is what the agent will read.

Don't some agents and agencies require a synopsis?

If they do, keep it short. Treat the synopsis as a tease, a mini Previews of Coming Attractions dedicated to seducing the agent into wanting to know more about the project. In this regard, the more information you provide, the less likely that the agent will want to read the script.

If an agent insists on a synopsis, double-space it and limit it to a fraction of a single page. Don't try to cram each and every tidbit of story and character into the synopsis. The purpose is to coax the agent into making those discoveries for herself in the script.

This query letter "system" was recently tested and fared quite well. A screenwriting instructor in a major metropolitan center—thousands of miles from Hollywood—conducted a survey at two different university film departments. Students in four screenwriting classes wrote query letters and sent them cold to a sampling of agents gleaned from the Writers Guild's list of franchised agencies.

Before the letters were mailed, however, they had to be approved by both the instructor and all the students in the class. The letters were painstakingly studied, with an eye toward economy and seduction. They went out to agents only after winning approval from the class.

The reported "take" rate (the proportion of favorable responses—invitations to submit the scripts): ninety-six percent. When query letters were adjudged to be properly, effectively written, without any connection to or recommendation from an industry insider, ninety-six out of a hundred agents agreed to consider the scripts. Moreover, a substantial number among them were agents who designate on the Writers Guild list that they do not accept unsolicited scripts.

Remember, they did not agree to represent the scripts but merely to consider them. Once an agent agrees to consider a script, it is the script's merit—or lack thereof—that will persuade her to represent it or, conversely, to pass.

If writers are reluctant to believe that agents want to consider their scripts, they find it even more improbable that agents actually want to like those scripts. It is as if the agents wake up each morning with an agenda to break as many writers' hearts as possible.

This is, of course, exactly the opposite of the truth. Should that come as a surprise?

Does not everybody prefer to read something they like rather than something they do not? Would not any agent covet the opportunity to launch a new writer, to say nothing of garnering the commission payable to her upon sale of the script?

This is one of those truths that is so obvious it is difficult to see. It obliterates the myth that agents are generally cynics whose greatest pleasure is to crush writers' dreams, dash their hopes, and bust their chops. On the contrary, agents want to respect what they read. Writers need to recognize that the relationship between artist and representative—as among all members of the creative film family—is not adversarial but collaborative. Writers and agents are not at odds with one another. Both need the same thing: a script that is marketable.

Once again, the simplest, most effective, most straightforward way to win an agent's consideration is simply to write a standard query letter. I stand behind that proposition today more firmly than ever.

Do not send the letter, or the script, return-receipt requested. Sometimes this results in a notice being left by the carrier instructing the addressee to report to the post office to pick up the script. It's damned frustrating for an agent to schlep there and stand in line only to discover that what awaits her is a letter from a writer seeking permission to submit a script, or the script itself. It creates an impression, all right; but not the kind that any smart writer seeks.

It is a wise idea, also, to avoid any fancy tricks or stunts when submitting scripts. Recently I received a huge box. Inside was nothing but packing foam. Amid all the foam I finally found a single fortune cookie. The "fortune" was the news (presumably lucky for me) that a new script by a new writer was on its way.

I admit it: I was annoyed at having squandered even a little bit of time searching through the packing material to see if there was anything in there, wondering whether or not something had been lost. Moreover, I was doubly disturbed at having to trek down the hall to the waste bin in order to ditch all that trash, with the Styrofoam peanuts flying all over the place. Did this take up a great deal of time? No. Still, all of the time it did take up—every second of it—was wasted; it achieved absolutely no purpose other than to create an unfavorable impression upon a potential reader.

The single most preposterous script submission I ever heard of involved a huge package arriving by special messenger at an agent's office. Inside was a birdcage containing a screenplay and a living, breathing bird: a homing pigeon.

Attached to its leg was a small leather pouch. A note pasted to the cage contained instructions: Upon reading the script, the agent was to check "yes" or "no" on a scrap of paper, insert it in the pouch, and release the bird out the window. Presumably, the bird would carry the notice to its sender.

Alas, however, as the script lay at the bottom of the cage, it already contained commentary from the bird, commentary that was both fowl and foul.

2) *Telephone Etiquette*

In fair weather and foul, however, instead of phoning, writers are still better off writing letters to agents. Indeed, screenwriters use the telephone entirely too much. They use it in movie after movie wherein characters narrate the tale via telephone conversations rather than act it out.

There is another way writers abuse the telephone: calling agents. There is simply too much telephone traffic for even the most diligent agent to handle. He can, on the other hand, easily handle his mail. That is why writers should write letters to agents instead of dialing their telephone numbers.

On those rare occasions, however, where it is appropriate to telephone an agent or producer, certain simple rules of procedure should be followed.

Never call merely to find out if a script was received.

I've already mentioned that it's a mistake to send material return-receipt requested. Alternatively, the writer can provide a self-addressed, stamped postcard for the agent to pop in the mail, but I regard this to be an error as well. It carries the rank air of amateurism.

How can one know if a script has been received?

First, make certain you get the mailing address exactly right. While you're at it, spell your correspondent's name correctly. Do I care a whole lot if my name is misspelled?

No.

Others, however, may take substantial offense and view the misspelling as a discourtesy and, worse, as an indication of the likely carelessness that went into the script. If the address is current and correct in all its details and specifications, and if it is clearly printed, the likelihood that it has arrived is overwhelming. There are, of course, exceptions, but they are just that: exceptions.

Additionally, be mindful that in Hollywood your first impression is your only impression. Be certain, therefore, that the proffered screenplay is truly ready.

Never call in order to tell someone to discard a script recently submitted because the draft has been revised. Such calls inevitably arrive immediately after the reader has finished reading the script. If the script needed to be revised it should not have been sent in the first place.

These days, no doubt thanks to the capabilities of word-processing software, there are no discrete first, second, and third drafts but instead just one wriggling, writhing, endlessly evolving draft. Writers hand me a script at ten in the morning and have a revised version at two o'clock that same afternoon.

I sometimes receive phone calls from writers advising me that I am about to receive a package with revised pages 8, 18, 22 through 25, 61, 73 through 78, and 109. Accompanying the new pages is a request, naturally, that I re-collate the script.

About the only legitimate reason to utilize the telephone to intrude upon an agent or producer is to return a call she made to you. Should you reach her voice mail, observe an important practice: Begin every message with your name and telephone number.

Make it your practice to leave your number even if you are absolutely certain the party already has it.

If this strikes you as petty, remember that underlying it resides respect for the receiver of the message, the person you hope will return your call. For one thing, he may be calling in for his messages from a remote location and not be in the practice of lugging around his ten-pound Rolodex everywhere he goes. Granted, these days the analog printed-on-cards Rolodex file has given way to the cell phone and the BlackBerry and other forms of compact, electronic personal organizers in which everybody has not only their address and phone files but also the blood types and hairstyle of everyone who ever lived going back all the way to Charlemagne. Still, instead of making it even just the littlest bit harder for someone to return your call, why not make it easier? Redundancy has no proper place in dramatic narratives but in our life it is often useful.

Even when I do not desire a call to be returned—for example, when I am merely imparting some requested information—I will announce my name, then state something like the following: "There's no need to call me back but, for your convenience, if you have any questions or comments, my number is . . ."

When you have to leave a message, keep it short.

It communicates a great deal about the writer's respect and consideration for his listener's time when the information he leaves is cogent and useful instead of rambling and incoherent.

Be certain that the outgoing message on your own voice mail, i.e., your own recorded greeting to callers, is straightforward and to-the-point.

A complex production with horns blaring and hooves beating, accompanied by a dramatized voice-of-doom narration, might be funny the first time—if at all—but thereafter it is just a pain in the neck, a waste of the caller's time.

Some people are reluctant to include their name in their voice mail's outgoing greeting, and that is just fine. Nevertheless, it is useful to let callers know that they have reached the correct number.

In your outgoing greeting, be certain to report your name and/or phone number, including the area code, so that the caller will know he has reached the intended party.

Area codes are now ubiquitous. Nowadays even local calls require eleven digits, absent any extensions that may also have to be dialed. Many people—myself, for example—may be calling through an institutional switchboard that requires yet another code to be dialed in order to access an outside line.

That could all add up to fourteen or more digits merely to call across the street. Under such circumstances, cannot everyone understand how easy it is to misdial?

It is useful, therefore, to let callers know precisely what number they have reached. It is frustrating, indeed downright maddening, in attempting to return someone's call—someone seeking my help—to reach voice mail containing no clue as to the identity of the party I have reached.

Bear in mind also that voice mail is now very much a part of our culture. There is no longer any need to indicate in an outgoing greeting that it is voice mail that has been reached, that we're either on another line or away from the desk, that your call is important to us, that we'll be back shortly, or any of that now all-too-familiar fluff. Nor is there any purpose in instructing callers to wait for the beep.

Of course, all this discussion regarding voice mail presupposes that the writer possesses such service. Personally, if I attempt to return a call and reach a line that rings without answer, I will not call again. The same applies to a busy signal. A writer who wishes his calls to be returned needs to be available even when he's unavailable. He requires, therefore, not only voice mail but also call waiting. What the savvy writer desires is to make it not difficult but easy to be reached.

Above all else, remember that the finest telephone etiquette is not nearly as effective, as considerate, or as smart as writing an old-fashioned letter.

These rules may seem petty, even silly. My hope is that they seem obvious. Ultimately they ought to derive from common sense. They promote practices that are helpful not only professionally but also personally. A writer can only have poor phone manners, for example, if he does not yet appreciate how he comes across. In screenwriting as in all creative expression, coming across is the name of the game.

3) A Foolproof, Shockproof, Waterproof, Tamper-Resistant Method for Reaching an Agent

If winning the attention and, eventually, the representation of agents for theatrical features is hard, gaining representation in television is still more difficult. While query letters may work for writers seeking representation for feature-length film scripts, it is trickier in TV.

Too many writers—like too many critics—are snobs about television. In certain corners of institutions of higher learning, television is referred to only in whispers and even then as "the T word."

In fact, television shares with all creative expression—film, theater, dance, music, painting, sculpture, literature—the fact that most of it is unworthy while some small portion of it is truly excellent. By "worthy" I mean that it has qualities within it that cause it to merit the time and attention of observers because it moves them, provokes them, disturbs them, upsets and frightens them, engages them, makes them laugh, makes them cry.

I quite agree with a *New York Times* article in recent years holding that for the most part TV is a whole lot more interesting than theatrical features. At the time of this writing, instead of exploring new and exciting ideas, major studios are reprocessing hoary, ancient product, producing sequels and prequels and remakes and new chapters of weary, old franchises. These are almost inevitably lean on story and character and rich in fireballs and weird vehicles and wardrobe and chases and shootings and special effects.

When the Writers Guild went on strike some years ago, I was assigned picket duty at a studio gate, where I ran into an old film school classmate from the University of Southern California, action/adventure meister John Milius (*Apocalypse Now*, among many other credits). Wielding bright Day-Glo STRIKE! signs, we tramped up and back before the entrance to NBC's facility in Burbank. Noticing our picket signs, several tourists approached us. "You guys writers?"

We nodded.

"How do you get into TV?" one asked.

"What you should ask," John said, "is 'How do you get out of TV?'"

In truth, television is the arena where writers are treated and paid most generously. A top screenplay price may be, say, four million dollars, but that is fairly rare; consider that for creating and writing the TV series *Family Ties*, Gary David Goldberg earned scores of millions of dollars. Joe Eszterhas sold a four-page treatment describing *One Night Stand* for, adjusted for inflation, seven or eight million dollars. However, Matt Groening and James L. Brooks have each earned literally hundreds of millions of dollars from *The Simpsons*.

The greatest show business fortunes consist of trillions of nickels and dimes: record and publishing royalties and television residuals. In a typical season, for example, an episode of a TV series will rerun in prime time at least once, and almost certainly twice. Each rerun under such circumstances pays the writer a hundred percent in residuals; that is to say, each time the show reruns he is paid all over again the whole amount he was paid in the first place. If that were the end of it, it would still be generous compensation by any standard. It is not the end, however; it is merely the beginning. In subsequent seasons the writer will continue to earn residuals, albeit on a declining scale. If, however, the show goes to syndication, even as the individual airings pay less and less, there are more and more of them, so that the overall amount of money actually soars.

Best of all, to earn all of these payments the writer has to do exactly this: nothing. The residuals that flow to him during his lifetime—and thereafter to his heirs—are payments for work he has already done.

Generally speaking, therefore, financial compensation in television is far greater than in film. The various collaborators in a television series that produces a sufficient number of episodes to qualify for syndication may well share more than a billion dollars among them.

A hit television series, then, is like *Star Wars*, *E.T.*, and *Jurassic Park* (Michael Crichton, David Koepp, adapting Crichton's novel) all rolled up in one. Plus, you can probably toss in *The Dark Knight* (Jonathan Nolan, Christopher Nolan, David S. Goyer, based on characters created by Bob Kane); *Up* (Bob Peterson, Pete Docter, Thomas McCarthy); and one or another or several of the *Transformer* movies (Ron Friedman), too.

As dizzying as such remuneration may be, writers in television are not only paid more generously but also treated better than feature film writers in a host of ways. This ought to come as no surprise, since it is television writers who constitute the majority of working Writers Guild members and it is natural to assume therefore that the rules and regulations would be designed to favor them.

Note, for example, that a writer at a pitch meeting for a film may be asked to return for further discussions regarding a particular proposal. Indeed he can be invited back again and again without limit.

Without compensation.

Some writers may consider that many meetings to be encouraging and flattering, but the experience grows old in a hurry and comes to resemble free brain-picking.

In television, on the other hand, after an initial pitch meeting, if a producer wants to discuss the matter further, he must pay at least Writers Guild scale for a story. These days that's something like ten thousand dollars minimum—and that for only a two- or three-page double-spaced outline.

Money aside, TV—in particular cable—is generally a lot more courageous than mainstream big-studio commercial Hollywood. For me, any given episode of *The Sopranos* is far more worthy of my time and attention than the vast majority of studio theatrical releases that I see. HBO, for example, is a company willing—even eager—to give a talent such as David Chase, *The Sopranos*' creator, free rein to do whatever it is that he wants to do. In presenting his timeless drama—replete also with wonderful comical moments—Chase did not have a dozen studio executive vice presidents looking over his shoulder, oppressing him, driving him crazy, telling him what to do and what not to do.

Earlier I mentioned my film school classmate John Milius. Notwithstanding decades of success as an action/adventure maven with hugely successful theatrical movies under his belt, in many ways his greatest triumph was the HBO series *Rome* (cocreated by Milius). This from the guy who opined that television is something not to get into but to get out of.

UCLA alumnus Darren Star found far more opportunities to be creative and experimental in his TV shows—*Sex in the City* and *Melrose Place*, among others—than he ever would have enjoyed in mainstream commercial features or broadcast TV.

No wonder the television market is cruelly competitive. Exacerbating this situation is the fact that over the past decade the freelance market in television has largely evaporated. Writers who break through and enjoy sustained success almost invariably are those who, after selling a handful of episodes, end up on staff at a particular show. This causes the availability of freelance work to shrink still further as staff writers consume more and more of the assignments.

Good news: There is a solution.

Upon encountering resistance from television agents, writers can take another tack altogether: write to the writers. Which writers? The writers of the shows they hope to crack.

How can one find out the names of these writers? Copy them from the tube. Watch the credits as they flit past; if they move too quickly, record the show on your DVR and exploit your freeze-frame capability so that there's ample time to read the name.

Once one has the name of the writer, how can one find out his address?

All film and television writers have the same address.

Here it is: c/o Writers Guild of America, West, Inc., Membership Department, 7000 West Third Street, Los Angeles, CA 90048.

What should these letters say? First of all, they should praise the writer. You'll never go wrong praising talent. You need to invent some breezy, respectful, affirmative opening gambit. For example:

> Dear [writer's name],
>
> Likely I watch more television than anyone ought to, but every once in a while a show comes along that makes it all worthwhile. Your episode [episode title] of [series title] changed my life forever.

Next, praise some specific aspect of the writer's work.

I recall in particular the way [character] confronted [character] over the question of [issue]. When she tells him [line of dialogue] and he responds [line of dialogue] I just about fell out of my La-Z-Boy recliner.

I even dropped the channel zapper (which my schnauzer promptly ate).

In what might otherwise have been but a mildly diverting half hour you were able keenly and precisely to posit profound insights into human nature. I'll never again view the question of [issue] in quite the same way.

Do not state that you are yourself a writer, and that you are willing to commit unnatural acts upon him if he'll only read your work and recommend it to his own or another agent. Instead, self-effacingly wonder aloud about some arbitrary and mundane aspect of the writer's work habits.

I've always wondered about the day-to-day methods of talented, disciplined artists such as yourself. I am curious to know, for example, whether you write with pencil and ruled yellow legal pad or utilize a word processor.

Of course, I have no right to presume you will respond to such questions; I recognize they're none of my business and, moreover, that you are undoubtedly too busy creating still more dazzling fare.

Therefore, I won't squander another moment of your time. Please know that I am forever grateful for your having touched my life. I offer you congratulations and thanks for sharing your considerable gift with me and millions of viewers all around the nation and the world.

Sincerely,

[your name]

I offer two promises: (1) The sun will set in the west tonight. (2) The writer will answer your letter.

There are two reasons you can count on a reply. The second reason first:

*Principle 63: Every established writer—without exception—
was once totally unknown and inexperienced.*

Lingering in the memory of even the hardest-bitten, steel-tempered veteran is the recollection of his scuffling days; he'll likely be eager to provide support to a fledgling scribe who approaches him in an engaging, sincere, and, most important of all, respectful manner.

The main reason, however, that virtually any experienced writer will choose to be helpful is this:

*Principle 64: Every writer will seek any excuse to avoid
working on the particular assignment in front of
him at the moment.*

That is why any writer will seize upon the opportunity to reply. It is the perfect outlet for him to avoid his own work. It offers him a double whammy: He gets to put off his own work and he also wins the chance (not without justification) to feel like a good guy, a caring, generous soul.

Ask yourself: If you were a successful writer and received such an inquiry, would you not reply?

Of course you would.

A dear old friend of mine, now an enormously successful writer and director, tells me that when he was completely unknown, fresh out of college and working a grim and tedious day job, he wrote a letter of appreciation—really nothing more than fan mail—to none other than renowned novelist, essayist, poet, and critic, the late John Updike, complimenting him on his latest book.

He mailed the letter on a Monday. Thursday of that same week he received a handwritten nine-page reply from Updike. No doubt there is solid testimony here to Updike's generosity. You can also be certain, however, that even John Updike wanted to avoid whatever writing project lay in front of him on his desk at any particular time.

In the proposed sample letter I suggest that after praising the writer you ask not about profound literary issues but, instead, about the writer's personal work habits. Are writers willing to discuss this subject with perfect strangers?

Just try to stop them.

Just try to get them to shut up.

Writers crave the opportunity to wax prolific, to rant and rave about their particular and peculiar quirks: what level of rag content they seek in their writing bond, how soft the lead in their pencil, which blend of coffee roast they favor in order to stay awake while slogging through their tedium.

In the movie *The Front* (Walter Bernstein), Woody Allen portrays a bartender who secretly fronts for blacklisted writers, writers who cannot work under their own names because they are politically out of favor. Woody's character thus receives screen credit for stories he did not write, then quietly passes the payment to the actual writers.

His girlfriend quizzes him about what she takes to be his writing. He is always understandably reticent. He asserts that he simply does not like to discuss it. "I don't get it," the girlfriend laments. "Generally you can't get writers to cease prattling on and on about their writing."

Amen to that.

Once the writer has replied to your letter, write back to him; thank him and perhaps ask yet another innocuous question or two. Eventually you will have established enough of a relationship gingerly and delicately to presume to ask him to read your script. Perhaps you'll write something like this:

> . . . *and finally, I want to let you know that you have so inspired me that I've actually written an episode. I do not tell you this in order to solicit your consideration of my wretchedly amateurish effort with an eye toward a recommendation to an agent (yours, for example) but merely to share with you how affirmatively your creativity has affected one particular member of your vast, grateful audience.*

I promise two things: (1) The sun will rise in the east. (2) The writer will volunteer to show your script to his agent or, at the very least, to recommend it to another agent or even a producer.

He may well do this even if he thinks the script stinks. Perhaps he wants to demonstrate to you—and to himself—that he has the power to get a script read. But whatever his motivation, your chance for success will come down to one thing alone: the script.

Let it, therefore, be worthy.

Speculating

When a writer writes a screenplay in exchange for only the hope but not the promise of remuneration, he is said to be speculating. He is guessing—speculating—that the script will sell.

It's a fancy euphemism for writing for free.

Notwithstanding the principle requiring that writers treat themselves as professionals, speculating can be the craftiest marketing move a writer can make. It is the way virtually every successful writing career is launched. This is because until a writer demonstrates that he can write—by writing something—no one is likely to hire him. Once he has written a screenplay, he alone owns one hundred percent of it.

If the script turns out to be terrible and nobody wants to buy it, or if it turns out wonderful and still nobody wants to buy it, the writer can sit himself down and speculate again.

What's more, after that he can speculate yet again.

While an agent almost certainly will not go out and peddle an unknown writer's services, if he feels the script is any good he may well hustle that same anonymous writer's existing screenplay. This is because even if the writer is unknown, the screenplay is not. Once it is written, it is there, in all its glorious (or not so glorious) pages. One can heft it in one's hand, thump it against a desk.

More important, one can read it.

Upon reading, one can love it, hate it, or a bit of both. One need no longer guess about it since it is there for all the world to see. It may eventually bring joy to the writer by winning him representation. There is a strong possibility also, however, that it will deliver only heartache.

Hollywood Nightmares

In the film and television business one never has to stand in line awaiting his ration of heartache.

To be sure, Hollywood abounds with dark stories about how cruelly its artists are cheated, mistreated, and abused. That's the good news, for there is something far worse than that: neglect. Infinitely more painful than the harshest criticism is the yawning, hollow silence that accompanies being ignored.

Tragically, too many Hollywood nightmares are true. There are popular perceptions, however, that are in fact false, one of which is that screenplays—and even mere ideas for screenplays—are commonly stolen.

A modest major studio movie is budgeted these days at scores of millions of dollars. What's more, money spent to shoot a movie is only the beginning. Those production costs are followed by additional scores of millions for promotion, advertising, and prints. *Avatar* (James Cameron) is said to cost half a billion dollars to produce and promote.

It ought to be evident that no movie studio is going to invest so much money in a movie for which the rights to the screenplay have not been secured. It makes no sense to run the risk of subpoenas, injunctions, and litigation of every kind from every corner, merely to avoid spending even as much as, say, a million dollars or even three or four million for the script.

From time to time, nonetheless, a screenplay is stolen, but this is exceptional. Far more commonly, a writer claims some particular film credited to others is in fact based upon his own script. In the studio's movie, say, a boy and a girl fall in love, break up, and then reconcile. In the writer's script the same occurrences play out.

What possible explanation besides larceny?

Why do so many people seem to think their idea was stolen? Probably because they misunderstand the value of an idea. They do not realize that ideas, basically, are just ideas—brief, unformed flashes of incidents or insights, broad bits and pieces of notions.

Trembling with excitement, a doctor pal of mine who happens to specialize in nephrology (you can look it up) recently told me that he had "a great idea for a movie." All that remained, he assured me, was "for it to be written."

I resisted the urge to say to him: "I have a great idea for a kidney transplant; all that remains is the surgery."

As asserted earlier and throughout, ideas are cheap. What has value is an idea worked out in detail, not merely thought up but written down.

New writers too often hesitate to show their scripts for fear they will be swiped. But new writers are best advised to "dazzle 'em with their footwork"—show their work to anybody and everybody who'll look. Even if readers don't respond in the desired fashion, the writer's name is paraded before the industry's eyes. The writer begins to build stature. He's current, he's in circulation, he's in the market.

A simple precaution writers can take is to register their scripts with the Writers Guild of America. Scripts can be registered in person or by old-fashioned postal mail or e-mail. At this writing the fee for writers who are not Guild members is twenty dollars. The Guild's Registration Office will accept a hard copy of the material or an electronic file and store it. Should it ever be necessary (as it is in a minuscule number of cases, far less than one percent), the Guild will testify in court that on a particular date at a specific hour they had in their possession the material in question. It is up to the court, then, to study the material and determine whether theft has actually occurred. Writers have enough to worry about without worrying about what they don't have to worry about. Character, dialogue, and story are subjects worth worrying about. Plagiarism is not.

Good Faith

Beyond agents, beyond lawyers, beyond personal managers, beyond convoluted contracts with complicated definitions of net profit, above all else what a writer needs is faith. The same faith necessary to write a screenplay is required also of writers who, having written that script, hope to navigate their way through the business. They have to be able to tolerate a certain uncertainty.

Without good faith, even the most carefully prepared, assiduously detailed contract is effectively meaningless. Even a major studio, for all its size, is often merely a cog among numerous enterprises owned by a far larger conglomerate. With its vast legal staff and boundless resources, it can embroil a writer in endless, costly legal procedures.

Some time ago a prominent writer enjoyed in his contract a uniquely rich participation in his film's profit. The movie turned out to be a thundering success, earning hundreds of millions of dollars. The writer, however, while paid his original fee, never saw a dime of that so-called net profit, which ought to have been a still far greater sum than the compensation he had already received.

After costly audits of the studio's books by his own accountants, the writer sued.

In a television interview the head of the studio, defending his company's position, told a reporter that the writer had already received hundreds of thousands of dollars for scripting the movie. Where was it written, he asked, that a writer should own part of the picture itself? I ached to hear the reporter respond: "In the contract your studio negotiated with him." The reporter, however, remained silent. Could it have been that the studio in question also happened to own the television network on which this interview took place?

The executive went on to challenge the writer. He had engaged the fanciest lawyers in all of Hollywood, hadn't he? They'd written him the lengthiest, most ironclad contract in show business history. Let him compel them now to enforce it. All parties could meet in court, the executive suggested, sometime during the next century.

Into what useful information does this translate for new writers? Simply that they should forget about agents, lawyers, rights, contractual clauses, and profit provisions altogether, at least during the period they're actually composing their script. They have their hands full worrying about good writing.

Once they have written a worthy script, they can engage capable professionals to worry about these details for them. As surely as they need to confront the possibility a script will not sell, they need also recognize there is the chance their rights will not be consistently upheld regarding a script that has won a contract. Writers—successful and not—had better be prepared from time to time to have their hearts broken. If their sanity absolutely requires a consistently honest accounting, plus unmitigated fair treatment, they should decline the dreams-for-dollars dodge and go to work delivering mail for the post office.

Acquiring an Agent

Certainly many agents have famously started their careers in their agencies' mail rooms.

The rule is that as long as you truly need an agent you'll never find one; conversely, if you don't need one, agents will queue up at your door pleading to represent you. Of course, this is a bit of an exaggeration, but only a bit. Agents are not evil; they are merely human. If they are any good, they are also busy.

A writer friend of mine who has changed agents at least a dozen times in the past several years told me recently he's finally found one with whom he is truly happy. The agent calls him, my pal boasts, several times a week, just to chat and see how things are going. Frankly, however, I urge writers to beware of agents who have time to gossip. A smart writer wants his agent to be too busy beating the bushes for bucks to have time for time-passing conversation about the weather or the Dodgers or the Lakers. It's perfectly fine, if rare, for agents and their clients to become truly close friends. What counts first of all, though, is that aspect of their relationship that is not personal but professional.

There are essentially two kinds of services an agent might realistically provide a client: find him a professional assignment and sell original material. For most writers, especially new writers, as a practical matter agents offer only one of these services, if they even offer that: selling original material.

Since we can dismiss it in a hurry, let us address the first service first. A writer without credits, much less a writer with no sample or showcase script, has a snowball's chance in Southern California of finding a commissioned assignment, that is, a paid writing job. That's why it's largely a waste of time trying to work up a pitch or even to write a so-called treatment.

I should quickly tell of a longtime friend, a former English professor who arrived in town with a proposal for a television series and questions for me regarding what he should do with it.

"Put it in a drawer," I recommended. "No studio or network is going to buy a proposal from an unknown writer."

"But isn't TV interested in new ideas?" he asked.

"Do you watch TV? Does it appear to you that they're interested in new ideas?"

I discouraged my friend even from sending his brief proposal to producers as I was certain it would be returned unopened and unread.

"If they aren't interested in new ideas," he continued, "what are they interested in?"

"In people," I told him.

"What people?"

"The people who did it before. The same people who got a show on last year. They do not want to take chances with unknown writers who might produce a program that is mediocre; they want people they can know for certain to be mediocre."

"The people who got a show on last year," my pal persisted, "each and every one of them at one time in their lives had never had a show produced."

I told him that as a writer lacking professional experience he should be speculatively writing a showcase feature-length screenplay, and accept the TV proposal as a warm-up, a worthy ten-finger exercise.

Disregarding my advice, he mailed his proposal blindly to a prominent television production company.

Two weeks later they bought the project.

I relate this incident because it is fair warning that any advice in this book may prove plain wrong. Bearing that in mind, I stand on my advice: The way to get an agent is to speculate on a screenplay.

With the virtual certainty that an unsolicited script submitted blindly to a studio will be returned unopened and unread, it is easy to conclude that not too many people in the movie business are eager or even willing to read a new writer's work.

Nothing could be further from the truth. First, as already suggested, it is probably a mistake for a writer to make his own submission directly to a potential purchaser. He's better off having an agent do that. While stamina is forever useful, connecting with agents is a simple procedure.

The Writers Guild of America, West (www.wga.org) publishes and regularly updates in hard copy and online its franchised agency list every month. The list contains contact information for scores of legitimate agencies. Some of these agencies are one-person operations. Many more involve several agents. Still others have dozens of agents representing writers. Collectively, then, the list provides access to literally hundreds of writers' representatives.

All listed agents are licensed by the state and certified to abide by covenants negotiated with the Guild. To put it another way, the listing confers a certain legitimacy upon the agency. This is not to suggest that all agents will satisfy every writer; it means simply that no writer should deal with any agent who is not on the list.

A glance at the list reveals that some agents indicate they do not accept unsolicited submissions unless they are recommended by persons known to them. Other agents indicate the reverse, that they welcome unsolicited scripts from first-time writers.

The majority, however, indicate nothing either way. For the most part, writers may ignore these indications. If they adhere to the simple method that follows, they should have relatively little trouble winning the consideration of agents.

First, permit me to make a suggestion that I touched on earlier in this chapter: Do not try to reach agents by telephone.

A former student of mine, now a prospering playwright and screenwriter, in her scuffling days got a part-time job working for a top agent. On one occasion, when his secretary was away from her desk, he asked the student to cover his phone during lunch.

Upon his return he asked if there had been any calls.

She handed him a list of one hundred and four calls; these were merely the calls that had come during lunch.

If Steven Spielberg were on the list, you can be certain the agent would promptly return his call. If a Doe calls (John or Jane) there simply is no earthly way the agent can return the call. It is impossible for a single human to return hundreds upon hundreds of telephone calls.

To be certain, Hollywood is phone-crazy, obsessed with telecommunications etiquette. Who calls whom? Whose secretary calls whose secretary? Who comes on the line first? There is no understating the important role the telephone plays in the film and television writing world. For agents, it is an especially critical tool. More than a tool, it is a weapon. A leading agent compares it specifically to a bayonet.

In the nineties, e-mail was added to the mix.

How then do you win an agent's consideration for your screenplay? You're a writer? Write a letter or send an e-mail.

The same top agent with a hundred and four calls during lunch, the one who routinely ignores but an infinitesimal portion of them, nevertheless answers all his mail and a decent portion of his e-mail.

How can that be?

As stated earlier, a writer's job is to place himself inside the minds and bodies of other people and think and act as they do. This is true, obviously, for the characters in a writer's scripts. It's true also for characters in the writer's life, including his professional life. Place yourself, therefore, in the mind and body of your representative, and think and act as she does.

Agents are by nature workaholics. Like them or don't like them—they work hard. If they feel particularly lazy one day, they'll delay their morning arrival at the office until six thirty. The phones are miraculously quiet for thirty minutes (until the East Coast calls roll in). It's an opportunity to catch up with neglected matters. Most important for writers, it's an opportunity for agents to read their mail.

An agent grabs yesterday's stack of mail, seizes his twenty-first-century version of the Dictaphone, and barks his responses. A phone conversation that would have eaten up fifteen minutes is disposed of in a terse nine seconds.

What about e-mail? No harm in giving it a try. Exactly as agents cringe under the weight of phone messages, however, these days they cringe under a barrage of e-mail. For this reason, an old-fashioned, retro, analog, ink-on-paper letter will stand out. It may win faster attention than an e-mail bearing the same text.

Even a letter from an unknown writer, a complete novice, gains its brief moment of scrutiny. If it's a lame letter, the agent may pay the writer the respect of instructing his secretary to send the formal we-don't-read-unsolicited-scripts response. An intelligent letter, however, will almost surely win the response the writer seeks: an invitation to submit the script.

Clearly, the wording of such a letter—in publishing it's called a query letter—is crucial.

The writer ought to be aware that his letter is the first evidence of his ability—or inability—to write. It's the place to start exercising infinite care; it's the place to demonstrate an appreciation for the way one comes to be perceived by others.

Be certain the letter is economical, efficient, direct.

Most important: Do not include the script with the letter.

The letter should appear to have been written quickly, even breezily, but in fact the writer needs to spend perhaps several hours on getting it exactly right. Happily, once such a letter is composed it can be copied and recopied, submitted and resubmitted to agent after agent.

This does not mean it can be a form letter, addressed To Whom It May Concern. Though the writer eventually may send this very same letter to scores of agents, there should be no hint of that fact in the letter.

To make the letter appear personal, the agent's name is required. You're writing to the agent, not the agency. Supposing you choose to approach, for no particular reason, Regressive Artists Agency, how do you know to whom to address it?

Here I renege slightly on my don't-use-the-phone injunction. Call the agency's switchboard and ask for the name of an agent at that particular agency. Should they stonewall you, should they refuse even merely to report the name of an agent, hang up and call back and ask for an arbitrary name. For example, "May I please speak to Barry Stein?" The operator may likely say something on the order of: "We have no Barry Stein but there's a Harry Steinberg. Is that you who mean?" The idea is to get her to suggest a name of an agent. You don't even need to speak to that potential representative. You've got a name. Politely hang up the phone and get ready to write a letter containing an offer they can't refuse.

Years ago a student in my UCLA workshop handed me a script that I recognized in only half a page as brilliant. I put away my notorious blue pencil and read the script just for fun. By the time I was halfway through the script I was on the phone to a hugely powerful independent agent whose clients at that time included William Goldman during his *Butch Cassidy* days and Robert Towne during his *Chinatown* period.

He took my call likely because he appreciated that if he did not I would immediately call another agency. "Put on your asbestos gloves," I told him. "This script is so hot it'll give you third-degree burns." I asked if I could send it over to him. He said, "No."

It's unusual in the extreme for an agent to decline to consider a script I refer. I was myself uncharacteristically speechless. After a while I heard the agent then say to me, "By 'send' do you mean as Priority Mail via the UCLA mail room? It'll take two weeks for it to get here if it gets here at all. Just sit tight. I'll send a messenger."

Within twenty minutes there was a knock at my door. I gave the messenger the script. The following day the agent called, saying he was declining to represent it. He said it was first-rate writing, but that the subject did not particularly appeal to him. This was no reflection on the writer or the script, he insisted. He explained that he was a fussy old man and preposterously particular about the projects he took on. He went on to tell me that he did not doubt for a second, however, that the script and writer would find representation and that it would all add up to a successful movie and writing career.

With my assistance the writer developed something resembling the following query letter.

Dear Mr. Lastfogel:

I am a student at UCLA in the Master of Fine Arts program in Screenwriting.

I have written a screenplay, SHADOW CLAN, an action/adventure story set in contemporary New York City and ninth-century Scotland.

May I send it to you for your consideration?

Cordially,

Note that the first paragraph—a single sentence—introduces the writer in a brief but engaging way.

The next paragraph, also a single sentence, hardly describes the screenplay at all. It establishes the setting and the style and virtually nothing else. Who could refuse to read an action/adventure screenplay set in contemporary New York and ninth-century Scotland, particularly if it's written by a writer enrolled in an institution that has produced the writers of a dozen films and TV shows produced and/or directed by Steven Spielberg?

On his own, following my instructions, the writer mailed his letter to several agents on the Writers Guild's franchised agency list. Every one of them responded affirmatively. What had previously been unsolicited material was now suddenly solicited.

All the agencies responded that they wanted to represent the script. The writer arbitrarily chose one—not a particularly prominent one at that—who nevertheless promptly sold the script to a major studio. I gave the writer an A in the course and 20th Century Fox gave him (adjusted for inflation) four million dollars.

Right there, as anyone can see, are two good results the writer got from the script.

Obviously, it's helpful in query letters to mention that the writer happens to be a student at a world center of higher learning, enrolled in the leading screenwriting education program. What about the vast majority of writers who can make no such boast?

Here is a variation on the theme.

Dear Mr. Lastfogel,

    I am a probation officer for the city of Dayton, Ohio, where I have written a screenplay entitled BOTTOM DOLLAR.

    It is a comedy about an AWOL marine's search for his long-lost father.

    May I send it to you for your consideration?

                                 Cordially,

Note that the final paragraph is identical to that in the previous sample. There is but a smidgen of information about the writer, just enough to make him appear interesting. Beyond the title is only the briefest description of the screenplay.

It is this last area where inexperienced writers get into trouble. They are all too eager to tell too much about their script. Instead, they should tease the agent, seduce him into wanting to know more.

The way to get him to want to know more is to tell him less.

The greater the detail you provide, the larger the target to shoot at. This is why you should never include a synopsis or outline of the script. If you provide a summary, that's what the agent will read instead of the script. If the agency insists on one, then make it as brief as possible, as I described earlier when discussing synopses. As eager as agents are to discover new talent, to say nothing of the prospect of earning generous commissions, they are also perpetually swamped with material and crave any excuse to avoid reading yet another screenplay.

Still, a well-crafted query letter will win nine out of ten agents' invitations to submit a script. It is in this manner, once again, that an unsolicited script becomes solicited.

Once the agent answers, agreeing to consider the material, the writer can send the screenplay with a quick cover letter. This second letter simply acknowledges the agent's own letter and indicates that, as requested, the script is enclosed.

Before we leave this section, allow me to include another example of an actual query letter that no agent could turn down.

> *Dear Mr. Lastfogel,*
>
> *On January 4, 2004, I walked into my apartment and found my fiancé "doing" my roommate. She had honey smeared on her chest and was handcuffed to the headboard.*

Can anyone imagine an agent—or anyone else—not reading further?

> *Unfortunately, what I did in response to finding them led to my arrest. Six years later I'm still dealing with the consequence of my actions. But you know what they say about lemons and lemonade.*

The letter went on to say that these events were the subject of a script the writer had completed. Is it any wonder that every agent who received this letter promptly solicited the screenplay?

The lesson: Find something personal about yourself, even if it's not felonious, and find something seductive also about your story. Report it succinctly—a sentence or two or three—in an old-fashioned, analog letter, and you'll receive the response you desire. Remember, however, there's no purpose in any of this, unless and until a writer is confident that she has a script that's truly ready to show.

How about e-mail?

E-mail is all right, but remember that many professionals, especially literary agents, receive hundreds of e-mails daily, and it's easy to get lost in the electronic slush pile. Since fewer and fewer writers send letters printed on paper in ink, doing so is one way to stand out.

Principle 65: Standing out is what it's all about.

Agents: Contracts and Law

Once a writer stands out and wins representation, will the agent truly and faithfully work for the client?

There is every chance that he will not. Still, it is nothing to lose sleep over.

The worst thing that should happen to a writer ought to be that she wants to separate from her agent but her agent doesn't want to let her go. This occurs only when the client is earning sizable fees and the agent is motivated, therefore, to keep her.

That's the exception.

Even in so unusual an instance, stuck with an agent she's come to dislike, the writer enjoys substantial protection. For one thing, literary agents in movies and television are by law limited to commissions of ten percent. I've never heard of an agent charging less, but under the law none charges more. Literary managers and lawyers may charge more, however, and sometimes a writer, once her career is really under way and there are offers on the table to purchase her scripts, may require a combination of the above. These multiple commissions can add up to a lot of money.

Commission, however, means just that: a percentage paid out of the gross once a sale of original material or an agreement regarding writing services is consummated and the funds actually paid. No writer, therefore, needs to spend money out of pocket. Her representatives withhold their commissions before sending the balance to their client.

No writer should ever send an agent any money. Neither should any agent bill a writer merely to consider representing a screenplay. No reputable agent asks for funds in advance.

Beyond the ten percent commission limit, the law also restricts agent/client contracts to ninety days unless there is a bona fide offer of employment. This means that even a writer not yet halfway through a two-year agency contract is free to leave if three months pass without an offer of a professional writing job.

The most common agent abuse by far is no abuse at all but, rather, neglect.

Agency Contracts

Many writers' contracts with their representatives are oral. Oddly, new writers often appear disappointed if they do not have a written contract with an agent, if they are not "signed" by the agent.

There is no reason in the world, however, for a writer to have a signed contract with his representative. While there is nothing wrong with having such a contract, neither is there any reason for the client to press the agent for papers, for it is primarily the agent who is protected by the contract.

This is a far cry, of course, from an agreement for employment. With employment, as opposed to representation, a contract is essential.

Cynical writers suggest that agents are like underwear: You should change them once a year whether you need to or not. Of course this disserves the legions of fine agents who capably and honorably support the professional screenwriting community. Still, it is worth noting that while there is something to be said for having a single representative throughout a career, in fact clients and agents frequently separate, often without hard feelings.

At the time of this writing, over a career in fiction, nonfiction, and screen I have had more than a dozen agents, some of whom I've genuinely forgotten (to be fair, surely they have forgotten me, too). Among all these agents, I signed papers over the years with perhaps a third of them. I'm not unwilling to sign an agency contract, but given my druthers, unsigned status is preferred. When agents have insisted I sign, without hesitation I have signed. Why wouldn't I? The contracts do not mean a lot since the salient features—commission, term—are generally fixed by law.

Likewise, there are similar protections for writers, who, long before any contracts are offered, are required upon submitting material to sign a release.

Releases

Should an unrepresented writer, in order to have a screenplay considered, sign a release?

Yes.

A release is a legal document of no real consequence. Lawyers insist it protects production companies against nuisance plagiarism suits, but this is largely unfounded.

By means of a release a writer acknowledges that he understands there may be scripts similar in concept and design to the one he is himself submitting. Should a disagreement arise regarding authorship of another of the producer's projects, the writer pledges not to litigate but to seek instead some sort of arbitration.

Studio releases run to various lengths, from less than a page to six or eight extralong legal-size pages of impenetrable party-of-the-first-part legalese in swarming 2-point microfont. The most benign represent a simple acknowledgment by the writer that there may exist similar projects; the most malignant state that should there arise a disagreement between the company and the writer, the sole discretion of the company prevails in determining whether or not the writer's material was purloined.

Leading entertainment business attorneys assure me that no judge in any jurisdiction will agree that a writer intended to assign away his screenplay's rights in exchange merely for a studio's agreement to consider the project. In practical terms, therefore, a signed release means nothing. Regardless of its wording, the writer does not surrender his right to litigate, nor does he award the studio the right to steal his material.

Why do production companies and studios and networks provide such releases if they are essentially meaningless? I expect there are two reasons. First, like any other constituency within a public bureaucracy or a corporation, the lawyers want to be certain that their end is wholly and responsibly covered; that on behalf of their employer they have performed due diligence. I suspect also that they hope to scare away frivolous lawsuits that may be brought by writers who overvalue mere ideas.

Until recently, the general rule has been that no release was required from a writer whose work was submitted to a studio through an agent. Lately, however, even that seems to be changing; companies increasingly insist on releases even when the work is submitted through an agent.

Releases should cause no concern. Since many companies flatly refuse to read material for which releases are not signed, and since such documents are harmless, there is every reason in the world to affix a signature. Ultimately it could lead to the sale of a script or a paid assignment.

Copyright and the Hydrant Effect

A writer working on a paid assignment—developing a screenplay based upon a producer's idea, rewriting somebody else's script, adapting for the screen material from another medium such as a novel on behalf of a production company—is considered a "writer for hire" who does not own the rights to the material upon which he works. If he did not originate the material he is merely a hired hand participating in a quid pro quo enterprise; the producer supplies the money, the writer provides the talent and, mainly, the toil.

Being a writer for hire, especially a well-paid writer for hire, is a wholly honorable enterprise. Creating original material—in the case of new writers this almost invariably involves speculation—automatically results in the material's rights accruing to the writer. As long as he doesn't base the work on anybody else's material, a writer owns what he writes.

Many writers—and many civilians, too—misunderstand the nature of copyright. What they think of as "copyrighting" material is actually the registration of the copyright with the Copyright Office of the Library of Congress in Washington, D.C. It is simply not necessary to do so. The copyright is in fact created as the work is written.

Regrettably, perhaps the most dreadful mistake writers made throughout the history of writing was to hand over motion-picture copyrights to producers. A novelist's copyright is owned by the novelist. A play's copyright is owned by the playwright. A screenplay's copyright is owned not by the screenwriter but by the studio that produces it. There comes a sweet and sour moment in every successful screenwriter's life when, upon selling an original screenplay, he is required to sign a statement affirming for the purposes of copyright that not he but the studio is the work's author. It's sweet because it'll never happen until a writer wins success. It's sour because the writer gives away a lot.

As the author of this book you are now reading I own one hundred percent of the copyright; I license the right to my dearly beloved publisher so that he can, well, publish it. The copyrights of the screenplays described in this book, however, belong not to the writers who wrote them but to the producers who produced them.

What's the difference?

There are many differences. Prominent among them is the fact that not a word of a play or a book can be revised or rewritten without the consent of the author. The publisher cannot unilaterally decide to bring in another writer or a team of writers to rewrite the author's drafts. In Hollywood, however, even highly paid and acclaimed screenwriters suddenly and routinely find themselves cast aside for other writers brought in to rewrite them and still others to re-rewrite the previous re-writers.

Few producers have the courage to look at a writer's script and declare it to be ready. There's safety in delay. Safety, as I have already argued, is fraught with danger. It's not all that unusual to have a dozen or even more rewriters of a script. It's not unusual to find that the final version is very much like the first. The story evolves through the early and middle rewrites and then returns in the final stages. We end up sometimes pretty much with what we started with. Often, in the rewriting process, damage is done to the original vision that inspired the purchasers in the first place.

Additionally, the hydrant effect I mentioned earlier means that every producer and every rewriter has to dribble a few drops on the script; that is, he has to leave his mark upon it so that later he can claim it was his suggestion, regarding this aspect or that one, that explains the success of the screenplay. He can claim credit, supposedly, for the script's avoiding turnaround.

Option, Purchase, and Turnaround

Should a screenplay be purchased and never make it to the screen (a major studio typically buys at least fifteen screenplays for every movie it produces), there is some arrangement for reversion, or turnaround, of the film's rights to the writer. Some years ago the Writers Guild negotiated automatic reversion for writers, based upon a complicated formula involving time and money. Essentially, after seven years during which time the script has failed to be produced as a film, the writer has a two-month "window" to return the money and reclaim the rights. Then, of course, she is entitled to sell those same rights to somebody else if she can find a new buyer.

Obviously, however, turnaround is something writers generally hope to avoid.

Once she's written an original script, a professional writer devoutly hopes to sell it. Best of all is to find someone willing to part with a fortune. Such an arrangement is characterized simply as "purchase." It is not much different from the purchase of anything else: a car, a coat, a pack of chewing gum. They have money, you have the product; they give you the money, you give them the product.

The purchase of original material for the screen is inevitably more complicated than that, to be sure. There are often bonuses based upon the material actually going into production. Perks and bumps—which is to say, more money—are awarded if the material earns a certain amount of profit or it is parlayed into one or more sequels or it spins off into ancillary products—toys, shirts, posters, coffee mugs. These extra benefits are not mutually exclusive; any combination of such happy occurrences may serve to enrich a writer who is skillful and insightful, to say nothing of lucky. The ancillary rights to *Star Wars*, as an example, were worth far more than the film's mere ticket sales, record-shattering though the latter happened to be.

Should a script go into turnaround, its chances for another sale are mitigated by the very fact of turnaround. You're marketing an entity that another company has declined to produce, even after what may have been a substantial investment. To no small extent, therefore, projects in turnaround resemble what in retail is called "distressed merchandise."

Nonetheless, many projects that go into turnaround are eventually resurrected and produced.

The rules surrounding reversion represent the recognition by writers and producers alike that a screenplay is in fact not a car, a coat, or a pack of chewing gum; that if a producer fails to produce the film, that may not be the end but merely the beginning. The writer has the right to try to get the project produced elsewhere.

One might expect that the original purchaser should not object to such an arrangement; indeed, he ought to welcome it. He gets his money back. In fact, however, many producers despair to see somebody else produce a project they once owned. In a business where appearance is everything, it looks bad for a producer to be unable to get a project filmed and then have some other producer succeed with the same material. Worst of all is for the movie, after being rescued from turnaround by another producer, to become a major hit.

Purchase of original material is rare, however, when compared to an option, which costs a producer a lot less than a purchase. It's like renting the rights. It enables him to treat the material in very much the same manner as if he had purchased it outright. A producer wins the right to purchase the original material later, within a specified period and at a predetermined price. A producer not willing to risk hundreds of thousands or even millions of dollars on a particular screenplay might find the writer willing to let him option the material for a period for substantially less money.

It might very well be to the writer's advantage to accept such an arrangement. For one thing, the writer likely has tried, on his own or through his agent, to find a buyer. As happens with the overwhelming majority of screenplays, this proves futile. If after several potential purchasers have turned down the opportunity to buy the script outright, the agent and/or the writer may be reluctant to have the property exposed all over town, only to demonstrate conclusively that nobody wants to buy it.

There might, however, be a producer who feels that perhaps properly "packaged"—more about this later—with the right director and a star or two, or in some way rewritten, or for any of a host of reasons, the property is worth acquiring at least temporarily, in order to determine whether a movie might eventually result.

Typically option payments are credited against the purchase; they are deducted from the final payment. The term is adjustable. It may be six months or a year, at a particular price. It may be renewable at the producer's discretion, perhaps at an adjusted sum for another period. Every aspect is negotiable.

More important than the money paid for an option is the fact that once a producer acquires material he may actually devote time and attention to showing the script around to organizations with the capability to get the project filmed, such as broadcast and cable networks and of course also studios. He may also expose the script to directors and actors. In so doing, he may succeed in getting the script to the screen. Even if he fails at that, the writer's name and writing skills are exposed in various offices where they might otherwise not have been known. This can go a long way to building a reputation. The writer can report truthfully that a particular company has acquired the rights, however temporarily, however cheaply, to his script, conferring professional status upon a writer previously considered amateur.

It is more prestigious to have a legitimate producer, who's gone to the trouble and expense, however small, of acquiring a script, peddling the property through the professional community, compared to having the author himself or the author's representative doing the same thing. It demonstrates that somebody besides the writer and his agent—both of whom have an obvious vested interest—believe the screenplay is worthy of an audience.

As an example, a student at UCLA optioned a comedy to a prominent producer. The producer, thanks to an extraordinary record of hit films, was able to have the script read promptly at the highest levels of the industry. Though no studio saw fit to produce this particular story, they were favorably impressed with the writing.

The producer never succeeded in getting the film made and eventually dropped out of the picture, allowing the option to expire, which is the fate of the overwhelming majority of options. Nevertheless, as a result of the script being read at a particular company, the writer won his first professional assignment: a rewrite of another project. He was paid ten thousand dollars a week with a six-week guarantee, all this merely to rewrite a script that somebody else had already written.

Not too shabby for a first job.

Moreover, he ended up spending not six but eight weeks on the rewrite, pocketing eighty grand and keeping the original option money for himself as well as the rights to his original script. This writer—in addition to the cash, plus the enhancement of his reputation—enjoys the prospect of eventually selling the script all over again.

In addition to all this, predictably, the writer also found representation. If a producer at a major studio wants to hire a new writer for ten thousand dollars a week, agents will line up at his door, and he can pick and choose. This particular writer chose wisely, and he has had a prosperous career under way now for many years. He had a major summer release from a big studio, and he had a huge success in a Christmas picture during a Christmas season that happened to be fairly dismal that particular year in terms of movie revenues.

Even if he doesn't eventually find a purchaser who'll acquire the script outright, there's always the possibility he'll find someone else who wants to option it yet again. A friend of mine wrote a script on assignment for a producer at a major studio more than fifteen years ago. Long before he finished writing, the producer was fired from the studio. The company, honoring the writer's contract, paid him all the money owed, then promptly put the project into turnaround; the rights reverted to my pal.

Of course, he wished the script had been filmed, but he had no serious cause to complain. He was paid the full fee as required in his contract, and he still owned the rights to what he had written. Over the subsequent decade he sold six options on that same script and was nearly disappointed when, finally, it was once again purchased outright by another studio. I say disappointed, because over the years he'd grown used to renting out the rights. He had come to regard it as a kind of annuity and over time it had begun to add up to a respectable sum.

Eventually the new studio changed administrations, and the script went into turnaround yet again, the rights once more reverting to the writer. Here's a script, then, that effectively has been sold outright twice, and optioned half a dozen times or more, to which the writer still retains all rights plus the possibility it will sell—or be optioned—yet again, and maybe even again after that.

Writers sometimes give options on material to producers virtually for free. Instead of stone-cold free, it's actually for one dollar. This is because legal agreements require that some sort of tangible exchange, however small, occurs between the parties.

Why in the world would a writer sell an option for his material for free (or for a dollar)? Because the producer may succeed in setting up the project to be filmed, in which case substantial remuneration accrues to the writer. Clearly one might be reluctant to permit the first person who reads material to option it; a writer with virgin material, a script shown to nobody, wants to get at least a sampling of opinions and reactions before agreeing merely to rent the rights for a relatively small sum instead of selling them outright for far more money.

If all else fails, if nothing comes of the optioned material, the writer has not hurt himself; he still retains all rights to the script and can hope to market it throughout his lifetime. There are scripts that have been around for many years before they finally became films.

It is demonstrated for us once again that the most precious commodity for writers is patience. Over time, a passed-over script may eventually be resurrected as part of a package.

Packaging

You may have thought a movie is a movie, but it's not; in contemporary Hollywood parlance a movie is actually a package. You may have thought writers are writers, actors are actors, and directors are directors, but they are not. An actor—especially a star—is an element. Likewise, in the scheme of movie things a director is not a director; he is but another element. Similarly, you may have thought a screenplay is a screenplay, but it is not.

A screenplay is a vehicle.

In the old days, into the late 1940s, when studios owned their own theaters, they also owned their own writers, actors, and directors. These artists did not operate freelance, picture by picture, studio by studio as today. Instead, they were on a single studio's staff and assigned by the studio to work on specific pictures.

Under such conditions some artists complained that they were no more than slaves, but no slaves were ever treated and paid so lavishly. What's more, thanks to requirements of the studio system, they enjoyed each other's companionship and support, a far cry from today's industry wherein screenwriters work in veritable isolation, closeted in their home offices, literally phoning in their scripts via a now-antique dial-up modem, or more likely sending it as an attachment to an e-mail, never having to interact directly with any other human.

This isolates writers from the richest source of their stories: the humanity all around them.

There is today at every studio a so-called Writers' Building, a structure that during Hollywood's "golden age" housed writers' offices but is now used for other purposes, usually quartering independent production companies. There also used to be at every studio commissary a writers' table where, by tradition, the writers all ate lunch together every day of the week. There the writers engaged in informal story conferences, bounced ideas and dialogue off one another, and consulted collectively on any and all aspects of their work, from specific quirks of character to basic questions regarding story structure.

In those times a studio decided to make a picture, assigned the various artists, and made the picture. Today, more often than not, a picture finally comes into being because bankable elements become attached to a vehicle and form a fundable package.

An element is considered bankable if it can be depended upon to deliver butts to seats in theaters. An example of a bankable element is a major movie star. Bankability, however, is in constant flux. As of this writing, Steven Spielberg continues to reign as a preeminent example of a bankable element. Spielberg's pictures can be counted on to earn vast profits, it is widely asserted. If he wants to make a movie based upon the text contained on the label of a pair of Fruit of the Loom jockey shorts (low bleach, tumble dry) it's a done deal.

The central underpinning, and most common misconception, regarding bankability holds that audiences can be counted on to buy tickets to see a bankable element's pictures. This is demonstrably a hoax. Our example, Steven Spielberg, while having directed some of the most commercially successful movies ever, has also made films that tanked: *Hook*, *Always* (Jerry Belson, Dalton Trumbo, Frederick Hazlitt Brennan, based on Chandler Sprague and David Boehm's story "A Guy Named Joe"), and *Artificial Intelligence* (Steven Spielberg, Ian Watson, based on Brian Aldiss's story "Supertoys Last All Summer Long") are examples.

Not bankable elements nor elaborate, expensive marketing campaigns, nor anything other than word of mouth—audiences' recommendations to friends—accounts for a movie's success at the box office. There is no "bankable" star who has not appeared in his or her fair share of flops. There is not a single writer, producer, director, or actor whose filmography lacks a number of disappointments. Not even George Lucas's name above the title could rescue *Howard the Duck* (Willard Huyck, Gloria Katz, based on a character by Steve Gerber).

Principle 66: The only factor that accounts for movies' box office success is word of mouth.

It is useful to remember, therefore, that what actually makes an element bankable is not that audiences will flock to movies in which it plays a role but that bankers will bank on it. If bankability is good news for this season's handful of hot elements, for movies in general it's no cause to rejoice.

Packaging, alas, is good news neither for writers nor audiences. The real reason for packaging is, first, so that packaging agencies receive a commission not merely for one element or another but for a collection of them. The second reason is that the practice provides the opportunity for studio executives to cover their tails in the event—no mere possibility, but the likelihood—they need to explain away the expected failure of their picture.

If her picture tanks, a producer does not have to justify squandering perhaps a quarter of a billion of the corporation's dollars if there were bankable elements in the movie. When a leading producer like Peter Guber mounts a movie like the notorious *Bonfire of the Vanities* (Michael Cristofer, adapting the Tom Wolfe novel), if it succeeds he's a hero. If it bombs he can claim, "It's not my fault. I had Brian De Palma directing. I had a screenplay by the hugely successful Michael Cristofer adapting a bestselling novel by superstar author Tom Wolfe. I had Bruce Willis and Tom Hanks and Melanie Griffith and Morgan Freeman, all in their prime. It's not my fault; it's theirs."

Bankable elements exist, therefore, primarily for the purpose of assigning blame.

Lamentably, too many movies today in too many cases are now only elaborate schemes to prepare the blame strategy for their predicted failure. Instead of exciting new ideas, studios search for packages of bankable elements to cobble together into vehicles that will provide cover for the decision to put money into it in the first place and explain to shareholders a film's poor box office even if it has not yet had a chance to fail. Is it any wonder so much movie fare appears stale and listless?

What does this all mean for writers?

Primarily, that a script submitted all by itself—regardless of its strengths—to potential purchasers, particularly at major studios and production houses, is not likely to sell, much less to be produced.

From a practical standpoint, however, for writers this changes nothing. We still need to write the freshest, most original material we can write, and we must at the same time be prepared eventually to deal with agents and packagers and, especially, options, because what typically occurs during the option period is that the bankable elements are assembled.

This provides writers with extra reason to create characters who are broad, rich, fleshy, the sorts of roles bankable actors would like to play. On the other hand, however, aren't worthy characters already a basic tenet of worthy writing?

Should a writer be represented by an agent who is also a packager? It's a strategic toss-up. The big, powerful packaging agencies understandably prefer to represent not merely a script alone but also the director and the stars since, as explained earlier, this provides not merely one but several commissions.

From the standpoint of writers, representation by such agencies has both strengths and weaknesses. The elements for a package may be right there in the agency, which might result in a better chance for a sale and an actual production. There is always the possibility, however, that one or another element will fall out of the package before production commences. In such an instance the blush is off the project. The agency sees now perhaps only a script, and what packaging mega-agency wants the relatively meager commission provided by the sale of a script alone?

This is why writers, especially new writers, may be best positioned with smaller, more boutiquelike agencies where a motivated representative might stage the sort of hand-to-hand combat with producers and executive vice presidents that is required to get a picture started. Additionally, at the bigger agencies the individual writing client is all too easily lost in the shuffle of actors, directors, writers, writers, and writers.

I have myself over the years been represented by agencies large and small. When signed with the former, it was not unusual for me to be sent to meet with producers in order to pitch my take on a particular prospective assignment. In the waiting room I would see a half dozen of my agency coclients, sent there by my own representatives in order to compete with me for the very same job.

Perhaps the ideal compromise is a new agent at an old agency. Potential purchasers know he's legitimate. Moreover, he is motivated to work hard to establish his reputation, and the way he does that is by establishing that of his clients.

At UCLA I frequently take calls from new agents just starting out at well-established agencies. They eagerly seek clients. I send them our best and brightest writers and for a brief period they do great things. Soon, however, their stables fill, their reputations solidify, and they have only limited time to work for new artists.

Big agencies gobble up the product of smaller agents. "Why should I work hard to establish an unknown writer when I can simply sail in and swoop up a writer whose reputation has been established by a smaller agency?" a major agent actually told one of our classes at UCLA. The producer Arthur Mayer, who was a beloved teacher at the USC film school, once commented that the problem with Hollywood is not that people steal but that they steal with impunity.

Writers should note an important caveat regarding loyalty, however. I mentioned before the once hugely successful writer who wrote one of the all-time Hollywood box office megahits and who confessed to me at that confessional altar of writers' conferences, the hotel bar, that he hadn't worked in years and it was all due to the way he had mistreated his agent His reputation had been built painstakingly by an independent agent who worked her butt off on behalf of her client. Once he had his blockbuster hit, however, he succumbed to the siren song of a larger agency whispering in his ear that he was now a bigger writer and required a bigger agent.

They put him into their informal and unofficial, unannounced "rotation." That is, while he was by far the leading client of his previous representative, here he was merely one among a stable of superstar screenwriters. They started him on the second-tier rotation; that is, his work and offers for his services were sent not to the top but the second-to-the-top companies du jour. After two or three months of tepid responses, they put him on Ignore. They stopped sending him out and refused even to take or return his telephone calls.

This is no anomaly but, unhappily, fairly routine in Hollywood.

Tail between his legs, he crawled back to his previous agent. "Now that you're out of work you want me to rebuild your career so that if I can get it soaring once more you can dump me for the big boys? Thanks, but no thanks," she told him.

The lesson: Be good to the people you meet on the way up as you will meet them again on the way down. Whether you're interested in a career making low-budget, independent films or mainstream blockbusters, the rules for courtesy and politeness always apply.

The Writers Guild

The mainstream motion-picture business is a union shop.

In negotiations with the industry in such matters as wages and working conditions, film and television writers are represented by the Writers Guild of America, which maintains branches in New York and Los Angeles. Although the networks and studios and legitimate independent production companies agree to employ union members exclusively, no potential employer will reject a writer simply because he's not a member of the Guild. This may appear to be a contradiction but it is not. Once he negotiates his first sale or assignment, the writer simply agrees to join the Guild.

Therefore, compared to new actors, directors, editors, cinematographers, carpenters, electricians, and makeup and wardrobe artists, new writers have a leg up. This is because the Writers Guild will admit any writer to membership as soon as he wins an assignment from a signatory company.

Moreover, every legitimate company engaging writers is signatory to the Guild standards and practices. As soon as a company hires a writer it promptly notifies the Guild. The Guild checks its roster. If the writer is not a member, he is promptly invited to join. The Guild will never propose to potential employers that they use instead writers who are already union members. It will simply welcome the writer into its membership. Full disclosure: The "welcome" is accompanied by a sizable bill for the initiation fee. When I joined in the early seventies the fee was two hundred dollars. At the time of this writing it is twenty-five hundred dollars. Upon joining, Guild members also pay dues of a hundred dollars a year or one and a half percent of their screenwriting earnings, whichever is greater. For a complete explanation of the fee and credit structure visit the website, www.wga.org.

The experience of a writer seeking work is quite different from that of, say, an editor. Impressed with the work of a new cutter, should a company desire to have her edit their movie, they cannot blithely hire her. The editors' union, upon checking its roster and discovering the proposed candidate is not a member, will try to get the producer to use instead one of its available (unemployed) current members.

New writers, having won their first assignment, may not want to worry about matters like union representation. All the same, the Guild is essential to guaranteeing standards and fairness in compensation and credit. Writers' rights to such representation were won only after years of heroic struggle against well-financed and frequently nasty opposition.

Until there was a writers' union, on-screen credit depended upon the whim of the producer. Producers could (and often would) arbitrarily assign writing credit to their spouses, siblings, children, friends, and dogs. For perhaps half a century now, however, credit has been determined exclusively by the Guild. Moreover, on-screen writing credit is no small consideration. For writers, far beyond the emotional and psychological implications, screen credit is also about money.

The Writers Guild of America represents, therefore, a win-win situation for screenwriters, even for first-time screenwriters who do not yet belong. These writers are afforded all the Guild's protections even though, since they don't belong, they pay no dues. On top of that, they are not discriminated against with regard to sales or hiring even though they don't yet enjoy Guild membership. Naturally, at the time of a sale or assignment they promptly join the Guild, pay the initiation, and look forward to regular bills for their annual dues over the years to come. There is also a ceiling on the amount paid. After a certain amount, no more dues are owed until the following year.

As with all other technical and business considerations, writers can forget about how to get into the union and concentrate instead upon writing their best screenplay. That's because writing their best screenplay is the way into the union.

The Gatekeeper Theory

Since the film and television industry is so competitive, so prestigious, and so glamorous, its lower-rank laborers are typically overworked and underpaid; they're willing to tolerate all sorts of abuse for the opportunity to work in so dynamic and (sometimes) creative an arena. This is particularly true of office personnel, particularly receptionists, secretaries, clerks, perhaps even janitors.

Surprisingly, these same people often wield substantial power.

In an effort to reach higher-ups—either by mail or telephone—it can be a serious mistake to run roughshod over them for two reasons. First, running roughshod over people is simply not acceptable behavior among civilized adults in enlightened societies. Second, these lower-echelon functionaries often hold the key to influence and attention far beyond their station.

When I was still a student at USC's Cinema Department in the late sixties, I worked briefly as a script consultant to the head of a major studio. Soon, my boss ran the studio into the ground and was fired. Of course he was then promptly hired by another major studio, where he lasted several years until he also ran that one into the ground. During his tenure at the second studio, I attempted to reach him so as to pitch a screenplay I'd written. I reached, instead, his secretary. In an aggressive, inconsiderate manner I figuratively tried to shove my way past her on the phone. The secretary hesitated and then, recognizing my voice, spoke my name. It turned out to be the same secretary he'd had at the previous studio, a woman I'd come to know well, and one capable of getting my script to the top of the pile of material on his desk.

Forgiving my rudeness, the secretary treated me generously, showing me more consideration than I deserved. She arranged to get the script to her boss immediately.

The boss read it promptly and just as promptly rejected it.

The lesson still holds, however. My firsthand familiarity with this particular secretary—and her uncommon toleration—spared me the wreckage of my bad manners. It pays, therefore, to be a decent, respectful human being, even in the movie industry. Agents' and producers' secretaries and their readers are generally abused by traffic at both ends of the line. That is, their bosses bark at them, and people trying to reach their bosses also bark at them. That may explain why they are open to kindnesses shown. These same badly treated folks often hold the key to the attention of very important people.

Make every one of them your ally.

When your call is first answered, ask for the precise name of the person with whom you're speaking. Jot it down for future reference. Kibitz with him or her for a moment; these folks are used to being pushed around and most will go the extra mile, therefore, for a struggling writer who treats them with respect. Remember that in correspondence it is he or she who'll open the mail and often also the e-mail, deciding which matters merit the attention of the boss and, more pertinently for our purposes here, which ones do not. It's not a bad idea, therefore, to remember them fondly to their boss when you correspond.

In Hollywood, as elsewhere, one's selfish best interest is served when he treats people humanely. It is all part of taking oneself seriously as a professional.

Professionalism

The difference between an amateur and a professional is that the former does it for free while the latter gets paid.

There is, of course, a significant difference between amateur and amateurish. A disciplined, talented amateur may write far more effectively than a particular pro, and a particular pro may write amateurishly. A professional's writing is not necessarily better than that of an amateur, it is merely more remunerative. If no screenwriter needs to apologize for reaching an audience, neither need he apologize for being paid to write.

At UCLA's School of Theater, Film and Television my telephone rings constantly with would-be producers seeking writers who are "bright, fresh, new, innovative, not creatively stuck in a rut, not yet caught up in the whole Hollywood maw."

What the caller really means is that he seeks writers willing to work for free.

When I inquire as to how much money they're willing to pay, there is usually an astonished silence and the telephone grows palpably cold in my hand. Invariably the voices on the phone mumble that they offer a new writer far more than mere money. They claim to offer access to studios and agents; they offer an almost ready-made deal that requires merely the "fleshing out" (a euphemism for writing) of an idea. They assert that the script will virtually "write itself."

My UCLA colleague Hal Ackerman likes to wonder at this point, "If the script will write itself, why won't it produce itself?"

When I'm meeting with producers who tell me a script will "write itself," I reach for a pencil and ruled yellow legal pad, hold the pencil aloft, its point touching the page. Then, gingerly and delicately, I remove my hand from the pencil, as if expecting it to start writing all by itself.

In all such experiences to date, as soon as I release the pencil, it falls down.

This provides me with the opportunity to say, "Looks as if this is another one of those scripts that will not write itself but will require an actual writer to write it."

"The whole story's set," many among these bottom-feeders tell me, and some writers may actually believe them. "The characters are there. All that remains is to invent some incidental, anecdotal action for them and then to jam some dialogue into their mouths. All you really need to do is connect the dots. The script doesn't need much more than that to be put into proper screenplay format."

I suggest they hire a stenographer—it shouldn't cost more than fifteen or twenty dollars an hour—and, since it's all "worked out," the apparent producer can simply dictate the script. The stenographer can get the whole thing done in a day for perhaps a hundred or a hundred and fifty bucks. As far as screenplay format is concerned, if the stenographer can't handle it there are affordable software programs that will format the script in an instant.

Inevitably the self-styled producers hem, haw, and then reluctantly acknowledge that perhaps a little more than mere stenography is required—for example, action, setting, conflict, theme—and, truth to tell, they can't in any case hire a stenographer because they lack even the hundred bucks for that. What movie, I ask them, with a budget of even just a couple of million dollars—at this writing a superlow budget—ever gets made that requires a script be written for free?

"If they're going to get into this business, students have to speculate," I'm informed gently and not so gently by my callers.

My students speculate all the time, I explain. The difference is they own one hundred percent of what they write. Why should they give time and toil and talent to a project that not they but you own and for which there's no guarantee of compensation?

Writers should never experience the least bit of shame for insisting producers pay them for their services. Oscar Wilde famously said: "Amateurs talk about art; artists talk about money."

As indicated earlier, writers should never become involved speculatively in projects they do not entirely own. They must not allow themselves to be conned into adapting for the screen a play, for example, or a novel, or anything in any form, if they do not possess the rights to the original material. Neither should they rewrite anybody else's screenplay on behalf of an erstwhile, would-be producer, in the hope that eventually they'll receive cash and credit.

Self-anointed producers love to promise naive new writers all kinds of screen credit. Every legitimate producer knows, however, and every writer absolutely ought to know, that screen credit is determined exclusively by the Writers Guild through a sophisticated system of confidential arbitration panels.

If the producer reneges on any aspect of the "agreement," or more likely, if the movie is never produced, the writer can't even market elsewhere the fruit of his labor because he does not own it.

The sometimes sweet, sometimes painful irony regarding money and writing is that the more a producer is required to pay a writer, the better he appreciates writing. It is a self-fulfilling prophecy that feeds on the Hollywood community's abundant narcissism: The more I spend, the more the product is worth. If this writer costs so much, she must be pretty good. Would a crafty, tasteful, artistic producer like myself pay folding money to a mere hack?

The converse is every bit as true. A producer for whom a writer works for free will likely figure he's getting his money's worth. If the writer doesn't think his stuff is worth anything, why would the producer?

New writers often expect that if they demand to be paid they will be ridiculed and scorned. To the contrary, however, the more confident a writer's insistence that he be paid, the greater the respect the producer will afford both him and his work.

Obviously, no serious professional should get into any kind of discussion about money with a producer; he should put the producer in touch with his representation. If a legitimate producer sincerely wishes to hire a writer, he should be not reluctant but eager to contact the writer's representative.

What if a writer is offered a paying assignment but has no representation?

This is a problem I wish upon all writers. No writer with a serious offer of employment ought to have any trouble engaging an agent. Indeed, if it's a legitimate offer from a respectable party, agents ought to line up at his door and he can pick and choose. This is because agents are understandably reluctant to expend the time-consuming effort required to shop material from producer to studio to network. No agent, on the other hand, will reject a writer who walks in off the street with a deal in hand.

Nobody turns away business at the door.

The writer is allowed to hope, even to expect, that the agent will negotiate a deal at least ten points better than the writer would have won on his own, thereby covering the commission.

A Final Word about Agents

Agents are people, too.

There is something fundamentally difficult in the nature of the agent/client relationship; it is in many ways a classic double bind. I expect it derives in no small part from the fact that there should be no real trick to selling material that's good, fresh, and innovative.

So it is all too perfectly human for the agent to downplay the quality of the writing he markets. At the same time as he wants the work to be good, he doesn't want it to be too good, because if it is, what's his job? Is he but a broker trading commodities? The better the writing, the paler the testimony to the agent's own prowess as a wheeler-dealer. Psychologically, therefore, he has a curiously vested interest in trivializing the quality of any client's effort.

As if that were not already sufficiently awkward, there is yet another bind, equally irreconcilable.

Writers and agents alike will tell you that the client employs the representative, not the other way around.

With whom, however, does the agent play tennis and loll in the sauna? The client? Rarely. More often than not, the agent socializes with management—producers, executives, studio wonks, network operatives. That's exactly as it ought to be, and it is exactly as every client ought to want it to be, because, as Willie Sutton replied when asked why he robbed banks, that's where the money is.

I submit that one obvious area of conflict between agents and clients could be quickly eliminated if the agent represented instead of the client merely the particular project at hand.

Typically, to represent even a single project, the agent takes on full representation of all of the client's writing. Among these projects are those for which the agent has great enthusiasm and those for which he does not. It is fair to neither agent nor client to have a project represented reluctantly. Agent and client alike ought to have the right to forgo representation regarding this item or that one, perhaps with the agent possessing a version of first-refusal rights. In other words, he should get a chance before anybody else to represent a particular script. He should also, however, have the right to decline to do so.

In too many ways an agent's lot is not a happy one; it's enough to evoke sympathy even among writers. Like the waiter who gets scolded by the kitchen (even though he didn't order the food) and scolded by the diners (even though he didn't cook it), agents take the heat from movie and TV producers for writers' shortcomings, and they take heat from writers who blame them not for their own but for the producer's (from time to time somewhat) unreasonable demands.

Even agents need love.

PART IV

. . . .

The Whole Picture

"This Other Guy We Went to Film School With"

A Case Study

No writer can resist a ringing phone.

When my own phone rang that April evening in 1971 I was rushing off to the Troubadour to hear some East Coast musician pals. I ran back up the steps to my house. The caller was my fellow USC film school alumnus Gary Kurtz.

"I'm producing George's new movie," Gary told me straightaway. "He just called from France. He wants you to write it. We have a development deal at United Artists for ten thousand dollars. It's all yours if you'll take the job."

Ten thousand dollars in 1971 was the equivalent of today's two hundred thousand or a quarter million dollars. At that time, however, even so princely a sum did not mean that much to me. I was well into my first Hollywood hot streak, writing four major studio feature assignments back to back and serving also as the dialogue director on the latest—and last—big-studio Jerry Lewis movie. I wasn't exactly rolling in dough, but I was making more money than I needed.

I did not have to ask who "George" was. Though not yet widely known to the general public—his first feature film, *THX 1138*, would come and go with little fanfare—George Lucas was already celebrated among film students for the miraculous original version of that same movie, produced while he was a student, *Electronic Labyrinth: THX 1138 4EB*. The movie's running time was fifteen minutes and proved to anybody with eyes in his head that George Lucas was a film graphics genius.

His final student film, *The Emperor*, a swan song to USC, is a quirky,

eccentric, brilliantly original quasidocumentary saluting radio personality Bob Hudson. The film represents the one time George and I worked
together in film school. At his request, I popped into the USC Cinema
Department's crude recording studio and, along with our classmate John
Milius, contributed dialogue to accompany snapshots of terrorists pur-
portedly in Central American jungles but shot actually in the cramped,
bamboo-overgrown patio outside the department's modest still-photo
darkroom.

By the time George Lucas was planning the teenage fifties rock 'n' roll
movie Gary had called me about, I had acquired a mini reputation among
the film school alumni for a conversancy with late fifties/early sixties pop.
I had appeared as an actor in a student film called *The Reversal of Richard
Sun* that was steeped in freeze-dried sixties politico babble. Even its
writer/director, Bill Phelps, had no idea what the film was about.

Richard Sun is a too-typical late sixties hippie-dippy freak-out extrav-
aganza treating trendy, naive notions regarding Liberation and Revolution. George had told me that the movie's brightest moment is the scene
featuring me sitting in the stairwell of a house flipping through already-
old 45 RPM rock records and improvising comments regarding the tunes,
the labels, the performers. I don't recall what Phelps had written in the
script but I remember discarding the pages and, with his encouragement,
voicing whatever thoughts came to mind.

Richard Sun marks perhaps the first filmed instance of anyone spin-
ning fifties pop culture in this fashion. The fifties seemed at the time
still too fresh, too recent to be plumbed for history and nostalgia, as
George now planned in his new film. I was thrilled that he wanted me to
write it.

I had already written a treatment for my own fifties/adolescent/nostalgia/
coming-of-age screenplay, *Barry and the Persuasions*, that had enjoyed substantial encouragement in the industry. As Dorothy Parker famously remarked, however, Hollywood is the one place on earth where you could die
of encouragement. For all of the praise *Barry* won me, I had been unable to
squeeze a nickel from any producer to develop it.

I asked Gary if George had a title for the United Artists project. He
said, "*American Graffiti.*"

"American who?" I asked.

Gary explained that it was only a working title.

"That's good," I said. The title seemed to represent everything George loathed. "People are never going to buy tickets to a film with a title that is so art house, so European," I told Gary. Was there ever so wrongheaded a prediction? *Graffiti*, of course, would eventually become—dollar for dollar—among the very most profitable films in history.

Gary told me that except for George everybody hated the title. "I hate it," he said, "you hate it, Willard and Gloria hate it."

"Willard and Gloria Huyck?"

"They were George's first choice to write it. They sketched out a couple of brief treatments. UA's legal department insisted there had to be something on paper to justify the development deal. Now Willard and Gloria have suddenly gotten their own film, a low-budget horror piece called *Second Coming*. They'll write it together, and Willard will direct. So they aren't available for *American Graffiti*, or whatever George's picture ends up being called."

At the USC Cinema Department in its heyday, the magical middle and late sixties, it was my privilege to mix with some of the most creative, imaginative, disciplined young artists who in no small way would come to dominate the film industry in the following decades. To my view there was nobody more brilliant than Willard Huyck. *Down These Mean Streets*, his ten-minute black-and-white film-noir tribute to the American movie detective, is still the best student film I've ever seen. Indeed, it is among my favorite all-time movies in any category.

On the telephone, Gary Kurtz explained to me that George and his bride, Marcia, were backpacking across Europe and would end up in Cannes where he would screen the feature-length version of *THX* for the international film market. George was expected back in Los Angeles within a couple of weeks and was unavailable to discuss *American Graffiti* until then. In the meantime Gary would provide me with whatever background was available.

The following morning I met with Gary and struggled mightily to talk him out of *American Graffiti*, not just the title but the whole picture. I handed him the treatment for *Barry and the Persuasions*, which, I assured him humbly, was far superior to any notion regarding George Lucas's cornflake coming-of-age in white-bread Modesto. Managing to keep a straight face, Gary explained with characteristic equanimity that for better or worse George wanted to make his own movie. It would take place over a single night, sunset to dawn, in a central California town like the one where he was raised.

Gary handed me two documents, one of which was four or five pages and the other perhaps eight. These were the treatments Willard and Gloria had written solely to satisfy United Artists' legal department's requirement that, for the purposes of the contract, there had to be at least a modicum of material on paper. Gary instructed me to pay no attention to these pages; he told me that they were strictly pro forma; they were to have no bearing at all upon the script.

Gary then handed me the top-ten hit lists from a decade's worth of *Billboard*, the record business trade journal. "Over the next couple of weeks while George is away," I told Gary, "I'll spend my time listening to music, scratching out some notions, and just preparing myself for his return. I'll milk the Huycks for whatever they know regarding George's plans for the script. Then, when he returns to town, I'll sit down with him and we'll write the script together."

Gary told me this would not work. He said it was essential that I have an entire draft ready by the time George returned from Europe. "I'm not about to guarantee a whole script in two weeks," I told him. "If you want fast, get somebody fast. If you want good, I'm your writer."

Gary told me to write as much as I could, as fast as I could. George had been taking too much time and the studio was antsy. We needed to get a draft on paper. This gave me cause for concern. A director like George, I told Gary, was not going to take a script that was handed him and go to a soundstage and shoot it. He would want to be closely involved in the writing.

Gary agreed. To address this issue, he explained, the deal had been structured in two tiers. I would be paid seventy-five hundred dollars for the first draft and twenty-five hundred for the revision. This way, when George came back to town I could hand him a complete first draft and then the two of us would rewrite it together. By working with me on the second draft, George would include in the script whatever he desired.

"I still prefer to wait till George returns," I said. "What difference can two weeks make?"

Confronting George with a draft upon his return, Gary told me, would challenge him to get off the dime and address the serious creative choices that lie at the core of every movie, particularly in their early stages. The scheme struck me as unsound. "I still say drop the whole damn thing and do *Barry and the Persuasions*," I told Gary, only half joking.

I invited the Huycks to the house for dinner. Willard and Gloria were excited about *Second Coming*. Regarding the Lucas project, they said that it was appropriate I should write the script. They based this, they told me, upon something George had told them.

They said that when they first discussed *Graffiti* he said he wanted the movie to capture the spirit of my scene with Milius and the 45 RPM records in *Richard Sun*. While they had never themselves seen *Richard Sun*, Willard and Gloria told my wife and me that George said it was the spirit of that scene that he wanted to capture in a film treating adolescent coming-of-age, rock 'n' roll, and fifties nostalgia. They also reiterated Gary Kurtz's prescription to ignore the treatments.

After breakfast the following morning I rose from the table, walked the three steps to my study, settled in front of my Hermes 3000 manual typewriter, inserted a sheet of paper, and typed "AMERICAN GRAFFITI (working title)." By evening I had written fourteen pages. I wrote all the next day, and every day thereafter, through the weekend and the following week, nine days in all, and was surprised to discover that I had an entire draft.

The challenge writing *American Graffiti* was to fulfill George's desire to capture the aimlessness, alienation, and dislocation that are the hallmarks of adolescence. This had to be accomplished, however, in the context of a story that was itself not aimless, alienating, and dislocating.

The reconciliation of diametrically opposed qualities—aimlessness and drift on one hand, direction and purpose on the other—posed problems requiring solutions that would prove elusive. Indeed, before the film would shine upon any screen, four writers at two different studios would write more than a dozen drafts in pursuit of this mission.

Additionally, the movie presented the special challenge of creating an ensemble piece, a film whose attention would be distributed over a wide array of characters at the same time as it presented a clear protagonist with a singular vantage and voice.

I was satisfied that I had crafted the foundation for the revised draft George and I would write together, as producer Gary Kurtz had instructed. The first draft's issues would be resolved in the rewrite.

At the top of the picture, according to this first draft, the Ron Howard

332 THE WHOLE PICTURE

character attempts to break up with his girlfriend as, come morning, he and his pal Richard Dreyfuss are to quit their dull-as-dust hometown and head for the big city. Instead of breaking up with the girl, however, Howard ends up engaged to be married.

"Engaged?" Dreyfuss protests.

"You and I are splitting this burg all the same," Howard reassures him. Later, however, when he goes to the girlfriend's house to bid her farewell, they end up driving to Nevada to be wed.

Scenes include the sock hop ball; the search for the mythical, mystical girl in the T-bird; the loaning and subsequent damaging of the car by Terry the Toad (exquisitely portrayed by the underappreciated Charles Martin Smith); the Toad's attempt to buy liquor without an I.D.; the subsequent holdup of the liquor store; the confrontation with the disc jockey at the radio station; and a host of other material, some of which is in the final film and some of which is not.

Instead of a drag race at the climax, as contained in the treatments I'd been instructed to ignore, I had the teens engage in a game of chicken. Think of it as an homage to the adolescent movie icon *Rebel without a Cause* (Stuart Stern, Irving Shulman, Nicholas Ray), wherein at the climax the kids drive their cars straight at each other in a reckless contest to see who veers first, that is to say, who chickens out.

George would later say, "We never played chicken when I was growing up. We had drag races."

Of course it was his call, but chicken seemed to me more appropriate than any drag race. I acknowledge that all across the land, legions of Americans are apparently hypnotized by drag racing. Still, it bores me to tears. I'm a New York City–raised kid. What did I know from cars and drag racing? We didn't have cars. We had feet. We had bicycles. We had the subway.

To my view, chicken represented not only better drama, but also an apt metaphor symbolizing the politics and culture of the Cold War, which was raging full-bore at the time in which the movie is set. President Eisenhower's first secretary of state, John Foster Dulles, even had a name for it: brinkmanship. Each side would bring the other to the brink of annihilation, and then see who blinks. It reduced foreign policy to an adolescent game of nuclear chicken.

To argue with the success of a critical and financial triumph like

American Graffiti is a self-defeating prophesy if ever there was one. Even if the final film's drag-racing sequence works splendidly—and I agree that it does—I still believe that for purposes of film what matters is not what actually happens in real life but, again, what constitutes the best drama.

Could George in any event have expected me in this draft faithfully to report the facts of life pertinent to coming of age in Modesto? Call the chicken decision a rotten creative choice if you will, but to fault me for failing accurately to portray precise and specific details of middle-California life is a bum rap. My only error was agreeing to write a draft solo, prior to George's return from abroad, at which time he would have been available to consult and collaborate.

It has been reported also that George took offense at the moist, throbbing teenage sexuality in which my first draft occasionally wallows. He has criticized this aspect of the script as lacking taste.

I will stipulate that from time to time I do indeed favor a taste of vulgarity in dramatic narratives. As observed elsewhere in this book, throughout the millennia sex has served drama well. A film treating adolescence but ignoring sexuality might miss something essential.

In light of Lucas's astonishing career and his vast influence upon public and popular culture, which influence I happen to regard as affirmative and nourishing in the extreme, it is certainly appropriate to take a look at his own sexuality, not insofar as it pertains to his personal life—even George Lucas is entitled to his privacy—but with regard to its expression in his films.

Lucas's sexiest film? After all these years that still has to be the USC student production *The Emperor*. Here and there are some tantalizing flashes of lush-lipped young women addressing the camera, erotically pouting, sighing, as they affirm their undying lust for "Beautiful Bob" Hudson, the Emperor.

When I brought the roughly typed, clipped, stapled, Scotch-taped, hand-corrected jumble of first-draft pages to Gary Kurtz's office early the next morning, George was still across the Atlantic. Gary made a photocopy for himself and sent the original to George's office. George was due back in town late in the week and would read the script over the weekend.

The next day Gary telephoned to praise the draft. He told me I'd done exactly what needed to be done. He said the script provided precisely the foundation the film required. Upon George's return in a few days we would get to work and create a revised draft that United Artists would green-light for production.

Early Monday morning when the phone rang I did not have to lift the receiver to know who was calling. From George's flat affect I knew immediately that he did not share Gary's sentiment. If he had nothing negative to say that morning on the telephone, neither did he have anything by way of affirmation. Indeed, of the script he said nothing at all. Instead he suggested that we talk face-to-face. I gave him the directions to my house. He arrived twenty minutes later.

"Nice place," he said, nodding grimly, looking around our cheery, modest bungalow. We chitchatted uneasily about old film school pals, about the weather, about his experiences with *THX* in Cannes. Incredibly, he offered not a single comment regarding my draft and I, still more impossible to believe, asked no questions. In retrospect, of course, it seems I had figured out that if he had anything good to say he would have said it.

I am well practiced in the art of denial. Throughout the week I would be able to delude myself into believing that this was just George's curious manner, his social style. There could be no doubt that soon we would sit down together and write the revised draft. At that time we'd have substantive discussions regarding the script. From his posture that Monday, however, also his tone, and from his sparse, spare language, it should have been readily apparent that he wanted to work on a new draft by himself.

I pointed out what he already surely knew, that contractually I owed him a second draft, just as United Artists owed me twenty-five hundred dollars for that draft. I was ready to collaborate with him. From the conversation's downward drift, however, it appeared that he wanted me to offer him what Hollywood calls "relief."

In my experience as a professional writer I have written dozens of assignments where money has changed hands. Among these are published books, both novels and nonfiction; feature-length screenplays for virtually all the major studios and also for independent producers; and prime-time television series episodes for the three major networks; also scattered rewrites and polishes, and articles for newspapers and magazines. Additionally, I have written dozens of short films: corporate image movies and political propaganda; commercials; industrial films; government films;

informational, instructional, and educational movies; travelogues; and even one elaborate, highly remunerative industrial slide show.

In all this experience there were only four occasions where anybody ever tried to deny me money I was owed. Happily, in each instance I succeeded in compelling full payment. Like most freelance writers I am sensitive to money issues. Uncertainty over whether or not a writer is going to be compensated inevitably sullies the relationship with his employer. Few experiences bother me more than a producer reneging on a payment that is due me.

All the same, I was sympathetic with George's plight. He had told me he was broke, that his fee for directing *THX* for Warner Bros., fifteen thousand dollars, represented his total recompense over the prior two years and was long spent. The reason he and Marcia had been backpacking in Europe was because they couldn't afford a hotel. He told me that at the moment, just to make his rent, he faced the prospect of having to shoot a soft drink commercial.

If he had changed his mind regarding our arrangement, if now he did not want me to write a second draft, that was surely his right. George averred that it had been a mistake for Gary Kurtz to promise me all the development money. I explained that I had never sought this assignment nor had I negotiated the terms. I had simply accepted the offer.

George was asking me to make good for what he characterized as someone else's mistake. My impression is that he took offense at my insistence that the contract be honored.

To me, more important than the money—and the money was important—was what the money represented. Money is, as I've argued earlier, a metaphor representing everything else; moreover, it's a metaphor with numbers on it. Here the money symbolized the commitment to collaborate on a second draft. Creative Management Associates, or CMA, the agency representing both George and me, had taken out a two-page ad in *The Hollywood Reporter* in August listing some of its writing clients and their then-current projects. Included among them was *American Graffiti* with George and me identified as the writers.

It became increasingly apparent at our meeting, even through my nervous spray of words and George's closemouthed remoteness, that he wanted no second draft. I rose to call Mike Medavoy, my agent at CMA, for clarification. George urged me not to call Mike. I did not call Medavoy, therefore, until George left the house. Mike reassured me that there was no doubt I would write a second draft and be paid as contracted.

A week unfolded. Friday, Medavoy telephoned. My period of denial abruptly ended. Mike told me that George hated the draft and was not interested in my writing a revised version. Coolly and calmly, I decided to gather some clothesline and hang myself from the avocado tree in the backyard.

Mike assured me, however, that I would be paid for the draft, as per the contract, and, since I had to be paid, George would require that I write another draft. I was told to wait for George's notes.

The weeks melted away. Mike Medavoy announced that he was leaving Creative Management Associates for International Famous Artists. He said I could accompany him to IFA or stay on at CMA with another agent there, Mike Wise.

Perhaps because I saw myself still bound to CMA over *American Graffiti*, or perhaps simply because of inertia, I remained at CMA. Sometime in July, instead of hearing from George, late one afternoon I heard from Jeff Berg, the newly appointed head of the agency. "Richie," he said when I answered the phone, "what's this bullshit about you insisting on the second-draft money for *American Graffiti*?"

"Apparently there is something wrong with this connection," I said.

"Don't be a crybaby," Berg told me. "You worked nine days, bagged seventy-five hundred bucks, that's what? Eight hundred and thirty-three dollars a day. And thirty-three cents. A day! Forget about a second draft and forget about the second-draft money."

What matter to Jeff Berg and CMA if I got paid or not? The agency represented not only me but also Lucas. However the payments were distributed among its clients, the agency would receive the same commission. I told Jeff Berg, "I've earned enough money in the past year to pay you guys thousands of dollars in fees to have you win me deals and enforce my contracts."

"The important thing is to get you working again," Jeff said. This is as close as I have come to hearing anybody actually pronounce a reasonable facsimile of the classic Hollywood threat: You'll never work in this town again.

I replaced the phone in its cradle. In another moment it rang.

It was my new agent, Medavoy's replacement, Mike Wise. "Richie. Thank God I caught you. This is ridiculous."

"Ridiculous is exactly what it is," I concurred. "You guys boast about finding me a great deal, though in fact the deal found me, and I carried it to you in my hot little hand. Then you brag about negotiating me great terms, which terms you negotiated in fact not at all. When I insist upon the contract being honored, Jeff insults me and threatens me with unemployment."

"What'll it take to get you off this berserk jag?"

"It'll take George Lucas," I said, "on this phone, within the next twenty minutes, promising me that there is no question regarding payment of the money owed me."

"George is out of town," Mike said. "We don't know where he is."

"The clock is ticking," I said, and I hung up.

In the clear light of hindsight I am appalled that I said what I said and did what I did. Certainly it is not my practice to hang up on people. I rose from my desk, stretched, and took several deep breaths. The telephone rang yet again.

"I'm coming to town tomorrow," George Lucas told me. "Let's have lunch."

(At this writing, decades later, thanks largely to my position at UCLA where I'm perpetually encountering new writers, I'm frequently in contact with ICM—the agency into which CMA eventually evolved—which Jeff Berg still runs, to recommend potential clients, confident that should the agency sign them they will be capably, responsibly represented.)

George Lucas and I met the next afternoon at Hamburger Hamlet at the west end of the Sunset Strip. He told me he was sympathetic with my situation. He acknowledged that I had been placed in an untenable position, that my script was capable and professional, but that reading it had demonstrated to him that in order to tell his story he had to write it himself. He recognized that I was owed money for a revised draft and that I also, therefore, owed him that draft. He assured me he would call me soon with his notes, and at that time I could get started.

Two or three weeks later, early one Sunday morning, the phone rang, waking me. "Am I calling too early?" George inquired from Marin County. "Not at all," I lied and, from between the sheets, no doubt annoying the hell out of my wife, I listened for perhaps ten minutes as George specified what he wanted in and out of my new draft.

"Leave the tunes out," he said. "I'll fill them in myself."

He was referring to the vintage rock numbers I had specified at ap-

propriate points throughout the script. My first draft contained many
such references. These songs were intended not to accompany the picture
merely as background music but to help drive the narrative. They reflected
the tale's twists and turns, constituting a component of the story itself.

"And in the end," he reminded me, "it's not chicken but a drag race."

"Not chicken," I assured him. "A drag race."

I took nearly a month methodically, deliberately rewriting, and when
I sent it to George he described it—perhaps sincerely, perhaps only out of
politeness—as "vastly improved."

He never did submit the draft to the studio. Instead, he waited until
his own version was finished. He then gave that to United Artists, which
promptly passed, ending forever his and *American Graffiti*'s relationship
with the studio.

In the subsequent months, Francis Coppola was able to resurrect the
deal at Universal. George had come to know Francis during the latter's
"rain period," the time during which Coppola directed *The Rain People*
and *Finian's Rainbow*. Francis had adopted George as something of a pro-
tégé. Francis took *Graffiti* to Universal. He persuaded the studio to develop the script and ultimately even to shoot it, as long as the budget was
rock-bottom.

By the time the new development funds for *Graffiti* were liberated
from Universal, the Huycks' *Second Coming* had fallen apart and therefore Willard and Gloria were available for *Graffiti*. They wrote some drafts
on their own, as I understand, and then further drafts in collaboration
with George.

The film was finally shot in San Rafael with a budget of seven hundred
thousand dollars, a sum that would not even buy breakfast for the drivers
on *Titanic*. Universal was so unhappy with the finished film that there
was substantial doubt as to whether or not they would even release it.
Indeed, even after *American Graffiti* had become not only a critical triumph but also, given its low cost, to that moment the most profitable film
in history, Universal declined the opportunity to make George's next film,
a science fiction epic called *Star Wars*. The studio apparently saw *Graffiti*
as a fluke. As for this new project, had not George already fallen on his
face at Warner Bros. with a science fiction picture, *THX*?

Prior to *American Graffiti*'s release, as with any film in which various
writers are employed, there remained the question of writing credit. His-

torically, as discussed earlier, the authority to determine on-screen writing credit resided solely with a film's producer. Sometimes a spouse, a pal, even a pet received credit for what a screenwriter had written. Over years of enormous effort, however, the Writers Guild of America had wrested that power from producers and today, as for many years, it has full authority over the matter.

It's not at all unusual in Hollywood for various writers to be hired to work on a script and not all of them to receive credit. Indeed, I understand that after *Graffiti* Willard and Gloria went to London to work with George on the draft of the first (or is it the fourth?) *Star Wars* chapter. They were well paid for their services but ultimately received no screen credit.

With a film such as *Graffiti*, where a key production executive—in this case the director, George Lucas—seeks writing credit, the Guild automatically conducts a confidential arbitration in which an anonymous panel of members reads all the drafts and determines the final credits.

More than mere ego rides on screen credit; there is also money. In the case of a megahit such as *American Graffiti*, substantial sums are involved. Writers' contracts typically award bonuses—often in the form of net profit participation—not only for screen credit but also for the manner in which such credit is displayed.

The system is complex. For example, writers' names linked by the word "and" earn more than those whose names are connected by the ampersand, "&." Additionally, solo credit pays more than credit that is shared with other writers. First position among the names confers more prestige upon the writer than second or third place. If the system is not always fair, it is certainly the least unfair method anyone has yet devised.

Certainly George, Willard, and Gloria were entitled to credit. Had I shared credit with them, the Huycks being an ampersand-connected team, I would have received one-third of the writers' net profit share of five percent, that is, one and two-thirds percent of the film's total net profit.

Didn't I say it was complicated?

I sometimes tell my students that the real creative writing in Hollywood occurs in studio accounting offices. The expression "net profit," I say, actually derives from the Russian *nyet*. That is, net profit really means no profit. Through all sorts of manipulations, for example a practice called cross-collaterization, hugely profitable movies can be made to appear actually to have lost money. This enables the producers to keep more of the money for themselves by denying net profit participants money that is rightly theirs.

Notwithstanding any of that, however, with a success as huge as *Graffiti* it is impossible to conceal all the profits. Net profit participants in such instances do receive some portion of what is owed them. In the case of *Graffiti* even a mere one and two-thirds percent of net profit adds up to over a million dollars, more than a hundred times the amount I was paid.

What's more, additional millions would likely have accrued as a result of future assignments and increased fees, the result of being associated with so successful a movie. Indeed, on the strength of *Graffiti* the Huycks sold a script, *Lucky Lady,* for four hundred thousand dollars, at the time the highest price ever paid for an original screenplay. Adjusted for inflation, four hundred thousand dollars then represents perhaps five million or even more today.

Years later I realized that I had been naive regarding the arbitration process. I assumed at the time that the various drafts constituted the entire body of material examined by the panel. Unbeknownst to me, I could have submitted additional material: comparisons, analyses, arguments, and other documentation in an effort to make my case. Stupidly, lazily, neurotically, self-destructively, beyond the screenplays I submitted nothing at all that might have buttressed my arguments for credit.

After its deliberations, the panel awarded me no screen credit, apparently holding that not enough of my writing had made it through to the screen.

Was I devastated? Call me a liar, but I was not. Don't I wish I were a millionaire superstar screenwriter? Of course I do. Had my career plummeted after *Graffiti*, I might have felt differently. Careers, even those of writers far more prosperous than I, run hot and cold at best. Notwithstanding intermittent frigidity over the years that followed, I continued more or less regularly to win writing assignments and comfortably to support my family exclusively from income I earned as a writer.

Ironically, not long after *Graffiti*'s release, the Guild changed the arbitration rules so that the writer of a first draft could not be wholly excluded from credit. Even if that constitutes for me cosmic bad timing, I managed well enough. Using my *Graffiti* drafts as writing samples, for a while I came to feel like Hollywood's go-to guy for adolescent coming-of-age, rite-of-passage, loss-of-innocence screenplays, writing feature assignments treating that subject at Warner Bros., Universal, Fox, Columbia, and elsewhere.

My success in winning these assignments had to do also with *Barry and the Persuasions*. I had ultimately used the screen treatment as an outline not for a screenplay but a novel, which promptly sold to a major New York publisher the year after *Graffiti* was released. *Barry*, along with my drafts of *Graffiti*, helped earn me these writing jobs. If the work didn't make me fabulously wealthy, neither was I anything at all like impoverished.

Not long after *American Graffiti*'s initial release, I won a lucrative, glamorous assignment writing a film in Italy. A Spanish, Italian, and French coproduction, it was the highest-budgeted film to be produced in Europe that year. They even threw in an additional ticket for my wife, so we could make something of a vacation of it.

I recall easing into my recliner in the first-class section of Alitalia's flight to Rome. As the cabin lights faded and the movie came on, it was plain enough to see that they were showing—what else?—*American Graffiti*. I had a terrifying notion that simultaneous to the writing credits' appearance on-screen the plane would be hurled against a mountain, and the writing credits, absent my name, would be the last vision in my life.

I was not thrown against any mountain. Moreover, there was a technical problem with the projector, and they were not able to show the end of the movie. I was spared, therefore, the experience yet again of watching the disputed drag race sequence.

Approximately twenty-five years after its original release, Universal screened *American Graffiti* as part of a weeks-long celebration commemorating the studio's classic releases. They set up in their amphitheater the world's largest movie screen. At each screening, someone associated with the particular film was invited to introduce the film. To my surprise, for the *Graffiti* screening I was invited to be the speaker.

Over the years I have from time to time read interviews given by George and the Huycks in which they discuss the history of *American Graffiti*. While George always cites me by name, Willard and Gloria persistently refer to me as "this other guy we went to film school with."

Not too many years ago, however, they gave an interview in which, again, they referred to me as "this other guy we went to film school with," but by this time my star had risen sufficiently to cause the reporter to ask: "You mean Richard Walter?" They graciously acknowledged that it was I. They then went on to express sympathy for the awkward position I had been put in, and also regret for their advice to me all those years ago to ignore the early treatments.

Hollywood is in many ways a constant good news/bad news joke. When a script does not sell, for example, it is not the end but only the beginning. All kinds of benefits may nevertheless accrue, and an unsold script may one day still sell. It could also lead to a development deal on another picture, or to a rewrite assignment.

Similarly, a movie made in which a writer who was paid for his writing services is denied credit may lead nonetheless to future employment and earnings, and even a certain sense of accomplishment and serenity.

To attach particular expectations to any action is a formula for frustration. To attach to the writing of a screenplay the expectation that it will sell is a recipe for disappointment. Writers have to write solely for the sake of writing since, as argued repeatedly, it is a privilege even merely to be mistreated in Hollywood. To traffic in one's own imagination, to swap one's dreams for dollars, has to constitute the highest creative calling. Few experiences mellow the spirit like getting paid to write.

How cool is that?

To George Lucas, Willard Huyck, Gloria Katz, and writers everywhere: May the Force be with you.

Appendix: A Story Craft Exercise

Creature Comforts: Theme and Identity

Let us now explore the unifying influence provided by theme. We'll study in close detail the beginning of a tale of my own invention. The idea for *Creature Comforts* came to me as I happened to stroll past a hotel in New York City. I glanced inside the lobby and witnessed a man and a woman at the front desk. I saw no luggage.

This observation occupied maybe a couple of seconds. Nevertheless, I continually thought about it: Who are these people? Where is their luggage? What is the nature of their relationship?

Eventually, it led to the following story.

A taxi pulls up to the entrance of the Javits Convention Center on Manhattan's West Side. The entrance is festooned with banners on which is emblazoned the legend: WELCOME BOOKSELLERS!!!

Out of the taxi steps our wimpy, geeky protagonist. Herb Castle is every bit as creased and crumpled as his olive-drab corduroy suit. His glazed, bleary eyes tell the viewer that he has just arrived via the so-called red-eye, the low-budget overnight flight from the West Coast.

The catch on his salesman's sample case slips open; its contents spill to the gutter. They appear to be books: obscure technical and scientific texts. Clearly, Herb is a specialty publisher's regional sales rep.

As he scrambles to gather the books, the impatient taxi driver complains, "Forty-five dollars, pal."

Herb pulls his wallet from his pocket, peers inside. Sheepishly he offers a bill to the driver, saying, "I hope a hundred-dollar bill is not a problem."

"Not for me it ain't," the cabby says, pocketing the bill, gunning the engine, and sprinting away into traffic.

"Officer!" Herb yells to a policeman directing traffic. "That cabby just split with my change!"

"The white zone," the cop recites in bureaucratic police-babble, "is for the loading and unloading of passengers only. Please do not obstruct ingress into, and egress from, the facility."

Using not so much dialogue as action, this introduction establishes important information regarding the protagonist. We see that Herb is a fellow who is often put-upon, abused, and cheated. He is the standard out-of-towner scammed by a New York cabby. Painful as it is, there is also a hint of humor.

We travel through the facility's central chamber, where mainstream publishers have their plush, fancy booths overflowing with promotions: pens, pencils, book bags, graphics, and galleys. The floor swarms with buyers, sellers, agents, editors, and authors.

One particular publisher features a boxed set, the reissued works of a reclusive bestselling author who writes under the nom de plume Page Turner. From posters it is apparent that at long last Turner plans to go public and actively promote the boxed set.

Off the main chamber, in the low-rent district, scientific and technical textbook publishers occupy downscale cubicles. Herb's cubicle is hardly even that; it's a spot against the wall with a card table and folding chair. On the table before him arrayed on their spines are his publisher's current offerings.

Herb dozes.

A beautiful woman appears. Her mere presence is powerful enough to waken Herb. "Thanks for stopping by," he blurts out. "We've just reissued Olivewood and Crawford's *Curvilinear Dysfunction in Crystalline Entropy Mechanisms*. It's part of our *Rotational Divergent Immunoglobulin* series. There's also an updated edition of *Nonperiodicity in Central Euclidean Tessellations* and . . ."

Herb grinds to a halt. "Laura," he says. "I hardly recognize you."

"Want to see some I.D.? Driver's license? Bloomie's charge plate?"

"You look beautiful. Radiant. A whole new person."

"A whole new person is precisely what I am, living a whole new life. Carl and I have split. I've moved out of the house in Brooklyn Heights."

"I'm so sorry."

"Don't be. My life hasn't ended; it's just begun. Take me to lunch and I'll give you all the gory gossip."

"Can't. I've got to hold down the fort here." They scan the empty aisle. There isn't much of a fort to hold down.

This little bit of dialogue shows readers of the script and viewers of the film that Herb and Laura go back a long way. For the purposes of story I need now to get Herb and Laura away from the convention.

One way I can achieve this is by crafting dialogue for Laura that persuades Herb to accompany her to the next scene. In fact, however, I do not have to waste even a minute on chatter. In a movie it is possible to have a character absolutely refuse to do something, yet promptly in the next scene do whatever it was he said he could not do.

Herb flat-out refuses to accompany Laura to lunch. Then, in the very next scene, they're seated at an East Side café, finishing lunch. Laura orders yet another bottle of wine, from the look of things perhaps their third.

Laura finishes the description of her marriage's crash landing: ". . . And so I said to myself, 'That's the final straw,' picked up my hat and coat, and walked out the door of our house in Brooklyn Heights."

Note the second reference to Brooklyn Heights. I hammer on Brooklyn Heights because it soon connects with an upcoming story angle.

"You and Carl are taking time off to allow each other a bit of place and space, as intelligent, advantaged, enlightened, aware couples do from time to time these days?"

"Spare me that mellow feel-good California new age drivel," Laura responds. "Carl and I hate each other."

"I see," Herb says, nodding. "Separation may be a little hairy at first," he says, "a little lonely. There may be moments you get to feeling shaky, even panicky. You may feel a certain despair, a dark and gloomy hopelessness."

"Shut up, will you?" Laura pours him more wine. "I feel great."

"I feel sloshed," says Herb, chugging the latest glass.

"We're both a little blotto," Laura says, "and it's a good thing, too, because there's something I've always wanted to tell you, and I'm just sloppy enough to say it straight out. I love you. I've always loved you."

"I'm fond of you, too, Laura."

"I'm not talking 'fond.' I'm talking love."

"I understand completely."

"Do you? Great. Then let's go to a cool, secure place. A hotel."

"What are you saying?"

"I'm saying let's get naked and ball till we're black and blue and blind."

Herb knocks over the wine bottle. He rights it, pours himself yet another glass. "You're merely reacting to the trauma of the separation," he says. "It's perfectly natural."

"You're turning me down."

"Of course I'm turning you down. This is all too fast for me."

"Fast? I've lusted after you for decades."

"Ridiculous," Herb insists. "I'm the selfsame nerd you knew in the neighborhood."

Laura leans forward. "It took tremendous courage for me to seek you out. You're in town for the day. We have a chance for a sweet, crazy moment together. Something special just for us. When it's over, it's over. You go back to Santa Monica; I stay here in New York. We never see each other again. But when we're old and feeble with Alzheimer's, after everything else has faded, this crazy afternoon in Manhattan is all we'll remember."

"I hadn't a clue you felt this way," Herb confesses.

"It won't even be any good," Laura says. "First times are inevitably clumsy, awkward, and inept, aren't they? Still, the issue looms between us like a wall. We can address it or ignore it but it is here, unfinished business, an ancient account to settle."

"I'm flattered," Herb says. "And tempted. Frankly, however, given your recent separation, I doubt you could handle such an event."

"Speak for yourself."

"You're absolutely right," Herb acknowledges. "I'm the one who couldn't handle it. It's not my style. I'm a middle-class kid. A married guy. You asked me a direct question; you're entitled to a direct answer. No. Impossible. Absolutely not. It's out of the question."

Just as I needed to get Herb and Laura away from the book fair, I need now to get them into bed. At the convention center I waived the dialogue for that. Similarly, here I choose not to squander language as Laura attempts to persuade Herb.

We do precisely what we did in the earlier instance: Herb flat-out refuses to join her at a hotel. Then, of course, we cut directly to the exterior of a hotel. Over this we hear the voice of the desk clerk saying, "And precisely how long will you require the room, Mr. Murphy?"

In the lobby, with Herb and Laura standing at the front desk, the clerk peers at the registration card Herb has fraudulently filled out.

"Only tonight," he tells the clerk.

"Where are your bags?"

Herb panics. Bags? To check in to a hotel without bags arouses suspicion. It's too easy to skip out without paying the bill.

Herb blurts out, "American."

Laura and the desk clerk ask Herb in unison: "American?"

"Airlines," Herb responds. "American Airlines. They misrouted or rerouted or something. The bags. Sent them to Cleveland or Buffalo or some such godforsaken place." Turning to Laura he says, "We'll have to purchase complete new wardrobes here in town, darling."

"Just the excuse I've longed for my whole life."

Here are two understandably anxious first-time lovers. Private banter between them brings them closer together.

"Don't worry about your bags," says the clerk. "Airlines lose luggage all the time, but they also find it." He reaches for the phone and prepares to dial. "I'll call American Airlines and have them deliver your luggage right here to the hotel as soon as it reaches Kennedy. What flight did you arrive on?"

Herb has no desire, of course, for the clerk to phone any airline in search of phantom bags on a phantom flight. "Actually," he says, inventing, "I have to call the airline myself to rearrange our return flight. While I'm at it, I'll tell them we're registered here. There's no reason, therefore, for you to call them."

"Excellent," the clerk says, hanging up the phone.

As soon as Herb figures he's outfoxed the guy, however, the clerk seizes a pad and pencil. "Describe the bags. I want to make sure the bell captain sends your luggage directly to your room the minute it arrives."

Herb can't shake this clerk.

"Describe the bags?" Herb asks. "Sure. Why not?"

He exchanges a covert glance with Laura. "There's an off-white vinyl

Samsonite piece, somewhat beat-up, and also a plaid fabric fold-over with a hard black double handle." The clerk scribbles furiously as Herb creates his fantasy luggage. "Oh, and also a little carry-on flight bag. Not American. Braniff."

"Front!" the clerk sings out, hitting the bell. A bellhop materializes.

We cut now to the room. Herb and Laura enter. They lock the dead bolt and hook up the restraining chain. They face each other. "I suppose the time has come," Herb says, "to be clumsy, awkward, and inept."

This, of course, echoes the line Laura used in her seduction of Herb at lunch. As we shall see with "Brooklyn Heights," this represents another facet of integration. It stitches together the story's various strands.

The lovers now slam together in an embrace.

Sensuality is more erotic when implied rather than expressed. Instead of playing out on-screen, the lovemaking unfolds where all art works best: in the mind of the viewer. The erotic scenes in *The Reader*, for example, where the sex is not explicit but implicit, engender greater arousal than any clinical hard-core porn sequence ever could.

Upon the lovers' embrace the camera tilts up to the ceiling. We hold there for a moment as the light dissolves from midafternoon to dusk. We know that a couple of hours have passed.

When we tilt back down to the bed, the lovers are intertwined in each other's arms, clothes and bedding scattered about the room, dead to the world, lolling in the afterglow of lovers' slumber. Herb awakens to a knock at the door. "Who is it?"

"Bellhop!" a voice rings out. "Good news, Mr. Murphy! Your bags have arrived!"

Herb makes his way to the door and opens only as far as the restraining chain allows. In the hall stands the bellhop with his luggage cart stacked high with bags: an off-white vinyl Samsonite piece, somewhat beat-up; a plaid fabric fold-over with a hard black double handle; a flight bag—Braniff.

These are precisely the bags Herb created only a couple of hours earlier at the front desk. Based upon the Prudent Person Principle, which requires that characters in the movie act the way members of the audience would act under similar circumstances, Herb has to take the bags into the room.

He does so and locks the door.

"What's all that?" Laura inquires as she wakens.

Herb and Laura must now open the bags.

Creating the bags' contents represents for the screenwriter the most critical kind of choice making, because those contents will drive the whole picture.

In my travels around the world addressing screenwriting groups, I often tell just this much of the story. Then, at this juncture in the narrative, I invite writers to imagine that Herb indeed opens the bags. I ask: What's in the bags?

Below are some of the answers I have received over several years. After analyzing them for strengths and weaknesses, we'll move on to my own version of the bags' contents.

Plane Tickets and Passports

Placing plane (or bus or train or steamship) tickets and passports in the luggage is smart story craft. The tale kicks forward instantaneously. If there are tickets to Paris (or anywhere else), rest assured one or the other or both members of the couple will eventually travel there, where, undoubtedly, there will be further adventures.

Like tickets, passports also imbue screen stories with forward motion. The names on the documents can be Murphy (the name created at the front desk) or they can be those of Herb and Laura. The documents' photos can be of Herb and Laura at an earlier age, perhaps in their college years, perhaps as preadolescents.

Such paraphernalia might well herald a journey through their earlier lives.

Key(s)

The bags could contain among other things a key that fits, say, a locker at Grand Central Station. Or it could fit the ignition of a car parked across the street. Or the key could open some door encountered later. In any case, keys suggest motion. A lock that the key opens will be found and will take the story to its next station.

A Body or Body Parts

Judging by the number of occasions in which mild-mannered writers come up with dead bodies or parts of dead bodies, one might well get the impression that the screenwriting landscape is awash in sadists and perverts.

That said, it has to be acknowledged that dead bodies can be clever components to pack into the bags. They imply violence, of course. Like it or not, as I've argued eternally, violence in emotion and often also in action has occupied the heart of drama since its earliest days.

A body or body part adds stress and tension and conflict. Beyond that, these items turn the tale on its head, and they do so quickly. What was up until now a mildly comedic and romantic romp instantaneously becomes a tale of murder, terror, and intrigue.

Photos or a CD or DVD

We've already touched upon the subject of photos. The I.D. pictures of the passport owners can be those of Herb and Laura. The photos can be contemporaneous or from another time in their lives, perhaps the past or, depending upon the story, even the future.

They can also be pictures of completely different people. If the writer has a good grip on story craft, whoever is portrayed in those passport photos ought eventually to appear in the flesh.

If instead of—or in addition to—photos there is a CD or DVD, eventually it will become necessary to pop that disc into a player and view whatever is recorded on it. It could be images of a crime committed by other characters, who will eventually surface in the script. It could be scenes from Herb's and Laura's earlier lives. It could be surreptitiously recorded images of Herb and Laura at the convention, at lunch, entering the hotel, perhaps even secretly recorded images of their lovemaking.

It could be scenes from portions of their lives that they have not yet lived, and eventually we see them live out these scenes.

Rhino Horns and/or Tigers' Penises

Similarly, the bags could contain contraband relating to endangered species. Andrew Bergman's *The Freshman* exploits such species both effectively and hilariously. Herb and Laura could have stumbled into a convoluted scheme to loot such treasures from some remote corner of the world. Or they could themselves be victims of the perpetrators of such a plot.

Wardrobe

There could be any and every kind of costume inside the bags.

Let us say, for example, that there are a bridal gown and a groom's tuxedo. Perhaps later in the tale Herb and Laura appear at a wedding as bride and groom.

Perhaps it is not just any wedding gown, but Laura's gown from her own wedding years ago. If this is the choice, there is the added responsibility of explaining it to the audience. It's easy enough to tell the reader of the script that the garment was worn by the character at her wedding, but how will this information be made available to viewers of the film?

This can be accomplished in any number of ways, such as scattered dialogue. Laura could say, "Wow! It's my wedding dress, and there's Carl's tux."

This is, of course, heavy-handed and too on-the-nose. That is, it is overly textual and insufficiently subtextual. A more appropriate way to reveal such information is to delay that revelation and then let it unfold visually. For example, Herb and Laura could eventually come upon a wedding photo album with the newly married couple wearing the clothes Herb and Laura discover in the suitcase.

If the clothes do not include a tuxedo and a wedding gown, how about underwater diving outfits—wet suits, maybe scuba gear—that the characters could eventually wear in a perilous dive into a flooded quarry where clues to an earlier mystery are revealed.

Nonsense Stuff, Condoms, Toenail Clippings

The bags can contain items that make no sense at all.

Condoms, of course, relate readily to sex, a dramatic narrative mainstay, and perhaps also to the scourge of AIDS, and to a substantial number of other naturally dramatic, weighty subjects.

Toenail clippings could eventually be subjected to scientific DNA analysis, revealing that they once belonged to, say, Albert Einstein or Adolf Hitler or John Kennedy or John Lennon or Sonny Bono or Pinky Lee.

Drugs

The suitcases could be stuffed with illicit drugs.

These could be out in the open—plain as day—in plastic bags, clearly visible upon lifting the suitcase's lid. Or there could be built into the luggage a hidden compartment. Luggage with false bottoms, however, seems wearily familiar.

Instead of drugs, the bags could contain other objects that are eventually discovered to conceal cocaine, heroine, or whatever other style of pharmaceutical contraband the screenwriter chooses.

If luggage with false bottoms strikes me as wearily familiar, however, what can I say regarding drugs? Want to guarantee that I won't attend a movie? Run its trailer with a voice-of-doom narrator talking about cops going undercover in order to bust some dope ring. Just thinking about it elicits from me a deep, gaping, spittle-popping yawn.

Take, for example, Eddie Murphy's sparkling performance in *Beverly Hills Cop*. The story rolls and rollicks along until the plot stumbles into cocaine smuggling, and then the movie becomes merely one more third-rate episode of some marginal TV police/action/melodrama.

Steer clear, therefore, of the shoals of familiarity. My advice to screenwriters: Avoid at all costs the subject of drug smuggling. It's been done to death.

Nothing

When I ask writers to contemplate what is in the bags, it thrills me when one decides that the bags are empty. Perhaps the bags themselves are the subject of the scheme. Has not everyone heard the story of the fellow who marches daily through a fortified international border checkpoint pushing a wheelbarrow loaded with dirt? Each day the guards sift through the dirt trying to figure out whatever it is that the guy is smuggling, but they come up empty. Eventually we learn, of course, that what he is smuggling is: wheelbarrows.

Perhaps the bags—much less their contents—turn out to be of no consequence. It is merely the fact that they arrived, and what the arrival says about Herb's elaborate routine played out earlier at the front desk when he first "created" the bags.

The Bags Cannot Be Opened

Another possibility is that Herb and Laura struggle to open the bags but the lids will not budge. The bags could remain sealed throughout the picture, representing some metaphorical aspect of the tale and its theme.

Or they could be opened later, perhaps by some other individual who possesses the key.

The Twilight Zone *Approach*

Perhaps the bags' contents change each time they're opened.

One writer suggested, for example, that when Herb opens the bags he finds whatever he finds; perhaps he finds nothing at all, the bags are empty. He closes the bags, he closes his eyes, he thinks carefully for a heavy moment, and he reopens the bags.

Inside one of the formerly empty suitcases there is now a diamond brooch.

He closes the bag again, thinks, then opens it again to find a hot cup of coffee, a steaming plate of scrambled eggs and bacon, home-fried potatoes, and lightly buttered whole wheat toast. Each time he closes and opens the bag it is found to contain whatever it is he has just thought of, exactly as he "created" the bags in the first place during his exchange at the front desk with the clerk.

In this same writer's version the film cuts suddenly to Santa Monica, where Herb is at home, in his study, wearing his bathrobe, seated at his desk before his word processor, thinking and writing, writing and thinking. Each time he writes anew, we return briefly to the hotel room, where the contents change precisely as Herb revises his pages back in Santa Monica.

Herb is revealed to be a writer constructing a tale—this tale—and creating the bags' contents exactly as real writers create within their stories whatever they wish to create.

This approach integrates into the story the field of writing itself. Herb is presented at the tale's outset, after all, as a member of the book community—a publisher's sales representative—on his way to attend an event that involves the world of books. Why not create him as a writer of books who is writing this very book—or movie—as he goes along?

I call these approaches *Twilight Zone* methods. They transcend the more familiar reality-based story notions and bleed over into the world of fantasy, magic, illusion, and imagination.

This does not mean that under such circumstances the rules for story craft are suspended. Indeed, folding fantasy and imagination into the tale places an even greater burden on screenwriters, since such stories still must manifest the same logic, the same balance, that any worthy story possesses. To fail to confront this challenge is the equivalent of resolving impossible circumstances by having a character wake up at the end of the movie to discover it has all been merely a dream.

What's wrong with that?

It's too easy.

When audiences fork over their time and attention—to say nothing of the fistful of dollars required for a movie ticket—they seek evidence that the film artists have kept their part of the bargain by working hard.

There is no end to the choices writers have at their disposal. The more choices a writer makes, the greater the potential for still further choices. The universe of choices does not contract but expands, just like the universe in which we live.

Here follows a portion of the tale just now described—the first several pages of the script—as it would appear in professional screenplay format. This allows us the opportunity to appreciate not so much what information ought to be included but, more important, what needs to be left out.

CREATURE COMFORTS

FADE IN:

EXT   JAVITS CONVENTION CENTER—NEW YORK   MORNING

Banners festooning the entrance read "Welcome Booksellers!!!"

A TAXI pulls up.

Harried, harassed, hassled HERB CASTLE, forty, stumbles from the cab lugging an unwieldy SALESMAN'S SAMPLE CASE.

Herb is as creased and crumpled as his drab cord suit; he looks like a man who has just stepped off the all-night, super-cheap, red-eye flight from the Coast.

The Sample Case promptly breaks open spilling TECHNICAL and SCIENTIFIC TEXTBOOKS into the gutter.

The CABDRIVER calls to him, pointing to the meter.

> CABDRIVER
> Forty-five dollars, pal.

Ankle-deep in books, Herb struggles to extract his wallet from his pocket. He removes his one-and-only bill, a crisp, new HUNDRED, and hands it sheepishly to the Driver.

> HERB
> I hope a hundred's not a problem.

> CABDRIVER
> Not for me it ain't.

The Taxi speeds away.

Herb turns to a nearby COP directing traffic.

> HERB
> Quick! That cabby just split with
> my change!

> COP
> The white zone is for the immediate
> loading and unloading of passengers only.
> Do not obstruct ingress into or egress
> from the facility.

INT   MAIN EXHIBITION HALL

Acres of display booths swarm with BUYERS and SELLERS.

Publishers hawk books on health and fitness, addiction and recovery, how to live, how to die, how to diet, how to prosper in economic hard times and laugh in your friends' faces while their children starve.

There is even a smattering of fiction.

Prominent in this latter group is the booth representing PENTANGLE PRESS.

The company's entire display—as its posters attest—is devoted to the upcoming release of a boxed set of the collected works of bestselling reclusive author Page Turner.

CORRIDOR—TEXTRON'S BOOTH

In a hallway off the main floor, clearly the convention's low-rent district, Herb dozes fitfully at his company's "booth": a card table and folding chair.

A stunning beauty, LAURA MAYER, midthirties, approaches. Her mere presence startles Herb into wakefulness.

> HERB
>
> We've just reissued Olivewood and Crawford's <u>Curvilinear Dysfunction in Crystalline Entropy Mechanisms</u>. It's part of our <u>Rotational Divergent Immunoglobulin</u> series and . . .

He runs out of steam.

> HERB
> (continuing)
> I hardly recognize you.

> LAURA
> Want to see some I.D.? Driver's license? Bloomie's charge plate?

> HERB
> You're beautiful. Radiant. A whole new woman.

> LAURA
> A whole new woman living a whole new life. For one thing, Carl and I are through. Finito. We've separated. I've moved out of the house in Brooklyn Heights.

> HERB
> I'm so sorry.

> LAURA
> Don't be. My life hasn't ended; it's just begun. Take me to lunch and I'll give you all the gory gossip.

> HERB
> I'd love to, but I've got to hold down the
> fort here.

They scan the empty corridor.

Our Own Solution to What's in the Bags

Now let's continue with what's in the bags. Herb opens them to discover, among the various items, all sorts of upscale duds: high-fashion
three-piece suits, silk shirts, ties, slacks, fancy-label socks, and underwear. He pulls out a cashmere sport coat and slips it on.

It's a perfect fit.

He looks at himself in the oval mirror inside the armoire door. Naked
now except for the jacket, for the briefest moment he poses, perhaps even
primps and preens. The coat appears custom-tailored to Herb's precise
measurements.

He rifles through the rest of the bags' contents. He withdraws a digital
recording device plus an army .45 automatic pistol. He finds also fresh,
neatly bound and bundled currency—a cool million dollars in lush, green
cash.

He reaches deeper and extracts a legal-size manila envelope and
dumps its contents—clipped and stapled documents—onto the bed. One
set of papers swarms with microprint legalese; it appears to represent
some kind of contract. Another sheaf is an apparent itinerary: dates,
times, locations, appointments. The listings include among other items a
signing at a bookstore, a TV interview, an appearance at a literary society
at an upstate college.

Let's pause here for a moment to consider the special problems that
arise in the attempt to show printed matter—here the apparent legal
documents—on the screen. It's all so easy in a novel simply to blurt it
all out. The author can state that these papers are an author's contract
and a listing of the events typical of an author on a book-promotion
tour.

On-screen, however, it's quite another matter. One cannot cavalierly
show the documents in close-up for audiences to read on the movie screen.
People do not go to the movies to read. If they want to read they can stay
home and curl up with a fine novel.

Or even a book on screenwriting.

In the screenplay *Creature Comforts* we can make the points that need to be made and drop a few clues via a glance at the overall shape of the documents. We can combine this with brief snatches of dialogue. For example, while inspecting the documents, Herb could mutter under his breath something on the order of: "Lots of legal mumbo jumbo. Some sort of contract, a travel itinerary, an expense-account ledger."

This would shed light into an otherwise dark corner of the film.

Film requires such illumination. In literature, as already indicated, we can exploit language to assert the nature of documents, stating outright precisely what they are. In film, we can only hint at what they might be.

Let us return to Herb and Laura in the hotel room. Herb sets down the legal documents and author's itinerary and reaches once more into the bag. His fingers fasten upon some object. He withdraws a ream of paper. He examines it and shakes his head in dismay. "Oh, no," he says.

"What?" Laura asks anxiously.

Herb passes her the pages. "It's some sort of manuscript," she says, thumbing through them. "Looks like a novel." She lets the pages fall closed and regards the cover. "*Creature Comforts*," she says. "The novel is called *Creature Comforts*. There's no author listed."

"That's me," Herb says.

"You? I don't get it."

"I'm *Creature Comforts*," Herb explains. "I mean I wrote it."

"You're a writer?"

"A closet author. I've scribbled several novels over the years. I haven't sold one yet, but don't count me out. Why do you think I beat my head against the wall as a regional sales rep for a fringe operation like this scientific and technical textbook publisher?" Herb asks her. "Because it's as close to publishing as I can get."

Laura contemplates the typescript. "*Creature Comforts*," she says. "What's it about?"

"It's about three hundred and twelve pages," Herb says.

"Now's hardly the time for wisecracks."

"I agree." Herb takes the script from her, hefts it in his hands. He opens the manuscript to the final page. "Just as I suspected," he says. "There are forty pages missing. The whole last act's been lopped off."

"What do you make of it?"

"Beats me."

"What do we do now?"

"One thing seems clear enough."

"What's that?"

"Let's get out of here."

At this juncture we can provide Herb with any number of choices. The sweaty lovemaking session just behind him might provide motivation for a quick shower. Considering the pressing nature of the circumstances, however, I cannot believe that he would take the time to shower. According to the Prudent Person Principle, he would be anxious to depart the premises promptly.

If an audience cannot believe that Herb would now pause to shower, it might nevertheless believe that he would take a few seconds to empty his bladder. Compared with showering, this act carries greater urgency and takes less time, at least for younger men.

So Herb stations himself in the bathroom before the bowl, at precisely the same moment as the sounds of commotion come from the room: rumbling and crashing, a woman's scream, a couple of gunshots.

Herb stumbles back into the room to find the door ripped from its hinges, dangling precariously from the still-connected restraining chain. On the bed lies Laura, limp and crumpled like a rag doll, two dark purple bullet wounds in her forehead, a crimson stain blossoming in the mattress beneath her. Numb with disbelief, Herb sinks to the foot of the bed, where lies the pistol.

Mindlessly he picks up the gun.

At precisely this point, of course, the bellhop charges into the room. "I heard shots!"

The bellhop looks at Herb—gun in hand, smoke still curling from its muzzle—and at the apparently lifeless Laura, spread before him on the bed. He cautiously backs away toward the hall.

"Don't get the wrong idea," Herb pleads.

The bellhop continues to retreat.

"I can see how this must all look suspicious," Herb concedes. The bellhop continues his nervous departure. "Where are you going?" Herb gestures toward the bellhop with the gun. "Wait!"

"Sure," the hop responds, halting in his tracks. "Whatever you say." He trembles, clearly fearing for his life.

At this moment, from the street below come the sound of a siren and the screech of brakes. Herb glances over his shoulder through the window, which provides a clear view of the hotel entrance several stories below. A nondescript dark brown sedan—magnetic-mount red light on its roof whirling and flashing—sits at a curious angle at the end of dark rubber arcs, four fat commas, skid marks just now inscribed on the pavement. The car doors fly open and several men, apparently plainclothes detectives, leap out and race for the steps to the lobby, drawing their guns.

It ought to be clear to the audience and to Herb alike: He's in trouble.

Herb brandishes the gun and abruptly orders the bellhop, "Get it off."

"What?"

"The outfit. That monkey suit. Off."

"I don't understand," the hop pleads.

"What's to understand? Take off that uniform. Get naked. Now."

The bellhop obediently removes his uniform. As he strips off each garment, Herb frantically dons it. The bellhop now starts to tug down his boxer shorts.

"Wait," Herb says. "That's not necessary."

A screenwriting educator once said of story craft that writers need only to set their protagonist in one place, put his goal in another, and throw up obstacles all along the way.

To me this seems overly simplistic. It leads to stories that are straightline instead of rounded, sculpted, shaped, kneaded, and finessed. Still, anything that adds stress is to be welcomed. It might be fun here, therefore, to have a mini battle between Herb and the hop over the issue of the latter's underwear.

"Wait," Herb says to the hop, who is tugging at his shorts' elastic band. "That's not necessary."

"You said, 'Get naked.'"

"I only want the uniform."

"I'm doing whatever you tell me to do. Please don't shoot me, please." He continues to tug at his shorts. "I have young children."

"Keep them on. I changed my mind."

"You ordered me to get naked. If you don't want me to get naked, if you want instead that I leave on my shorts, you have to order me to do so."

"Okay," Herb barks. "I order you to leave on your shorts."

Dressed now in the hop's ill-fitting uniform, Herb orders the man into the closet and closes the door behind him. He places his shoulder against the armoire and pushes the bulky item in front of the closet door, sealing the hop within.

For the purposes of our story, I need Herb to keep the bags with him throughout the next several scenes. Wouldn't the Prudent Person, however, care not a whit about the bags? Would he not want to flee as quickly as possible? Would he not abandon the bags, which might otherwise slow him down?

Based on what we see and hear, Herb's plan ought to be clear: He intends to escape from the hotel disguised as a bellhop.

To this end, audiences would be willing to believe he would fetch the luggage cart just outside the door where the bellhop left it, stack the bags high upon it to provide concealment as he vacates the premises.

He wheels the loaded dolly down the hall to the elevator.

No sooner does he press the "down" button than the doors open, disgorging the apparent plainclothes detectives—guns drawn—whom he'd viewed moments earlier exiting the unmarked car at the hotel's entrance. They move right past Herb and down the corridor toward the room he has just now fled.

Herb passes onto the elevator and the doors slide closed behind him.

Herb emerges in the lobby.

He wheels the cart past the front desk and the bell captain's station, through the front doors and out into the street, where lined-up taxis await passengers. He sweeps aside an elderly couple who are about to board the first cab. He tosses the bags into the taxi, leaps in, slams the door, and orders the driver: "Drive!"

Of course we could have the cabdriver simply drive off as commanded. Here arises, however, yet another opportunity to ratchet up the tension by throwing an obstacle in a protagonist's path.

A preferable choice, therefore, is for the driver to challenge Herb over his cutting in line.

"Pardon to me, my friend, but there is no excusing for such rudeness," the Russian cabby says. "I am not to permitting hooliganism inside my taxi motor vehicle. It is precisely such barbarian behavior that gives to Large Apple its unseemly repute. So say I, Slavko Vorkapich."

Note that we've captured in print something resembling a foreign accent without ever transliterating any of the dialogue, that is, without spelling out the pronunciation or the mispronunciation.

At this point we can underscore the stress still further by tossing in protests from the elderly couple who've been pushed out of line and cheated out of their cab. While foul language on-screen has long ago achieved full-tilt tedium, some vulgarisms here could be both surprising and funny. The little old lady who has been denied her rightful taxi appears thoroughly proper and prim. We don't expect her to rap the cab's window with her umbrella and squawk at Herb, "Ass-wipe! Dick-wad! Slime-sucking scumbag!"

It might provide a chuckle.

It might not.

What's clear enough is that Herb has to flee. How is he going to get the cab moving? He pulls the gun out of one of the bags but before the driver sees it; he quickly replaces it. Now, instead of brandishing the gun, Herb grabs a fat wad of cash from the Braniff bag and drops it on the front seat beside the driver.

"Drive," Herb says again.

The cabby drives.

Herb and driver Slavko Vorkapich clatter along the Manhattan streets. In transit, Herb strips off the bellhop's uniform and dons a sporty outfit extracted from the luggage. Finished dressing, Herb tosses the hop's outfit through the window and into the street.

Perhaps a homeless person picks it up and measures it against himself, and then calls after the departing taxi, "You got this in a forty long?"

In the cab, driver Vorkapich speaks to Herb. "It requires not profound insight to perceive you are fellow on—what is idiom?—the lam. In United States by America am humble cabdriver but in Russia was psychologist. And comes with cabdriver's territory—as with barber or bartender—to practice just little bit psychotherapy. It appears you are not criminal type. You have no chance to elude felon-finding apparatus of NYPD. Suggestion: for to facing—what is the idiom?—the music."

Herb thinks it through; he nods his head slowly. "Brooklyn Heights," he instructs the driver.

Recall that earlier in our tale, when Laura first confronted Herb at the booksellers' convention and told him about the breakup of her marriage, she mentioned that she had moved out of "the house in Brooklyn Heights." The repetition of that location here represents integration. Something is referred to in one place and, later, referred to again.

What chance has Herb Castle as a felon in flight? Clearly, his only hope is to go to Laura's residence—the place in Brooklyn Heights—and inform the estranged Carl of her death, attempt to figure out what's going on, and perhaps even to devise a solution.

The taxi deposits Herb before a nineteenth-century townhouse in historic Brooklyn Heights. Herb drags the bags up the several steps leading to the front door. He knocks cautiously and, surprisingly, the incompletely closed door swings open in response to his touch.

He steps into the dim entryway and sets down the bags. In the distance he hears voices in muffled conversation. Herb steps into the living room, where the voices are louder, closer. From the dining room through the slightly ajar kitchen door, he sees several figures engaged in anxious discourse.

There is a middle-aged man, Carl, and a handful of other individuals in the kitchen, among them the purported plainclothes detectives seen earlier at the hotel. Herb hesitates.

The front door is heard flying open and smacking hard against the suitcases Herb parked there only moments earlier. There is also the sound of a large body tripping over the bags and then crashing to the floor. A moan follows. Herb, still lurking in the darkened dining room just outside the kitchen door, now backs away and sequesters himself beside a tall piece of furniture—a highboy containing tableware—as the figure who stumbled over the bags in the entryway emerges, rubbing his sore hip. He limps past Herb into the kitchen.

It is the desk clerk from the hotel.

Herb watches and listens as the clerk joins Carl and the others. "He got away!" the clerk exclaims.

"Tell us something we don't know," Carl says.

"You told us he was a wimp who would just roll over and play dead," the clerk says. "Instead, he shows some initiative and manages to skip the joint."

"You were supposed to keep him at the hotel," Carl says.

The clerk responds, "At least you've got him here now."

"Here? Now?"

"The bags," the clerk explains, "the suitcases you had us prepare. They're here in the house. I practically broke my butt just now tripping over them in the entryway."

En masse, the entire group moves to the entryway.

No bags.

They step out onto the stoop and peer up the street. It is deserted. Now they peer in the other direction.

A half block away, sprinting as best he can while lugging the bags, Herb approaches the entrance to a subway station. Carl, the desk clerk, and the "plainclothes detectives" take off in hot pursuit.

Inside the subway station a half dozen people wait in line to purchase subway cards at the booth. Herb, frantic, takes his place at the end of the queue for a split second before suddenly rushing to the front. He is about to cut into the line. The person at the head of the line, however, a big galoot of a guy, offers Herb a menacing New York glare that translates: You got a problem?

Herb, desperate, reaches for the gun, but comes up instead with another fistful of cash from the Braniff carry-on bag. "I'll buy your place in line," he says.

"You got a deal," the man responds, clearly impressed with the money clutched in Herb's hand.

Before he can accept the cash, however, another patron chimes in. "Hey, never mind no place in line. I'll sell you my MetroCard."

"Quit queering my deal!" the first dude says.

Competition breaks out among the customers. "You want a Metro-Card that bad?" a woman asks Herb. "Give you my own right now for ten bucks."

"Nine!"

"Eight fifty!"

Herb tosses a fistful of bills into the air, seizes a MetroCard from the nearest available hand, and rushes through the turnstile toward the platform, where a train is just pulling in.

Around the turnstile people scramble, flailing to pluck bills fluttering to the ground and squabbling over those that have already landed.

At precisely this moment, of course, Carl, the desk clerk, and the "plainclothes detectives" rush down the stairs from the sidewalk. Spotting Herb as he boards a car of the waiting train, they leap the turnstiles and hurtle toward the platform.

The doors slide closed in their faces. Huffing, puffing, they watch Herb glide with the train into the deep, dark recesses of the Metropolitan Transportation Authority's labyrinth.

I normally caution writers against providing any special effects—such decisions belong generally to editors and directors—but a slow FADE-OUT or FADE TO BLACK might be appropriate at the end of this scene.

This, naturally, is followed by a slow FADE-IN. We find the screen dimly aglow in dawn's dreary light. The pale vista that unfolds depicts a vast subway train yard in the north Bronx where the MTA stores subway cars at off-peak hours.

Now we are inside one such car. Except for Herb, the car is deserted. He sleeps sitting upright, his chin on his chest, the bags balanced precariously in his lap and at his feet. Clearly, Herb rode from the end of the previous scene to the end of the subway line, then spent what must have been a fitful night.

This scene, however, prompts a reasonable question: Can one truly stay the night in an off-line New York City subway car?

Even in anarchic, chaotic, lawless New York City, while it is possible to ride the trains endlessly, it is impossible to spend the night on a car that is taken out of service, as Transportation Authority police routinely sweep through the trains to roust any citizens who might still be on them.

One way to get around this is to insert several brief shots showing Herb hiding out somewhere—say, a track-repair worker's safety alcove in the dark tunnel—then sneaking back onto the car. In fact, however, this is unnecessary. Show Herb riding the subway, then cut directly to him here, and audiences will accept that one way or another he eluded the system and managed to hide all night on the train.

You just don't need all the fill-in material. To provide it denies the audience the opportunity to fill it in for themselves.

Parenthood (Lowell Ganz, Babaloo Mandel, Ron Howard) contains a splendid example. A friend of Steve Martin's wife has told her that she revitalized her own tedious marriage via the sudden and unannounced administration of oral sex upon her husband.

One evening while they're traveling along the highway in their van, Martin's wife decides to try the same thing. We see her lean down toward her husband's lap.

Instantaneously, we cut directly to the van, now wrecked, at the side of the road. A police officer, pen poised above his notepad, takes down a report from Martin and his wife. The cop asks them, "You folks want to explain that to me again?"

It earns the biggest laugh in the movie. Lesser writers would have crammed in views of the van skidding and swerving and just generally going haywire in traffic. There would have been hair-raising near collisions with other vehicles, a host of slapstick car stunts.

Such extra footage could appear to offer excellent opportunities for grand movie fun. In fact, however, far better than any of these shots is no shot at all. Cutting from the wife's erotic gesture directly to the van crumpled at roadside implies all the other stuff.

Without a lot of unnecessary filler, then, we return now to our protagonist, Herb, fitfully dozing in the subway car at dawn's earliest light, the luggage stacked precariously on and about him.

Herb's car is now suddenly coupled to another as trains are assembled for the morning rush hour, causing the car to lurch. The bags fall from Herb's lap to the floor and he is jolted awake.

The audio recorder spills out of one of the bags and lands on the floor, triggering the machine into action. "Harriet went to the door, period," an unfamiliar man's voice oozes from the speaker. "Quote, Who's there, question mark, close quote, she asked, period." It sounds very much like someone dictating material for a typist to transcribe.

Perhaps the voice could have certain quirks. It mispronounces "et cetera" as "eck cetera" and "often" with a hard *t*: "off-ten."

Later in our tale we'll meet someone who speaks precisely that way. Thanks to the clues contained in these vocal eccentricities, we will know upon meeting him that it is his voice that is recorded here.

This device also integrates the tale by connecting one thing to another. It connects something early in the picture to something occurring much later. It prevents the script from appearing episodic. It prevents the narrative from resembling a string of pearls, lending it a shape that is pleasingly round and whole.

Our tumbling recorder presents also an example of the "plausible impossibility." Let's face it: One could drop a digital recorder on the floor ten thousand times and it would never, ever be triggered into playing. Indeed, it will turn to puree of recorder before it ever plays whatever is recorded on it.

Regardless, if the actor drops the device to the floor and it promptly begins to play, the audience—even though intellectually it knows better—will never challenge the action's authenticity.

In the very first screenwriting class I ever attended, I pitched a story in which a young thief, wielding a glass cutter, slices out a rectangular pane from within a larger plate-glass window, so as to be able to reach through to unlock the door.

"Glass doesn't cut like that," a classmate volunteered.

Someone else in the class responded, "In movies it does."

Indeed, the beauty of screenwriting is that many things that cannot happen in life occur in movies quite readily, if only the writer needs them to do so.

To have Herb deliberately turn on the recorder renders the hand of the writer visible. The writer needs the recorder to play; he orders his character to turn it on. Isn't it more natural in appearance to have the recorder start up apparently on its own, propelled by action?

Herb, then, sitting aboard the train, listens to the recording, and then spends but a brief moment reviewing some of the bags' other contents.

At last, he appears to come to a moment of decision.

Now, it is easy to relate items like "moments of decision" to the reader of a screenplay. It is quite another matter, however, to communicate such information to folks in a theater watching images unfold on the screen.

Description of mental processes in screenplays challenge even the most experienced practitioner. Whenever I read screenplays in which someone "thinks" or "decides" or "remembers" or "realizes" something, I know I am in the hands of an amateur.

We know, therefore, of Herb's "moment of decision" only because of the material that precedes it, the expression on his face, and the material that follows it.

What follows Herb's "moment" is an exterior shot of Barry's Bookshop in Manhattan's East Fifties. A large crowd waits in line out front along with hordes of reporters. Signs in the bookshop window boast: IN PERSON TODAY: RECLUSIVE AUTHOR PAGE TURNER GOES PUBLIC!!!

A bookstore is the first stop on the author's itinerary that was among the documents Herb found in the luggage.

Inside the bookstore, mobbed by fans and media, a wary, uneasy Herb signs stacks of boxed sets of the reissued Page Turner volumes first encountered when we toured the booksellers' convention at the Javits Center.

Viewed from the back, we now see a woman make her way through the throng. She maneuvers up close to where Herb is stationed. Herb's eyes widen in shock when he sees her.

As the camera tracks around for a clearer look at the woman, we see that it is Laura, whom we left for dead back in the hotel.

In the introduction to this book, "The God Game," I argued that to write is to play God.

This is precisely what we do here by bringing Laura back to life. Of course, she was never really killed in the first place. She was instead part of a scheme in which for some reason—to be revealed later in the tale—Herb had to be set up to portray bestselling reclusive author Page Turner.

Laura was not fully informed of all of the scheme's aspects. At the same time as she misled Herb, she was herself deceived by Carl.

She is similar in ways to the character portrayed by Eva Marie Saint in *North by Northwest*, who first deceives Cary Grant but then changes sides, crossing over to join him in love and adventure. A similar romantic crossover involves Ingrid Bergman in *Notorious* (Ben Hecht).

Likewise, the musical *Damn Yankees!* (George Abbott, Douglass Wallop, adapting a book by Wallop), based upon the Faust legend, contains an element wherein Satan's seductress, femme fatale Lola, falls in love with her intended victim, and crosses over to become in the end not his antagonist but his ally.

The same sort of crossover occurs right here in *Creature Comforts*.

Let us now leap to the end of the tale and work our way backward. Our purpose is both to articulate a story-craft principle and to see how identity and theme inform each another. We'll draw from the central idea of the third chapter, that a sincerely personal, wholly integrated screenplay will merit audiences' attention and consideration regardless of its subject.

To that end imagine a prisoner at some correctional institution in, say, upstate New York—the notorious Attica—who happens early during his incarceration, some ten years before our movie starts, to join a prisoners' creative writing workshop. There he writes a romantic thriller. His instructor—an English professor from the local community college—is impressed with the prisoner's talent.

"This stuff's really good," the instructor tells the prisoner. "Let me send it to a publisher."

"But I can't publish," the prisoner says. "Have you never heard of the Berkowitz law?"

David Berkowitz is a convicted serial murderer imprisoned in New York State. He is more notoriously known as Son of Sam, the nom de crime under which he killed his various victims.

Upon his incarceration, the authorities were afraid he would profit from his crimes by publishing a bestseller, thereby capitalizing upon his notoriety and exploiting his criminal behavior. To prevent this, a law was passed that restricts prisoners' rights to market their writing.

Imagine that the incarcerated felon's writing instructor tells him that he can avoid the Berkowitz restrictions by writing under a nom de plume, for example, Page Turner. In that way, the instructor continues, no one can accuse him of trading on his outlaw reputation, since no one will know who he is. Furthermore, Turner will not write accounts of his crimes. He will write fiction.

Under such circumstances, if his books sell, the success will be attributed not to profiteering from his skill as a writer.

Indeed, ten years pass and Page Turner, the prisoner, writes perhaps a dozen novels, all of them bestsellers. Some become hit movies; others are successful television series.

What to do about all the money he earns? It goes to his estate.

What kind of "estate" can a lowlife convicted felon have? Only his mother, a housekeeper in, say, Rochester, New York. Every six months or so when she visits her son in prison he asks, "Mama, are they sending you the money?"

"Son," she responds, "they send me so much money! Why, last year alone they sent me nearly five thousand dollars!" Five thousand dollars is actually one-hundredth of what she should have received.

Eventually, our prisoner is released from confinement.

I am not sure how best to craft this particular turn in the tale. Perhaps "Turner" is found to have been wrongly imprisoned. Frankly, that strikes me as too pat, too familiar. That might not make a bad movie but it's not this movie. Perhaps, instead, he escapes from prison. That also strikes me as too broad a development. Might as well have UFOs appear in the sky and have it morph into a sci-fi epic.

Perhaps he is pardoned. There are possibilities here for drama, to be sure, but overall it strikes me as an unnecessary complication representing so radical a twist as to make it into a whole other movie.

Perhaps he simply serves his time and is released.

Upon getting out of prison, Page Turner learns that his publisher has been ripping him off for a decade and confronts him, demanding the millions he is owed.

The publisher responds by hatching a complex scheme in order to avoid paying. He'll select a bogus Page Turner—the ideal candidate would be some nerdy, geeky, wimpy guy from the other side of the country who is peripherally involved in the publishing business. It should be someone no one will likely miss. Next, he'll parade the bogus Turner around in public for a while in order to establish his identity as that of the bestselling reclusive writer.

Finally, of course, he'll have him killed.

The schemers intend that the body will be found in an alley along with the bogus baggage. Police, upon inspecting the luggage, will identify the author as Page Turner, and the news will go out that he is dead. This, of course, forever discredits any and all individuals who claim Turner's work as their own.

Among those discredited will be, of course, our prisoner/author, the true Page Turner. He can scream and yell all he wants. With Page Turner's works newly and publicly attributed to another figure, no one will take him seriously.

Let us say that the publisher orchestrating this scheme is Carl himself. Let us assume also that after Herb's escape from the hotel, the real Turner, our prisoner, confronts Carl. Carl then shows him TV news footage of Herb signing all those Page Turner boxed sets at Barry's Bookshop, figuring that Turner, a convicted criminal, will himself pursue and eventually eliminate Herb once he has seen him on TV claiming credit for the prisoner/author's work.

Somewhere along the way, of course, Turner and Herb and Laura join forces and defeat their oppressors.

Eventually they make their way to the jail where Turner was imprisoned. There, in a conversation with the warden, they recognize the eccentricities of diction on the audio recorder—"off-ten" for "often" and "eck-cetera" for "et cetera." They realize that the warden is himself one of the conspirators. The last pages of Herb's latest manuscript were ripped off—literally—from the end and "dictated" into the recorder in an attempt to simulate a work-in-progress, which then became one more item in the luggage of a purported author on a book tour.

In *Creature Comforts* Herb finds imposed upon him an identity he views as not his own. At first he resists. Eventually, however, he surrenders to it, exactly as all of us must at long last resign ourselves to our own destinies and identities.

Herb has, after all, struggled futilely his whole life to be a bestselling author. Now, suddenly, scoundrels attempt to impose precisely that identity upon him. First he resists; but before long he earnestly embraces that identity.

The real Turner, now that he is free, has no interest in writing anymore. "I can understand why a prisoner locked in his cell would want to be a writer," he tells Herb, "but why would a free man want to write?"

In the end, therefore, Herb and the true Turner cut a deal. Herb will take over the franchise and write the Turner books. He and the former prisoner will divide the money between them.

After all is said and done, we have here an example of identity as theme. Herb has an identity imposed upon him. Reiterating, at first he resists, but eventually he accepts it. Indeed, he comes not merely to accept it but, ultimately, to embrace it.

Isn't this the story of all of us? Of course our DNA is an important aspect of who and what we are. Beyond that, however, we arrive on earth pretty much a blank slate. Our circumstances, experiences, and acquaintances ultimately shape our identity. In the end they define for us who we are. Like Herb, we may resist at first, but eventually our identity asserts itself and we can only surrender to it.

In one form or another, in one way or another, this is what lies at the core of both real life and dramatic narrative.

Recommended Reading

If there is anybody out there who is not writing a screenplay, it is probably because he has taken a break to write a book about writing screenplays.

The authors of screenwriting books do not really compete with one another. People do not purchase either my book or someone else's; instead they buy several. In this way screenwriting titles compare to cookbooks. Perhaps we authors are actually contributing to writer's block: Screenwriters read our books instead of writing their scripts.

The same can be said for the flurry of screenwriting seminars and workshops that have been sweeping the nation and the world now for decades. Instead of attending to their screenplays, writers attend these events. It is so much easier to spend a weekend sitting in a chamber with a group of folks listening to a skillful speaker—or even a lousy one—than to sit alone in a room, hour after hour, endeavoring to fill blank pages or glowing LCD screens with dramatic material meriting the time and attention and consideration of audiences.

Recently I met a writer who had attended one such popular seminar. I asked him his opinion of the event and he said that he found it to be worthy in the extreme. "I took over a hundred and fifty pages of notes," he told me proudly.

"How's your script coming along?" I asked him.

He hesitated, and then admitted sheepishly that he was still collating the notes.

Having said that, let me assert my firm belief that there is no such thing as too much education. The more books and screenplays you read, the more courses you take, the more seminars and workshops you attend, the more you expand your opportunities for success.

With a new screenwriting book being published these days approximately every twenty minutes, there is still none that touches Aristotle's *Poetics.* There is no small irony, of course, in the fact that this screenwriters' bible—really not much more than the surviving fragment of a pamphlet—was written over two millennia before film was invented.

Screenwriters should not expect ever fully to understand the *Poetics.* Rather, they have to make it part of their writing lives. It need not be read straight through from beginning to end; one can skip around at random. The trick to using the *Poetics* is not to try to extract timeless principles, though they are surely there, but rather to follow it closely in a practical, hands-on way.

Nothing beats the original, but Michael Tierno's *Aristotle's Poetics for Screenwriters: Storytelling Secrets from the Greatest Mind in Western Civilization* is a worthy companion volume. Notwithstanding a somewhat cloying, gosh-all-golly voice, this volume provides useful insights into issues regarding story structure and every other aspect of dramatic narrative.

Hal Ackerman's *Write Screenplays That Sell: The Ackerman Way* is an authentic standout. Full disclosure: Hal is a dear friend and longtime colleague at UCLA. He is a master teacher whose students have enjoyed phenomenal professional success over decades. I quote Hal and his book all the time. Moreover, I sneak into his lectures in search of material to steal. What greater testimony to my admiration than that?

Lew Hunter's Screenwriting 434 has been in print now for almost twenty years. Hunter is a UCLA professor emeritus and longtime colleague. Writers have no better friend. His book leads readers week by week through his own version of our bread-and-butter course, Advanced Screenwriting Workshop. Because he knows better than to winter in Nebraska, he comes to Southern California every January for three months to continue his legendary UCLA workshops. Throughout the year he also presides over a week-long screenwriting colony at his home in Superior, Nebraska, and around the world. Reading his book is the next best thing to enrolling in his class.

Professor Brian Henderson is a screenwriting scholar from the University at Buffalo. He is the world's leading expert on 1930s and 1940s screenwriter Preston Sturges and has written two books examining his scripts: *Five Screenplays by Preston Sturges* and *Four More Screenplays by Preston Sturges*. Each of Henderson's books contains the screenplays exactly as Sturges wrote them, not gussied up for publication but in the straightforward, professional format Sturges used. Studying a master like Sturges can carry a writer a long way toward excellence.

The Fifty Worst Films of All Time (and How They Got That Way), out of print now for perhaps thirty years and therefore hard to track down, remains among my favorite screenwriting resources. Harry Medved and Randy Dreyfuss burst a lot of bubbles regarding screenwriting hoaxes. My favorite quote: "The average filmgoer should trust his own instincts in reacting to film. The fact that a movie is overwrought and boring does not mean that it is somehow edifying or 'good for you.'" On the surface, this book seems like a throwaway gag but it is not. It posits truly profound insights into the nature of movies and screenwriting in an engaging, affectionate fashion.

I still love the late critic Walter Kerr's book *How Not to Write a Play*. While aimed at playwrights, it is useful for any writer dealing in dramatic narrative.

William Goldman's *Adventures in the Screen Trade* and its follow-up volume provide often painful, frequently hilarious accounts of the Hollywood writer's life. It also has cogent advice regarding story, character, and more. Be forewarned, however, that his script for *Butch Cassidy and the Sundance Kid*, contained within, should not be a model for new writers. Goldman is a bestselling novelist and supremely honored screenwriter who can get away with writing that is wordy and overly descriptive in a way that newer screenwriters cannot.

The late Irwin R. Blacker's The *Elements of Screenwriting—A Guide for Film and Television Writers* consists of notes compiled by his former students, myself among them, who were fortunate enough to sit in his classes at USC. The book is modeled after Strunk and White's timeless *The Elements of Style*, which treats not screenwriting in particular but writing in general. In the late sixties swamp of narcissism, negative-heel Earth shoes, and psychedelic tie-dye tees, Blacker was a throwback, a warrior for discipline and structure, strong characterization, and dialogue that is to-the-point.

I have preached here and elsewhere that real writing is rewriting. Paul

Chitlik, a UCLA screenwriting instructor, has written a volume that deals exclusively with issues pertinent to second and third and subsequent drafts. Writers of not only screenplays but stage plays and novels will find *Rewrite: A Step-by-Step Guide to Strengthen Structure, Characters, and Drama in Your Screenplay* supportive of their attempts to slog through the challenges confronting them once they realize that the first draft is just that: the first draft.

Screenplay: Writing the Picture, by Robin U. Russin and William Missouri Downs, takes a fresh look at the issues facing writers across the broad spectrum of the writing experience. Russin and Downs have a collective voice that is warm and accessible, and for all its discipline and its straightforward point of view it resonates nonetheless with affirmation and encouragement, and also humor.

I recently reread *Understanding Media: The Extensions of Man* by Marshall McLuhan fully expecting it to appear wan and weary, just so much groovy sixties pop-chatter. Instead, it shines more brightly than ever. McLuhan was no shuck-and-jive artist; as clearly as anybody he saw the Whole Picture in expression and perception across formats. He is an authentic seer who appreciates the way things break apart and, more important for artists, the way they come together.

Another book that does not focus directly upon screenwriting but is of inestimable value to creators of narratives is *The Ascent of Man* by Jacob Bronowski. This world-famous scholar is the first to cite the ancient European caves at Lascaux and Altamira with their astonishing murals as the earliest movie theaters. He is a great synthesizer who unites all scientific and artistic disciplines, illuminating the underlying principles that all among them, screenwriting included, share.

Prof. Richard Walter
UCLA Dept. Film, TV and Digital Media
102 East Melnitz Hall
Los Angeles, CA 90095-1622
www.RichardWalter.com